Publication Number 43

Duke University Center for Commonwealth and Comparative Studies

Pakistan: The Long View

Pakistan:
The Long View

William J. Barnds
Craig Baxter   Norman D. Palmer
Lee L. Bean   Stephen *and* Carroll McC. Pastner
Ralph Braibanti   Khalid B. Sayeed
Gilbert T. Brown   Anwar H. Syed
S. M. Burke   Wayne A. Wilcox
Shahid Javed Burki   W. Howard Wriggins
Hafeez Malik   Lawrence Ziring

Edited by
Lawrence Ziring, Ralph Braibanti,
and W. Howard Wriggins

Number 43 in a series published for the
Duke University Center for Commonwealth and Comparative Studies
Duke University Press, Durham, N.C.
1977

© 1977 Duke University Press

L.C.C. card number 76–4320
I.S.B.N. 0–8223–0363–9

Printed in the United States
of America by Kingsport Press, Inc.

In Memory of
Wayne, Ouida, Kailan,
and **Clark Wilcox**

Contents

Contents

Contributors

William J. Barnds, born in Oak Park, Illinois, in 1927, is a graduate of the University of Michigan and the Georgetown Law School. Presently Senior Research Fellow, Council on Foreign Relations, he was employed by the Central Intelligence Agency from 1952 until 1966. He is the author of *India, Pakistan and the Great Powers* (1972) and has contributed articles to *Foreign Affairs, International Affairs, Europa-Archiv, The World Today, Problems of Communism,* and *Worldview.*

Craig Baxter, born in Elizabeth, New Jersey, in 1929, received the Ph.D. in Political Science from the University of Pennsylvania. He was Counselor of Embassy, Accra, Ghana. As a Foreign Service officer he has held posts in India and Bangladesh as well as Pakistan and was detailed to the U.S. Military Academy from 1971 to 1974. He is the author of *The Jana Sangh, a Biography of an Indian Political Party* (1969) and *District Voting Trends in India* (1969).

Lee L. Bean, born in Salt Lake City, Utah, in 1933, received the Ph.D. in Sociology from Yale University. Presently chairman of the Department of Sociology, University of Utah, he has held several positions on the Population Council and was associate director of its Demographic Division. During the last two years of his appointment at Yale he was on leave serving as the demographic advisor to the Pakistan Institute of Development Economics under the sponsorship of the Population Council. He is the author of *A Decade Later, Population Projections for Pakistan: 1960–2000*

(1968) and *Population and Family Planning: Manpower and Training* (1972).

Ralph Braibanti, born in Danbury, Connecticut, in 1920, received the Ph.D. in Political Science from Syracuse University. He is James B. Duke Professor of Political Science at Duke University. A frequent consultant to the Agency for International Development, the Ford Foundation, and the United Nations, he served from 1960 to 1962 as Chief Advisor to the Civil Services Academy in Lahore, and at various times was consultant on administrative development in Pakistan, Turkey, Saudi Arabia, Malaysia, and other countries. He was president of the American Institute of Pakistan Studies. He is the author of *Research on the Bureaucracy of Pakistan* (1966) and is editor and co-author of several volumes including *Asian Bureaucratic Systems Emergent from the British Imperial Tradition* (1966).

Gilbert T. Brown, born in Tampa, Florida, in 1926, received the Ph.D. in Economics from Yale University. He was senior economist, Pakistan Division, International Bank for Reconstruction and Development, he has held several academic positions as well as positions in business and government. He has served as economist for the Federal Reserve banks of Boston and New York, and for the First National City Bank of New York. For ten years he was with the Agency for International Development both in Washington and South Korea. He is the author of *Korean Pricing Policies and Economic Development in the 1960's* (1973).

S. M. Burke, born in what is now Pakistan in 1906, took his M.A. in History from the University of the Panjab and studied jurisprudence, law, economics, and Persian at the University of London for two years. He was professor and consultant in South Asian Studies at the University of Minnesota. A member of the Indian Civil Service before partition, he opted for Pakistan and joined the Foreign Office in 1948. He has been a Minister, Ambassador, or High Commissioner for

Pakistan in eleven different countries. He is the author of
Pakistan's Foreign Policy: An Historical Analysis (1973)
and *Mainsprings of Indian and Pakistani Foreign Policies*
(1974).

Shahid Javed Burki, born in what is now Pakistan in 1935,
is currently on deputation by the Government of Pakistan to
the International Bank for Reconstruction and Development.
After graduating from the University of the Panjab, he spent
two years as a Rhodes Scholar at Oxford University. From
1967 to 1969, he was a Public Service Fellow at Harvard
University. He is a civil servant in the Pakistan government
and prior to reorganization belonged to the Civil Service of
Pakistan. He is the author of *A Study of Chinese Communes*
(1969), *Pakistan: A Demographic Report* (1973), and *Population Burden and Public Policy* (1974).

Hafeez Malik, born in Lahore, Pakistan, in 1930, received
an M.A. in Journalism and a Ph.D. in Political Science from
Syracuse University. Now Professor of History and Political
Science at Villanova University, he was White House correspondent for the *Nawa-I-Waqt* and *Shahaz.* He is Director
of the American Institute of Pakistan Studies and Chairman
of the Pakistan Council of the Asia Society. He is the author
of *Muslim Nationalism in India and Pakistan* (1963) and the
editor of *Iqbal: Poet-Philosopher of Pakistan* (1971).

Norman Palmer, born in Maine in 1909, received the Ph.D.
in International Relations from Yale University. He is
Professor of Political Science at the University of Pennsylvania. In 1973–74, he was Visiting Distinguished Professor
of Political Science at Duke University. He has been a senior
associate of the Foreign Policy Research Institute and is a
former president of the International Studies Association.
He is the author of *International Relations: The World
Community in Transition* (with Howard C. Perkins) (1953,
1957, and 1969), *The Indian Political System* (1971), *South
Asia and United States Policy* (1966), *Sun Yat-sen and Com-*

munism (with Shao-Chuan Leng) (1961), and *Elections and Political Development: The South Asian Experience* (1975).

Carroll and Stephen Pastner are Assistant Professors of Anthropology at the University of Vermont. They received their Ph.D. degrees in Anthropology from Brandeis University in 1971. They have done field work in the Makran District of Baluchistan, 1968–69. They jointly wrote "Agriculture, Kinship, and Politics in Southern Baluchistan," *Man* (1972) and "Aspects of Religion in Southern Baluchistan," *Anthropologica* (1972).

Khalid B. Sayeed, born in Belary, India, in 1926, received the Ph.D. in Political Science from McGill University. He is Professor of Political Science and Director of the Institute of Commonwealth and Comparative Studies, Queen's University. He has taught at the University of Dacca, the University of New Brunswick, Duke University, and McGill University. He was a United Nations consultant in Iran and has been a Visiting Fellow at Harvard University and London University. He is the author of *Pakistan, The Formative Phase* (1960) and *The Political System of Pakistan* (1967).

Anwar H. Syed, born in Batala, India, in 1926, received the Ph.D. in Political Science from the University of Pennsylvania. Now Professor of Political Science at the University of Massachusetts, he has also held positions at the Universities of Karachi, Panjab, and Pennsylvania. He is the author of *Walter Lippmann's Philosophy of International Politics* (1963), *The Political Theory of American Local Government* (1966), and *China and Pakistan: Diplomacy of an Entente Cordiale* (1974).

Wayne A. Wilcox, born in Pendleton, Indiana, in 1932, received the Ph.D. in Political Science from Columbia University. Before his death he was Cultural Attaché, United States Embassy, London. He had held the position of Professor and Chairman of the Department of Political Science,

Columbia University. He was the author of *Pakistan: The Consolidation of a Nation* (1963), *India, Pakistan and the Rise of China* (1964), *Asia and United States Policy* (1967), and *The Emergence of Bangladesh* (1973), and (with Leo Rose and Gavin Boyd) was co-editor and co-author of *Asia and the International System* (1972).

W. Howard Wriggins, born in Philadelphia in 1918, received the Ph.D. in International Relations from Yale University. He is Professor of Political Science and Director of the Southern Asia Institute, Columbia University. In 1958, he was Chief of the Foreign Affairs Division of the Legislative Reference Service of the Library of Congress, and in 1973–74 he was the Rhodes Fellow at St. Anthony's College, Oxford. From 1961 to 1967 he served on the Policy Planning Council of the Department of State and the National Security Council Staff of the White House. He is Director and Coordinator for the National Seminar on Pakistan/ Bangladesh, and is the author of *Ceylon, Dilemmas of a New Nation* (1960) and *The Ruler's Imperative* (1969) and editor (with J. F. Guyot) of *Population, Politics and the Future of Southern Asia* (1973) and *Pakistan in Transition* (1975).

Lawrence Ziring, born in Brooklyn, New York, in 1928, received the Ph.D. in Political Science from Columbia University. Currently Professor of Political Science at Western Michigan University, he was Secretary of the American Institute of Pakistan Studies and Chairman of the Pakistan Studies Development Committee of the Association for Asian Studies. He served as a lecturer in the Department of Political Science, Dacca University, 1959–60, and as an advisor to the Pakistan Administrative Staff College, 1964– 66. He was an ACLS Fellow in 1974–75 and lectured at several branches of the Institute of Oriental Studies, Academy of Sciences, USSR in 1974. He is the author of *The Ayub Khan Era: Politics in Pakistan, 1958–1969* (1971) and (with C. I. Eugene Kim) *An Introduction to Asian Politics* (1977).

Preface

On September 27–29, 1974, the Wayne Ayres Wilcox Memorial Symposium, "Pakistan After 1971," was held at the Quail Roost Conference Center in Rougemont, North Carolina. This volume represents some of the papers that were read at the conference. All the papers presented have been edited and several have been rewritten for this publication. The symposium was dedicated to the memory of Wayne Wilcox, who died with his wife and two eldest children on March 3, 1974, in a plane crash near Orly airport outside Paris.

In slightly more than a decade Wayne A. Wilcox had established himself as a leading scholar of Pakistan affairs. His training and interest centered on political systems and foreign policy; he was also an amateur economist and sociologist. As his colleagues can attest, Wayne Wilcox produced a series of important publications that will continue to light the path of those who seek an understanding of South Asian nations. We who knew Wayne Wilcox lost a great friend. Our field of scholarship lost a unique and perceptive commentator.

Our principal purpose in this volume is to examine the "new" Pakistan that emerged after the Indo-Pakistan War of 1971 and the loss of East Pakistan. The authors of the chapters that comprise this book have sought to place contemporary developments in historical perspective and to suggest prospects for the future. While the book does not represent the last word on Pakistan, it is an attempt to produce a comprehensive analysis of a country whose experience in nation-building has been generally neglected by the scholarly community.

A project such as this is extremely complicated and our gratitude extends to more people than can be identified in this space. Both the conference and this volume that results from it received support from several sources. The Program in Comparative Studies on Southern Asia at Duke University provided the major financial support for the symposium. The South Asia Regional Council of the Association for Asian Studies also helped finance the symposium. Publication of this volume was made possible by a generous contribution from the publications fund of the Center for Commonwealth and Comparative Studies of Duke University and by a contribution from the Southern Asian Institute of Columbia University. Both the SARC and the Southern Asian Institute have received generous support from the Ford Foundation. The Center for Commonwealth and Comparative Studies of Duke University has received general support from the Carnegie Corporation, and a small part of its contribution to this volume is derived from a Carthage Foundation grant for South Asian Studies.

The indebtedness of all of the authors for support by these organizations is hereby gratefully acknowledged. None of the organizations mentioned above is responsible for data or conclusions presented in this volume. Such responsibility rests solely with the authors.

LAWRENCE ZIRING
RALPH BRAIBANTI
W. HOWARD WRIGGINS

February 23, 1977

Pakistan: The Long View

Introduction

Lawrence Ziring

The literature on Pakistan does not adequately examine the country's raison d'être. Indeed, what has been written on this subject is mostly negative. Fear of a Hindu-dominated Indian state raised the cry "Islam in Danger," and from this call issued the "Two Nation Theory" of the Muslim League. Pakistan is therefore in large measure a manifestation of acute emotion and fear as much as ambition and human aspirations. The communal bloodletting prior to and following the partition of British India provides ample evidence for this view.

Although the "Two Nation Theory" is useful for understanding the emergence of Pakistan as an independent state, it was more a reaction to Muslim–Hindu antagonism, suspicion, and hatred than a positive expression of national existence. In this volume both Wayne Wilcox and Hafeez Malik examine the formative period. And while they do not necessarily agree, their individual contributions offer new insights into the philosophical and practical underpinnings of the Pakistan state. They also help us to understand why the nation has groped for, but has never quite resolved, the question of its national identity.

Few countries have expended so much energy in an effort to identify national ideology as has Pakistan. The term most commonly employed to describe the Pakistani ideology is "Islamic Socialism," but neither government practitioners nor intellectuals have successfully detailed its intrinsic

properties. As Anwar Syed's chapter suggests, even Zulfikar
Ali Bhutto's political party manifesto, which is the most
systematic attempt to date, remains a vague declaration. It
is interesting that Hafeez Malik believes the dilemma may
resolve itself as the people of Pakistan are compelled to
come to grips with the geopolitical realities of their post-
1971 existence.

To many Pakistanis, the sense of nationalism remains
rudimentary. Provincialism continues to be a more profound
force, and this provincialism also dramatizes the current
divisiveness within the country. Repeated mention is made
in this book of the inability of the leadership to engender national purpose or to reduce interprovincial rivalry. It can be
argued that Bangladesh was made possible in part because
the negative has usually been accentuated. If the different
ethnic and linguistic groups had been drawn into a national
framework promoting interdependence, instead of one in
which fear, not only of Hindus, but also of one's fellow-
Pakistani Punjabis, Bengalis, Sindhis, and Pathans was frequently nourished by local leaders, the country might well
have avoided the agony of Bangladesh.

A significant limitation of Pakistan's leaders, however,
has been their tendency to provoke but not control subnational ethnic, regional, and religious group controversy.
Few if any leaders have chosen to grapple with the fundamental dilemmas of national integration, and Khalid B.
Sayeed's presentation is a suggestive commentary on this
subject. Force or intimidation, not persuasion, has all too
often been employed to control the "provincialists," "miscreants," and "opportunists." It should not surprise us
therefore that even Prime Minister Bhutto cannot escape
this legacy. As recently as 1974, the Ahmediya community in
the Punjab was legislated out of the Islamic faith. Ralph
Braibanti points out in his chapter the potential risk of this
action to the cohesion of Pakistan as a nation. Moreover,
increasing strains between the Muhajirs and indigenous

communities, especially in Sind, seem to have developed a momentum that the present government can hope only to contain, not overcome.

The question may then be asked: Can Pakistan discover its positive national purpose and cement its disparate peoples? Clearly, there is no easy answer to this conundrum. What is obvious, however, is that the cry "Islam in Danger," and the real and imaginary fears that it generates, was not a sufficient unifying concept to transform Pakistan into a coherent national entity; a more positive, constructive theme is clearly essential if the current centrifugal tendencies are to be reversed. It remains then for leadership, whether in government, in the political opposition, or outside either element of the explicitly "political" realm, to renew its commitment to the national well-being and ultimate progress of the nation. Without such a commitment the future of this still very young Muslim state cannot be projected with certainty.

Islamic unity in the unique context of Pakistan may be considered a positive goal, but it should not be confused with the dream of Pan-Islamism. Simply put, unity suggests that varying ethnic and denominational Muslims, whatever their place of origin, and inhabiting the northwestern segment of South Asia, can draw themselves together under a single national flag, not because they are concerned with Hindu, Afghan, or some other form of alien domination, but because they sense that their future is enhanced by membership in a community called Pakistan. In part, then, one of Pakistan's more basic requirements is the communication of national pride and a sense of honorable common destiny for all its inhabitants. In sum, Pakistani unity depends on the ability and willingness of the nation's leaders to develop the positive side of pride in national experience, a pride that manifests itself in belonging to a multidimensional and heterogeneous nation. Such a feeling harbors its own power, and it is leadership's challenge to find the well-

springs of unity and channel this sense of purpose throughout the nation.

Those who saw Pakistan emerge as an independent sovereign state, and followed closely the efforts made at erecting
a nation, are compelled by the nature of their interest to
weigh the consequences of the East Pakistan secession.
The trauma associated with the 1971 dismemberment is not
necessarily visible, but it permeates the attentive public's
psyche. Jinnah's epochal creation has already been given a
severe blow, and no politically conscious Pakistani can
ignore or conceal the pain that secession has caused. Furthermore, Zulfikar Ali Bhutto is the heir to a noble but nonetheless uncertain vision. He and his Pakistan People's Party
were summoned to restore the nation's confidence, provide
a new political framework, and both motivate and direct
progressive change. After many years of military and bureaucratic rule the politicians had obtained a new mandate. But
the bonds that hold Pakistan together are subject to strain,
and the numerous regional and ethnic groups that now seek
political expression are a distinct challenge to the Bhutto
administration. Several chapters in this volume emphasize
the importance of coping with the autonomy syndrome and
give special attention to Prime Minister Bhutto's policies
and techniques.

Syed suggests that no observer can do more than speculate
on how well or how poorly Bhutto will perform. He does
believe, however, that the Prime Minister is fully conscious
of the problem he faces. Bhutto's attempts to find a middle
ground, to neutralize his detractors while not overly antagonizing former supporters, are aimed at strengthening
the body politic behind his leadership. It is certainly too
early to make forecasts; however, the maintenance of Pakistan's territorial integrity appears uppermost in his public
declarations. Moreover, the Prime Minister took quick and
firm action following the assassination of Hyat Mohammad
Khan Sherpao. Not only did the Prime Minister order the

banning of the National Awami Party and the arrest of many of its leaders, but he implied that foreign forces were again seeking the destruction of the state.

I

Pakistan's twenty-nine-year history is marked by a remarkable search for national expression. The country was thrust into history by a congeries of forces and accelerating events that left little if any time for a "citizenry" to acclimate itself to new circumstances and situations. It has been argued by Wayne Wilcox that the refugee community "pushed" their way in, while others, indigenous to the territories that became Pakistan, were "pulled" into a new political and economic structure. But no matter how this formative period is viewed, it is clear that no war of national liberation galvanized the Indian Muslims. Few among them were aware of the magnitude of the "Freedom Movement," let alone fathomed the difficulties of establishing a new state in South Asia. Apparently the greatest enthusiasm for an independent Pakistan came not from the people residing in those regions that would ultimately form the new state's territories, but from those Muslims living in the northern and eastern stretch of Hindu-majority provinces. The Muslim League proved to be the organizational expression of this latter group and its battle cry "Islam in Danger" rallied both the fearful and the sentimental. But the Muslims inhabiting traditionally strong Muslim regions were not similarly motivated. Because they looked to local leadership, the dominant figures in the Muslim League (with the possible exception of Mohammad Ali Jinnah) were either suspect or soon were reduced to ordinary stature. Wilcox, Sayeed, Malik, and Craig Baxter all allude to these differing perceptions and the consequences that flowed from them, especially after the death of Quaid-i-Azam, Mohammad Ali Jinnah, in September 1948.

The "flowering" of nationalist movements in Baluchistan, the Northwest Frontier, and Sind have their roots in Pakistan's past. The Bhutto government, by its own admission even more so than its predecessors, must struggle with the forces that compelled Pakistan's creation as a nation. In order to understand Pakistan's present problems, it is therefore necessary to shed light on the difficulties inherent in sustaining an idea amid the complexities aroused by deep-seated, historic centrifugal tendencies. As Wayne Wilcox comments in concluding his presentation, Pakistani reality has always been different from the Pakistan dream.

Craig Baxter's chapter supports the view that the Punjab was the key to the formation of the new state, and that the Muslim League ably managed the traditional factionalism in the province so as to establish its own hegemony. Baxter explains that support for the Muslim League in the Punjab elections of 1936–37 was negligible, yet by 1945–46 the party was able to win all but a handful of the Muslim seats in the provincial legislature. The transference of popular allegiance and sentiment from the domiciled Unionists to the "carpetbagger" Muslim League was primarily a story of personalities and promises, mixed well with human emotion. In many respects it was also a contest of rural versus urban interests. Moreover, the Unionists were more concerned with class problems while the Muslim League sought to construct a new community upon a formidable Islamic foundation. Thus the Unionists opposed the partition of British India, lost popular appeal, and faded into history. Under Muslim League tutelage the Punjab became the linchpin for the new Pakistani state, and the Punjabis became preeminent in political, bureaucratic, and military circles. Efforts were made to Punjabize the Muslim League, and the other regions of Pakistan were, in a manner of speaking, required to adjust their hopes to satisfy Punjabi claims of superiority. During the first decade following independence, only East Bengal was in a position to voice its dissatisfaction with this unsubtle program. Delays in constitution-making have been traced to these interprovincial conflicts; and the One Unit scheme that eventually amalgamated all the provinces of West Pakistan stirred the embers of anti-Punjabi sentiment in Sind, the Northwest Frontier, and Baluchistan.

Linked with interprovincial tensions and prominent in Pakistan's history is the rivalry among Punjabi families, *baradaris*, and their respective supporters. There were no overwhelming powerful figures in the Punjab at Pakistan's birth, and the picture is complicated by a number of influential personalities around whom a variety of groups were formed. Baxter provides the antecedents for these developments. Shifting alliances made agreements between these leaders tentative exercises, and almost as soon as one gained prominence the others moved to weaken and displace him. In this way the Punjab and the nation were exposed to frequent crude struggles for personal power and position. In this maelstrom of conflicts the Muslim League splintered and eventually lost control of the government to the civil-military bureaucracy.

Pakistan's future is dependent on a reasonably stable Punjab. And Prime Minister Bhutto, a prominent Sindhi, will face serious difficulties in governing if the province's present factional leaders find his policies unacceptable. Anwar Syed dwells on this theme and analyzes the organization of the Pakistan People's Party in the Punjab. The PPP is the left-of-center heir of the Muslim League in the province, but it too is caught in a web of local and cross-provincial rivalries. It seems unlikely that the PPP can overcome the characteristics that make the Punjab a unique region. Islamic or secular ideologies are no match for traditional arrangements; projects aimed at altering the life-style of the general populace have failed before, given the inability of local leaders to transcend family or baradari competition. In other words, progressive intentions are not enough to carry the PPP beyond the private goals, aims, and ambitions of its individual leaders. The unchecked striving for personal power and its concomitant self-aggrandizement intensify corrupt and/or ruthless practices. This striving also threatens to undo the PPP just as it destroyed the Muslim League, Republicans, and Conventionists in earlier periods. Syed's chapter is helpful in assessing this proposition.

II

Another important theme, therefore, is the nature of the political opposition in Pakistan and how it is perceived by the party in power. It appears that the opposition is being equated with anti-state and treasonous activities. The Bangladesh affair has reinforced the conviction that evil men in collusion with foreign governments are plotting the dismemberment of the remainder of Pakistan. Ultimately, their intention is alleged to be the dissolution of the country as a national entity. With some noticeable exceptions, the loss of East Pakistan has intensified an acute sense of personal and collective insecurity. In political terms this is translated into a growing fear of opposition motives and purposes.

Given these perceptions of the political opposition, Prime Minister Bhutto's PPP government acts as if it is justified in using whatever means seem appropriate to protect its own political interests, which, incidentally, have become synonymous with the territorial integrity of the country: hence, the banning in early 1975 of the National Awami Party and the incarceration of its national and many of its regional leaders. This action may or may not propel Pakistan toward becoming a one-party state. The PPP, in spite of its internal organizational problems, has demonstrated it has the legal and physical power to sedate political opposition. Experience elsewhere, however, would argue that coercion is only a partial and usually a temporary answer. Regional problems in Baluchistan and on the Northwest Frontier are quite different from those that provided the impetus for the Bangladesh movement in East Pakistan. While the opposition leaders in these frontier states are viewed with increasing suspicion, and indeed many of the most prominent of them have been jailed at this writing, the Bhutto administration must still contend with the principle of succession in a democratic society or give up all pretenses of genuine multi-party politics in Pakistan.

Thus, while the political situation remains in a characteristically volatile state, the immediate concern of the PPP government is to dramatize the channeling of developmental funds into areas long neglected by previous regimes, and, at the same time, recruit previously dissident elements into the political system. The integration of Baluchistan into the overall national structure, the Pastners assert in their presentation, is essential to the PPP as well as to Pakistan's quest for political unity. The PPP has not yet demonstrated a capacity to win Baluchi support at the ballot box, and the continuing tribal unrest necessitates the use of forceful means and adroit political manipulation to bring the province under firm central control.

Earlier Pakistan governments sought to displace local Baluchi rulers with bureaucratic officials, but the Bhutto government is following a policy more like that of the British *Raj;* the program involves exploiting the *sardari* system, hence allowing Baluchistan's traditional rulers ample opportunity to neutralize each other. And while the Sardars are engaged in protracted conflict with each other, the PPP is promoting economic development that it hopes will bring sufficient economic opportunities to the politically ambitious so that they can free themselves from their conventional tribal patrons. Naturally, many of the traditional leaders fear that these measures will deprive them of their historic followers, and resistance to change is pronounced in the more rugged interior. Carroll and Stephen Pastner consider these problems from the perspective of anthropologists who conducted field work in the Makran division of Baluchistan in 1968–69.

Prime Minister Bhutto is committed to quieting his turbulent frontier population. On October 15, 1974, an offer of amnesty was made to all dissident Baluchis surrendering to regular Pakistan forces. In his proclamation the Prime Minister insisted that the military operations conducted in the province only sought to restore law and order, not to punish the "misguided tribals." Moreover, the Bhutto strategy is to follow the stick with the carrot. More money was earmarked for Baluchistan in 1974–75 than at any time in Pakistan's history. In addition to developing roads, electrification, and new water supplies, programs are being aimed at abolishing feudal institutions — institutions that the Pastners examine in considerable detail. The success of this strategy rests upon numerous interrelated factors, but in no small measure it is a question of political and economic decision-making, which is investigated by Shahid Javed Burki in a subsequent chapter.

There is an obvious but complex relationship between Pakistan's variety of social groups, political groups, and governmental policy. Attention must be given to economic decision-making and the political considerations that determine who gets what, when, and how much in Pakistan. An examination of the five periods of Pakistan's history is made by Burki. He identifies these as: (1) The Jinnah Period (1947–51); (2) The Social Group Coalition Period (1951–58); (3) The Ayub Khan Period (1958–69); (4) The Military Period (1969–71); and (5) The Bhutto Period (1971 to the present). According to Burki, each period brought certain social groups into positions of prominence, but these groups proved more successful in promoting their own interests than in promoting the nation's well-being.

Since becoming independent, Pakistan has experienced little if any social equilibrium. And perhaps this helps to explain why political stability and nation-building programs repeatedly have broken down. In each of the periods mentioned above, those groups with powerful connections, or the decision-makers themselves, seldom if ever broadened the process to include either regional interests beyond what appeared to be the dominant political idiom of the time or those with varying ideas and philosophies. Politics by consensus has never been seriously explored in Pakistan, and therefore economic decision-making has been monopolized by those with narrow vision. It now remains for Prime Minister Bhutto to cope with this legacy. Burki's paper examines the distributive problem and the differing approaches to economic development prior to the Bhutto regime.

At the time of this writing, Bhutto's coalition is in flux. Originally his PPP was composed of urban factory workers from the large cities of Sind and the industrializing regions of the Punjab. To this mass were added ideological leftists with collective bargaining persuasions, elements of the landed aristocracy from Sind, and middle-level farmers from the Punjab. Also joining were the sharecroppers of the Northwest Frontier, heterogeneous student groups, and middle-class urban consumers. Strenuous efforts have been made to satisfy the demands of these different groups, but the PPP has been badly shaken by inflationary dilemmas and the high cost of essential imports. Organizationally, it has also found itself unable to manage complex socio-economic questions. Therefore, despite its monopoly of power, the PPP is not yet an effective government.

The problem is apparently both institutional and ideological. The PPP is dependent on the civil service for the management of state affairs, and that bureaucracy is in the process of being reorganized and politicized. But the core of the service is still dominated by men from the older conventional services who resent the loss of their special stations and privilege. And PPP dependence on the professional civil bureaucracy could provide the latter with the

leverage that is calculated to insure its continuing importance, no matter how well-intentioned the reforms may be.
If this should happen, many of the social groups in the
original PPP coalition are likely to remain unsatisfied.

In addition, the PPP is somewhat divided between those
who profess a higher ideological commitment and those who
are more attached to the personality and dynamism of Prime
Minister Bhutto. PPP purges have generally followed this
division, with the more doctrinaire among the leftists being
separated from the party. Lessened ideological fervor has
caused student disenchantment and apparently has also
provided a fillip for a resurgence of religious fundamental-
ism.

Burki and other contributors to this volume concur in the
view that Prime Minister Bhutto alone gives the PPP coherence and cohesion. The PPP, and the coalition that
identifies with it, is primarily Bhutto's own creation; he is
without question the supreme decision-maker in all aspects
of current Pakistani life.

III

The problems suggested above commingle with an economic picture not wholly of Pakistan's making. Worldwide
economic dislocation, spiraling inflation, and sharply increased prices for such necessary imports as petroleum and
foodgrains compound the difficulties of decision-makers the
world over. In the face of severe economic strains caused by
the secession of East Pakistan, the Indo-Pakistan War of
1971, the floods of 1973, and the global economic downturn,
the Pakistan government, in the view of Gilbert Brown, has
performed better than many other Third World countries.
Even the balance-of-payments crisis expected to follow the
loss of East Pakistani jute has not proven overly burden-
some. Indeed, Brown says that import earnings rose in FY

1973 by some 27 percent due to buoyant foreign demand and favorable world prices for Pakistani cotton, textiles, and rice. Brown argues that Pakistan appears to have a viable economy, but rising import demands, extremely high import prices, along with low investment and savings rates, could signal a decline in the rate of growth. Furthermore, fear of nationalization dampens the enthusiasm of those who would otherwise plow back a good portion of their profits into the economy. Government investment in the economy is small because of a lack of financial resources, and this requires that new incentives be offered to a private sector wary of government promises.

In the immediate period, however, inflation is perhaps the most serious problem facing the Bhutto government. Although the administration has raised the salaries of low- and middle-income groups, the increasing costs of virtually all commodities threaten to wipe out would-be gains. Pakistan's annual inflation rate during the Ayub years, Brown notes, was approximately 3 to 4 percent. But between January 1972 and December 1973 prices had risen by 20 percent. Price controls could go only so far to hold down prices in the face of worldwide inflation, and restrictive fiscal and monetary policies would only intensify unemployment and discourage economic growth.

Pakistan's economy can grow and it can sustain the country's population, but much depends upon the policies that the nation's leaders pursue. The administration's managerial ability is undergoing a public testing; few believe the PPP has the expertise to implement the economic programs that are being planned. The government has nationalized basic industries, insurance companies, and domestic banks. But as noted above it is also attempting to encourage the development of private establishments, especially small industrial plants, middle-level farms, and small businesses. Although the administration has swerved from its earlier proclaimed socialist course, the private sector will remain cautious and is not likely to commit itself, given continuing uncertainty about long-range government intentions and unpredictable policy changes. Pakistan's mixed economy will continue, however, and foreign investment will be encouraged as Prime Minister Bhutto endeavors to explain to his constituents how socialism and capitalism can coexist in his new system.

Lee Bean in his chapter examines the structure of Pakistan's labor force and the efforts of government to maximize employment. The labor force in Pakistan, as in other less developed countries, has increased at an unprecedented rate. Bean insists that the essential problem is finding employment in a relatively backward economy for a grossly unskilled and underskilled population, and this feat must be accomplished in an urban rather than an agricultural setting. The implications are obvious, though answers are elusive or difficult to implement. Socio-political instability is unavoidable unless the high unemployment projections are in error. It is wise, Bean argues, for the Bhutto administration to recognize the actual rates of population increase. He feels the Pakistan government may be underestimating the size of its potential labor force in 1985 by 4.6 to 7 million people.

The government appears to be encouraging emigration in order to earn foreign exchange. Such is the case with Pakistanis working in the countries of the Persian Gulf. But emigration is also being promoted in order to relieve some of the pressures on the job market. Such a policy could be counterproductive, for it would have little impact on the larger mass of people, while those Pakistanis with specialized skills would be among the first to leave. Other governmental policies that would result in delayed entry into the labor force are stopgap expedients. In the short run, such expedients can produce potentially adverse effects, especially when escalating demands are placed on selected job categories.

New schemes for inducting the educated unemployed into the PPP system are described by Brown. The National Development Volunteer Program is envisaged providing job opportunities to young scientists, engineers, and technicians. In addition, the Education and Social Services Corps, modeled somewhat after the experience of Iran's Literacy Corps, is to be organized and trained for work at the village level. The People's Work Program, the Integrated Rural Development Program, and the Agrovilles also aim at utilizing the energy and folk skills of the uneducated or undereducated population. Neither Brown nor Bean are sanguine about these programs, but they both agree that the times call for action. It has been stated repeatedly by the authors of this volume that the right commitment and the right leadership could register successes in spite of other inadequacies or shortcomings in the government's domestic policies.

IV

Pakistan's foreign policy is shaped by the demeanor, philosophy, and attributes of the country's leaders. During the Liaquat Ali Khan period, reports S. M. Burke, collective decision-making and consensual foreign policies were managed with reasonable success. Following Liaquat's assassination, however, Ghulam Mohammad, Iskander Mirza, and Mohammad Ayub Khan committed Pakistan to Western military alliances, and the civil-military bureaucrats virtually eliminated influence from the politicians. Whereas the alliances sought to protect Pakistan from the perceived Indian threat, they also isolated the country from its coreligionists in the Arab Middle East and Afghanistan, while apparently antagonizing the communist powers. Military ties to the West came in for severe criticism in Pakistan after the 1956 Suez Affair. And when the United States rushed weapons to India during the Sino-Indian border conflict in

1962 the Pakistanis were especially incensed. Demands that Pakistan quit the Western alliances were whipped up during the Pakistan presidential campaign of 1964–65, but when the United States imposed an embargo on arms to Pakistan during the Indo-Pakistan War of 1965, anti-Americanism reached a peak. Pakistan, it was said, had been betrayed by the United States. Forced to negotiate, Ayub Khan reluctantly signed the Tashkent Agreement, which his foreign minister, Zulfikar Ali Bhutto, allegedly refused to be associated with. It was soon after this event that Bhutto left Ayub's cabinet and began to attack his former leader.

Demonstrations organized by the political opposition focused on the foreign policy that now became blamed entirely on Ayub Khan. Bhutto led the demonstrators who insisted that Pakistan sever all ties with the United States. Given attacks from the student community and growing general restlessness in other sectors, Ayub was forced to step down. But he refused to pass power back to civilian control. General Yahya Khan received the transfer of authority and quickly assumed the presidency. It was only after the disaster that culminated in the civil war in East Pakistan and the subsequent Indo-Pakistan War of 1971 that the politicians again had a free hand in the fashioning of Pakistan's foreign policy. Burke's treatment of the way Pakistan's political personalities conducted the country's foreign affairs in the pre-Bhutto era is further informed by his own earlier positions within Pakistan's foreign service.

The Bhutto period is distinguished by the Prime Minister's personal diplomacy and his insistence on going directly to the people before certain major policies are formalized. Examples of the latter are Bhutto's efforts to obtain public sanction for both the 1972 Simla Agreement with India and the 1974 recognition of Bangladesh. Burke, Howard Wriggins, William Barnds, and Norman Palmer all appear to agree with the view that Bhutto's style is more populist than that of his predecessors. As with domestic administration, the management of Pakistan's foreign policy has been significantly politicized. Pakistan's quest for leverage in the international political arena remains largely unchanged in spite of the loss of East Pakistan. One man again dominates the governmental process, but the military establishment has been subdued and the civilian element is more pronounced.

Fear of India holds an important place in the nation's foreign policy, although this does not prevent Pakistan from pursuing ambitious goals. Barnds notes in his presentation how surprising it is that so poor a country should have sought security through confrontation rather than accommodation; moreover, that it should have declared so loudly and so consistently its intention to "wrest a sizable piece of territory [Kashmir] away from a neighbor several times its size." What is even more confounding is the awareness that this posture was established as early as 1947, when the country could not have anticipated receiving large-scale external military assistance.

As William Barnds and Norman Palmer explain, emotion, pride, and a strong sense of honor were more instrumental in shaping Pakistan's foreign policy than was rational, objective evaluation. Furthermore, Pakistani leaders were so convinced of the rightness of their cause that they naïvely assumed the Muslim world as well as the Commonwealth nations — or, at the very least, the United Nations — would come to their assistance in the Kashmir dispute. Indeed, it was with this same unrealistic expectation that Pakistanis looked to the United States and then finally to China in hopes of realizing their lofty aims. Even the East Pakistan crisis reveals the Pakistani disposition to expect too much from its "friends."

When Prime Minister Bhutto succeeded to the leadership of the country, he was called upon to uplift a discouraged and thoroughly confused nation, rebuild a political structure, revitalize a dismembered economic system, and cope with the consequences of a military defeat that swept away all illusions about the formidable regional power of India. All the same, there are some Pakistanis who still sense their showdown with India lies somewhere in the future. Nevertheless, since the Indo-Pakistani War of 1971 Pakistan's weakness in foreign affairs is observed not only in its position vis-à-vis India, but in its difficulty in acquiring support from significant major powers. The Soviet Union will not back Bhutto, given his continuing embrace of China and the United States, and Moscow's link with India. China is limited in what arms it can supply, suggest Barnds and Wriggins, and only the United States could, if it would, recreate a substantial, more up-to-date military establishment. (Given large sums of Iranian and Arab petrodollars, Pakistan has been making military purchases from the French, and these may exceed what it is likely to buy from the United States.) The detonation of India's nuclear device in May 1974 and Prime Minister Bhutto's "successful" Washington visit in February 1975 led the Ford administration to lift the arms embargo that the United States imposed on the country in 1965. It remains to be seen how this policy reversal, which places Pakistan in the same category as other countries able to buy arms from the United States, will affect Pakistan's military capability. But it is doubtful that it signals a resumption of large-scale military assistance, although some Indian publicists seem to fear this.

Discussing Pakistan's search for additional outside support to help balance the much greater power of India, Wriggins notes that Pakistan has always had a minor role in the state system, and Prime Minister Bhutto has the difficult task of educating his people to accept a clearly subordinate position vis-à-vis its primary enemy. Bhutto knows that his principal problem lies in how he adjusts Pakistan's weakness to India's strength without endangering his country's security. The handling of this delicate matter will also influence his control of the nation's domestic conditions. It is in this latter context that India's quasi-annexation of Kashmir must be examined. Even if Prime Minister Bhutto was moving toward a slow recognition of the status quo over that disputed territory, the Indian decision to unilaterally determine the region's future severely complicates further progress toward an Indo-Pakistani rapprochement.

The role of Pakistan's military in national policy-making has been ambiguous. Although reluctant to become embroiled in domestic politics again, the military may not always accept Bhutto's handling of the country's security. It has been asserted by Barnds that soldiers have rarely accepted a plowshare philosophy. Pakistani military leaders still believe Muslims are superior to Hindu soldiers, he comments, and even the 1971 defeat is being explained in ways that are not likely to bring about a fundamental change in outlook. In the short term at least, much depends on how successfully Prime Minister Bhutto manages the country's domestic life. And the expanded police establishment, especially the Federal Security Force, is concerned not only with controlling internal strife, but also with checking the temptation of the military to interfere in civilian affairs. Clearly, foreign policy and domestic policy are inextricably linked.

Given its fear of India, Pakistan has lived in the shadow of major war since its inception. Moreover, it fought large-scale encounters with its larger neighbor in 1965 and 1971; nor has the extended conflict in Kashmir between 1947 and 1949 been forgotten. Hence, India has been at the center of all Pakistan's foreign policy calculations. Without ignoring the historic, cultural, and psychological dimensions of the Indo-Pakistan conflict, one discerns a classic example of a weaker, smaller state's fearing its larger, stronger neighbor. But if the Pakistanis have feared India, the latter has often, by word or deed, reinforced these apprehensions as Pakistan's efforts to gain security through association with outside powers have raised Indian anxieties. In other words, there is sufficient self-fulfilling prophecy on both sides of the border. Although discussing different aspects of Pakistan's foreign policy, Wriggins, Barnds, and Palmer stress the balance-of-power scenario. And just as Pakistan has sought to balance India's might by allying itself with the United States, India has entered into an agreement with the Soviet Union to maintain a balance in its favor within the Indian Ocean region. Added to this equation is the factor of Communist China, which threatens India as it befriends Pakistan. Rather than producing a new balance in favor of Pakistan, however, China's role further complicates rivalries in South Asia. Moreover, these rivalries are not likely to dissipate despite the renewal of diplomatic relations between India and Pakistan, and India and China in 1976. And as Barnds explains, the ouster and death of Mujibur Rahman in Bangladesh has apparently strained Bangladesh's relations with India while improving those with Pakistan.

Pakistan's foreign policy cannot be examined without understanding the Pakistan–United States alliance, and Wriggins' paper is the most detailed in this area. It soon became obvious to both governments that neither could be expected to serve the interests of the other at the expense of its own interests. The Pakistanis were less concerned with the containment of international communism, while the Americans could see no point in making an enemy of India. As the Wriggins chapter brings out, both countries pursued balance-of-power objectives, but the United States was fixed on a global balance, whereas Pakistan's goal was regional at best. Curiously, in spite of these significant differences, Pakistanis and Americans were drawn to each other, and despite two decades of strain and considerable uneasiness they have maintained a surprisingly close association. Nevertheless, like the United States, Pakistan does seek other options, and China plays an important role in this search. Pakistan must acquire support wherever it can find it. However, the country profited only slightly from its

Chinese connection during the 1965 war with India, and China was of no help whatsoever in the 1971 conflict.

In conclusion, Bhutto's foreign policy is generally more conciliatory than bellicose. On the rhetorical side, both India and Afghanistan were in early 1975 the targets of increasing official attacks. Nevertheless, it is apparent that Pakistan wishes to avoid an incident that could precipitate conflict with one or both of these neighboring states. Moreover, the Prime Minister's emphasis on a policy of bilateralism seems to suggest that Pakistan refuses to take sides in any conflict involving the great powers. Pakistan remains in CENTO because the association helps Pakistan sustain close relations with Iran and Turkey and also keeps open a channel for the possible passage of United States arms shipments. It need only be noted that the CENTO military exercise called MIDLINK '74 in November 1974 involved Pakistani forces for the first time in almost ten years. Pakistan's overtures to the Muslim states of the Middle East, especially to Iran and select Arab states in the Persian Gulf area, are aimed at establishing and legitimating Pakistan's southwest Asian orientation. The close ties that Bhutto hopes to cement with the Middle East countries may provide Pakistan with diplomatic leverage in conducting future relations with India, but this is at the moment problematical.

If Pakistan senses that it may be outflanked by Indian diplomatic maneuvers, it could be right. Prime Minister Bhutto has worked arduously at cultivating improved relations with the Arab states. His numerous visits to Middle East countries have sought to emphasize Pakistan's new orientation away from the subcontinent. His dependence on Iran is dramatized in the $580 million credit that the Shah pledged Pakistan in July 1974. But the Middle East states do not base their policies on sentiment or common Islamic ties, as Palmer points out. Each nation has its own wider interests to consider. For the moment, however, while Iran seeks a wider role beyond the Persian Gulf and hopes to draw closer to India, it apparently views Pakistan as being of considerable importance.

V

The concluding chapter by Ralph Braibanti is a detailed theoretical examination of Pakistan's development as a political system. It is also a critique of the literature on political development and Pakistan's place therein. The authors of this volume would agree with his observation that without a thorough understanding of Pakistan and its unique place in the constellation of Third World countries, knowledge of the nation-state system in the latter quarter of the twentieth century is bound to be faulty. Appropriately placed as the final chapter of this volume, it points the way to subsequent research on Pakistan. After outlining in his synoptic chart thirty different paradigms of political development, Braibanti, using his own paradigm (architectonics, institutionality, participation, innovation) as an example, explores the salient characteristics of Pakistan's development. In so doing, he analyzes the relevant literature and various modes of analysis. His comments on polycommunality and on the Ahmediya issue put in a somewhat broader perspective the issue of national integration, treated by the Pastners, Malik, and others in these pages.

This introduction has attempted to select many of the themes discussed in this volume. *Pakistan: The Long View* is an examination of Bhutto's Pakistan in historical perspective, that is, Pakistan after the emergence of Bangladesh. Chapters are devoted to historical, political, economic, socio-political, and socio-economic as well as foreign policy subjects. The book looks at the complex issues challenging Pakistani government and society. Each chapter has been prepared by a scholar with long experience in Pakistan. Together, they represent a distinctive enquiry into many aspects of Pakistan's national existence.

2

The Wellsprings of Pakistan

Wayne A. Wilcox

The search for the true wellsprings of the idea of Pakistan is a difficult task. Authorities on the subject are divided in their evaluation of the importance of various factors, and very different criteria are used in examining oftentimes sparse evidence. This is not surprising since the Pakistan movement was such a short, complex phenomenon, and its outcome so dramatic. Explanations of Muslim nationalism in India involve many of the basic questions of social science and historiography, none more difficult than the problem of attributing particular outcomes to specific causes in a historical process. This article is not a history of pre-1947 subcontinental life, and it would be convenient if the story could begin on August 14, 1947. However, general interpretation of Pakistan's development must begin with the realization that differing interpretations about the roots of the state had important consequences after its creation.

The basic division of opinion and outlook is concerned with whether the seeding of Islam in the Indian subcontinent from the seventh century to the twelfth century produced a social dynamic that prefigured the emergence, in an age of nationalism, of an Indian Muslim state or states. The alternative view is that Pakistan emerged for a number of reasons, and from a number of processes, unique to British India in

Editors' Note: Wayne Wilcox was working on a history of Pakistan. This is a very lightly edited version of the first and only chapter he completed before his death.

the twentieth century—such as the British view of minority rights, declining public authority, wartime mobilizations and demobilizations, inflation, social change, the frustrations of limited provincial democracy, and severe rivalries between communal parties and commercial groups. Many of these tensions were displaced to, or justified in terms of, religious identification. Thus, the demand for Pakistan, expressed in terms of a Muslim identity, may have been an accumulation of more mundane social identities.

Neither of these overall theories or explanations satis-factorily accommodates the complexity of the last decade of the Pakistan movement (1937–47), nor allows for the undoubted fact that different participants in or against that movement had conflicting ideas and interests. Yet a more fundamental question is missing from these two grand histor-ical explanations: did a new set of political loyalties, focusing on an idea of Pakistan, emerge, and if so, why? More particu-larly, in the minds of its adherents, was "Pakistan" merely the political manifestation of a deeper loyalty to a "threat-ened" Islam, or was it, rather, a wholly secular concept in which Islam was a symbolic component? These are, in a way, the personal dimensions of the "movement" explanation.

These several basic questions cannot be definitively resolved. Their partial exploration, however, should be conducted with an awareness of the wide differences of class, region, and ideology that characterized the Indian Muslims.[1] The post-hoc–propter-hoc fallacy of the inevitabil-ity of Pakistan's emergence must also be eschewed to permit an appreciation of the external circumstances in response to which the various Muslim leaders in India acted. The stimuli that lay behind the Pakistan demand propelled people into a separate semi-free political process of great fluidity, and

1. This is made clear in the brilliant scholarship of Peter Hardy, *The Muslims of British India* (Cambridge: Cambridge University Press, 1972).

brought together demands and opportunities in a historically unique outcome—the Islamic Republic of Pakistan.

The "Pull" Hypothesis

A large number of Indo-Muslim thinkers and historians, led in recent times by Ishtiaq Husain Qureshi,[2] have argued that the nature of the Muslim social order requires a religiously supportive state. It was necessary for the Indian Muslims, therefore, to ensure that their faith shaped the society and its expression. During the era of Mughul rule, regardless of the peculiar interpretations of the emperors, the civic order was "Muslim." British rule in India, first thought to be hostile to Islam, was later accepted as religiously "neutral." This was a bitterly contested point, but a "non-statist" Islam did exist and was allowed to prosper modestly.

When British rule became demonstrably weakened and Indian independence became an immediate prospect, Indian Muslim leadership split along new lines. One body of opinion held that an independent India would provide a "neutral" environment in which Islam could continue to play its historical role. Another body, which had always held that British rule was hostile to Islam, argued that an independent Indian government where Muslims were a minority would be detrimental to a Muslim social order. A third group, many of whom accepted British neutrality, could not accept the view that a "Hindu India" could be neutral. It was the latter two groups who for quite different reasons coalesced behind the Pakistan movement.

Scholars who argue that the outcome was inevitable—or, at least, highly likely—base their view on an interpretation of Muslim history that is "corporatist." Islam is a total way

---

2. See I. H. Qureshi, *The Muslim Community of the Indo-Pakistan Subcontinent, 610–1947* (S-Gravenhage: Mouton, 1962).

of life, and the Muslim's values cannot be separated from the tradition by which he rears his children, earns his living, expresses his art, or makes his political decisions. The separation of church and state for a Muslim, therefore, is not only impossible, it is undesirable. Hence, in this era of nationalism, leading thinkers of Muslim India demanded that their state be governed by Islam.

The "Push" Hypothesis

A second factor undergirding this judgment was a reading of Hindu-Muslim relations that interpreted them as philosophically hostile: the conflict between monotheism and polytheism; between dietary habits that found the Hindus revering the livestock that the Muslims consumed; between heroes and villains who were from the other community. Even if Islam had not demanded its distinctive form of political society, there were reasons for its creation because of the differences between the two great communities of British India, especially because the Hindus outnumbered the Muslims in a ratio of more than three to one. The arithmetic of democracy would assure the Hindus a commanding position from which to ensure that their distinctive tradition dominated that of the Muslims.

It is difficult to determine how many Muslims, and who among them, held these views. Objectively speaking, neither argument was wholly true or widely accepted. Corporate Islam might have been a historic ideal, but it was rarely if ever practiced. Muslim-Hindu cultural confrontations were only part of a relationship that also witnessed aspects of sympathetic cooperation. The intertwining of religious idealism and social competition did, however, provide a remarkably strong set of ideas for political leaders to use in different settings, and it also came to be the dominant view of those politicians and ideologues who came together in the Muslim League and Pakistan movement. The question remains whether Pakistan was "inherent" once Islam had penetrated Indian society.

The "Secular Interests" Hypothesis

Perhaps a majority of those scholars studying the emergence of Pakistan believe the dominant factors at play were those of self-interest rather than those of socio-religious conscience. Like the other hypotheses, however, it is equally impossible to prove. Nonetheless, the evidence is quite extensive. An economic class argument has been made by Wilfred Cantwell Smith,[3] and, though subsequently disclaimed, it continues to attract adherents. This view holds that by the beginning of the twentieth century, a Muslim bourgeoisie was emerging. This class found many of its avenues of opportunity blocked by British and Hindu firms, and its members could not develop large-scale capital. Hence, its interest lay in a Muslim state where both British and Hindu competitors would be at a disadvantage, and in which Muslim businessmen would have considerable influence.

It should be noted that the Muslim commercial class was exceedingly small. Many Muslim businessmen were associated with British or Hindu enterprises and most Muslim entrepreneurs were located in territories that did not have Muslim majorities and thus were unlikely to be included in any new Muslim state. In these Muslim enterprises the fear persisted that any contraction in the market area, or any interruption of trade between regions in India, would be economically costly. This was of little consequence to the Muslims who *after* independence moved from India into Pakistan, and it is significant that most of the great commercial houses of Pakistan of the 1960s were not in existence in the 1940s.

3. Cantwell Smith, *Modern Islam in India* (London: Gollancz, 1946).

A more powerful argument for the economic interest hypothesis in the Pakistan movement focuses on the role of "feudal" landholding classes. When the Muslim League was founded in 1906, its membership was inclusive of the Indian Muslim feudal elite. This group was not particularly interested in the Pakistan movement until the eleventh hour, but it did perceive that "land reform" could be used as a weapon against it should the rival community seize power.[4] The Muslim League's economic policies before independence were vague but certainly more conservative than those of Jawaharlal Nehru's wing of the Congress party. Moreover, the number two man in the Muslim League hierarchy, Liaquat Ali Khan, had been leader of the United Provinces Agriculturalists' party. There was, therefore, less to lose with a Pakistan than with a Congress-dominated India that professed socialism.

Perhaps the most important interest group in the Pakistan movement was the Muslim professional middle class.[5] The educational progress of the Muslims in the 1920s and 1930s was quite rapid, and many teachers, doctors, lawyers, professors, military officers, and bureaucrats were recruited from this group. Their interests in an independent state are clear and direct, especially among those who were members of the civil and military services. Opportunities would abound in an independent Muslim state for other careers as well. The professional classes would suffer the least discomfort from political discontinuity when the British left, as their skills and credentials were uniquely mobile. Moreover, the occupations of this middle class were particularly governmental, and the more responsive a government to a Muslim

4. This did indeed happen. Land reforms in East Pakistan were easily passed since most large landholdings were owned by Hindus; the reverse was true in Uttar Pradesh, India. In the Pakistani Punjab and in the Indian Punjab, where landlords were of the majority community, land reforms have been weak and indifferently implemented.

5. This line of approach relies upon the excellent analysis of B. B. Misra, *The Indian Middle Classes* (London: Oxford University Press, 1961).

claimant, the greater the guarantee of high-grade employment opportunity. This helps explain the urban strength of the Muslim League and its popularity in colleges and universities.

Not all Muslim professionals were pro-Pakistan, however. Many in the cultural elite found India at least as congenial as Pakistan, and the idea of puritanical "mullah-rule" had no appeal to Lucknow and Bombay sophisticates. Highly successful Muslim lawyers, doctors, and even civil servants were less concerned with Hindu competition. In many cases, the affection for a particular region in India, the maintenance of historic lands, the familiarity of a regional idiom and a circle of friends undercut any support for the creation of a country that would have implied emigration and the liquidation of a personal heritage. Thus, when Pakistan was created, many families divided over whether to leave for the new land or stay behind in India.

A decisive group in the creation of Pakistan was the political leadership of various Muslim parties and provinces. Mohammad Ali Jinnah, leader of the Muslim League and, after 1946, an irreconcilable separatist, was a giant among his colleagues in terms of his intelligence and organizational ability. Jinnah's potential competitors in the Muslim community could claim only provincial status, and none could match his charisma. By 1946 he had brought all the provincial leaders under his sway, and those who opposed him found themselves undercut by the pro-Pakistan plebiscite votes taken in that year. When Jinnah decided to create Pakistan he gave all his energy to the task. Had he not led the movement, it is likely a federalized India and not partition would have been the outcome of the independence demands. It has been argued Jinnah hungered for authority, and in order to satisfy it he needed his own state. Reading his critics, "arrogant" appears to have been the most customary adjective used to describe him in the postwar period. Yet Jinnah was willing to accept the federal proposals set forth by the

Cabinet Mission Plan in 1946, proposals that would have foreclosed the creation of Pakistan.

The "Divide and Rule" Hypothesis

A number of historians have argued that Pakistan was the logical fulfillment of a British policy of "divide and rule," seduously followed from the late nineteenth century. In order for this policy to work, the British first had to convince the Muslims and Hindus that they were entirely different and could not get on together, and then to convince the Muslims that the British were their true protectors, "holding the balance." In the first part of their Indian rule, the British appear to have discriminated against the Muslim aristocracy, representing as it did the talent of the preceding political regime. It was only after the founding of the Indian National Congress in 1885 when the Hindus developed a new militancy that the British took care to rehabilitate the Muslims.[6]

Exploiting animosities was a natural enough imperial strategy, but it would be a mistake to see British policy as pitting one community against another, let alone as encouraging one community to create its own state (at the cost of British-built markets and industrial patterns). Until the Second World War, the nationalists in both camps were a minority and the British had ample power to manage them. The strength of British authority in India was magnified by the weakness of its opposition. As long as the enfranchisement of propertied classes kept politics in the hands of moderates, and as long as the British could decentralize the management of their subcontinental empire to ensure that no all-India movements developed, there was no reason to provoke intercommunity conflict. Moreover, the British were hard-

6. As Ainslie Embree has written, "Jinnah did not strengthen the Muslim League through an appeal to religious emotion. He built his case substantially on the formal recognition by the British in 1909, 1919, and 1935, through the creation of a Muslim constituency, that any political settlement would have to take the Muslims as a sub-nationality into account." *India's Search for National Identity* (New York: Knopf, 1972), p. 110.

pressed to contain the destruction and hatred caused by communal riots since the 1920s.

The Second World War weakened the British, mobilized all-India movements, extended political and social power downward from the moderates to the more extreme, and forced the British to work for intercommunal harmony in the interest of the war effort. It was an optimum period for the organization of powerful agitational parties, a period seized by the Muslim League, which did not oppose the war effort and which said it spoke for the 40 percent of the Indian army that was Muslim. The Congress party opposed India's being declared a belligerent and launched its "Quit India" movement. It paid for these disruptionist activities by having its leaders imprisoned in the crucial wartime years of mobilization. But the termination of hostilities did not ease the British burden.

Postwar India was turbulent. The British government faced military mutinies, severe inflation, and intensified political agitation. The election of a Labour government and its announcement that India would become independent before July 1948 intensified the struggle between Indian political groups at precisely that moment when governmental authority was weakest. Hence, instability and violence punctuated the decision-making environment. Moreover, group insecurity increased and members of the Muslim community, especially in the minority areas, were drawn together. In these circumstances the Muslim League became spokesman for the Muslim community on an all-India level. Provincial leaders either followed its lead or fell from power. The Congress leaders came to believe that the risks of including an alienated and discontented Muslim community of 100 million people in a free India were too great, and they rejected the goal of national unity. The Congress party granted Pakistan, not the British.

A strong case can be made for arguing that if the Second World War's dislocations had not weakened British authority, and had its effects not changed crucial relationships within the subcontinent, Pakistan would not have been created in 1947. If independence had been given to India early in the war, as advocated by a number of American statesmen,[7] the Pakistan movement would have been stillborn. The aftermath of war and the British decision to leave India produced a vacuum of authority and very ambiguous expectations — a kind of historical discontinuity — in which the Pakistan movement, complex and weak as it was, could flower.

The "Party Leaders Competition" Hypothesis

Whatever might have been the loyalties, interests, and predicament of Indians in the 1940s, political interplay was independently important in clarifying (and muddying) the issues and choices. The most powerful, well-organized, and well-led political "party" was the British government. From the Simon Commission to the Government of India Act, 1935, until the transfer of power to the Congress party and Muslim League in 1947, the British government occupied a pivotal position in the Pakistan movement. It could have blocked the establishment of the state either by arresting or detaining Jinnah and his lieutenants (which was never done), or by transferring power to an Indian authority without regard to Muslim League claims.

The British did not use their power in this way because they needed Muslim support in India in the 1930s, and especially during the war years. Given the Indian National Army crisis,[8] and the naval rating mutiny at Bombay, the British needed all the support they could muster from the 40 percent of the army that was Muslim. Any British action directed against the Muslim League and Jinnah was per-

7. See Stephen Hess, *America Encounters India, 1941–1947* (Baltimore and London: The John Hopkins University Press, 1971).

8. A force recruited by the Japanese from prisoners of war and armed to invade India as a quasi-nationalist liberation force.

ceived as causing an explosive reaction in the Punjab, the prime recruitment ground for the armed forces. Moreover, Prime Minister Churchill did not intend to grant India independence. During the years of conflict, his view was that the war came first, that India's role in the war was decisive, and that any political change would harm the war effort. Therefore, the British clamped down on the Congress and other outspoken nationalist groups, eased up on the Communists who were now allies in the "great patriotic war" effort, and had cordial relations with the Muslim League.

After the war when Prime Minister Attlee sent Louis Mountbatten to India to replace the soldier-viceroy Archibald Percival Wavell, British policy was reversed. Now there was no special interest in encouraging the Muslims or repressing the Hindus. Jinnah clearly saw that the British "party" had an interest only in maintaining its commercial lodgment, in cutting the costs of imperial management, and in getting out. Moreover, the Congress replaced the British as the dominant political power in the subcontinent, and the Muslim League had to deal with that new reality.

The leadership of the Indian National Congress was never really unified, and this was true after the war as well. Gandhi refused to play an institutionalized role within the party, preferring to lead by example from his unique pulpit. The most powerful figure in the party was Sardar Vallabhbhai Patel, the "organization man" who built Congress power and wealth and had allies throughout the states of India. Jawaharlal Nehru was the third member of the trinity—handsome, articulate, and thoughtful. These were important attributes in a country dependent on great leaders.

Gandhi's India was, like so many of his conceptions, rather vague. The imagery that he used, however, was entirely Hindu. He breathed life into the nationalist movement by reaching beyond the bounds of caste, class, and region and by energizing ancient symbols and popular culture. Muslim

League attacks against Gandhi were few, although his style and approach were totally antithetical to that of Jinnah and the Muslim League. To many Muslims, Gandhi was a pious Hindu "throwback." Moreover, Gandhi did not want India partitioned.

Sardar Patel was a party politician of little ideological conviction. He probably stood closer to Jinnah on economic and foreign policy matters than to Nehru, but he also represented the conservative Hindus. He is supposed to have made his views on Pakistan known with a terse "When one has a diseased extremity, one amputates it." The Indian Muslims were his diseased extremity, a view his outspokenness could never hide.

Nehru's views on Pakistan were as complex as those of Gandhi, but for other reasons. He believed that the Muslim League was engaged in some sort of medieval obscurantism, that the call "Islam in Danger" was bogus, and that a large number of expedient politicians had joined the religious bigots to serve their selfish interests. His model of a future India was a continuation of the British "neutral" state, more active in social and economic planning but wholly disinterested in religion. But he was realist enough to know that the Muslim League's power and appeal among the masses was genuine, and that Jinnah meant, after 1946, to have his own country.

It was Nehru who sabotaged the Cabinet Mission Plan, the last British proposal for a federated India before the Pakistan demand was accepted. The Muslim League had agreed to the division of India into three zones, with one corresponding to most of what is now West Pakistan. When queried about Congress acceptance of the plan, Nehru told a group of reporters that the plan would be accepted but only after power had been turned over to the Congress-dominated Indian parliament, thus giving them the sovereign power to modify it. This response triggered violent reactions throughout Muslim India and confirmed the "tricky" image that

Muslims have of Hindus. It was left for Mountbatten to announce that Indian unity was beyond reach and partition inevitable.

On Origins and Identities

The emergence of Pakistan was the product of exceptional circumstances and unprecedented conditions. It is clear that as a social movement Muslim separatism in midcentury India was propelled by powerful emotions. It is also clear that in its 1947 form Pakistan was an expression of forces that crystallized around the notion of an Islamic state, or Muslim government. It all led to the curious "two-part" federation, with West Pakistan essentially delimited by the Indus valley, and East Pakistan being comprised of the lower Gangetic delta. These two disparate areas shared a Muslim faith, a few common leaders, many similar views about the threat and cost of Hindu dominance, and to some extent a national language — English.

The reality of Pakistan was different from, and less than, the idea of Pakistan. If the Indian Muslims were to have their own society, it should be inclusive, but the territorial division of the British Indian empire left one-third of all the Indian Muslims in India. The Indo-Muslim architectural and cultural heritage was almost entirely concentrated in the upper Ganges valley, the heartland of modern India. The Muslim League's leadership was drawn from Bombay, Delhi, and the United Provinces, but the territories of Pakistan were Bengal, the Punjab, Sind, and the Northwest Frontier Province. Urdu, which some promoted as the national language of Pakistan, was practically unknown in Bengal and was little used in the Indus valley. At least, Pakistan should have insulated the Muslims from their Hindu rivals, but within a year of independence Hindu and Muslim armies were fighting for Kashmir.

The creation of Pakistan cost an estimated one million lives, and millions took flight to avoid the communal carnage.

The economy of the eastern Punjab and eastern Bengal was disrupted by the drawing of arbitrary frontiers. Property was destroyed and lifelong scholarly projects burned. Pakistan's creation was sealed in blood and fire, and Hindu-Muslim enmity attained a new level of intensity. By the summer of 1947 those who doubted the depth of primordial hatreds were forced to reconsider their positions. Nevertheless, the people of the new Muslim state had different ideas of why Pakistan emerged, and what it meant. Peasants in Sind or Baluchistan were little touched by the emergence of Pakistan, whereas the refugees had suffered enormous trauma. People inhabiting the border districts between West Pakistan and India, and between the parts of Bengal, saw a torrent of destruction and recoiled from efforts at reconciliation. To most of these people, whatever their views of Muslim separatism, Pakistan was *necessary.*

Given that Pakistan was necessary, most refugees felt it should be the center of their loyalties. They had left the past, the legacy of their fathers, oftentimes their families, and arrived in the new world, Pakistan. For the people who already lived in what became Pakistan, however, there was no change except that there were fewer Hindus and many more poor, dispossessed people. Like farmers everywhere, they resented any plan to give their land to "foreigners," their loyalties remaining local or, at best, regional. This unavoidable contradiction soon became a poisonous social division, making it exceedingly difficult to fashion a coherent set of national policies. Moreover, this multidimensional divisiveness has carried down to the present Bhutto period in Pakistan's history.

It is perhaps enough to know the complexities and forces that brought Pakistan into being. It is useful to remember that the historical process is inherently untidy, and that countries are the most complex of a whole range of social institutions. If Pakistan was tenuous at birth, so too are most other new countries. If Pakistan lacks a settled national patriotism, so too do many countries much longer in history. What Pakistan continues to have is a faith, made the more poignant by desperation. This was the promised land, and the only land as well.

3

Union or Partition: Some Aspects of Politics in the Punjab, *1936–45*

Craig Baxter

The Government of India Act, 1935, was in keeping with the gradual transfer of power to Indians enunciated by Edwin Montagu as secretary of state for India in 1917 and carried forward by the Government of India Act, 1919. The new constitutional arrangements—largely imposed by the British after the failure of the series of round table conferences—were fully acceptable to none of the political groups in India, but all prepared for the election to be held in the winter of 1936–37 if for no other reason than the vote by an expanded electorate would be a measure of the level of support for each party. To the British and to many Indians, the powers of provincial autonomy would be a testing ground for eventual self-government. Events—particularly the resignations of the Congress ministries following the Viceroy's declaration in September 1939 that India was at war—led to a much less than full experience with provincial autonomy prior to independence. However, one province, the Punjab, did maintain a ministry of the same party throughout the life of the first provincial assembly.[1]

The importance of the Punjab in this period was, in several ways, greater than that of any other province. Without the Punjab, or a portion of it, the concept of partition could not

---

1. For an account of the working of provincial autonomy in other provinces, see Reginald Coupand, *Indian Politics, 1936–1942* (London: Oxford University Press, 1943).

have worked, whether in the framework proposed by Iqbal at the 1930 session of the Muslim League, the acronymic suggestion of Chaudhury Rahmat Ali, or the form that grew out of the Lahore resolution of 1940. The Punjab was, and is, the sine qua non of Pakistan. Support for the Muslim League as such in the 1936–37 election in the Punjab was almost nonexistent, yet by the 1945–46 election the League was able to win all but a handful of the Muslim seats in the province.

This chapter examines briefly six events or trends that contributed to the change in the allegiance of the Muslims of the Punjab from the Unionist Party to the Muslim League, from a party dedicated to a multi-communal and socio-economic approach to politics to one that, by 1945, seemed unalterably committed to ending the unity of India. These events are (1) the difference in approaches to the 1936–37 election by the Unionists and the Muslim League and the ensuing triumph of the Unionists; (2) the pact concluded between Sir Sikandar Hayat Khan and Mohammad Ali Jinnah at Lucknow and its effect on the politics of the Punjab; (3) the role of Sir Sikandar in the Lahore resolution and his reaction to the meaning placed on it by Jinnah; (4) the death of Sikandar and the succession of Malik Sir Khizr Hayat Khan Tiwana and its implications for the Sikandar-Jinnah pact; (5) the impact of the behavior, alleged or real, of the Congress ministries and the rise of a new generation of politicians; and (6) the contest between the League and the Unionists in the 1945–46 election and the victory of the League.

The 1936–37 Election

As the time for active election campaigning drew near, clearly the first among political figures in the Punjab was Mian Sir Fazl-i-Husain.[2] He had been a minister and an

---

2. See the excellent biography by his son, Azim Husain, *Fazl-i-Husain, a Political Biography* (Bombay: Longmans Green, 1946), which serves also as a record of Unionist politics up to Sir Fazli's death.

executive councillor following the Montagu-Chelmsford reforms, and in 1930 he was named to the Viceroy's executive council. In 1935 his term in New Delhi expired and he returned to Lahore to lead the Unionist Party in its preparations for the forthcoming election. Although Fazli had played an important role behind the scenes in Muslim politics, both nationally and in the province, while in New Delhi he was necessarily inhibited from becoming involved in the day-to-day political activities of his home province. His national stature, however, was sufficiently high that he was invited by the Muslim League, through Jinnah, to preside over the League's 1936 session, a request he declined owing to differences with Jinnah.[3] He had served as an unofficial adviser to leaders of the All-India Muslim Conference during their attempt to bring together disparate Muslim political leaders as well as an adviser to Muslim representatives under the leadership of Sir Muhammad Shafi at the round table conferences.

On his return to the Punjab Fazli found a party that was divided into two loosely formed factions. One of these was headed by Sir Sikandar Hayat, who had replaced Fazli both as a minister and as executive councillor, and included as Sikandar's principal lieutenants, Nawab Muzaffar Khan, Mir Maqbul Mahmud, and Mian Ahmad Yar Khan Daultana. Opposed to this group was that generally described as the Noon-Tiwana faction, headed actively by Malik Firoz Khan Noon, a minister in the Punjab, and, behind him, the aging but long-active Nawab Malik Sir Umar Hayat Khan Tiwana.[4] Intermarriage as well as political allegiance bound the factions together. For example, Sikandar was brother-in-law to both Muzaffar Khan and Maqbul Mahmud and once considered the marriage of one of his daughters to the son

3. *Ibid.*, pp. 306–7, contains the text of Jinnah's letter.
4. In the last section of this chapter I will allude to the continuing rivalry between the Noon-Tiwana and Sikandar-Daultana factions.

(Mian Mumtaz Mohammad Khan Daultana) of Ahmad Yar Daultana, who in turn was related to a number of members of the faction.[5] Noons and Tiwanas were also intermarried. Fazli acted to break the factional dispute by "exiling" both leaders from the Punjab. Sikandar was dispatched to the prestigious but non-political position of deputy governor of the Reserve Bank of India, and his place in the executive council was taken by Muzaffar Khan. Noon was found an even more remote but perhaps more prestigious position as High Commissioner of India in London and was replaced as minister in the Punjab by Fazli himself. Fazli also attempted, with mixed success, to set up a party secretariat (at the head of which was Nawab Sir Shah Nawaz Khan of Mamdot) to establish formal procedures for the selection of candidates and to provide means to raise funds for the campaign.

Fazli and Jinnah, however, had diametrically opposite views of the role of the Muslim League in the election. To see this in relation to the Punjab, it is necessary to look at the "communal award" made in 1932 by the British prime minister and how it affected the province. The award followed closely the suggestion of Sir Mohammad Shafi at the last round table session, a plan that presumably had the approval, if not the joint authorship, of Fazli. The Punjab was to have an assembly of 175 members, of whom eighty-six would be elected from territorial constituencies specifically designated for Muslims. The elections would be under a separate electorate system, a point that both Fazli and Shafi

---

5. For a more detailed discussion of the family connections of the Hayats of Wah, the Daultanas, and the Noon-Tiwana family group, see Craig Baxter, "The People's Party vs. The Punjab 'Feudalists,'" *Journal of Asian and African Studies*, VIII, Nos. 3–4 (July–Oct. 1973), 166–89. The Wah family was under consideration in a study in progress by Herbert Feldman, to whom I am indebted for permitting me to see portions of his draft. There is a family connection between Fazli and Noon—one of Fazli's daughters is married to Noon's brother. Also, in this chapter the titles listed for individuals are those received during their lifetimes and not necessarily those held at the time of the events being described.

had strongly supported in the past, even when Jinnah appeared willing (in the late twenties) to enter a joint electorate system. But the eighty-six seats would, even if won by a single political party, fall short of a majority. Muslims could reasonably expect to win two or three special seats for landholders and thereby push just beyond the 50 percent mark.[6]

At the Bombay session in 1936 Jinnah received a mandate from the League to set up a parliamentary board that would select candidates to contest Muslim seats; the intention was that the League would contest all seats in its own name. Fazli demurred and put forward another plan. He foresaw that no party in the Punjab, be it Muslim League or Unionist, could expect to win all seats assigned to, or presumed to be safe for, Muslims. With the very close margin in the communal award it seemed but logical to assume that the principal Muslim party could not win a majority on its own. Therefore, said Fazli, it would be necessary for the Muslims to ally themselves with non-Muslims who had similar economic and social goals and to campaign on a non-communal basis for these goals. In the Punjab such a group was available and already allied within the Unionist Party. These were the Haryana Jats under the leadership of Chaudhury Sir Chhotu Ram. In addition, there was an unwritten understanding with the Khalsa National Board, of which Sardar Sir Sundar Singh Majithia was the nominal provincial leader. In the Muslim-majority provinces, according to Fazli, the important immediate task was the formation of governments under Muslim leadership but including other communities. If successful, it would demonstrate that maximum provincial autonomy with a confederal and limited center was the pattern to be followed in an independent India.

Under the Fazli program the Muslim League would become the representative body of Muslims in the Central

6. One of these seats was certain, that for Baluch *tumandars*, since the tiny electorate was composed entirely of Muslims.

Legislative Assembly and would be the national forum for the expression of Muslim views to the British and the Hindus. It would not, however, be involved in provincial politics directly. Rather it would be a loose coalition of the Muslim segments of the multi-communal parties in the provinces. The basis of this coalition would be a post-election meeting of Muslim legislators called, if he agreed, by Jinnah; if not, by Fazli himself.[7] The two men met in Lahore in April 1936, during the final illness of Fazli. When Jinnah left the house he commented that the two had agreed to disagree on the conduct of the election but would meet following the convening of the new assemblies. Fazli's death in August precluded this, but his successor, Sikandar, carried out much of the post-election portion of Fazli's plan.

The death of Fazli brought Sikandar back from his post in Calcutta to assume the leadership of the Unionist Party. The party went ahead with election preparations designating single candidates in most of the eastern and central Punjab. In the western districts, where no other party existed, many of the contests assumed the character of a preferential primary among several persons, each of whom was committed to the Unionist platform. Fazli had recognized that some urban Muslims, notably Iqbal and Malik Barkat Ali, opposed his plan and they ran candidates against the Unionists, as did the Congress and several other Muslim groups, including the Ahrars and the Ittehad-i-Millat. The League won one seat, Barkat Ali's, and two other Muslim groups won two each, all in urban areas, while the Congress took two rural seats. These results gave further support to Fazli's contention that placing all bets on Muslim seats would not produce a majority in the Assembly. However, by adding thirteen Hindu seats to its Muslim victories, the Unionists

---

7. Sir Fazli presented these proposals formally at a meeting of the executive committee of the All-India Muslim Conference at Delhi on February 16, 1936, at which the Aga Khan presided. See Nur Ahmad, *Martial Law-se Martial Law-tak* (Lahore: Din Muhammadi Press, 1965), p. 175.

were able to win a total of ninety-five seats and were assured the support of a number of independents as well as those elected on the Khalsa National Board Ticket.[8]

The Sikandar-Jinnah Pact

Following the election, on April 1, 1937, a provincial ministry was installed under the leadership of Sir Sikandar Hayat Khan. Sir Chhotu Ram, the leader of the Hindu Haryana Jats in the Unionist Party, became de facto number two in the cabinet, while Sir Sundar Singh Majithia of the Khalsa National Board was included as a representative of the Sikhs. The urban areas were represented by both a Hindu and a Muslim. Sikandar included as the sixth member the Assembly leader of the Noon-Tiwana faction, Malik Sir Khizr Hayat Khan Tiwana. The cabinet pledged itself to a program of further advance in the province's rural areas, expansion of educational opportunities, elimination of the disabilities of the backward and scheduled castes, and prosecution of new development schemes.[9] Urban Hindus were concerned by the prospect of further legislation protecting rural landholders against the activities, real or imagined, of the largely Hindu trading classes, but Sikandar was able to maintain cordial relations with the leaders of the Hindu Election Board, the rubric under which the Hindu Mahasabha campaigned in the Punjab. Relations with the more conservative Sikhs were cemented through the inclusion of Majithia in the cabinet, while relations with the Akali Dal

---

8. Election results given here are taken from official reports and in some cases disagree with press and other unofficial reports. For example, the official report for the first Assembly election lists Raja Ghazanfar Ali as a Unionist, although it is known that he accepted the Muslim League ticket and switched to the Unionists only after the results were in. However, for uniformity, the official reports are used as these are the only formal record available. For the first election: Great Britain. India Office. East India. Constitutional Reforms: elections. *Return showing the results of elections in India, 1937* (London: H.M.S.O., 1937). Cmd. 5589.

9. Lajpat Rai Nair, *Sikandar Hyat Khan, the Soldier-Statesman of the Punjab* (Lahore: Institute of Current Affairs, 1943[?]), pp. 66–70, contains the text of Sikandar's April 1, 1937, speech that details the program.

became closer when the "Sikandar-Baldev Pact" was concluded in 1942.[10] Sikandar used his principal lieutenants well. Muzaffar Khan worked closely with the Sikhs, while Maqbul Mahmud and Sikandar's brother, Nawab Sir Liaqat Hayat Khan, were conduits in dealing with the princes whose territories intertwined with those of the province. Communal disputes were not absent but were kept under close control.

After the building of an intricate system of supports within the province, it was still necessary for Sikandar to find a means through which he could link the Muslims of the Punjab with the national Muslim movement. More importantly for him, he had to do this in such a way that he would have control of any provincial manifestation of a national movement. Many in the Unionist Party felt they should have a part in the national movement, and Sikandar would be hard-pressed to keep his colleagues in check, especially after the Congress refused to form coalition governments with the Muslim League in the Hindu-majority provinces. The specter of "Hindu Raj" was very real for Muslims in these provinces.

Just as Sikandar needed some kind of association with the Muslim League, Jinnah needed the assistance of the regional parties in the Muslim-majority provinces. The League had done quite poorly in the election.[11] While the official results are clouded by the large number of independent Muslims returned to public office (some of whom were members of the League but chose not to run on the party's ticket), it was only in the United Provinces that the League could claim any real success; it was there that the Congress' refusal to form a coalition was most strongly felt. The League session in Lucknow in October 1937 was hardly expected to be a victory celebration; even the president of the previous session at Bombay had deserted the League. Several mem-

10. *Ibid.*, pp. 58–65.
11. Source as listed in n. 8 above.

bers of the Unionist Party had been and, constitutionally, still were members of the Muslim League Council, and they were invited to attend the Lucknow session. Mamdot and Raja Ghazanfar Ali Khan were among those who dealt with the League and arranged for Sikandar himself to attend as a "special invitee." The existing Muslim League in the Punjab also attended the session, represented principally by Barkat Ali since Iqbal was in too poor health to attend. Thus, the Punjab sent what amounted to two delegations, one of primarily rural Unionists, the other of urban Leaguers. Similar negotiations enhanced the session with the presence of Maulvi Fazlul Huq, leader of the Krishak Praja Party and premier of Bengal. Jinnah's session thus commanded more attention than might have been expected, but the allegiance of the two premiers was yet to be gained.

Barkat Ali prepared a draft for an agreement between Jinnah and Sikandar that, in effect, would have dissolved the Unionist Party and brought the Muslim members into the League, thereby hindering the prospect of a continued coalition government in the Punjab. The arrangement would have been similar to that offered the League by Nehru in the United Provinces. Sikandar rejected it out of hand. Then Maqbul Mahmud undertook to write a formula for cooperation that was successful. Both Sikandar and Jinnah signed this "pact," and it was ratified by the council of the League.

The terms of the agreement were straightforward. It arranged for Muslim Unionists to participate in the League on national matters, while they would remain Unionists in regard to provincial questions. Sikandar would ask all Muslims in the Unionist Party in the Assembly to join the League and to place themselves under the discipline of the League's central and provincial bodies. Future elections and by-elections would be held under the banner of the Unionist party, and successful Muslims would form a Muslim League party in the Assembly separate from but in coalition with the overall Unionist Party. Although these members were to be subject to the provincial board of the League, the final paragraph of the pact said that this body would be "reconstituted," which was simply another way of saying that control of the League in the Punjab would pass from Iqbal, Barkat Ali, and their associates to Sikandar and the Unionists.[12] The result was a boost in morale for Jinnah. The League could now claim as members the ruling party in the Punjab (and in Bengal as a similar arrangement was made with Fazlul Haq), but for Sikandar it would end the opposition of the League and provide a means to control Muslim sentiment. Often looked upon as a victory for Jinnah, it was equally one for Sikandar. The Lucknow session was not the meeting of all Muslim legislators envisaged by Fazl-i-Husain—the absence of the Khudai Khitmatgars from the Frontier was the most notable—but on paper, at least, the majority of the Muslims were on the same team.

The reconstitution of the Punjab League Board was not painless. Iqbal spent much of the last year before his death complaining to Jinnah about the usurpation of the offices by Sikandar's men.[13] Sikandar met Iqbal, who then wrote to Jinnah opposing the transfer of control of the League to the Unionists. Malik Barkat Ali, professing his staunch devotion to the leadership of Jinnah, and admitting at the same time his concern at the rural takeover of the League, attacked Sikandar on several occasions. He described Sikandar as an "autocrat" and added "it is wrong to say that any political principles bind the members of the Unionist Party."[14] Barkat Ali also wrote that were Sikandar to disband the Unionist Party "the charge that he is really untrue to the Muslim League and is covertly advancing the cause of his erstwhile Unionist Party to the permanent detriment of the Muslim

---

12. Text in Nair, *op. cit.*, p. 57.

13. *Letters of Iqbal to Jinnah* (Lahore: Sh. Muhammad Ashraf, 1942). Foreword by M. A. Jinnah. Esp. pp. 26 ff.

14. M. Rafique Afzal, *Malik Barkat Ali, His Life and Writings* (Lahore: Research Society of Pakistan, 1969), p. 126.

League shall then have no foundation."[15] The opposition
of those formerly in control of the League was in vain. The
Unionists took over the organization, placing Mamdot at
the head, and used it to their advantage so long as Sikandar
and his close associates lived. Barkat Ali, however, was to
make a prediction that came true soon after Sikandar's death
when he wrote "there is a great deal of discontent and dissatisfaction brewing beneath the surface and any day a storm
may break out."[16]

Sikandar and the Lahore Resolution

Sikandar's concept of the constitutional arrangements of
an independent India have already been mentioned. Following the ideas expressed by Fazli prior to the election, he
desired a high level of provincial autonomy as a guarantee
that Muslims would be the principal members of intercommunal coalitions in those provinces where they were a
majority; in turn, the automatic Hindu majority at the center
would be severely limited in its power. In the late thirties
and early forties a number of politicians and writers, many
of them Muslim, put forward proposals for the post-independence period in India. Among these were Sikandar and
Nawab Sir Shah Nawaz Khan of Mamdot.[17]

Sikandar's plan, published in 1939, was anything but the
model of a democratic constitution. It retained much power
in the hands of the viceroy, who would head the executive
and serve also as an arbiter among the various communities
in India. A key suggestion was, "Only those subjects, the
retention of which is essential in the interest of the country
as a whole and for its proper administration, shall be allo-

15. *Ibid.*, p. 127.
16. *Ibid.*, p. 126.
17. Syed Rais Ahmad Jafri, *Rare Documents* (Lahore: Muhammad Ali Academy,
1967), contains the texts of Sikandar's plan (II, 249–53) and that published by
Mamdot (II; 263–65). Whether Mamdot was simply the publisher of the latter, or
the writer, or stimulated the writing by a less prominent Punjabi, is a matter of
speculation; at any rate, his name is associated with it.

cated to the centre, e.g., defence, external affairs, communications, customs, coinage and currency, etc." He also envisaged an intermediate government between the provinces and the center in the form of seven zonal administrations, two having Muslim majorities. The Cabinet Mission Plan of 1946 would have three zones, but otherwise there were many parallels in the two proposals. The zonal administrations would take the powers allotted to the federal administration under the 1935 Act, except for those that were agreed to be included under the new central government. Checks on the central exercise of power included specific allocation of places in the cabinet among the zones and among the communities, an interzonal advisory committee for defense and another for external affairs, a one-third membership in the central legislature for Muslims, and communal voting on matters having communal aspects. Both central and zonal legislatures would be elected indirectly by the members of the provincial assemblies, ensuring that those named to higher bodies would be responsive to the provincial legislatures and, presumably, less likely to be caught up in schemes that might increase the power of the center and decrease the power of the zones and the provinces. Provincial autonomy and communal representation thus were the keys to Sikandar's plan, but division of the country was not contemplated.

In February 1940 the League decided to hold its annual session the following month in Lahore. During February Jinnah had conversations with the Viceroy in which he referred to the possibility of a Muslim demand for the division of India on the basis of the "Two Nation Theory." Sikandar was quickly made aware of this and decided to propose a resolution for the League's consideration in Lahore. He and Maqbul Mahmud drafted a document, the exact text of which is not available, but which can be reconstructed from Sikandar's speech to the Punjab Assembly on March 11, 1941. The Sikandar text contained two basic points: first, each province would become a sovereign state; second, these sovereign states would cede minimal powers (defense, communications, foreign affairs) to a central body that would act as the agent for the sovereign states in these areas.[18] This formulation, of course, was much more acceptable to Sikandar and the Unionists than the one passed at the session. Assuming the political alignment in the Punjab continued, it would give full local control to the multi-communal body, would all but eliminate the Muslim League as a factor in the province, and nationally would reduce the League to a loose pressure group.

The resolution that was passed—the so-called Pakistan Resolution—was a model of how not to draft a document. It left many points unclear and, in places, was internally contradictory. It was soon denounced bitterly by Sikandar and other old-line Unionists. The lumping of the Punjab with other provinces in the northwest and the inferred lopping off of the part of the territory belonging to the province were the immediate points of objection. Separation from the rest of India also held no appeal, and, as Khizr Hayat Khan Tiwana was later to point out, separation could be detrimental to those Muslims who would remain in Hindu-majority provinces. Even more basic, many Unionists considered the "Two Nation Theory" to be nonsense. In the Punjab castes and tribes were divided among Hindus, Sikhs, and Muslims. For example, it was difficult to assert that a Sikh Bajwa Jat belonged to a different nation than a Muslim Bajwa Jat. Sikandar's speech of March 11, 1941, was perhaps his strongest attack on the resolution and on the concept of Pakistan:

If that is what Pakistan means, I will have nothing to do with it. Let us join hands in order to preserve and maintain peace and harmony within the province, and unite with the rest of India to face with courage and confidence the danger from without. And let

18. Nur Ahmad, *op. cit.*, p. 199.

us above all show to the rest of India that we in the Punjab stand united and will not brook any interference from whatever quarter it may be attempted. Then and only then will we be able to tell meddling busybodies from the outside, "Hands off the Punjab!"[19]

The meddling busybody foremost in Sikandar's mind was Jinnah, with whom the Punjab premier was to have another brush. Lord Linlithgow had decided to set up a representative Defense Advisory Council and consulted Jinnah about its make-up. Jinnah's intransigence about the number and method of naming the Muslim members and the refusal of the Congress to participate delayed the implementation of the Viceroy's plan until July 1941. Linlithgow wrote to Jinnah to inform him of the Muslims selected, but Jinnah interpreted the letter to mean that the persons chosen were taken as representatives of the Muslims, in his view under his ultimate authority, and not because of their other political capacities. Three who were challenged were Sikandar, Maulvi Fazlul Huq of Bengal, and Sir Mohammad Sa'adullah of Assam; all of them assumed they were asked to join as premiers of their respective provinces and accepted the invitation with that understanding. All were members of the Muslim League, however, and Jinnah directed that each be served with a show-cause notice to explain their violation of League discipline.

Sikandar reacted strongly. He decided to resign from the League rather than from the council, and he went to Bombay to attend a meeting of the working committee armed with the resignations from the League signed by seventy-three members of the Punjab Assembly. However, when Sikandar and Jinnah met in Bombay, the latter showed the Punjab leader the letter from Linlithgow. Sikandar was taken by surprise and agreed with Jinnah's interpretation. He then agreed to resign from the council, as did Fazlul Huq and Sa'adullah. The heavy hand used by Jinnah in this episode

19. Coupland, *op. cit.*, p. 252.

was not calculated to endear him to Sikandar. It was also a major factor in driving Fazlul Huq from the Muslim League.

The Death of Sikandar and the Succession of Khizr

On December 26, 1942, Sir Sikandar Hayat Khan died unexpectedly in Lahore. Earlier that year, on March 28, Nawab Sir Shah Nawaz Khan of Mamdot, the provincial League president, had died and was replaced in that post by his son, Nawab Iftikhar Husain Khan. Another of Sikandar's close associates, Mian Ahmad Yar Khan Daultana, had died in 1940.

The question of the succession to Sikandar is one on which more information is needed. The second-ranking minister in the cabinet was Chaudhury Sir Chhotu Ram, but the political reality that a Muslim-majority province required a Muslim premier eliminated him from consideration. With the death of Sikandar, only the Noon-Tiwana faction of the Unionist Party was represented among the surviving members of the cabinet, by Malik Khizr Hayat Khan Tiwana, in age and experience the youngest of the five remaining. However, the Sikandar-Daultana faction, which bore their names even after the deaths of the two men, claimed several experienced and important political figures. Among these were Nawab Muzaffar Khan, a member of the Assembly and a former executive counselor; Mir Maqbul Mahmud, a parliamentary secretary with much experience in the princely states; and Chaudhury Sir Shahabuddin, the speaker, a former minister and a brother-in-law of Daultana. Outside the Assembly, Nawab Sir Liaqat Hayat Khan, then premier of Patiala state, was a strong figure who merited consideration. There is reason to believe that Muzaffar Khan was consulted closely by the governor, whose task it was to select a successor who in his judgment could command a majority in the Assembly. It seems possible that an offer was actually made to the nawab, who declined it. With hindsight it would appear that the experience of Muzaffar Khan might have enhanced the possibility of the Unionists' staying together. He had many of the political skills of Sikandar and had assisted the late premier in his political negotiations with Sikhs and Hindus of the coalition. Another potential premier was Malik Sir Firoz Khan Noon, who by this time had returned from England and was a member of the Viceroy's executive council. Noon has written that Governor Glancy offered the premiership to him, but that he declined and recommended the governor choose Khizr.[20] This writer has been unable to locate independent confirmation of Glancy's "offer," and Noon himself implied in another passage in his autobiography that his summons to Lahore in 1953 was the first time he was offered power in the province.[21]

Khizr was appointed premier and gained the support of the Assembly. He was faced with the question of filling the vacancy in the cabinet created by Sikandar's death and by his own promotion. It seemed that he must select a rural Muslim from the Sikandar-Daultana faction, but his choice was unexpected. He named Sardar Shaukat Hayat Khan, the son of the late premier. Shaukat had taken little part in politics and was indeed on duty in the Indian army. He was released from service, returned to Lahore to take up his post in the ministry, and soon began to clash with Khizr.

Jinnah quickly sensed that he had a weaker person with whom to contend in the Punjab than Sikandar, and he also was aware that the younger Unionists were more firmly with the Muslim League and its announced program for the partition of India. Regardless of what may have been said in the Sikandar-Jinnah pact, it was obvious that Sikandar ruled the Punjab with a Unionist ministry and not with one in which something called the Muslim League Assembly party was in coalition with other groups. At no time during Sikan-

20. Firoz Khan Noon, *From Memory* (Lahore: Ferozsons, 1966), p. 187.
21. *Ibid.*, p. 235.

dar's regime did the Muslim League party as such ever meet; decisions were taken at caucuses of the Unionists. The elder Mamdot served obediently as provincial president and was, if anyone was, the leader of the almost mythical Assembly party of the League. His son, however, drew about him some younger members of the Assembly along with leftover Leaguers like Barkat Ali. They demanded of Khizr that meetings of the League Assembly party be held. Khizr, with the support of the other ministers, refused to accept this interference in cabinet affairs.

In April 1944 Jinnah trekked to Lahore to investigate the situation. The upshot was an order from Jinnah to Khizr to designate his ministry the "Muslim League Coalition Ministry" rather than the Unionist ministry. Nothing could have been more disastrous to the carefully arranged multicommunal government of the Punjab. Khizr recognized this and by his silence refused to comply, citing the Sikandar-Jinnah pact, which he considered binding both on Jinnah and on himself as Sikandar's successor. The refusal initially was a silent one in that Khizr simply did not respond to a message from Jinnah delivered by the younger Mamdot and Mumtaz Daultana. An angry Jinnah had Khizr expelled from the League and his Muslim ministers were urged to quit his cabinet. Khizr jumped first, however, and dismissed Shaukat from the cabinet. Two parliamentary secretaries, including Raja Ghazanfar Ali, resigned.[22]

Khizr prepared a statement in which he refuted Jinnah's action.[23] The essence of Khizr's argument was as follows:

22. Nur Ahmad, *op. cit.*, pp. 222–23. Nur Ahmad also expanded his treatment of the Jinnah-Khizr dispute in a lecture given at Government College in April 1967 in response to a series of lectures delivered by Ashiq Husain Batalvi on March 11, 12, and 13, 1967, at the same place. The Batalvi lectures, entitled "Iqbal and the Pakistan Movement," were published in an Urdu pamphlet by Government College; Nur Ahmad gave me the text of his reply.

23. Sir Khizr supplied me with a copy of the statement and also with a copy of an unpublished manuscript on his political career. The quotation in the next sentence is from the unpublished manuscript.

"Was this arrangement [the Sikandar-Jinnah pact] . . . a bilateral agreement or pact between two parties, binding on both, or only a unilateral statement by Sir Sikandar, binding only on him, and not binding in any way on Mr. Jinnah?" In Khizr's opinion, it applied to both parties and Jinnah had violated the agreement. Jinnah's defenders maintain that the circumstances, especially following the Lahore resolution, had changed and that a common Muslim front was required at all levels, including provincial legislatures and ministries.[24] In fact, it seems that Jinnah was making a power play with the assistance of some active younger Muslims. While it failed in 1944 to bring down the Khizr ministry and destroy his coalition, it did set the stage for the Muslim League victory in the 1945–46 election.

Growing Solidarity with North Indian Muslims

It was indeed correct that political circumstances had changed considerably from those of 1937, and this fact had a growing impact on the attitudes of Muslims in the Punjab. Increasingly the younger Muslim politicians in the province were giving their allegiance to the Muslim League rather than to the Unionists. The three most important of these politicians were Mian Mumtaz Mohammad Khan Daultana, Sardar Shaukat Hayat Khan, and Nawab Iftikhar Husain Khan of Mamdot.

The expansion of the electorate under the 1935 act, while falling far short of universal franchise, had politicized a larger number of people throughout the country. The mass base of the Congress, developed under Gandhi in the twenties, was continuing to grow. As Gandhi expanded the Congress, Muslim concern increased. This has been well described by Percival Spear:

To make the movement [for Swaraj] strong enough it must be nationwide, and this meant a mass appeal. . . . But a mass appeal

24. This position was taken by Nur Ahmad in the talk referred to in n. 22 above.

in his hands could not be other than a Hindu one. He could transcend caste but not community. The devices he used went sour in the mouths of Muslims. They inevitably became suspicious that they would be outside the pale, in imagination as well as in hard bargaining and material interests. . . . Gandhi's mass movement inevitably led to a supplementary Muslim mass movement which as inevitably became a counter mass movement.[25]

Spear goes on to say that there might have been—how much this verb form is used by historians!—an alternative, and he suggests that had the political movement been kept in the hands of the middle class "the two sides could thus have worked together on a secular nationalist and British parliamentary platform."[26]

What might have been, was not. The large Congress victories in the 1936–37 election in the Hindu-majority provinces led that party to claim the rewards of victory and to form ministries excluding the representatives of the Muslim League. The reaction to this was felt in the Punjab, and we have already seen that the feeling among Muslim Unionists for their coreligionists in other provinces was part of the pressure placed on Sikandar—and felt by him as well—that led to his bringing the Unionists into the national political arena as part of the Muslim League, while retaining local control in provincial matters. The announcement by Nehru that the Congress would undertake a mass contact program among Muslims stimulated the counter movement by the Muslim League, and this was made more credible by the façade, at least, of support from the provincial ruling parties in Bengal and the Punjab.

Another stimulus to Muslim solidarity was the behavior of the Congress governments in office, at least as reported—and, no doubt, exaggerated—by investigative bodies set up by the Muslim League. It must be noted, of course, that

25. Percival Spear, "Mahatma Gandhi," *Modern Asian Studies*, III, No. 4 (1969), 299.
26. *Ibid.*, pp. 299–300.

what is is not nearly so important in politics as *what is thought to be*. The major investigation was carried out by a committee appointed by the League at its March 1938 council meeting in Delhi, which was headed by Raja Syed Mohammad Mehdi of Pirpur. The Pirpur report is a catalogue of grievances culled primarily from the United Provinces but also from other provinces under Congress control.[27] Other reports included the Sharif, which centered on Bihar, and one on a broader base by Fazlul Huq. Collectively these reports and the publicity given to them served to increase sympathy among Muslims in the non-Congress provinces for those who lived under Congress rule. The reports detail how Muslims were forced to honor the Congress flag and the *Bande Mataram*, deprived of adequate representation in municipal and other bodies, asked to accept cow protection, and subjected to harrassment and communal rioting. Many Punjabi newspapers added to the publicity, notably *Zamindar* under the editorship of Maulana Zafar Ali Khan.

About this same time a number of young Punjabis, Muslims and non-Muslims, completed their education in England. While there, they had imbibed new social ideas that did not correspond to those favored by their elders. Some became closely associated with communist organizations; most stopped short of this, retaining Islamic moorings but desiring social and political change away from the traditionalist rural setting of the contemporary Punjab. Most prominent of these men was the younger Daultana, who, although ironically elected first from a landholders' constituency, took the lead in preaching a more liberal platform for the Muslims. He became general secretary of the Punjab Muslim League under the presidency of the younger Mamdot, and Daultana and Mamdot served as Jinnah's messengers when the ultimatum was delivered to Khizr. Shaukat joined the group along with a number of less prominent but locally

27. Text of the Pirpur report is in Jafri, *op. cit.*, pp. 151–226.

influential young men. In the electoral campaign of 1946–47 they would be in the vanguard of the Muslim League's revolt against the Unionists.

The 1945–46 Election and Its Aftermath

To Jinnah and to his followers in the Punjab, the 1945–46 election took the form of a referendum on Pakistan. A strong Muslim League victory would strengthen the hand of the League's chief as the final rounds of negotiations toward independence began. He could demand to be recognized as the sole spokesman of the Muslims, and he could insist on major concessions up to and including the partition of the country, although at this time it appears that partition was only a last stand. But all this would be of little value unless Jinnah could win major victories in the Muslim-majority provinces, particularly Bengal and the Punjab.

Although defections from the Unionist Party in the Assembly swelled the ranks of the Muslim League group to about twenty, Khizr was able to maintain a majority in the legislature and his ministry completed its term. The three-two-one Muslim-Hindu-Sikh balance was upset in 1944 when Khizr added two Muslim ministers to replace the dismissed Shaukat. They were Nawab Sir Mohammad Jamal Khan Leghari, a Baluch *tumandar*, and Nawab Ashiq Husain Qureshi, of the important Multan religio-political family and a relative of the Wah family.

Opportunism seems to have vied with conviction as the election approached, and many who had been elected as Unionists in 1936–37 switched their allegiance to the Muslim League at the last moment. Of the seventy Muslim Unionists elected in 1936–37 and who survived until 1945, thirty chose not to contest in the new election. In a few cases retirement was in favor of sons or other relatives who ran on the Muslim League ticket. Age was also a factor in their retirement, but for many the decision was caused by their inability to accept either the new circumstances and joining with the Muslim League or the prospect of challenging the League and facing defeat. Of the forty who did run in the new election, thirteen jumped to the Muslim League and all were elected, although in some cases they were elected from seats other than the ones from which they were returned in 1936–37. Two straddled the fence and ran as independents, and one of them was elected. The remaining twenty-five chose to remain with the Unionist Party, and of these only six were successful. Khizr won from two seats, thereby giving the six winners a total of seven seats. All of the seats won were in the area that was to become West Punjab, and two of them were in landholders' constituencies where a more limited franchise obtained.

Not only those Unionists who sat in the Punjab Assembly changed parties. Firoz Khan Noon resigned his seat in the viceregal executive council and campaigned as a Leaguer. He has written that his first call after resignation was on Khizr, at which time he invited the Premier to join the League and assured him that he, Noon, would not be a rival for the premiership after the election. He justified his own departure from the Unionist Party by citing the changed circumstances following the first Assembly election. He wrote that the Muslims now desired Pakistan and that it would come whether the Unionists supported or opposed the idea. He also noted the enthusiasm of the younger League workers (not omitting a reference to their suspicion of older men like himself who had been staunch Unionists) and their devotion to Jinnah.[28]

The League and other parties with more specifically Islamic programs had been strong in the urban areas, but now, as Noon stated, the active campaigning in rural areas on the program of partition was a challenge to the traditional voting pattern. The Punjab Muslim League manifesto was, by then valid standards, radical in that it advocated a measure

28. Noon, *op. cit.*, pp. 188–89.

of land reform and other changes in rural areas as well as urban. It had been prepared under the leadership of Mian Muhammad Iftikharuddin, a former president of the Punjab Congress who was elected in 1936 on that ticket. He resigned from the Congress to join the League in 1945, and became president of the Punjab League in 1947. He was assisted by several who had leftist connections, including Danial Latifi, to whom some have ascribed the actual writing of the manifesto.

The first election results to be announced were those for the Central Legislative Assembly. That body was soon to be superseded by the indirectly elected Constituent Assembly, but the results are important for their indication of the League's strength and because they were available before all polling was completed for the provincial assemblies. The Muslim League won all of the thirty seats specifically designated for Muslims. Eight of those elected were returned unopposed; in the elections for the other twenty-two seats the League won an astonishing 86.7 percent of the votes. Even more encouraging to Jinnah and his associates, the League had performed well in the Muslim-majority provinces. In Bengal it won all six seats with 94 percent of the vote. In Punjab it also won all six seats, and in the three that were contested took 83 percent of the vote. Sind recorded only a 68.5 percent majority in the election for its single Muslim seat, but the party was divided and the opponent was of the unofficial faction of the League led by G. M. Syed. Disappointment did come, however, in the Frontier where the League was unable to field a candidate for the single seat, designated "general," and a Congress Muslim was elected. A Congress Muslim also won the Delhi general seat.[29] Thus, based on the limited franchise of the Central Assembly, the Muslims of India gave Jinnah an overwhelming

29. India. Information Services. "Central Legislature Elections, Analysis and Full Results" (Washington, D.C., 1946).

mandate, and the first step of the referendum on the question of Pakistan was completed. These results inevitably had an effect on the voting for the provincial assemblies.

The result in the Punjab Assembly election was largely corroborative of the national trend. Of the eighty-six seats specifically designated for Muslims (including urban, rural, and women's) the League won seventy-three, while the Unionists won but eleven, all rural, with two seats going to independents. In the eighty-three constituencies that were contested, the League won 65.4 percent of the vote and the Unionists, who only contested in the rural seats, 26.7 percent. The League faced non-Unionist competition, particularly in urban areas, from the Ahrars, Khaksars, and independents. The Unionists added to their strength five Hindus from the Haryana area, four from landholders' constituencies, and one from a Christian seat for a total strength of twenty-one. The final total for all 175 seats read: Muslim League, seventy-three; Congress, fifty-one; Unionist, twenty-one; Panthic Party (i.e., Akali Dal), twenty; and independents, ten.[30] The relative strength of the Unionists in the rural areas, where they polled 31 percent of the vote, can perhaps be explained by the continued traditional voting pattern which was not completely offset by the enthusiasm for some form of Pakistan. This was especially true in the western districts with their presumably stronger appeal of *baradari* connections. Moreover, the western districts were less developed economically and socially than those in the eastern and central Punjab.[31]

Retrospect

With the 1945–46 election the question "Union or Partition" was settled. The Muslims of the Punjab had given

30. India. *Return Showing the Results of Elections to the Central Legislative Assembly and the Provincial Legislatures* (Delhi: Manager of Publications, 1948).
31. For a discussion of the Unionist vote in the areas that became part of Pakistan, see Baxter, *op. cit.*, pp. 179–80.

their mandate to the Muslim League program and to Jinnah personally to work out a solution that would answer the demand for Muslim autonomy within or outside an Indian union. The mechanics of how this would be done could be left to the *burra sahibs*, who would work out the timing and details. The inability of the Muslim League to form a ministry in the Punjab was in the future, although it must be said that the governor did not invite Mamdot as leader of the largest party to attempt to form a coalition government. Although the League's supporters claimed there was a plot to deprive it of the fruits of victory, it was extremely unlikely that any of the other parties would have joined a coalition with the League which was — so it said — bent on the division of the country. Thus, so long as the Congress and the Akalis were willing, the only course open to the governor was to ask Khizr to form a ministry in a Unionist-Congress-Akali coalition. Some Muslim Unionists deserted the premier, but it was the Muslim League agitation that brought down his ministry a year later and left the province under governor's rule at the time of partition.

What lay behind the failure of the Unionist Party to maintain its control over the politics of the province? One reason was the decline in the power wielded by the leader. Sir Fazl-i-Husain had two preeminent qualities. First, he was a recognized leader on the national scene, perhaps not so well known as Jinnah, but one who could deal with Jinnah on equal terms. He had demonstrated his ability to administer — something Jinnah had not done — and he was loyal to the Muslim cause even when Jinnah was toying with such ideas as the yielding of separate electorates. Second, Fazli was above faction within the Punjab. He was recognized as *the* leader in the province and was able to keep both the Sikandar-Daultana and the Noon-Tiwana factions working together. The stature of Sir Sikandar Hayat Khan was enhanced nationally only after his election victory and elevation to the premiership. He was and, to an extent, continued to be the leader of a faction. Khizr Hayat Khan Tiwana inherited rather than won his office as premier. Before 1937 he was not even the leader of his faction, and he rose to prominence only when Malik Firoz Khan Noon was away from provincial politics. Khizr was unable to control the Sikandar-Daultana group, and the lineal heirs of both men rebelled against his leadership. It is a matter of speculation whether the choice of a senior member of the Sikandar-Daultana faction, perhaps Nawab Muzaffar Khan, might have preserved the Unionist Party. Whatever the might-have-beens, it was not possible for Khizr to save it.

The much greater politicization of the mass of Punjabi Muslims and the failure of the Unionists to meet this development is another aspect of the party's loss of strength. The propaganda that inundated the Punjab from the Muslim-minority provinces, although it was often exaggerated and occasionally false, fostered a high measure of Muslim solidarity with which Khizr and his associates were unable to cope. Jinnah's recognition of a weaker premier in the Punjab and his insistence that times had changed—as they indeed had—enabled the League's leader to pressure Khizr to the extent that he was driven from the League. The short-term loss of the Punjab premier's support was offset by the long-term gain of support from the Punjab Muslim electorate. As the possibility of independence and partition became more real, the stakes for which the politicians were playing became greater.

"Union or Partition" was not a question that could be settled in the context of Unionism. The party in its earliest manifestation as the "rural bloc" in the Punjab Legislative Council was organized to preserve the rights and privileges of the landholding rural Punjabi against both the government and the urban trader, generally a Hindu. It was pledged to protect and advance the economically backward classes, to encourage local self-governing institutions, to allocate taxation equitably between rural and urban rate payers, to

improve educational institutions, and to secure a fair distribution in the public services for all classes and communities.[32] This program was primarily economic and social — in
current terms, secular — and was one in which substantial
portions of the Muslim, Hindu, and Sikh communities could
join. The Unionists were not prepared for a situation in which
community became a more important factor than class. Their
record displayed considerable advance in the areas where
their program was directed. Separation from the Hindu
portions of India did not enter the equation when the uplift,
as defined rather paternalistically by the Unionists, of the
rural and backward groups was considered. More than this,
the full name of the party was National Unionist Party, and
to a large extent the "national" referred to the Punjab. The
earlier leaders were proud to be Punjabis, as can be seen
from Sikandar's speech quoted earlier. It was worth something to be the breadbasket of India and the home of the
martial races.[33] These were successful men in military,
agricultural, and administrative fields who did not look
kindly on "meddling busybodies" — especially effete UP-
ites and Bombaywallahs.

The Unionists were defeated in 1946, but they were not
dead. The Punjab Muslim chiefs have tended to give their
support to strong governments — the Mughals, the Sikhs in
the time of Ranjit Singh, the British. They also hasten the
demise of weak governments. They have been quick to seize
opportunities in order to protect their status, whether it
meant a sudden change of allegiance as in 1945 and 1946,
or pulling together to support governments which came to
power without their initial assistance, as with Ayub Khan
in the early 1960s. The name Unionist was not to reappear.
Instead, new names emerged: the Noon faction of the Muslim

32. Azim Husain, *op. cit.*, pp. 154–55.
33. The martial background can be seen in the full title of Nair's work on Sikandar
and in the several introductory pages of Khizr's unpublished manuscript devoted
to the place of the Tiwana Lancers.

League when he became chief minister of the Punjab in 1953, the Republican Party later in 1956, and the Pakistan Muslim League of Ayub Khan in the 1960s. All enjoyed the open or covert support of former Unionist families. And the factions continued to be important. The Noon-Tiwana group continued to oppose the Sikandar-Daultana faction; in the 1970 election, distrust between the two groups was a key factor in the failure of the several splinter Muslim Leagues to unite. In the next chapter we witness the contemporary continuation of this unrelenting rivalry.

Biographical Notes on Punjab Personalities
(In order of mention)

Mian Sir Fazl-i-Husain (1877–1936). M.L.C., 1916–25. Minister, 1921–25. Member, Executive Council, the Punjab, 1925–30. Member, Viceroy's Executive Council, 1930–35. Founder and leader, Unionist Party.

Mian Sir Mohammad Shafi (1869–1932). President, Muslim League, 1913. M.L.C., 1908–19. Member, Viceroy's Executive Council, 1919–24. Leader of Shafi League in opposition to Jinnah, 1928–32, later the All-India Muslim Conference. Leader, Muslim delegation, round table conferences.

Sardar Sir Sikandar Hayat Khan (1892–1942). M.L.C., 1921 and 1923–30. Member, Executive Council, 1930–35. Twice acting governor of the Punjab. Deputy Governor, Reserve Bank of India, 1935–36. Premier, 1937–42.

Nawab Muzaffar Khan (1879–1951). Punjab civil servant to 1934. Member, Executive Council, 1935–36. M.L.A., 1937–46.

Mir Maqbul Mahmud (d. 1948). M.L.C., 1923–30. Employed in Patiala, Rampur, Alwar, and Jhalawar in various offices. Aided princes at round table conferences. M.L.A., 1937–46. Director, Secretariat, Chamber of Princes, 1946–47.

Mian Ahmad Yar Khan Daultana (d. 1940). M.L.C., 1921–23 and 1926–36. M.L.A., 1937–40. Chief Parliamentary Secretary, 1937–40.

Malik Sir Firoz Khan Noon (1893–1970). M.L.C., 1921–36. Minister, 1931–36. High Commissioner for India in London, 1936–41. Member, Viceroy's Executive Council, 1941–46. M.L.A., 1946–48 and 1953–58. M.C.A., 1947–58. Governor, East Bengal,

1950–53. Chief Minister, the Punjab, 1953–55. Foreign Minister, 1956–57. Prime Minister, 1958.

Nawab Malik Sir Umar Hayat Khan Tiwana (1874–1944). M.L.C., 1904–9. Member, Imperial Legislative Council, 1909–20. Member, Council of State, 1920–25 and 1926–29. Member, Council of the Secretary of State for India, 1929–34.

Mian Mumtaz Mohammad Khan Daultana (b. 1916). M.L.A., 1943–48 and 1951–58. M.C.A., 1947–58. Minister, 1947 and 1955. Chief Minister, 1951–53. Defense Minister, 1957. M.N.A., 1970–73. Ambassador to the United Kingdom, 1972– .

Nawab Sir Shah Nawaz Khan of Mamdot (1883–1942). M.L.A., 1937–42. President, the Punjab Muslim League, 1937–42.

Chaudhury Sir Chhotu Ram (1881–1945). M.L.C., 1923–36. Minister, 1923–36. M.L.A., 1937–45. Leader of Haryana Jat element in Unionist Party.

Sardar Sir Sundar Singh Majithia (1872–1941). M.L.C., 1909–15. Member, Imperial Legislative Council, 1915–21. Member, Executive Council, 1921–26. M.L.A., 1937–41. Minister, 1937–41.

Allama Sir Mohammad Iqbal (1877–1938). Poet-philosopher of Pakistan. M.L.C., 1926–30. President, Muslim League, 1930.

Malik Barkat Ali (1885–1946). Muslim League M.L.A., 1937–46. Leading member of urban Muslim group.

Malik Sir Khizr Hayat Khan Tiwana (1900–75). M.L.A., 1937–48. Minister, 1937–42. Premier, 1943–47.

Sardar Baldev Singh (1902–61). M.L.A., 1937–46. Minister, 1942–46. M.C.A. (India), 1947–52. Minister of Defense, 1947–52. M.P., 1952–61.

Nawab Sir Liaqat Hayat Khan (1887–1948). Elder brother of Sikandar Hayat. Member, Indian Police Service. Detailed to Patiala, 1923. Prime Minister, Patiala, 1930–42.

Raja Ghazanfar Ali Khan (1895–1963). Member, Central Legislative Assembly, 1924–30. Member, Council of State, 1933–37. M.L.A., 1937–48. Member, Interim Cabinet, 1946–47. M.C.A., 1947–48. Central Minister, 1947–48. Afterward ambassador to Iran, Iraq, Turkey, and Italy, and High Commissioner to India.

Nawab Iftikhar Husain Khan of Mamdot (1906–69). M.L.A., 1942–48 and 1951–55. Chief Minister, 1947–48. M.C.A., 1947–58. Governor of Sind, 1953–55. Minister, West Pakistan, 1955.

Chaudhury Sir Shahabuddin (d. 1946). Member, Central Legislative Assembly, 1921–23. M.L.C., 1923–36. President, Council, 1923–36. Minister, 1936. M.L.A. and Speaker, 1937–45.

Sardar Shaukat Hayat Khan (b. 1915). Son of Sikandar Hayat. M.L.A., 1943–47. M.C.A., 1947–54. M.N.A., 1970–

Maulana Zafar Ali Khan (1873–1956). Editor and publisher of *Zamindar*. Associated in 1937 with the Ittehad-i-Millat. Member, Central Legislative Assembly, 1946–47, as Leaguer.

Nawab Sir Mohammad Jamal Khan Leghari (1894–1960). M.L.C., 1921–36. M.L.A., 1937–48 and 1951–58. Minister, 1944–46.

Nawab Ashiq Husain Qureshi (1900–47). M.L.A., 1937–47. Minister, 1944–46. Killed at time of partition riots.

Mian Mohammad Iftikharuddin (1907–62). M.L.A., 1937–48. Elected first on Congress ticket. Resigned from Congress, of which he was provincial president, 1945. Later president of the provincial League. Minister, 1947. M.C.A., 1947–58. Founder, Progressive Papers, publisher of *Pakistan Times*. Press taken over by Ayub regime, 1959.

Danial Latifi (b. 1917). From Bombay family temporarily settled in the Punjab. Grandson of Badruddin Tyabji. Associated with leftist movements, including Democratic Lawyers, in India after independence.

4

The Pakistan People's Party: Phases One and Two

Anwar H. Syed

Lenin regarded organization as the proletariat's main weapon in its struggle for power. More recently, Huntington, agreeing with Lenin, concluded his argument regarding political modernization and development with the observation that organization not only opened the road to political power but provided the preconditions of political stability and liberty. "In the modernizing world he controls the future who organizes its politics,"[1] Huntington writes. He argues that when institutional development does not keep pace with the expanding demand for political participation, anomic politics, instability, mass movements, violence, and bureaucratic and military interventions may be expected. Without denying the efficacy of other institutions, it may be said that political parties are the most important agency for managing participation in a modernizing polity.[2]

Organizational debility is probably a key explanation for the familiar disarray in Pakistani politics. One might suggest

1. Samuel P. Huntington, *Political Order in Changing Societies* (New Haven: Yale University Press, 1968), p. 461.
2. By "participation" I mean access to the various lawful and/or customary processes and procedures of influencing political decision-making, including the freedom to support or oppose the government of the day through the exercise of voting rights and freedoms of speech, press, assembly, and organization. Thus, when a ruling party rigs elections, puts opponents in jail or bans their organizations, disrupts their public meetings, penalizes critical journalists and their newspapers, closes colleges to prevent students from demonstrating, it may be seen as curbing participation.

that Pakistan never quite progressed beyond the stage of factional or "pre-party" politics to that of party politics. The Muslim League, a mobilist party at the time of independence, neglected to adopt the goals or the organizational behavior capable of accommodating or managing the participatory urges that mobilization had generated. It opted to function as an adaptive and pragmatic-hegemonic party within the context of a small number of political actors. It sought to control and limit participation, and, in trying to roll back the train of modernization, it split into a large number of factions mirroring the personal rivalries of factional leaders.[3] With the dismissal of Nazimuddin in 1953, politics in Pakistan came under the sway of bureaucratic-military leaders and stayed there until the nation's defeat and dismemberment in 1971. Political parties and factional groups did exist, but politics remained in low key during much of this period: many politicians spent more time in jail, or trying to stay out of jail, than in doing political work.

The Pakistan People's Party (PPP) appeared on the Pakistani political scene at a time when the deepening crises of integration, distributive justice, participation, and legitimacy were less than a year away from erupting into a massive revolt against the Ayubian order. The party's founder, Zulfikar Ali Bhutto, played a significant role in bringing about Ayub's fall. Later he led the party to victory in the 1970 general election, capturing the majority of National Assembly seats reserved for West Pakistan, a majority in the provincial legislature of the Punjab, and a plurality in the legislature

3. For a detailed account of factionalism in the Muslim League, see Safdar Mahmood, *Muslim Leeg ka Daur-e-Hakumat* ["The Period of Muslim League's Rule"] (Lahore: Sheikh Ghulam Ali and Sons, 1973). Briefer references will be found in Keith Callard, *Pakistan: A Political Study* (London: Allen and Unwin, 1957), chaps. 2 and 4, and his *Political Forces in Pakistan 1947–1959* (New York: Institute of Pacific Relations, 1959), pp. 23–25. Also see Khalid B. Sayeed, *The Political System of Pakistan* (Boston: Houghton Mifflin, 1967), chap. 4.

of Sind.[4] The PPP has been governing the country since December 20, 1971. It has made some moves to alleviate problems in the realm of distributive justice, but their full impact will take more time to materialize. On the other hand, the crises of participation and legitimacy have reappeared, while the crisis of integration never came fully under control. Consequently, the party has suffered a substantial loss of popularity, especially in urban Pakistan.

This chapter will examine the PPP's ideological posture, which gave it its mobilist character and carried it to electoral success and governmental power, and will look at the problems of factionalism, corruption, repression, and violence that have been threatening the party's organizational viability since shortly after it came to power.

The PPP's design for social and economic change—presented in its Foundation Documents and later in its Election Manifesto—represents a mix of traditional and modern values that the majority of Pakistani voters ratified in 1970. It merits study not only because it will serve as a reference point for constituent evaluation of the party's own performance, but because it is likely to dominate the value framework

4. The PPP won 86 of the 144 National Assembly constituencies in West Pakistan (including the six seats reserved for women), taking 65 in the Punjab, 19 in Sind, and one each in NWFP and Baluchistan. It polled 41.66 percent of the vote in the Punjab, 44.95 percent in Sind, 14.28 percent in NWFP, and 2.38 percent in Baluchistan. In the provincial legislatures it won 119 seats out of 186 in the Punjab, 30 out of 62 in Sind, three out of 42 in NWFP, and none out of 21 in Baluchistan. (These figures include seats reserved for women.) In the provincial elections it polled 39.07 percent of the vote in the Punjab, 39.11 percent in Sind, 14.29 percent in NWFP, and 1.88 percent in Baluchistan.

The PPP's performance was impressive as compared with that of other parties. In the National Assembly elections Wali Khan's NAP received 18.5 percent and JUI 25.45 percent of the vote in NWFP. The Council Muslim League, the second strongest party in the Punjab, polled 12.66 percent of the vote in that province. The Qayyum Muslim League polled 22.64 percent in NWFP and 10.7 percent in Sind. NAP's performance was much better in Baluchistan where it polled 45.23 percent of the vote. See Pakistan Election Commission, *Report on General Elections 1970–71* (Karachi: Manager of Publications, 1972), I, 202–5, 416–19, and, regarding women's seats, I, 167–68.

to which other Pakistani political actors will have to address themselves. Factionalism deserves attention, for it is not merely symptomatic of organizational incoherence; it also aggravates the deficiency already present. But of all the crises that have afflicted Pakistani politics, that of legitimacy is the most inclusive and far-reaching. Legitimacy refers to citizen assessments of a ruling authority's behavior in terms of its concordance with norms the community considers appropriate. It involves not only the legality of the process by which the ruling authority came to power, but its continuing adherence to rules of lawful governance, its propriety of personal conduct and life-styles, and the relevance of its policy goals to salients of the political environment in which it is operating. It is coeval with the crises of participation, distributive justice, and integration, and interacts with them, which is to say that a visible fall in the status of the regime's legitimacy will not only mirror but intensify these other crises. Pakistani experience, and that of many other developing societies, suggests that corruption and repressive limitation of participation will, more than normal policy failures, destroy the legitimacy of those in power.

Phase One: Developing a Viable Ideology

The Founder: A Window on Mr. Bhutto

The emergence, successes, and frustrations of the PPP cannot be understood without some attention to its founder and chairman, Zulfikar Ali Bhutto. One of the more controversial statesmen of our time, he has a way of arousing intense loyalty and passionate hostility toward himself. Countless characterizations of him have appeared in the Pakistani and foreign press, and especially in the Indian press. Yet, it is too early to attempt a full-scale assessment of this most unusual and exceedingly complex leader. At this stage it may be sufficient to present the following partly impressionistic interpretation of how he came to found a new political party.[5]

There can be no doubt that, first and foremost, Zulfikar Ali Bhutto is a political man who understands not only that politics is the art of attaining and retaining power but that politics in Pakistan must now be mass-oriented and mass-based in order to succeed. He is the only politician in recent years to have recognized the political necessity of learning, in adult life, a Pakistani language (Urdu) other than his native tongue. While he speaks the King's English well enough to overawe those Pakistanis who might consider such an accomplishment a hallmark of sophistication, his Urdu speech is refreshingly pedestrian and his Sindhi rural. When he addresses mass meetings, his idiom, metaphors, jokes, gibes, and even gesticulations are those of the ordinary folk. He is fluent in all three languages. Verb endings may not agree with number and gender in his Urdu speech, but words, even if sometimes mispronounced, come out like a torrent. His lapses of diction are in fact a political advantage: they enhance his rapport with his audience by amusing

5. A number of books on Bhutto have already appeared: Mahmood Sham, *Larkana Se Peking* ["From Larkana to Peking"] (Karachi: National Forum, 1972); Khalid Kashmiri, *Awam ka Sadar* ["President of the Masses"] (Lahore: Munib Publications, 1972); Yunas Adeeb, *Quaid-e-Awam* ["Leader of the Masses"] (Lahore: Maktaba-e-Pakistan, 1972); Qazi Zulfikar Ahmad and Rana Mahmood-ul-Ahsan, *Zulfikar Ali Bhutto* [Urdu] (Lahore: Moallam Publishing House, 1973); Rana Rahman Zafar, *Zulfikar Ali Bhutto* [Urdu] (Lahore: Khyber Publishers, 1973); Fakhar Zaman and Akhtar Aman, *Z. A. Bhutto: The Political Thinker* (Lahore: The People's Publications, 1973). Two Indian biographies of Bhutto should be mentioned. His old friend Piloo Mody, currently president of the Sawatantra party, has written *Zulfi My Friend* (Delhi: Thomson, 1973); Dilip Mukerjee, a noted journalist, published *Zulfikar Ali Bhutto: Quest for Power* (Delhi: Vikas, 1972). Briefer reference to Bhutto's political career, along with some characterization, may be seen in Lawrence Ziring, *The Ayub Khan Era: Politics in Pakistan, 1958–1969* (Syracuse, N.Y.: Syracuse University Press, 1971), pp. 47–48, 93–97, and *passim;* and Herbert Feldman, *From Crisis to Crisis: Pakistan 1962–1969* (London: Oxford University Press, 1970), pp. 313–18 and *passim.* Characterizations of Bhutto, not always hostile, are most frequently to be found in one of Pakistan's most distinguished and readable journals, namely, *Outlook.*

the better-knowing and by giving peasants and workers the good feeling that he speaks the same kind of Urdu or Sindhi as they do. As he goes along in his speech, he informs, instructs, flatters, and, on occasion, even scolds his audience. That he is often quite repetitive may be an act of choice, for it enables his message to sink in, maintains his oratorical flow, and gives him time to phrase his next sentence when dealing with a complex issue.

The supremacy of the people has been a recurring theme in Bhutto's speeches ever since he launched his battle against Ayub Khan. He presents himself as the people's servant, their friend, their brother. His government is their government, their will his will, and his achievements their achievements. On occasion, he will express his identification with them, and presumably theirs with him, in terms of completeness suggestive of a union of spirits or souls that students of mysticism or other devotional themes would readily recognize. Twice in the fall of 1973 I heard him tell his audiences that there were two Bhuttos: one that lived in his own body and the other that resided in each one of them. They and he were thus united in an unbreakable bond and made inseparable. He declares that, being human, he is capable of making mistakes, but that if he makes any, he will own up to them and seek the people's forgiveness; he will take off his hat and place it at their feet (a gesture of humility in Pakistani culture after which the unforgiving is the more blameworthy).[6]

Perceptive students of history, among whom Bhutto may be reckoned, know that emperors and kings, presidents and

6. He said this at a mammoth public meeting in Rawalpindi on December 20, 1973 — the second anniversary of his government. He spoke extemporaneously in Urdu, but he may have planned this statement in advance, for he was actually wearing a hat — a "Jinnah cap" — on this occasion (though he normally does not wear a hat) and took it off while saying it. He mentioned the "two Bhuttos" in this speech and earlier in a speech at the Lahore airport on September 29, 1973. I was among the audience on both occasions and, later each day, also watched the proceedings on television.

prime ministers, are often no more than moderately competent, and sometime quite foolish, notwithstanding the forbidding majesty with which protocol invests them. After a few years as minister in Ayub Khan's government, Bhutto saw that the president was by no means a giant, and that most of his colleagues were men of modest accomplishments. The talents of those few who were truly capable were preeminently legal, bureaucratic, or military rather than political. His own qualifications, including a zest for politics, may have appeared more substantial than those of his associates, including the President. The time to dissociate himself from the Ayub regime came when the 1965 war with India produced nothing better than a stalemate. The government-controlled media had earlier persuaded the nation that it won the war, but since the peace terms would show no evidence of any victory, Bhutto's dissociation from the cease-fire agreement and the subsequent Tashkent accord cast him in the role of a national hero while Ayub Khan looked like a virtual traitor. Bhutto's anti-India posture and his policy of friendship with China enormously increased his popularity at home, especially after the Chinese ultimatum to India during the war, as did the rumor, current at the time, that Ayub Khan was discharging him from the cabinet at American insistence.

After his departure from the Ayub government, Bhutto briefly considered the possibility of establishing a "Forward Bloc" in the Convention Muslim League. But the elders in that organization, such as Khuda Bakhsh Bucha (who now serves Prime Minister Bhutto as an advisor on agriculture policy), rebuffed him. On the other hand, leftist friends and admirers urged him to form a new political party. The Pakistan People's Party was declared established—and "democrats," friends of the downtrodden, men of patriotism and goodwill invited to join it—at meetings on November 30 and December 1, 1967, at Dr. Mubashir Hasan's house in Lahore.

The Foundation Documents

The new party's ideological and programmatic positions were first set forth in a series of papers called the *Foundation Documents*. The Urdu version is composed in elegant literary style, representing a blend of Islamic, socialistic, and liberal democratic values and vocabulary.[7] The second part of *Document 7* (pp. 64–68) is especially noteworthy for its scriptural style of poetic prose. The *Documents*, purporting to be Bhutto's covenant with the people, spell out the party's analysis of Pakistan's developmental journey during the previous regimes, the rationale for its coming into being, its basic principles and commitments, and the case for socialism.

The PPP argued that despite appearances of growth during the Ayubian decade, the national economy had remained essentially weak. Heavy industry and the development of advanced technological competence had been neglected. Investment choices were made on the basis of availability of raw materials, for such was written in the Anglo-Saxon books on economics. The Pakistani entrepreneur was not the tough, adventurous "captain of industry" one might read about in the annals of Western industrial development. He was a weakling, unwilling to take risks, who financed his enterprises, at least partly, with public funds and received abundant government protection at the public's expense: liberal foreign exchange allocations at an advantageous rate, bonus vouchers, low taxes, tolerance of fraud, industrial peace through repression of labor, depressed agricultural prices that kept the "subsistence wage" and, therefore, his payroll expenses down. By limiting production and raising prices in collusion with fellow industrialists, he was able, in some cases, to recover his entire outlay in a year or two. These crooked practices, amounting to a wholesale plundering of the nation, could not be called progress. As the PPP

7. *Foundation Documents of the Pakistan People's Party* (Lahore, November 1967).

saw it, the Pakistani industrialist had been wholly without any sense of national purpose.

Beyond economics, the party saw a general decline in the quality of Pakistani life: a state of aimlessness and rootlessness prevailed among students, workers, and peasants; false and decadent values had made the intellectual apathetic and sterile; corruption, nepotism, and self-aggrandizement pervaded the power centers; politicization of the bureaucracy had eroded its competence and public service orientation; national integrity appeared more fragile than ever. Political parties were split into factions. The conservatives (Council Muslim League, Jamaat-i-Islami, Nizam-e-Islam, and a faction of the Awami League) were insensitive to the needs of economic and social change while professing to value democracy. A polarization of political forces — conservatives on one side, progressives on the other — would rationalize the political situation and might even facilitate cooperation in restoring democracy. The progressives must therefore come together in a new party unencumbered by the personality orientations, conflicts, and prejudices of the past. That would be the Pakistan People's Party.

Document 4 asserted that socialism alone could cure Pakistan's economic and political crises. It projected the Leninist view that Afro-Asians need not travel the same developmental road, and stop at the same way stations as the Western capitalist societies had done, before arriving at socialism. The road to socialism was not necessarily the same for all; each nation's peculiar circumstances, values, and usages would influence its design. Other people's experience might provide useful suggestions, but, in the end, Pakistan must have her own kind of socialism, accommodating her religious and cultural values. Looking to the future, Pakistanis did not wish to disregard their past. Armed with knowledge and determination, the Pakistani socialist *mujahid* (crusader) would rediscover the native springs of his culture and civilization and reassert his national honor and destiny. There were many stages in this struggle and "an appointed time for each stage," indicating a gradualist approach.

The PPP believed that the enterprises basic to industrial development must be nationalized so as to be employed for the welfare of the entire nation. These would include banking and insurance, iron and steel, metallurgy, heavy engineering, machine tools, chemicals and petrochemicals, shipbuilding, armaments, automobiles, gas and oil industries, mining, generation and distribution of electric power, shipping, railways, and air and road transport. Competent and genuinely competitive private enterprise would be allowed to function and earn reasonable profits.

Social justice and the establishment of a classless society were said to be the party's guiding principles. Then there were the following "programmatic" commitments: a constitutional democratic order based on universal adult franchise; civil rights and liberties; full remuneration to peasants and workers for their labor; further elimination of feudalism and landlordism; encouragement of self-help projects and voluntary cooperative farming; development of nationwide unions in certain industries; minimum wages and the workers' right to strike; free health care for peasants and workers; mobilization to utilize the unemployed manpower's productive potential; reorganization of education to bring about a classless society; encouragement of regional languages expressing the people's cultural personality; separation of the executive from the judiciary; and the establishment of a national militia, trained and commanded by professional soldiers, to supplement the regular army.

The PPP came out strongly for the freedoms of belief and expression, press, organization, and assembly. The denial of these rights and liberties produced a "slave" society afflicted with dictatorship, corruption, police oppression, cultural and moral decay. It compelled free men to resort to violence. The party demanded withdrawal of the proclamation of emergency and the Defense of Pakistan Rules, abolition of the Press Trust of Pakistan, restoration of academic freedom and repeal of the University Ordinances, and repeal of all other laws curbing the freedom of the press.

The PPP chose to soft-pedal some issues. Apart from a fairly routine call for withdrawal from CENTO and SEATO and a continuation of the confrontation with India (in pursuing which Pakistan should support the people of Assam who wished to be liberated from Indian rule!), the statement on foreign policy was brief and tepid. The party opposed the Awami League's Six Points on the ground that, apart from being subversive of national integrity, they were irrelevant to East Pakistan's economic deprivation that only socialism could alleviate. On other constitutional issues the party wished to reserve judgment in order not to aggravate the current political turmoil! It is significant also that at this time the party did not wish to agitate the landed interests. It adopted the rather peculiar position that Ayub Khan's land reforms had largely eliminated feudalism and landlordism and that, now, only a few remnants had to be removed. Furthermore, agricultural problems, or many of them, could not be solved by direction from above.

Islam gets a place of high honor in the value system projected in the *Documents*. This was easily done since some of the major socialist values—egalitarianism and outlawry of exploitation—are also preeminently Islamic values. Other socialist emphases—nationalization of the means of production, class struggle, neocolonialist dominance of the developing world—are balanced by terms of democratic liberalism. Consider, for instance, the following observations in *Document 7:*

In the name of God, who rules the entire universe, we submit that when a degenerate social order stifles the values of human decency; when opportunism and hypocrisy become part of the national character; when flattery of the rulers is identified with wisdom, honesty with foolishness; when men become apathetic and close their eyes to reality; when men of learning mislead others for personal advantage, and fountains of creativity dry out; then surely men have left the path of righteousness, and for those who do and should care, time for Jehad [crusade] has come.

Jehad means eternal struggle for the expansion of man's creative capabilities and the safeguarding of decent values. It means abolishing artificial distinctions and making righteousness the criterion of honor among men, establishing a democratic and egalitarian social order. . . .

And for this Jehad, we invite the masses of Pakistan to unite with us to abolish ignorance, hypocrisy, oppression, exploitation, and slavery; to uphold and advance knowledge, honesty, probity, justice, equality, liberty; and to throw into this struggle our talents of expression, money, labor, and indeed our very lives, until this land brightens up with the divine light of God. [My free translation of the Urdu text.][8]

Not wishing to invite widespread hostility when it was just getting off the ground, the PPP preferred to be seen more as an adaptive and pragmatic party, rather than an ideological one; it was to be an agent of social change but not of a socialist revolution. There is little revolutionary or otherwise militant vocabulary in the *Documents*. It is clear that, at this time, the party wanted to attract as many and alienate as few interests as possible in order to prepare for the struggle for power that lay ahead. Nothing would be lost, and possibly much gained, by adhering to the established political custom of professing one's dedication to Islam; nor would it necessarily be farcical. It would be unwise to alarm the middle landlords in the countryside or the shopkeepers in towns by launching a major attack on landed property or private enterprise. The party promised to demolish the edifice of exploitative capitalism, already under fire from several quarters, but otherwise it chose to project itself as a progressive nation-builder dedicated to the gentle values of humane and civil conduct.

8. *Documents*, No. 7.

The Election Manifesto

By early 1970, when the PPP *Election Manifesto* appeared, Zulfikar Ali Bhutto had already established himself as the most popular political leader in West Pakistan. He spent much of 1968 building opposition to the Ayub regime by addressing students, peasants, workers, lawyers, and other groups all over the province. As his mass appeal increased, PPP offices sprang up in a great number of towns and cities. These developments — his and his party's enhanced status and self-confidence — are reflected in the *Manifesto*.

Written in fluent, readable English, its crisp and hard-hitting sentences are laced with militant socialist vocabulary — class struggle, monopoly capitalism, the idea of labor as the author of all value, theory of surplus value, a Leninist interpretation of imperialism — much more than the *Foundation Documents* were in 1967. It would be repetitive to cover the programmatic positions taken in the *Manifesto*, for they are substantially the same as those in the *Documents*. The discussion below will focus on the *Manifesto's* distinctive features.

The party was now ready to specify the dimensions of the public sector under its regime. Eventually, "all major sources of the production of wealth," to the extent of *80 percent* of the economy (excluding agriculture) would be nationalized. The remaining 20 percent would comprise small industry and retail trade, but even here the possibility of urban and rural consumer cooperatives need not be excluded. The *Manifesto* asserted that, all production of wealth being the result of human labor, landlords and capitalists were "functional superfluities." They contributed nothing that peasants and workers and public authorities could not provide. They only exploited the labor of others and pocketed the "surplus value." The earlier, rather generous interpretation of Ayub Khan's land reforms now gave way to the assertion that by granting state lands to privileged groups —

notably high civil and military officials—the Ayub regime had expanded landlordism, saddling the economy with "consumption-oriented non-producers." His land reforms had not broken up the large estates or the power of feudal lords, who continued to be a formidable barrier to social change. The PPP would appoint a new ceiling on holdings: fifty to 150 acres of irrigated land, depending on yield per acre. It would protect the interests of the peasantry "in accordance with the established principles of socialism." It would encourage the establishment of multipurpose "social cooperative farms" on a voluntary basis and develop some two hundred "Agrovilles"—small towns functionally linked with the surrounding countryside. Tenants and poorer peasants would pay no land revenue.

The *Manifesto* offered many specific commitments in the areas of health, education, local government, administrative reforms, labor welfare, civil rights, electoral reforms, national defense, and foreign policy. A few instances may be noted. The "socialist regime" would provide housing, adequate transportation, paid holidays, recreation camps, free medical aid, minimum wages, participation in decision-making to workers. There would be day-care centers where working mothers could leave their children, scholarships for workers' children, old-age pensions, and homes for the disabled and retired. In order to reduce the power of money in electoral politics, the PPP recommended a system of voting for party lists rather than individual candidates. In the area of education it would combine book learning with manual skills, give mathematics—the basis of all science and technology and, more than any other discipline, a contributor to the power of rational thinking—a place of honor in the school curriculum and provide for its teaching by the most modern scientific methods. The young Pakistani must understand not only the universe around him but the "inexorable processes" of history and the nature of social change.

The *Manifesto,* like the *Documents* before, offered a splendid defense of the freedom of belief and expression. One must not insist that only approved beliefs be expressed. "Bigotry is an insult to faith and intelligence alike." The party would lift the blinkers that the previous regimes had placed on the nation's eyes. It suggested that, in an earlier era, Muslim intellectual life had deteriorated because of the rise of "dogmatic fanaticism." Under the "socialist regime," therefore, "no book shall be proscribed merely on the ground that its contents differ from the tenets or beliefs of any religion or faith." Nor would there be any censorship of "true" news items.

The *Manifesto* is much more than a general statement of the party's principles and goals. It reads like a plan, with an amazing amount of specificity and detail. The reader will see, among other things, reference to toys and their contribution to children's mental development; comparative life expectancy statistics; elements of fats and proteins in Pakistani diet; expense accounts; truth in advertising; forests and woodlands; poultry farms and cattle ranches; training and diplomas for artisans; rental of floor space in factory halls; revocation of civil awards; bonus vouchers; counterpart funds; tax evasion; trash collection; water rates; the brain drain. The character and dimensions of social change proposed in the *Manifesto* were revolutionary. The existing system, which permitted "outright plunder" of the people, was "rotten." Therefore, the party would "abolish the system itself."

A Note on Islamic Socialism

The PPP designates its ideological position as "Islamic socialism." The phrase, as such, did not figure in the *Documents* or in the *Manifesto,* even though the party's advocacy of socialism was predicated on its professed harmony with the Islamic ethos. There may have been some reluctance to adopt the term, for it had been employed not only by the

Quaid-e-Azam and Liaquat Ali Khan but also by Ayub Khan.[9] In his public speeches during 1968 and 1969, Bhutto said repeatedly that there was no tension between Islam and socialism. On January 29, 1968, he told the party's women workers in Lahore that "the first seeds of socialism [had] flowered under Islam," that Islam had given "birth to the principles and concepts of socialism." This was the Islam of the Prophet and the first four Caliphs, which should be "our Islam, the Islam of the people of Pakistan."[10] Had there been any conflict between the two systems, he would have given up socialism, being first a Muslim. But in the socio-economic sector there was no conflict, and those who claimed that Islam and socialism were mutually antagonistic were only propagandists who wished to "exploit the people and suck their blood."[11] Bhutto began using the term Islamic socialism within a few days of launching his election campaign in January 1970. He reminded his audiences that in advocating this system he was "merely following the doctrines of the Quaid-e-Azam" and of Liaquat Ali Khan.[12]

It should be noted that the term Islamic socialism has been current in Muslim political discourse in the Indian subcon-

9. In a speech at Dacca on August 26, 1964, Ayub Khan, asserting that the Muslim faith had nothing in common with Hinduism, advised that "we should practice Islamic socialism." *Speeches and Statements* (Karachi: Pakistan Publications, n.d.), VII, 19. On March 26, 1948, the Quaid-e-Azam had told a Chittagong audience: "you are only voicing my sentiments and the sentiments of millions of Mussalmans when you say that Pakistan should be based on the sure foundations of social justice and Islamic Socialism which emphasises equality and brotherhood of man." Jinnah, *Speeches as Governor General of Pakistan* (Karachi: Ferozsons, n.d.), p. 98. At a meeting in Lahore on August 25, 1949, Liaquat Ali Khan said: "There are a number of *isms* being talked about nowadays but we are convinced that for us there is only one *ism* namely, 'Islamic Socialism,' which, in a nutshell, means that every person in this land has equal right to be provided with food, shelter, clothing, education and medical facilities." *Speeches and Statements of Quaid-e-Millat Liaquat Ali Khan 1941–1951* (Lahore: Research Society of Pakistan, 1967), p. 267.
10. Zulfikar Ali Bhutto, *Awaking the People: Statements, Articles, Speeches 1966–1969* (Rawalpindi: Pakistan Publications, n.d.), p. 54.
11. See the speeches in Sherpao and Peshawar on November 3 and 5, 1968, in *Ibid.*, pp. 179, 193.
12. Bhutto, *Marching Towards Democracy: Statements, Articles, Speeches 1970–1971* (Rawalpindi: Pakistan Publications, n.d.), pp. 21, 30, 157 and *passim*.

tinent and the Arab world for several decades. It represents, among other things, a sympathetic response to the value of egalitarianism and opposition to exploitation — including the imperialistic variety — that socialists urge. In an article published in 1920, Rashid Rida (1865–1935) saw socialism as a way of liberating workers from governmental and capitalistic oppression and thought Muslims must hope for its success.[13] Mustafa al-Siba'i, a leading intellectual of the Muslim Brotherhood and head of the Muslim Socialist Front in Syria in the late 1940s, called himself an Islamic socialist and wrote on the subject.[14] Even when the term is not used, the connection between a Muslim people's socialism and its Islamic culture continues to be made. Abdel Moghny Said, a contemporary Arab socialist intellectual, observes that Arab socialism is rooted "deep in the soil of Islam and the cultural heritage of the Arabs."[15]

The purists among some Pakistani Islamic parties, and others sympathetic to their persuasion, contend that the phrase Islamic socialism is a contradiction in terms, a mere deception, for Islam and socialism relate to each other as do light and darkness.[16] They take this position partly from a belief in the inviolability of private property but, more importantly, from their view of the strongly anti-religious and materialistic biases of Marxist ideologies. Some PPP intellectuals further invite this conservative attack by claiming that they are "scientific" rather than Islamic socialists.[17]

13. Albert Hourani, *Arabic Thought in the Liberal Age 1798–1939* (London: Oxford University Press, 1967), p. 304.

14. See al-Sibai's piece entitled, "Islamic Socialism," in Kemal H. Karpat, *Political and Social Thought in the Contemporary Middle East* (London: Pall Mall, 1968), pp. 122–26.

15. Said, *Arab Socialism* (New York: Barnes and Noble, 1972), p. 24.

16. This position is characteristic of the Jamaat-e-Islami but has also been taken by others, e.g., Mufti Mahmood. See his interview with Riaz Batalvi in the latter's *Leedran-e-Karam* ["Respected Leaders"] (Lahore: Al-tahrir, 1970), p. 272.

17. At a "seminar" on Islamic socialism at the Pakistan Administrative Staff College in Lahore on January 26, 1974, Khurshid Hasan Meer, the party's deputy secretary-general, said the PPP wished to establish scientific socialism "in consonance with the fundamental tenets of Islam." But at a party workers' meeting on the same day he said the party advocated scientific socialism and *not* Islamic socialism. Both reports appeared in *Pakistan Times*, Jan. 27, 1974.

Nevertheless, several Muslim *ulema* (religious scholars) in India and Pakistan — Ubayd-Allah Sindhi and Hifz al-Rahman Sihwarwi in the 1940s and Ghulam Ahmad Parwiz since independence — have advocated varieties of Islamic socialism.[18] While leaving it to the reader to decide whether a truly Islamic society would be socialistic, Khalifa Abdul Hakim, one of Pakistan's more notable writers on philosophy and Islamic ideology, seemed to have no doubt that such indeed would be the case.[19]

The PPP's linkage between Islam and socialism is substantially the same as that made by the writers referred to above, to wit, that both systems place a high value on egalitarianism and cooperation as principles of social organization.

The ultimate objective of the party's policy is the attainment of a classless society, which is possible only through socialism in our time. This means true equality of the citizens, fraternity under the rule of democracy in an order based on economic and social justice. These aims follow from the political and social ethics of Islam. The party thus strives to put in practice the noble ideals of the Muslim faith.[20]

The party argues, as do some other exponents of Islamic socialism, that the right to private property is subordinate to the interest of the community, which transcends that of the individual, so that property may be nationalized if and when there are compelling public reasons for doing so.[21]

18. See chap. 11 ("Three Theories of Islamic Socialism") in Aziz Ahmad, *Islamic Modernism in India and Pakistan 1857-1964* (London: Oxford University Press, 1967).

19. See chap. 12 ("Islamic Socialism") in Hakim, *Islam and Communism* (Lahore: Institute of Islamic Culture, 1962), esp. pp. 175-98.

20. *Election Manifesto of the Pakistan People's Party 1970*, p. 13.

21. Khalifa Abdul Hakim says: "Islam does not prohibit the holding of private property or the accumulation of private capital altogether, but all rights are subject to duties or, as the Muslim classical jurists say, there is no right in which Allah has not a share. Allah, in Islamic jurisprudence, is taken to mean the public weal. Private ownership is not absolute; it cannot be permitted if it stands in the way of general wellbeing." *Op. cit.*, p. 189; also pp. 179-80 regarding nationalization of land. See also Said, *op. cit.*, p. 28.

Bhutto himself sees no tension between Islam and science or, for that matter, between Islamic socialism and scientific socialism. Responding to my reference to scientific socialists in the party, during an interview on December 15, 1973, he observed that he too was a scientific socialist and not some "airy-fairy" kind. At the same time he insisted that his party had no intention of bringing communism to Pakistan and that it would draw on Marxian economic ideas and values selectively.

The PPP *Manifesto* assured its readers that the "socialist regime" would countenance no laws repugnant to Islam. The 1973 constitution accommodated the nation's Islamic sentiment in larger measure than the constitutions of 1956 and 1962 had done. Yet it is likely that the Islamic provisions of the constitution will, as before, have little practical consequence. In what way then will Pakistan be Islamic beyond the elements of compatibility between certain Islamic and socialist values referred to earlier? Even though Islam has now become Pakistan's "state religion," it is clear that the state will not enforce Islamic injunctions other than those made into law. It is likely also that some injunctions, such as the obligation to pray, will not be made into law. Nor, on the other hand, will the socialist regime embark on a systematic program of discouraging prayer, fasting during the month of Ramadan, pilgrimage to Mecca, circumcision, Islamic festivals, and a myriad of other observances and usages having an Islamic content.[22]

There is a more profound sense in which Pakistan may become Islamic. Western capitalism is said to have derived some of its motivational impulse from the "Protestant ethic." Debates and institutional development in the Christian church—led and urged by men such as William of Occam, Nicholas of Cusa, John of Salisbury, and later Luther

22. See Ralph Braibanti's chapter in this volume, pp. 430–79 for analysis of the Ahmediya issue, which is relevant to this discussion of Islam.

and Calvin—contributed to the development of Western democratic liberalism. In other words, Western economic and political ideas and institutions are the product of a culture whose values were, to a significant degree, Judaeo-Christian. The professed value system in Pakistan is largely Islamic, and there is a considerable Islamic element not only in the observance of rituals, ceremonials, and festivities, but also in day-to-day social interaction. With the passage of time, the thin veneer of westernization, characteristic of the Pakistani elite, will wear out. New generations of elites—rooted in the native culture, speaking native languages rather than English, subscribing to native values—will dominate political discourse and behavior, jurisprudence and laws, institutions and their dynamics. This nativization of Pakistani politics will necessarily involve some Islamization, especially in its cultural dimension. In that sense Pakistani socialism will be Islamic socialism.

Phase Two: Problems of Organizational Debility

As the 1970 election results indicated, the PPP has devised an effective ideological mix with which to mobilize the people. The durability of mobilization is partly a function of the goals to which it is related. Many reform movements—good government leagues, neighborhood beautification campaigns, and the like—come and go, often unable to sustain citizen participation. Such endeavors, inviting the citizen to *give* of his time and energy in behalf of his "enlightened self-interest," should be distinguished from a mobilization drive that urges the great majority of a people to *take* that which should have been its all along, save for the "thievery" of an exploitative class. When the appeal is directed to the basic elements of self-preservation—food, clothing, and housing—mobilization once done cannot be undone. The moral basis of the status quo having been destroyed, the mobilized people must now be led toward the proclaimed goals if extralegal political action and violence are to be avoided. While the Pakistani majority has accepted the PPP's model for social change, the party's organizational capacity for directing the mobilization it produced has been declining.

Mr. Bhutto has been presiding over the government of Pakistan since December 20, 1971, and PPP governments have been functioning in the provinces of the Punjab and Sind. For about ten months — May 1972–February 1973 — a NAP-JUI coalition ruled Baluchistan and the Northwest Frontier province. Coalitions more receptive to Bhutto's advice have since been governing these two provinces. Therefore, credit or blame for governmental performance during this period must largely be addressed to the PPP. As might be expected, the record is mixed. Bhutto's successes in clearing away the debris of the 1971 fiasco have been impressive. In return for an "apology" to Bangladesh and promises of peaceableness, possibly goodwill, to India, he has got back some five thousand square miles of Pakistani territory and 93,000 POWs (including the 195 whom Bangladesh wished to try for "war crimes"). In the fraternal spirit of an Islamic summit meeting, he recognized Bangladesh and greeted Sheikh Mujib-ur-Rahman in Lahore without any serious loss of face. At home he was able to produce a constitutional settlement. In addition, he launched a series of reforms concerning land, labor, health, education, law, police, and administration, among others. The most important of these — relating to land, the administrative structure, education, and labor — are in various stages of implementation. In addition to a number of basic industries, Bhutto has nationalized the "vegetable ghee" (cooking oil) industry, export trade in cotton, life insurance, and banks. The state of these nationalized enterprises is a matter of considerable controversy in Pakistan.

But there is no controversy about the fact that the "socialist regime" has failed to halt or control inflation. In his Rawalpindi speech on December 20, 1973, the Prime Minister not only conceded failure but suggested that the problem might be insoluble. It was like foul weather, he said, that had spread all over the world.[23] Bhutto is aware that the rising prices impose intolerable burdens on consumers, especially the urban poor and middle classes, and that a politically explosive situation might result. Dozens of notes and memoranda to his ministers and civil servants, which I was able to see on file in his secretariat in November and December 1973, reveal his intense concern and anxiety.[24] Except for the language riots in Sind in the summer of 1972, uncontrolled inflation is the single most important policy failure pulling the party down in public esteem. But the PPP's internal dynamics also contribute to its loss of popularity in no inconsiderable measure. The public sees the party as engaging in factionalism, corruption, and high-handedness in its dealing with dissidents. These aspects of its political style are discussed below.

Factionalism in the PPP

Discussing factionalism in the *Federalist No. 10*, Madison wrote:

So strong is the propensity of mankind to fall into mutual animosities, that where no substantial occasion presents itself, the most frivolous and fanciful distinctions have been sufficient to kindle their unfriendly passions and excite their most violent conflicts. But the most common and durable source of factions is the various and unequal distribution of property.

This analysis is just as relevant to post-independence politics in Southern Asia as it might have been to the early American scene.[25] Ideological differences, property and

23. My notes of his speech.
24. A note, dated December 24, 1972, asking the cabinet secretary to call a meeting of the Punjab and Sind ministers and officials to discuss a developing wheat shortage, includes the observation that while "the majority of the people live in the countryside. . . cities and towns bring the revolution."
25. See Craig Baxter's chapter in this volume for a discussion of factionalism in the Punjab prior to and immediately following independence.

class differentiations, caste distinctions, ancestral rivalries, clashes of personal ambition and interest, and even "frivolous and fanciful" reasons generate factionalism. For a quarter century Congress politics in Uttar Pradesh suffered from factional conflict, including allegations of political murder and other violence, *partly* because one day in 1941 Thakur Malkhan Singh had closed an argument by slapping Mohan Lal Gautam across the face while the two Congressmen were in the Agra jail.[26] Within moderate bounds factionalism might be a welcome sign of pluralism in party management. Therefore, the question we ask is not whether factionalism exists, but whether it exists to a degree that the party cannot rise above it—whether it will decay into a loose coalition of warring factions, incapable of moving as a body to conceive and implement coherent programs of social change.

There has been some "indiscipline" in the PPP, resulting in expulsions, and there seems to be considerable factional conflict at all levels. Soon after the 1970 election, Ahmad Raza Kasuri, a PPP MNA, revolted against Bhutto's leadership—specifically, against his decision to stay away from the National Assembly session scheduled for March 3, 1971, in Dacca—and, on being threatened with expulsion, proceeded to expel Bhutto from the party! For a time Kasuri acted like a factional leader, but eventually he joined Asghar Khan's Istiqlal party. Mukhtar Rana—a militant socialist from Lyallpur, a labor leader and an effective *gherao* organizer who had been speaking of "fascism" within the party, lost his National Assembly seat in April 1972 after having been sentenced to five years' rigorous imprisonment under Martial Law regulations on charges of inciting violence. At the time of this writing he remains in jail. Dissatisfied with Bhutto's socialism, Meraj Mohammad Khan, once a student leader in

26. Paul R. Brass, *Factional Politics in an Indian State: The Congress Party in Utter Pradesh* (Berkeley: University of California Press, 1965), pp. 89–92.

Karachi with considerable influence among labor, left his post as minister of state for political affairs. He too calls the PPP a "fascist" organization and, in May 1974, was placed in jail. On any given day a visitor to the National Assembly will notice a small group of PPP "rebels" criticizing the government while retaining their seats on the "treasury benches." In August 1972 the party leadership demanded undated letters of resignation from all PPP MNAs by way of strengthening party discipline; the implication was that if and when necessary in the judgment of the "high command," a letter might be dated and made effective. Fifty MNAs were said to have rejected the demand. On September 15, 1972, thirty PPP MNAs joined the opposition in condemning the appointment of Najaf Khan, a retired police officer, to an important post in the Special Police Establishment on the ground that controversy over his alleged role in the assassination of Liaquat Ali Khan in 1951 and certain political murders during the Ayub regime had never been satisfactorily settled.[27] Mahmood Ali Kasuri, law minister and "Leader of the House" in the National Assembly, developed numerous differences with Bhutto—mostly over aspects of the constitutional design then being prepared and on issues relating to the "rule of law." He resigned his cabinet post in October 1972[28] and now sits with the Opposition.

In May 1974 the newly appointed president of the Punjab PPP conceded that the party had been made ineffective by petty factional disputes and fights. Readers of Pakistani newspapers, especially those relatively free of government control, had been seeing references to factional conflict within the PPP for quite some time. In May 1972, for instance, rival groups fought and broke up the furniture in the

27. See Asrar Ahmad, "Cracks in the Ruling Party," *Outlook*, Sept. 23, 1972.
28. The official version of the circumstances surrounding Kasuri's resignation may be seen in *Pakistan Times*, Oct. 5 and 6, 1972. Kasuri's own version will be found in a long account of Ishrat Bokhari's interview with him in *Outlook*, Nov. 25, 1972. Also see "Kasuri's Pregnant Trail," in *ibid.*, Oct. 21, 1972.

party office in a small town near Wazirabad. A few days later a factional fight occurred in the nearby district town of Gujranwala, in which fists and kicks were freely exchanged until the police came in to restore order.[29] Many similar incidents have since been reported in the press. High party dignitaries are not above factional rivalries. *Shahab*, an Urdu weekly controlled by Kauser Niazi, the information minister, denounced Meraj Mohammad Khan as a pro-Moscow communist while the latter was still in government. Sheikh Rashid (health minister) was ridiculed for his allegedly old-fashioned views on socialism by fellow "scientific" socialists and, for a time, was deprived of influence in party affairs.

The internal politics of the Punjab PPP is illustrative of factionalism.[30] To date, party elections have not been held, with the result that party management is vested in appointed officials (presidents and general secretaries) and executive committees at the provincial, district, city, and town levels. During the 1970 election campaign, many enthusiasts and faithfuls — left-of-center elements impressed by Bhutto's promise of an egalitarian order — opened party offices throughout the province with or without the "high command's" specific authorization. Sheikh Rashid, president of the Punjab PPP at the time, did much organization work, gaining the loyalty of a large number of party workers in the province. Ghulam Mustafa Khar, once Bhutto's friend and confidant, was the secretary general. Before long the two men — Rashid and Khar — were seen as rivals. After the PPP

---

29. See *Jang* [Urdu], May 15 and 22, 1972. (This and subsequent references to *Jang* relate to the paper's international edition issued from London.)

30. The following discussion is based partly on information gathered through interviews with party functionaries — former and current (September 1973–January 1974) — and partly on the following articles in the weekly *Outlook*: Hussain Naqi, "How Sails the PPP?" June 2, 1973; Ishrat Bokhari, "PPP and Party Democracy," Aug. 7, 1973; Hussain Naqi, "Will Khar Survive?" Feb. 16, 1974; "Khar's War," Feb. 23, 1974; "Exit Khar, Enter Ramay," March 16, 1974; "Khar Bounces Back," March 30, 1974; Marghub Siddiqui, "The Gathering Storm," and Muzaffar Qadir, "The Story of Enrichment," April 20, 1974; Abdullah Malik, "The Power Tussle," May 11, 1974; and a "commentator's" "Bhutto-Khar Patch Up," June 1, 1974.

became the ruling party, Khar took over as governor of the Punjab while retaining his post as the party's secretary general. In an apparent display of hostility, he moved his party office away from the building where other PPP offices, including that of Rashid, were located.

Partly because of his friendship with Bhutto, Khar enjoyed the support of several party dignitaries at the center: Mubashir Hassan (Bhutto's old friend and the finance minister, once head of the Lahore city PPP), Abdul Hafeez Pirzada (education minister whose wife is related to Mrs. Khar), Ghulam Mustafa Jatoi (minister for political affairs), and Kausar Niazi (information minister). Khurshid Hasan Meer (minister without portfolio and Bhutto's assistant for establishment matters) would seem to have been a quiet, but not wholly inactive, supporter of Shaikh Rashid. So were Malik Meraj Khalid and Hanif Ramay, the provincial chief minister and finance minister, respectively.

During 1972 and the first half of 1973, many pro-Rashid elements were harassed, intimidated, and/or thrown out of the party hierarchy at various levels throughout the province. By May 1972 only one branch organization in the city of Lahore—the one in Baghbanpura—was said to have any pro-Rashid functionaries. These measures were facilitated by the fact that Khar, as governor, controlled not only government patronage but the police. Add to this the impact of his reputation as Bhutto's personal friend and that of Rashid's image as one whom Bhutto barely tolerated. A "reorganization" in the summer of 1973 made Mian Mohammad Afzal Wattoo—a Khar supporter, who had lost the 1970 election while contesting from a Bahawalpur constituency—president of the Punjab PPP despite numerous allegations of "misconduct" made against him by MPAs from Bahawalpur and neighboring areas. His appointment meant that Khar would be the effective head of both the party and the government in the Punjab.

Here it should be noted that during the 1970 election

campaign many of the landed aristocracy and gentry—along with "opportunists," self-seekers, and gangsters whose presence in the party is now freely admitted—came into the PPP. They sensed Bhutto was a winner and hoped his commitment to socialism was vastly overstated. More of them came in after Bhutto had become the chief executive. Peasants, workers, and leftist intellectuals, on the other hand, expected substantial social change. During 1972 there were many bloody clashes between peasants and landlords, workers and employers, and these have never quite ended. The landed gentry, interested in order and tranquility, looked to Khar, himself a middle landlord, for protection from the full impact of Bhutto's land reforms.

Governor Khar suppressed the "extremists," dissidents, and opponents—in short, "miscreants"—within and without the PPP with a ferocity reminiscent of Kalabagh's rule in the 1960s. That some of his ministers, notably Mian Iftikhar Tari, were widely alleged to have underworld connections damaged the regime's legitimacy. Mumtaz Bhutto's government in Sind operated in like fashion. By the fall of 1973 Prime Minister Bhutto concluded that he must dissociate himself from their heavy political style. He asked Khar to drop Mian Tari from the Punjab cabinet, and in December he discharged Mumtaz Bhutto from the chief ministership of Sind. As the Prime Minister's cabinet colleagues came to know his thinking, they began to withdraw support from Khar. According to some reports, Mubashir Hasan stopped seeing him and so did Pirzada.[31] At the Rawalpindi meeting on December 20, referred to above, Khurshid Hasan Meer criticized Khar's projection as "Quaid-e-Punjab" (leader of the Punjab) on the ground that it detracted from Bhutto's status as the "Quaid-e-Awam" (leader of the masses, which surely included the Punjabis). At a subsequent meeting in Lahore he criticized Tari and by implication Khar, who had been Tari's patron. Toward the end of January 1974, as re-

31. Marghub Siddiqui, *op. cit.*

ports circulated in PPP drawing rooms that Khar might soon be dismissed, forty Punjab MPAs submitted a petition to Bhutto, alleging numerous cases of corruption and other malfeasance on Khar's part. In early February five MPAs attacked Khar on the floor of the Punjab Assembly and engaged in a free exchange of colorful Punjabi vocabulary with some of his supporters.

Khar resigned his post on March 10, 1974, and Bhutto designated Hanif Ramay—the soft-spoken, civil, professedly propertyless painter and former journalist—to succeed him. Khar first appeared to accept his ouster with good grace, professing infinite loyalty to Bhutto with only a subdued expression of a sense of grievance. Amid shouts that he withdraw his resignation, he made the following declarations at a meeting of party workers in Lahore: He regarded Bhutto as his "father" and mentor; he had stood by Bhutto when others deserted him; he would make any personal sacrifice to preserve this "tower of friendship"; time would show that his enemies were in fact Bhutto's enemies; he "relished" his ouster from office, for it was a defeat inflicted on him by none other than Bhutto himself; he prayed that God might bestow still higher stations on Bhutto.[32] He suggested that he might withdraw from politics and resign his seat in the Punjab Assembly.

On his part, Bhutto tried to soften the blow by indicating that he still valued Khar's friendship: he took him to Al-Murtaza, his home in Larkana, and stayed at Khar's house during visits to Lahore. Ramay declared that he and Khar had always had a relationship of mutual respect, adding that the party could prosper only through unswerving loyalty to Chairman Bhutto and complete obedience to his dictates.[33] The new chief minister accommodated two Khar supporters — Abdul Khaliq and Mian Afzal Watoo—in his cabinet.

But thoughts of retirement soon gave way to a decision to

32. *Pakistan Times*, March 14, 1974.
33. *Ibid.*, March 13, 1974.

fight it out with Ramay and show the party chairman who really mattered in the Punjab. Khar toured the province to meet and organize his supporters in the party. He began to criticize the Ramay government, claiming that it was not a government at all, and that he, not Ramay, commanded majority support in the Assembly. He let it be known that he would organize a May Day procession of his own, separately from the official PPP procession to be addressed by Ramay. However, this plan had to be given up following a singularly unpleasant incident. On April 30 a veteran labor leader, Abdul Rahman, was murdered in the Kot Lakhpat industrial area on the outskirts of Lahore. Khar went there to visit with the workers and offer condolences but ran into a hostile crowd that beat him up and tore his clothes. The police, present on the scene, did not rescue him until after he had been manhandled.

Khar claimed that the Ramay government had engineered the Kot Lakhpat incident. If so, it may have been a way of conveying to him that "gentle" Ramay was not entirely incapable of the methods Khar himself had employed against his adversaries. But it is more likely that the Ramay government, unsure of Chairman Bhutto's mind on the subject, did not wish to treat Khar with the harshness customarily reserved for political opponents. There were some factional disruptions of his meetings and a moderate amount of police harassment during his tour of the province. The provincial labor minister accused him of fomenting labor and student unrest and disrupting the public peace.[34] Sheikh Rashid alleged Khar had bought a London restaurant worth £100,000 with funds illegally transferred abroad. Other charges of corruption and misconduct were made, and some local PPP organizations demanded his expulsion from the party. The provincial committee, without specifically naming him, condemned his indiscipline and opposition to the party

34. *Ibid.*, May 16, 1974.

government. But these were mere pinpricks compared to the treatment Khar's government had meted out to its opponents. Ramay took the unusual position that charges against Khar had best be left to the court of public opinion where he would stand exposed in due course of time.[35]

Khar made contact with the opposition parties and dissidents within the PPP outside the Punjab. He kept in "constant touch" with NAP leaders, entertained the Talpur brothers at his Clifton home in Karachi, and visited Meraj Mohammad Khan. He claimed to know of lapses by Bhutto that were much worse than anything Ayub might have done at Tashkent. On May 21 he and ten associates voted with the opposition in support of an adjournment motion to discuss a vegetable ghee shortage. His supporters claimed that Khar had asked *only* ten PPP members to vote against the government and that he did not wish to reveal the true size of his following. These developments moved J. A. Rahim, the party's secretary general, to send Khar a notice asking him to "show cause" why he should not be expelled from the party. At the same time Khar was reported to be seeking a meeting with Bhutto, who was in Lahore watching the political scene. Before seeing Khar, Chairman Bhutto dissolved the Punjab PPP organization and appointed Malik Meraj Khalid, one of Khar's opponents, as president with a mandate to reorganize the party in the province. On May 22 Bhutto met Khar, and after two extended meetings a "reconciliation" was announced.

It has been noted in this and the previous chapter that factionalism in the Punjab is a complex phenomenon. The numerous factors contributing to factional conflict, mentioned above, are all at work. But one should not underestimate the ideological division within the party. Sheikh Rashid, K. H. Meer, Taj Langah, and J. A. Rahim — to name a few — were socialists even before the PPP came into

35. *Ibid.*, May 6, 1974.

being. They would like to carry forward the mobilization begun in 1969–70. The PPP conservatives prefer a slower rate of social change and would like to see the party develop more as an agent of interest aggregation than as a mobilizer for class struggle. Related to, and often transcending, the ideological differences is the elemental struggle for political survival. Above all these divisions and rivalries stands Zulfikar Ali Bhutto. Party notables have repeatedly declared that they are his creatures, owing their legislative and ministerial roles to his personal popularity with the electorate. Factionalism, therefore, involves competition for a higher rating in the order of merit and precedence that he builds from time to time. Legislators and party officials at the district and local levels make estimates of where contending dignitaries stand in Bhutto's esteem, and they shift support accordingly. But if his charisma fades so that he is not expected to carry the Punjab in the next election to the extent that he did in 1970, factionalism in the province will proceed on local, and not his, terms.

Bhutto's reconciliation with Khar does not necessarily terminate the latter's factional role. But why the reconciliation? It might have been embarrassing to suppress him, but the Punjab police are ingenious enough to have surmounted that problem. The factor of personal friendship with Bhutto may also be discounted: during my interview with the Prime Minister referred to earlier, he observed that his friendships were all "in the public interest." (By now Khar may also have discovered this.) The best explanation may be found in Bhutto's preference for a balance-of-power strategy in party management. He gave the "scientific socialists" the upper hand to see what they could do. But he did not want to destroy Khar as a power in Punjabi politics.

Corruption in the PPP

Parties need money to do their political work. The worker at the base and functionaries in the party offices must have some income, even if they are seasoned, ideologically mature, and ascetically inclined men and women—a description that does not yet fit most PPP members. Funds are also needed for organizing meetings, demonstrations, processions, welcoming and farewell ceremonies for visiting or departing party dignitaries, and, of course, for contesting elections. Having declared itself an enemy of feudal lords and capitalists, the PPP cannot raise money in these quarters. Mr. Bhutto's memoranda to party associates indicate he has spent considerable sums of personal funds for party purposes. Other PPP notables, who happen to be prosperous, may have done the same: Khurshid Hasan Meer told this writer that many party men had become "bankrupt" spending personal funds for party work.[36]

In the absence of regular and systematized funding, legitimized by law or tradition, party influentials may resort to means of income and advantage broadly identified as "corruption," a transnational phenomenon that has received ample consideration in the literature on political development.[37] In the South Asian context, proceeds of corruption do not normally go into the party treasury; they profit the individual collector. Some observers endorse this practice as a necessary "cement" for party-building. Party men who get to be ministers receive handsome salaries and perquisites. But legislators are not so well paid, and many party functionaries receive no salaries at all. As a consequence, corruption is a way of keeping underpaid and unpaid politicians attached to the party. When political modernization and development have advanced to a point where individuals, gainfully employed elsewhere, are available

---

36. Interview on Dec. 26, 1973.

37. See Arnold J. Heidenheimer, ed., *Political Corruption: Readings in Comparative Analysis* (New York: Holt, Rinehart, and Winston, 1970). This is a massive compilation containing many essays, old and recent, on both sides of the issue. See also James C. Scott, *Comparative Political Corruption* (Englewood Cliffs, N.J.: Prentice-Hall, 1972).

for party work on a volunteer basis, corruption can be expected to diminish.[38] (I have discussed this matter in some detail elsewhere.[39])

In the interview mentioned above, K. H. Meer contended that charges of corruption against the PPP were merely "enemy propaganda." Yet only a few days later it became not only permissible but fashionable in party circles and government-controlled newspapers to acknowledge the existence of widespread corruption within the party. Many types of corruption were apparently involved: grant or sale of permits to operate ration depots for distributing necessities such as wheat, sugar, rice, and kerosene at controlled prices, with possibilities of making extra money through adulteration, bogus ration cards, and black marketing; informal delegation of authority to national and provincial assembly legislators to nominate persons for appointment to a variety of lower-level jobs (in primary education, family planning, and the People's Works Program); intercession with police and other officials in behalf of constituents, which might be done gratis for friends and relatives and on a fee basis for others; the entire gamut of "permit raj"—building and other government contracts, industrial and commercial licenses, foreign exchange allocations, import permits, access to subsidized fertilizer and agricultural machinery, low-interest credit. Beyond these lay the gratifications resulting from tolerance of organized crime such as smuggling. Proceedings at the Sind party convention on December 1, 1973, as well as comment in the press indicated that some ministers were engaged in corruption and other serious violations of the penal code.

---

38. For instance, Huntington says that "for an official to award a public office in return for a contribution of work or money to a party organization is to subordinate one public interest to another, more needy, public interest. . . . Corruption varies inversely with political organization, and to the extent that corruption builds parties, it undermines the conditions of its own existence." Huntington, *op. cit.*, pp. 70–71.

39. See my "Bureaucratic Ethic and Ethos in Pakistan," *Polity* (Winter 1971), pp. 160–94, esp. pp. 183–91.

Prime Minister Bhutto assured the Sind convention that he would proceed against all corrupt elements in the party regardless of their rank or status. A few weeks later, Abdul Hafeez Pirzada told the National Assembly that he would soon move a bill to deal with corrupt legislators and ministers.[40] Khurshid Hasan Meer called on party workers to purge "opportunists" who had forced their way into the PPP through "sheer goondaism."[41] Ghulam Mustafa Khar, some of whose own cabinet colleagues had gained considerable notoriety in connection with corruption and other types of lawlessness, declared that some PPP men were amassing wealth through illegal means and professed to have begun a crusade against them.[42]

Despite the ubiquitous nature of political and bureaucratic corruption, it is not inappropriate to ask why a political party committed to Islamic-socialist egalitarianism should become afflicted with massive corruption so soon after coming to power. It would be an oversimplification to conclude the matter by saying that the party's commitment to egalitarianism is bogus. Nor would it do to focus attention exclusively on the "opportunists" and gangsters who, according to Meer, have gate-crashed the party. There is also the deeper problem of failure at all levels, including the "high command," to have internalized the implications of egalitarianism concerning elite life-styles and consumption orientations. Without promoting elite asceticism and depressing the values of acquisitiveness and conspicuous consumption, egalitarianism will not function in an environment of widespread scarcities. The connection between elite asceticism and egalitarianism was well understood and made operational in early Islam.[43] The PPP dignitaries, however, appear to be oblivious not only to this connection but to Machia-

40. *Pakistan Times*, Jan. 27, 1974.
41. *Ibid.*
42. *Ibid.*, Jan. 13, 1974. From the beginning of January until his resignation on March 10, Khar's anti-corruption statements were almost a daily occurence.
43. See my essay, "Towards an Islamic View of Public Service Ethic," *Pakistan Administrative Staff College Journal* (June 1972), pp. 1–15. For further study, see

velli's eminently sensible emphasis on the role of appearances in politics.[44] The MPAs and lower party officials are entitled to know why they must combine "service to the people" with self-denial while party dignitaries pursue grandeur.

There is, for instance, no rational explanation of Khar's decision to be governor, rather than chief minister of the Punjab, other than that he wished to enjoy the splendid amenities and style—including the military secretaries and ADCs—of the Governor's House in Lahore. Since he also wanted to be the effective head of the provincial government, a role that constitutionally belonged to the chief minister, he usurped the latter's powers, subverting the constitution in the process. When the 1973 constitution came into force, and he had to be chief minister in order to have effective power, he moved the Civil Service Academy out of the "Residency"—the palatial house where the British Resident (overlord of the princely states in Punjab) used to live—in order to make it his official home. Prime Minister Bhutto ordered him away from the Residency but not until the scandal had further damaged the PPP's image.

To return to the matter of party funding, it should first be noted that membership dues have never amounted to any significant sum of money in the Pakistani experience. Moreover, after several "reorganizations," which plainly meant factionally motivated purges, it would be difficult to say who the PPP's members were. A major issue of membership policy—selective or open—remains to be settled. An ideological party might ask its relatively prosperous members to donate a given percentage of their monthly or annual

Khursheed Ahmad Farooq, ed., *Hazrat Umar ke Sarkari Khatut* ["The Official Letters of Umar" (the second Caliph of Islam)] (Delhi: Nadwatul Musannafin, 1959); the administrative policy letter of Ali ibn Abi Talib (the fourth Caliph) to Malik ibn Ashtar (letter 53) in Syed Mohammad Askari, trans., *Nahjul Balagha: Sermons, Letters and Sayings of Hazrat Ali* (Karachi, n.p., n.d.); Shibli Nomani, *Al-Faruq* (many editions), II, sections 226, 422, 522–24.

44. *The Prince*, chap. 18.

incomes to the organization. The SDP deputies in the West German Bundestag were, at one time, required to pay 20 percent of their salaries into the party treasury.[45] Certain non-political sectarian organizations in Pakistan follow similar practices. That the PPP legislators can be persuaded not only to give up the extralegal rewards of electoral success they now allegedly enjoy but to denote percentages of their legal incomes to the party may be wishful thinking.

The problem of funding is simplified in one-party systems: the party being an organ of the state, its expenses can be met from the public exchequer. But considering that opposition parties do perform a public function vital to the maintenance of a democratic order—a value to which the nations concerned have committed themselves—public funding can be made available in multi-party systems also. In the 1960s, the Federal and Länder governments in West Germany appropriated annual subsidies to political parties — in proportion to their representation in the legislatures—to help cover not only the costs of their "political education" and electioneering work but also their operating expenses.[46] The principle of public financing of election campaigns has gained a measure of acceptance in the United States. Under proper safeguards, including administration by an independent agency, a formula for the public funding of political parties in Pakistan might be more facilitative of party-building than corruption.

The parties might also engage in business enterprises, the profits of which would go to the party treasury. One might recall that in the late 1950s and early 1960s the Italian Communist party received as much as 30 billion lire from its numerous businesses, which included export-import cor-

---

45. Ulrich Duebber and Gerard Braunthal, "West Germany," *Journal of Politics*, XXV (1963), 776.

46. In the mid-1960s direct public subsidies to political parties amounted to about DM 50 million a year. See Arnold J. Heidenheimer and Frank C. Langdon, *Business Associations and the Financing of Political Parties* (The Hague: Martinus Nijhoff, 1968), pp. 78–88.

porations and "cooperative societies." One of the latter, "Federazione Reggiana delle Cooperative" in the town of Reggio Emilis, had "16,000 employees, a working capital of 12 billion lire and transactions amounting to 32 billion lire."[47] This method of building financial viability might also commend itself to the PPP and possibly other parties.

Political Intimidation and Violence

Some reference must also be made to political intimidation and violence that are relevant to the PPP's internal coherence and its standing in public esteem. For a long time the concept of public tranquility in Southern Asia has been understood to include suppression of political adversaries or "troublemakers." In recent memory, governments in the area have not been without preventive detention powers nor the jails without political prisoners. In the current tradition of political repression there is also the more blatant practice of implicating opponents in bogus criminal cases for one or more of the following purposes: putting the opponent away for a period of time; harassing him; ruining him financially by imposing on him the necessity of defending himself—sometimes right up to the Supreme Court—in an interminable succession of such cases; humiliating him among his constituents and/or his peer group as, for instance, when he may be accused of petty theft or cattle-lifting or when his father, or uncle, in his seventies or eighties, may be held for abduction or rape.

The PPP governments in Sind and the Punjab have used these weapons not only against troublesome outsiders but against dissidents within their own party. A few references should suffice. A petition before the Sind and Baluchistan High Court in May 1972 alleged that, as a punishment for opposing the party leadership on a policy issue, Abdul Hamid Jatoi, PPP MNA from Dadu, had been placed in

47. Giovanni Sartori, "European Political Parties: The Case of Polarized Pluralism," in Joseph LaPalombara and Myron Weiner, eds., *Political Parties and Political Development* (Princeton: Princeton University Press, 1966), pp. 145–46, n. 13.

preventive detention after earlier arrests on criminal charges could not be maintained.[48] His relatives and friends, including MPAs Mohammad Bakhsh Jamali and Amir Bakhsh Junejo, were also said to be threatened with arrest. Another petition before the same court in February 1974 alleged that, for his refusal to abandon the NAP, MPA Sher Ali Khan Nowsherwani was being implicated in criminal cases on various charges (including "dacoity" and murder), for some of which he had already been tried and acquitted.[49] In the Punjab, a few days after Mahmood Ali Kasuri had resigned and Governor Khar had threatened him with dire consequences, a procession appeared outside the Governor's House in Lahore, alleging that many months ago a man had been found dead on Kasuri's lands and that he was involved. Khar undertook to have the matter "investigated" and "justice" done. The case did not go forward, presumably because of Kasuri's international eminence as a jurist and the patent grotesqueness of the charge.

An incident at the local level might be of interest: on January 20, 1974, the *Pakistan Times* reported that three *former* PPP officials in Hasilpur (Bahawalpur district) had been arrested under the Defense of Pakistan Rules for making "objectionable" speeches. According to one account, Chaudhury Zahur Ilahi, a veteran opposition MNA from Gujrat, had been implicated in *twenty-seven* cases on charges including fraud, burglary, adulteration, cattle lifting, and gunrunning. His wife's property in Gujrat was said to have been demolished for alleged violations of the building code and some of his land taken over to provide low-cost housing for the poor.[50]

Many other instances might be cited, but reference to one recent case should be included. In early February 1974,

48. *Jang*, May 23, 30, 31, 1972.
49. "The Tale of an MPA," a correspondent's report in *Outlook*, March 2, 1974.
50. See Yusaf Lodi, "The Strange Case of Ch. Zahur Illahi," *ibid.*, Feb. 2, 1974. Numerous other references to political arrests and harassment, including the case of Altaf Gauhar, may be seen in "Season for Arrests" and "Twilight of Justice" in *ibid.*, Sept. 1, 1973, and Feb. 4, 1974, respectively.

PPP MPAs Yaqub Maan, Nawab Khakwani, Raja Munawwar, Khalid Ahmad, and Abdul Qayyum launched a campaign against the chief minister, Ghulam Mustafa Khar. Maan distributed posters and pamphlets urging Prime Minister Bhutto to investigate Khar's corruption and high-handedness. He and Khakwani also attacked him in the Punjab Assembly. Khar responded, first by ordering an "inquiry" into Maan's "malpractices." Two days later processions in Qasur and Multan, home towns of Maan and Khakwani, respectively, were organized to denounce their "anti-people," "anti-party," "pro-capitalist," and "pro-imperialist" activities. At a public meeting in Qasur on February 12, Khar canceled Maan's "illegal" possession of more than one hundred acres of land and ordered the same to be immediately seized and distributed among tenants and landless peasants in the area. Khar accused Maan of having manipulated bogus criminal cases against innocent citizens, ordered the withdrawal of all such cases, and apologized to the people of Qasur who, he lamented, had suffered from Maan's mischief!

The incidence of political violence in Pakistan has perceptibly risen during the last two years.[51] In May 1974 a labor leader in Lahore was murdered. In March the deputy speaker of the Baluchistan Assembly, Maulvi Shams-ud-Din, who belonged to the opposition JUI-NAP group in provincial politics, was shot dead. Before that the pro-Bhutto Pakhtoon Khwa leader, Abdus Samad Achakzai, was assassinated. Four attempts have been made on the life of Abdul Wali Khan, the NAP leader. Asghar Khan, leader of the Istiqlal party, has been assaulted. In 1972 Usman Kennedy, a Jamaat-i-Islami MPA in Sind, was almost beaten to death; Khawaja Rafiq, an opposition leader in Lahore, and Dr. Nazir Ahmad, a Jamaat-i-Islami MNA from Dera Ghazi Khan, were murdered.

---

51. Cf. Asrar Ahmad, "Language of Bullets," *ibid.*, March 31, 1973; "Stately Hooliganism," *ibid.*, June 9, 1973; "The Trail of Violence," *ibid.*, Oct. 13, 1973.

No conclusive evidence has come out linking specific politicians or political parties with these crimes of violence. But it is clear also that the provincial governments concerned have not investigated these crimes with any great vigor. The accused in the murder of Dr. Nazir Ahmad were acquitted for want of sufficient evidence. A High Court judge, looking into the case of Khawaja Rafiq's murder, reported to the Punjab government in February 1974 that the police had done a poor job of investigating the case.

A few cases of factional violence within the PPP were mentioned earlier. A commentator in the *Pakistan Times* (January 24, 1974) recalls some other incidents: in February 1972 disgruntled party workers forcibly seized the party secretariat in Karachi; in March a faction disrupted Prime Minister Bhutto's public meeting at the Gaddafi Stadium in Lahore to discredit those (the Ramay group) who had been in charge of the arrangements for the meeting; another factional fight disrupted a "tea party" at the Shalimar Gardens (Lahore) in honor of the newly appointed chief minister of the Punjab, Malik Meraj Khalid. In May 1972 an MPA from Lyallpur, an MPA from Hafizabad, and an MPA from Lahore were alleged to have been involved in cases of criminal violence, including, in two cases, murder. Lawyers, law clerks (including those of Kasuri and Rashid), and hired gangsters were alleged to have assaulted functionaries of the Young Lawyers' Association opposed to the government's new law reforms. In Vehari (Multan) a local PPP factional leader got a severe beating from a rival group; in Gujjar Khan an MPA and some party workers were injured in a clash.[52] In January 1974 a PPP MPA from Lahore Cantonment was reported to have hired gangsters to beat up lesser party functionaries and workers.[53]

It should be noted that misgivings about the presence of

52. *Jang*, May 12, 17, 24, 26–27, 29, and 31, 1972.
53. *Pakistan Times*, Jan. 17, 1974.

gangsters in the party were not voiced until recently. The incident at the Gaddafi Stadium merits a further word. According to *Jang* of March 29, 1972, the Lahore police had registered a case against Mian Iftikhar Tari and an associate for having shot and critically wounded one of the People's Guards posted at the stadium in anticipation of Bhutto's arrival. A factional fight broke out inside the stadium and the People's Guards came out running. In "hot pursuit" of the Guards, as it were, Mian Tari and his associate, Mazhar Ali, pistols in hand, came out at the head of another group. Mian Sahib allegedly fired two shots at one of the guards, Shahzad Ahmad, who told his story to the police on regaining consciousness five days after the incident. That Mian Tari soon became a minister in the provincial government would suggest that the police had not found evidence of wrongdoing on his part.

Bhutto's Role

Critics such as I. H. Burney, editor of *Outlook* (banned in July 1974), assert that, as an organization, the PPP is a shambles — "a picture of strife, squabbling and factionalism"; a mere "shadow of its former self."[54] One might dismiss Mr. Burney as a hostile critic but for the fact that his judgment is confirmed by current "self-analysis" in the party. A week after his appointment as president of the Punjab PPP, Malik Meraj Khalid declared that "internal conflicts . . . have not only discredited the party in the eyes of the general public" but brought suffering upon the entire nation. The party must be purged of corrupt elements, he said, and tolerance, a sense of justice, and respect for the rule of law must be cultivated. "We are pledged to restore democratic norms and principles," which alone can produce "real solidarity." He added that the people had so far been ignored — "for obvious reasons" — and must now be served.[55] And

54. See "Opinion" in the issues of May 11 and June 8, 1974.
55. See Meraj Khalid's statements in *Pakistan Times*, May 30 and 31, 1974.

all this, he insisted, would be done under the guidance of Chairman Bhutto.

It cannot be asserted that corruption, factionalism, and violence in the party have proceeded without the Chairman's knowledge. The files in his secretariat reveal not only that he has been aware of them but that, from time to time, he has commended civility and moderation to his associates. For instance, a note to Mumtaz Bhutto (May 20, 1973) regarding the Sind government's plan to import four hundred buses cautions: "Please see that no hanky-panky takes place and that everything is done above board." Complaining to his finance minister about corruption in a government lending institution (July 3, 1973), he says: "The loans must go to genuine persons and the genuine persons must be the poor people." Many other notes on file contain the statement: "I will not tolerate this corruption." A letter from Senator Agha Ghulam Nabi Pathan (dated November 22, 1973) informs him that the party's involvement with ration depots, and the associated black-marketing and smuggling, has lowered its standing so that most party workers cannot face the public or do their political work. They are "no longer visible on the public platform." Noting that "for quite some time I have been receiving similar complaints," the Prime Minister circulated Pathan's letter to members of the central committee eliciting their views and suggestions.

Bhutto has likewise been aware of violence and gangsterism in the party. A note to Mumtaz Bhutto (December 27, 1972) refers to the people of Shikarpur's complaining to him of "utter lawlessness" and the "reign of terror" that gangsters patronized by the party had unleashed. A memo to Governor Khar (August 16, 1973) opens with the following observation: "Pistols to the right of us, pistols to the left of us, pistols all around us. This seems to be the motto of the party. For the most trivial of things pistols are drawn and flashed." The Prime Minister goes on to say that the gangsters who do this sort of thing must feel they "have protection, because this was not their brave habit before we assumed office. How are we going to end if this becomes the order of the day?" Speaking of a specific incident and the person responsible, he urges: "I hope out of deference to my strong feelings, stern action will be taken against him." Another note to Khar on the same day seeks to instruct the governor in the virtue of moderation. Apparently one of Khar's ministers and three PPP MPAs from the old Bahawalpur state, one of them allegedly a known smuggler and the other two recent joiners in the party, were harassing a PPP MNA, his family, and friends by having the local administration institute bogus cases against them. Mr. Bhutto wrote that at one time he too had been unhappy with this MNA and that it might, on occasion, be necessary "to bring such individuals back to the right path *but, in making this effort, the path itself should not be broken.*"[56]

But why these suggestions, appeals, and gentle remonstrances? Were stronger measures not available? Several considerations are relevant. Mr. Bhutto is preeminently a political realist. Like many other politicians, he probably believes that in his craft an excess even of virtue is to be avoided, and that a certain amount of factionalism, graft, and arm-twisting are not only unavoidable but useful. Second, he does not, and cannot, control the government and the party in a monolithic fashion. Even though his associates and lieutenants flatter him by insisting that they respect his word as law, it is a "law" they often neglect to implement. His files contain many notes to ministers, provincial governors, and chief ministers, even civil servants, reminding them of things he had asked them to do and which they had not done. He urges them in the name of Pakistan's "toiling masses"; recalls the pledges made in the party's *Election Manifesto* and reminds them that "men of conscience" must be answerable to the electorate; and warns them of the

---

56. Names of individuals concerned are omitted because this information comes from the Prime Minister's files and not from published sources.

consequences of the party's falling popularity. Sometimes he does threaten. Protesting that the governments of the Punjab and Sind were not spending the development funds made available to them, a note (November 19, 1972) addressed to Mumtaz Bhutto, Ghulam Mustafa Khar, and some central ministers contains the following statement: "If the Chief Minister of Sind and the Governor of Punjab are very great men and cannot be touched, I will certainly take action against their Ministers for Finance and their Ministers for Development. I am going crazy trying to get things moving, to clear the slums and to have more roads and to have more construction." At a cabinet meeting on December 14, 1973, at which governors of the Punjab and NWFP, chief ministers of Sind and Baluchistan, and their respective officials were present to discuss a progress report on the implementation of land reforms, and which I was permitted to observe, the Prime Minister warned that if the provincial governments did not act more vigorously, he might call for a new general election, and then "we will see who gets elected!"

Mr. Bhutto's relatively low profile in party reformation cannot be understood without some reference to the aftermath of Pakistan's dismemberment in December 1971. The nation was seized by disillusionment, pessimism, indiscipline, and lawlessness. The Supreme Court declared that the Yahya regime had been a usurper and that its acts had no standing in law. Even though it later blessed the Bhutto government as legitimate, many commentators remained openly unconvinced, suggesting that the country was in fact without a legal government. Capital fled on a massive scale, unsure of its future. In the first half of 1972 an excess of egalitarian sentiment produced protracted industrial unrest in the major cities; "Awami Adalats" (people's courts) in the Punjab and Sind tried individuals for being pro-capitalist, or anti-labor, or "disrespectful to Chairman Bhutto," and passed sentences. Railway workers in Rawalpindi occupied bungalows meant for higher officials. Rival student groups in Lahore fired several thousand rounds of amunition at each other during student union elections. The police in Lahore and several other towns went on strike, which under the circumstances amounted to an act of revolt. There were severe problems in the area of foreign relations. On top of this, many prominent commentators reckoned Bhutto among those responsible for the nation's defeat and dismemberment. Z. A. Suleri, an old critic and accuser, came close to calling him a traitor.[57]

One might argue that in this situation Bhutto's options were severely limited. He would still use the civil and police services, but as subordinate agencies, not as allies. They would behave as subordinate agents not because the law said so but because the new configuration of power compelled obedience to political authority. The PPP had emerged as a great center of power inasmuch as it commanded a vast reservoir of physical force resident in the mass, which could be mobilized to subdue hostile power centers. Khar's success in breaking the police strike in March 1972 is a case in point: armed with the resounding support of a tremendous crowd at a Mochi Gate (Lahore) meeting, he warned that if the police did not return to work within forty-eight hours, he would discharge them all and recruit a new force. In this context of power politics even the gangster had a role: he possessed considerable expertise in organizing and employing capabilities of physical coercion. A campaign to throw out the "rascals," of whom there appeared to be many, would have to be deferred until after the more difficult domestic and foreign policy problems had been resolved. By the fall of 1973 the time was thought to be propitious for such a move.

57. See Suleri's column in *Jang*, June 3, 1972. In 1968 also he had questioned Bhutto's patriotism and urged suitable constraint. "It will be a poor nation that will pay the price of independent existence for the sake of fulfilling the boundless ambitions of a half-baked politician, to whom the only cause that matters is the personal cause. One might condone his other sins but the sin of perpetrating insurrection will not be overlooked." See his piece, "Mr. Bhutto's Rejoinder: An Analysis," *Pakistan Times*, Oct. 29, 1968.

But even now the option of making a clean break with the managers of political coercion was avoided: Mumtaz Bhutto's services to Sind and the nation were praised; Khar was showed continued friendliness; even Tari was allowed the honor of an audience, presumably to spare him loss of face among his "peer group."

The above interpretation does not imply that other strategies might not have been more promotive of domestic peace and cohesion or the PPP's own vigor. The excessive emphasis on coercion, entailing an irresistible "demonstration effect," worked to the political system's disadvantage. If Opposition leaders and PPP dissidents challenging the party dignitaries were to be denied the civilities of democratic procedure and the protections of the rule of law, actual or potential rivals of party notables at lower echelons would likely be treated in similar fashion. It is not surprising then that crises of legitimacy and participation have reappeared. Mr. Bhutto still dominates the Pakistani political scene and commands considerable mass support. But as Machiavelli would say, he may not be far from joining the ranks of "unarmed prophets": with the PPP, his "army," in disarray, the balance of power in the political system may once again tend toward the pre-1972 model. The regime's increasing reliance on the traditional enforcers of public tranquility for solving its political problems suggests this possibility.

During the first phase, the PPP became a movement to overthrow the existing political order on the basis of a winning ideological posture. Phase two has been a period of decay. The movement failed to convert itself into a party. Party-building in phase three, which is said to have begun with the latest "reorganization" in the Punjab, will have to contend with some serious problems, two of which may briefly be mentioned. If the party is to resume a mobilist role, which Meraj Khalid is advocating, a policy of selective rather than open membership will have to be adopted in order to preclude subversion from within. This could involve a purge of those existing members who do not meet the new criteria. But if the purge were to extend to PPP legislators, party governments would be endangered. Reformation must therefore be slow and cautious until the "high command" is ready for a new election. Over the long run, a certain delinking of the party's organizational personality from that of Chairman Bhutto is also necessary. Organizational viability cannot develop in the absence of leaders with some autonomy of role and status in the party and in their constituencies.

Editors' Note: Phase Three has focused on Chairman Bhutto's efforts to eliminate virtually all opposition to his rule, both within and outside the PPP. J. A. Rahim, Hanif Ramay, Mustafa Khar, K. H. Meer, and others either have been expelled from the PPP and imprisoned, or simply removed from positions of responsibility. The National Awami Party (NAP) was banned in 1975 and its leaders arrested and put on trial. A state of emergency was imposed on the country which remained in force during the general election campaign in February–March 1977. Bhutto has continued his mass mobilization program but the bureaucracy, and especially the expanding police bureaucracy, has become an important pillar of his regime.

· 5 ·

Adaptations to State-Level Polities by the
Southern Baluch

Stephen and Carroll McC. Pastner

One of the major goals and a defining feature of modern
nationhood is integration—the incorporation of regional
entities and cultural groups into a single functioning political
unit. With its diversity of regional cultures and languages,
Pakistan is one modern nation that has had more than its
fair share of difficulty in the attempt to achieve political and
societal cohesion. The integration of Baluchistan into the
national structure is one of the thorniest problems now faced
by Pakistan in its quest for political unity.

To illustrate specific aspects of this problem, we here focus
on the Baluchi-speaking people of Makran,[1] a notably insular
cultural sector in Pakistan's multi-ethnic mosaic, and we
depict historically the ways in which state-level polities have
interacted with the local-level social and political system. We
hope to demonstrate that because the southern Baluch and
their land were so difficult for central governments to administer, the resulting willingness of state authorities before

1. Anthropological field work was conducted by the authors in Makran, primarily
on the oasis of Panjgur, in 1968–69. Library research was carried out in Quetta and
in London at the India Office Library, the Royal Asiatic Society, and the School of
Oriental and African Studies, University of London. Financial support for the project
was provided by the National Institute of Mental Health and the Society of the
Sigma Xi. Contrasts from other relevant areas can be found in Robert Pehrson, *Social
Organization of the Marri Baluch* (Chicago: Aldine, 1966), for the eastern Baluch,
and Philip C. Salzman, "Adaptation and Political Organization in Iranian Baluchistan," *Ethnology*, X, No. 4 (1971), 433–44, for the Iranian Baluch.

the emergence of Pakistan to grant both de jure and de facto authority to indigenous elites exacerbated this insularity. The policy of indirect rule pursued by both the Brahui Khans of Kalat and by the British to maintain order on their rugged but strategic Baluch frontier fostered the problems presently encountered by their Pakistani heirs, who now find themselves faced with governing a population long inured to cultural conservatism.

Thus, a traditional, stratified social order, rooted both in tribalism and feudalistic patron-client ties between a hereditary power elite and subordinate retainers (an order manipulated and indeed strengthened by Kalat and the British), continues to exert a powerful hold on the southern Baluch at the expense of more "national" orientations.

We further suggest that the Pakistani civil-military bureaucracy, charged with administration at the local level in Makran, often has been less than effective in the pursuit of political and social integration. A policy of expedient, rather than benign, neglect by state authorities and the ineffectiveness of direct administration when it did exist created an atmosphere of sectionalism that (as of the time of our research in 1968–69) dominated southern Baluch interaction with the national polity. More recent events indicate this sectionalism is being reinforced not only by internal factors but by outside sources as well.

General Background[2]

Approximately 23,000 square miles in size, with a population of about 150,000, Makran is one of the largest, least populated regions in all of Pakistan. It is bounded on the north by the Siahan Range, which separates it from the deserts of Kharan; on the east by the mountains of Jhalawan

---

2. Summary histories of Makran are located in the *Baluchistan District Gazeteer* (Bombay, 1907), Vol. VII, and Henry Field, *An Anthropological Reconnaissance in West Pakistan* (Cambridge: Harvard University Press, 1959).

and Las Bela; on the west by Iran; and on the south by the Arabian Sea. The majority of the populace is Baluchi-speaking, although Brahui- and Jadgali-speaking enclaves are also present.

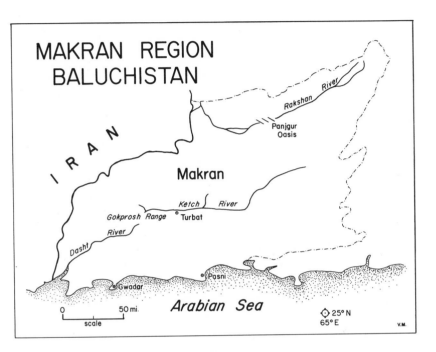

The coastal towns of Makran are trading and fishing ports, while the hinterland supports a scattered population relying on dry crop cultivation and sheep and goat pastoralism, either separately or in combination. Crucial to both the economic and political history of Makran is irrigation agriculture, with an emphasis on date arboriculture. In the stark and arid region of Makran, the oases have always been the focal points of population density and political centralization. Control over these oases, notably Panjgur in the Rakshan river valley of northern Makran and the settlements in the Ketch valley of central Makran, means control over the entire region.

Throughout its history, Makran, like the rest of Baluchistan, has witnessed continuing encounters with outside powers. Among the groups laying nominal claim to Makran at various periods were the Macedonians, Sassanid Persians, Arabs, Sindhi Brahmins, Ghorid Afghans, and Mongols. While these invaders sought control over Makran in order to secure routes between the Indus and points west, actual political power in the region remained in the hands of local groups. In the early part of the eighteenth century the Gitchkis, a tribe composed of a number of related lineages tracing Rajput ancestry, gained a brief hegemony over the oases of Makran; today they remain one of the foremost indigenous political groups. In the latter part of the eighteenth century the Ahmadzai Brahui Khans of the Kalat region of northeastern Baluchistan incorporated Makran into their confederacy. The Gitchkis agreed to share one-half of all collected revenues with Kalat, and from this time forward Makran's history has been one of continual involvement with state-level polities.

The British penetrated the region in the nineteenth century, and the first of several treaties between Kalat and the British was signed in 1854. The Khan of Kalat agreed to act in subordinate cooperation with the British, while the latter guaranteed the independence of the Khanate. In the 1870s, the autonomy of Kalat and its confederate chiefdoms was somewhat modified by Sir Robert Sandeman's so-called Forward Policy, whereby tribal administration was exercised through chiefs under British supervision. British policy in Makran up to 1947 oscillated between intervention and nonintervention in local affairs. Makran remained an administrative division of Kalat state until the Kalat dominions joined Pakistan in 1948. In 1952 the former Khanate became the semi-autonomous Baluchistan States Union, but in 1955 the BSU along with the Punjab, Sind, and the NWFP combined into the province of West Pakistan. At that time Makran became a separate District of the Division of Kalat and was administratively carved into first two, then three subdivisions, each in turn composed of a number of *tehsils*. After the creation of West Pakistan, Makran witnessed the era of Ayub Khan, which included a period of martial law as well as the institution of Basic Democracies. In March 1969 another period of martial law was imposed by Yahya Khan, and in July 1970 West Pakistan was dissolved and the original provinces re-established. Baluchistan was again identified as a distinct entity and given provincial status.

Social Stratification in Makran

The traditional social structure of Makran is a feudal one, based on the extraction of revenues and the operation of patron-client ties between three ascribed social strata: the *hakim*, the *baluch*, and the *hizmatkar*.

The *hakim* are a traditional ruling elite that includes the aforementioned Gitchkis as well as the Nausherwanis, the Bizanjos, the Buledis, and others. None of the *hakim* form groups in the corporate or cooperative sense. Indeed, as will be shown, the Gitchkis in particular have traditionally provided the main lines of social cleavage in Makran, contending among themselves for political and economic power and the support of other segments of society.

While the term "Baluch" is used to designate a distinct cultural status vis-à-vis other cultural groups in Pakistan, such as the Pathans, the Brahuis, etc., in Makran *baluch* also refers to a specific social status within a stratified social system. That is, the cultural status of Baluch is shared by all Baluchi speakers and by all social strata, but the social status of *baluch* refers to the broad middle layer of society — pastoral nomads in the hinterland and independent agriculturalists on the oases. While there are a number of named *baluch* tribes in Makran, each boasting a pedigree derived from a founding ancestor through the male line, in actuality such tribes play little corporate role in social life. Instead, it is place of residence, economic interests, and allegiance to individual *hakim* or their local representatives (headmen, usually

baluch) that traditionally have determined the lines of political activity in Makran. As such, kinship ties are crosscut with
or even superseded by political and economic activities.[3]

The *hizmatkar* constitute the lowest of the social strata in
Makran and comprise up to a third of its population. Tenants
and craftsmen (known as *nakib* in the north and *darzadag* in
the south of Makran) are the majority of this status category,
while others include *loris* (tinkers and metalworkers), *meds*
(fishermen on the coast), *palawan* (epic singers and musi-
cians), and *ghulam*, a category of slaves who were freed in
the late 1920s. The often negroid appearance of Makrani
menial classes derives from the African slave trade. Since it
is this group that makes up the bulk of migrants from the area,
urban Pakistanis who encounter these impoverished refugees often characterize all Makranis as *habshi*, or Blacks.

Political History

Historical and ethnographic data indicate specific continuities in the ways in which the Makrani Baluch have adapted
to the state systems of the Khanate of Kalat, the British Raj,
and the contemporary Pakistani nation.

Makran Under the Khanate of Kalat

Prior to the intrusion of the Brahui Khanate into the affairs
of Makran, the history of the area had been dominated by a
succession of local factions, with the Gitchkis emerging as
the foremost power in the early eighteenth century. After the
Khanate gained control of the area, attempts by the Gitchkis
to throw off its yoke commenced. In the original agreement
the Gitchkis retained the right to administer Makran, but by

---

3. For a more detailed discussion, see Stephen Pastner and Carroll McC. Pastner,
"Agriculture, Kinship and Politics in Southern Baluchistan," *Man*, the Journal of
the Royal Anthropological Institute, VII, No. 1 (1972), 128–36.

1816 they were forced to accept the presence of the Khan's own representative, the *naib*.[4]

The Khan's delegates in Makran oversaw the collection of taxes based on a tithe levied on landholders, as well as payments known as *zar-i-shah* (rulers' price). Nonetheless, the Gitchkis retained their position as rulers of the area and continued to receive their own share of traditional revenues. "The Gitchki chiefs had no hesitation in alienating the revenue to those who sided with them against the Naib, and the better class of Baluch . . . in this way obtained exemption from payment."[5]

As the Sardars of Makran, the Gitchkis divided their administration between Panjgur in northern Makran and the Ketch river valley to the south. Although sharing a common genealogical charter, the Gitchkis did not constitute a group in the corporate sense. The main lines of political cleavage in Makran emanated from within the Gitchki lineage, with different branches contending among one another for the right to rule and act as revenue agents for the Khan. However, as a social category, the Gitchkis maintained overall control.

One important (and still utilized) mechanism in the establishment of Gitchki control was the use of marriage alliances. Known as *shalwar* (trousers), such alliances linked the Isazai Gitchkis of Panjgur to the ruling house of the Khanate, while the Dinarzai Gitchkis of Ketch intermarried with the Shahizai Mengals of Jhalawan, a powerful military arm of the Khanate.[6] Other alliances were contracted with the Nausherwanis from the deserts to the north, whose military aid was influential in the power politics of Makran.

By the latter part of the nineteenth century it was clear the Khanate's political and economic hold on Makran was by no means uniformly maintained. Two British reports from the

4. *Baluchistan District Gazeteer*, VII, 49.
5. *Ibid.*, p. 249.
6. Denys Bray, *The Life History of a Brahui* (London: Royal Asiatic Society, 1913), p. 35.

period make this point. The following summary was made in 1868:

> It has been seen that the eastern half of Makran has fallen to the share of the Kalat state, and now forms part of what may be termed "Independent Baluchistan." The western part is more or less subject to Persian sway. The Kej division is at present day under the general supervision of . . . the Khan's Naib, and Panjgur under that of . . . a Gitchki chief.[7]

A further interpretation was offered in 1877:

> There is a gentleman called the Khan's Naib, but he is not the governor and does not pretend to govern the country or even collect its revenues. He is, in fact, only the receiver of such revenue as the actual governor may have agreed to pay the Khan . . . that actual individual exercising the functions of governor being either he who is the strongest or he who has agreed to pay the most.[8]

It should not be concluded, however, that the Gitchkis were always able to exert consistent political control. Indeed, in areas beyond the irrigated oases, their control was often marginal. The jockeying for power that took place among the *hakim* was paralleled among the baluch headmen (*komash, kaudai, motaber*) who served as revenue collectors for the Khan and the Gitchki Sardars. Headmen located on or near the oases came under the authority of the Gitchkis in return for tax exemptions, land investitutes, and financial rewards. In regions remote from the oases, local *baluch* chiefs often remained autonomous.

Forms of political recruitment were similar for the various aspirants to power in Makran. Whether it was a Gitchki at feud with his own kinsmen, the headman of an oasis village attempting to ingratiate himself to a Gitchki Sardar, or the local chief of a hinterland region, attempts would be made to build up a retinue of supporters known as *posht* (back, referring as well to kin related through the male line). So, for example, *baluch* headmen beholden to a Gitchki Sardar were

7. J. A. Saldanha, *Precis of Makran Affairs* (Calcutta, 1905), p. 41.
8. *Baluchistan District Gazeteer*, VII, 237.

obliged to provide *lashkars,* or levies of fighting men, under a system known as *lank* or *suren bandi* (the girding of the loins). Consequently, patron-client ties, particularly between Sardars and *baluch,* came to dominate political activity in Makran.

The presence of military retainers was a prerequisite for the achievement of political power, which, once obtained, was often arbitrary in its exercise. "The strong man's water can flow uphill" (*zuraki ap sha jhala borza ro:t*)—the politically powerful can contravene natural law—is the way one folk adage conceptualizes the nature of traditional Makrani politics.

Physical descriptions of nineteenth-century Makrani oasis settlements depict a scene of chieftains' mud forts, surrounded by the flimsy mat tents and brushwood huts of followers who, even if not fully pastoral-nomadic, could still pick up and move both their abodes and their loyalties elsewhere if the political fortunes of their overlord waned as another's waxed.[9]

Zikrism and the Kalat Period in Makran

During the early days of Kalat rule, religion and ideology as well as the more blatant forms of power politics related the Makrani Baluch to a wider political universe. In the seventeenth century the non-orthodox Muslim sect of Zikrism gained importance in the political events of Makran. The Zikris were followers of a sect founded in the fifteenth century by Said Mahmoud of Jaunpur, a *mahdi*—or Islamic messiah—who traveled extensively and drew many converts in the northwestern sector of the subcontinent. Tradition states he came to Ketch, near the present town of Turbat in central Makran, preaching for ten years and converting the entire populace before his death in the early sixteenth century. Despite this story, it is more likely that Zikrism was

9. See Henry Pottinger, *Travels in Beloochistan and Sinde* (London: Langman Reese, Orme and Brown, 1816), and Maj. Gen. C. M. Macgregor, *Wanderings in Baluchistan* (London: W. H. Allen, 1882).

brought to Makran by a number of disciples of the *mahdi* and not by the *mahdi* himself.[10] Individual and collective ritual serves to set off Zikrism from the mainstream of Sunni Muslim orthodoxy, which in turn views Zikrism as idolatrous.[11]

The historical connection between the rise of Zikrism and political events in Makran is clearly marked. The establishment of the sect is linked to the rise in power of an indigenous Makrani group, the Buledis. By the mid-eighteenth century the Buledi ruler of Ketch had quit the Zikri faith but was supplanted in political dominance by the spiritual leader of the Zikris, Mullah Murad, and his son, Malik Dinar Gitchki, who incited a revolt and wrested the main fort of Ketch from the Buledis and subsequently established their authority in two other major centers of Makran, Panjgur and Tump.[12]

Important changes in the religious affiliation of the Makrani population took place at the time of Brahui intervention. Under Nasir Khan of Kalat, who first threatened Gitchki hegemony, the son of Malik Dinar Gitchki was reconverted from Zikrism to Sunni Islam. The ruler's decision to change his religious allegiance influenced large sectors of the Makrani population, and by converting to Islamic orthodoxy the Gitchkis gained favor with Nasir Khan. As an orthodox Muslim, Nasir Khan viewed his campaign against the Zikris as nothing less than a *jihad*. By currying the Khan's favor, the Gitchkis retained control over their local autonomy, but the development of a distinctively Baluch religion was thwarted.

Makran and the British

When the British entered into treaties with the Khanate of Kalat, it was clear their primary concern in Makran, as with

10. Field, *op. cit.* p. 60.
11. More detail on the rituals of Zikrism and its contemporary status in Makran is found in Pastner and Pastner, "Aspects of Religion in Southern Baluchistan," *Anthropologica*, XIV, No. 2 (1972), 231–41.
12. E. C. Ross, *Memorandum of Notes on Makran* (Bombay: Transactions of the Bombay Geographical Society, 1868), Vol. XVII.

the rest of Baluchistan and adjacent Pathan territories, was the frontier. The location of the Kalat Khanate was important vis-à-vis Afghanistan, while Makran was said to "represent generally the line at which Persian aggression and intrigue have rested."[13]

The British often intervened in Makrani internal affairs. They formulated a number of policies, none with totally satisfactory results. First they attempted to settle disputes without using any specific means to enforce the results of settlement. Sandeman pursued such a policy in a major dispute between the Gitchkis and the Nausherwanis during an expedition to Panjgur in 1884. In 1891 this "let alone" policy was discarded and a British force was established in Makran. The "let alone" policy was revived briefly in 1894 after the British support force was withdrawn. However, four years later, any reliance on "Kalat responsibility" was abandoned when disputes between the Rinds (a turbulent tribe on the Persian border) and the Persians made British intervention imperative.[14] Makrani affairs were chaotic during this period. Colonel Sir T. H. Holdich made a reconnaissance in the area in the 1880s and recorded the following: "In no part of North-Western India from Persia to the Pamirs, have I heard expressed such a thirsty longing not only for the pax, but for the lex Britannica; and such confidence in the power of the British Sirkar to remove the yoke of misrule and anarchy from the necks of the people."[15] The British tactic of indirect rule reached its most progressive form with Sandeman's Forward Policy.[16] Sandeman used diplomacy chiefly to resolve feuds that undermined the Khanate. He also promoted the *jirga*, or council system, for settling disputes. This represented an

13. Saldanha, *op. cit.*, p. 27.
14. Sir W. Lee-Warner, *Memorandum on Makran*, Letter from India #214, 1898.
15. Col. Sir T. H. Holdich, *The Indian Borderland* (London: Methuen, 1901).
16. See esp. Lee-Warner, Thomas Henry Thornton, *Col. Sir Robert Sandeman: His Life and Work on Our Indian Frontier* (London: John Murry, 1895), and Olaf Caroe, *The Pathans: 550 B.C.–A.D. 1957* (London: Macmillan, 1965).

improvement over the often arbitrary rule of local political leaders and helped bring a degree of stability to the region. The coming of the British to Makran served to freeze leadership statuses and, theoretically, should have decreased the amount of sparring among the *hakim* and their allies. By their military support of the Khanate and their desire for stability on the frontier, the British encouraged the establishment of what amounted to virtually statutory chiefs. This same policy, however, provoked revolts by numerous havenot aristocrats who felt thwarted in their political aspirations. One such revolt was led in 1898 by Mir Mehrab Khan, brother of the British- and Kalat-supported Gitchki Sardar of Ketch. This insurrection was ended in the Gokprosh hills of Southwest Makran by a force of native troops under British officers, and led to the establishment of a more rigid administration by the Kalat-British condominium.

This administrative system was headed by a Nazim, the representative of the Khan, assisted by four Naibs stationed at strategic points within Makran. The first Nazim, a Brahui delegate of the Khan, was later honored with the high title of Nawab. After his death this rank reverted to the Gitchkis. Troops were maintained at three different forts. Civil and criminal cases were handled either by Shariat, by *rawaj* (local custom), or in a *jirga*. Civil cases involving land and inheritance were referred to Qazis. The Naibs and local notables handled criminal matters, the more important cases being submitted to the Nazim with the recommendations of *jirga*. Other serious cases were decided by the Nazim and a *jirga* of Sardars.

The British recognized that in areas as remote as Makran the use of force, either directly, or indirectly through local intermediaries, was an impractical method for keeping the peace. Instead, the British gave bribes for good behavior. Assorted grants in land and money, as well as titles such as "Sahib Bahadur" and O.B.E.s, were granted to those local headmen considered to have the greatest troublemaking potential. Cases in point are Sahib Bahadur Mehrab Khan,[17] the rebel of Gokprosh, and Sir Nauroz Khan, K.C.I.E., a chief of the Nausherwanis who in the latter part of the nineteenth century terrorized large areas of Makran with a band of desperadoes and a camel mounted with a cannon.[18]

In 1904 a continuous, albeit minimal, physical British presence in Makran was established. The Makran Levies, headed by a British commandant-cum-political officer, was permanently posted at Panjgur oasis. The cost of the force of three hundred was borne by the British, while the purpose of the corps was to keep the peace and patrol the Persian borderland.[19] Although traditional elites continued to enjoy great influence, this direct British presence remained until 1947.

Between 1904 and 1947 one of the major concerns of the British with regard to Makran was the border with Persia. In the early 1920s the Makran Levies were the only disciplined armed force along the Persian border or in the whole of Kalat State.[20] Nevertheless, the weakness of British authority on the border was demonstrated by the murder of a Gitchki Sardar at Tump. While "confidence was restored" by the dispatch of a Political Agent to Makran,

it appeared . . . that a division of authority in Makran . . . between the representative of the Kalat State on the one hand and the Assistant Political Agent on the other was a source of weakness to the administration, and before the close of the year proposals were submitted to the government of India by which the Kalat State would play a larger part in the direction of internal affairs.[21]

Moreover, there was no relaxation on the Persian-Makran border in the 1930s, given internal unrest in Persian Bulchistan.

17. *Administration Report of the Baluchistan Agency* (Calcutta, 1916–17), p. 131.
18. *Kharan District*, Vol. A, West Pakistan Gazetteers, comp. Malik Saleh Muhammad Khan (Karachi: West Pakistan Government Press, 1966), pp. 28–29.
19. *The Imperial Gazetteer 1908* (Oxford: Clarendon Press, 1908), XVII, 50.
20. *Administration Report of the Baluchistan Agency* (Calcutta, 1920–21), p. 10.
21. *Administration Report of the Baluchistan Agency* (Calcutta, 1921–22), p. 5.

Pakistani Makran until Martial Law 1969

In March 1948 Ahmad Yar Khan, Khan of Kalat, and his dominions acceded to the new state of Pakistan. Four years later the Baluchistan States\Union, composed of Kalat, Makran, Kharan, and Las Bela, was formed, and the Khan became the Khan-i-Azam. In 1955 the former provinces of the Punjab, Sind, Northwest Frontier, and Baluchistan became the administrative province of West Pakistan. Baluch antagonism against One Unit developed early. The Khan of Kalat was especially unhappy with the new arrangement and in 1958 he sought to separate Kalat from Pakistan. The Pakistan army quickly subdued the Khan's troops and sent him into temporary exile, but by 1962 he was restored to his former status and power.[22]

Meanwhile, One Unit brought direct administration to Baluchistan. Makran became a separate district within the Kalat Division of Baluchistan, with, eventually, three sub-districts (Kech, Panjgur, and Gwadur), further subdivided into seven *tehsils*. Ayub Khan's Basic Democracies system was established in Baluchistan in 1959. Units of self-government, known as Unions in non-urbanized areas such as Makran, were composed of elected representatives who sat on Union Councils and participated directly in the activation of public works programs. These representatives acted as liaisons between their constituents and the appointees of the central government who also sat on the Union Councils. Further up the pyramidal structure of Basic Democracies, however, the number of elected representatives diminished, thus increasing the power of the government bureaucrats. Ultimate decision-making powers therefore rested with the administrative officers, not the indigenous leadership. A commissioner oversaw Kalat Division, while Makran was headed by a deputy commissioner

22. Herbert Feldman, *Revolution in Pakistan* (London: Oxford University Press, 1967), p. 42.

(D.C.). Lower administrative echelons included three nazims, and below them, *tehsildars*, and still lower, *naib tehsildars*. The deputy commissioner chaired the District Council, and the commissioner headed the Divisional Council of the Basic Democracies. All higher levels of administration were dominated by non-Baluch, and above the level of nazim all positions were staffed by non-Baluch. As of 1961 there were no elected members in the District Council or in the seven Tehsil Councils of Makran.[23] This interrelationship between central government and local-level polities revealed two glaring shortcomings. One was the ethnic political gap between the Baluch and the power structure composed largely of Punjabis and Pathans. Second, there was "the immense cultural gulf that exists . . . between the Anglo-oriented bureaucratic elite on the one hand, and the tradition-directed masses and lower-ranking civil servants on the other."[24]

In spite of the bureaucracy's heavy hand, time-worn methods of administration were not completely abandoned in Baluchistan. Until 1969 the British practice of applying special legal codes to the Baluch was continued over the opposition of the legal community and the Western-oriented elites in Pakistan.[25] The Quetta-Kalat Ordinances of 1968 are modified versions of the customary laws contained in the British Frontier Crimes Regulations, which grew out of Sandeman's Forward Policy. Qazis continued the use of Shariat law and *jirgas* continued to function. The Makran *jirgas* handled criminal cases as well as those civil cases not clearly under the jurisdiction of a Qazi. Members of a *jirga* were often, but not always, Basic Democracies representatives. The stipulation that the president of the *jirga*

---

23. Office of the Census Commissioner, Ministry of Home and Kashmir Affairs, Home Affairs Division, *District Census Report, Makran: Population Census of Pakistan 1961* (Karachi: Educational Press, 1962), p. 9.

24. Ralph Braibanti, *Research on the Bureaucracy of Pakistan* (Durham, N.C.: Duke University Press, 1966), p. 134.

25. *Ibid.*, pp. 189–99.

always be a magistrate, however, altered the composition of the tribunal.

But the formation of the One Unit of West Pakistan clearly eroded the power of the traditional *hakim* elite. They no longer had explicit de jure political authority in their home regions. For example, the Nawab of Makran moved his residence to Karachi and received an allowance from the government large enough to persuade him to stay out of Makrani affairs.

In theory, the institution of universal suffrage under the Basic Democracies program opened the way for social mobility, especially for those social classes traditionally excluded from power. In fact, there was some upward mobility among members of the *hizmatkar* stratum of ex-slaves and menials. A handful of these people managed, through education and sheer determination, to move into the ranks of the lower-level civil service. However, the *hakim* and many higher-status *baluch* retained many traditional attitudes about the old social order, and they sought new means of manipulating their changing environment. The ballot box replaced the *lashkar* as a method for gaining and retaining political power. But the old idea of *posht* — of supporters and their patrons — was still present, now bolstered by the buying of votes and the dispensation of assorted favors by power-seeking traditional elites who continued to dominate local-level political life in Makran in 1969. In Panjgur, for example, the overwhelming number of elected ward and union officials were either *hakim* elites or members of *baluch*, chiefly families.

Non-Baluch Pakistani officials, recognizing the entrenched feudal tenor of contemporary Makrani political affairs, were also willing and able to turn it to their own purposes. Although generally expressing disdain for the Makranis, their land, and their customs, the urbanite Punjabis and Pathans posted to the area generally had solid working arrangements with indigenous elites. In return for the latter's promises of support, the government provided them with economic rewards, i.e., preferential loans, grants for irrigation projects, jeeps, etc.

A nominal if often shallow acceptance of the new spirit of social egalitarianism was shown by the indigenous elite. This was illustrated at a *diwan* attended by one of the authors at the home of an elderly Gitchki who was prominent in local politics. Also present were a number of *nakibs* of the *hizmatkar* class who had some influence in nearby hamlets. When questioned about the traditional social order, the Gitchki replied that although the *hizmatkar* were at one time slaves, they were now as good as any one else. In contrast, bazaar gossip had it that this same individual kept a number of aging daughters secluded in purdah and unmarried for want of sufficiently high-status suitors. Where are the ultimate loyalties of such elites? All too often the sentiments expressed by a leader of the Marri Baluch of Eastern Baluchistan apply equally well to the Makrani case: "I touch the political agent's boots and get a thousand to touch mine."[26]

Makran Since 1969 and the Future

After martial law was withdrawn in 1962, opposition to One Unit continued to mount in several quarters of Pakistan. Given the vastness of the Baluch territories and the low population density of districts such as Makran, problems of administration were, and are, understandably complex. Those people in remote areas believe that they are at a distinct disadvantage in government planning for economic development. In Makran many local people are embittered by the favoritism practiced by the civil service toward local elites. These same elites are known to work against their constituents in return for personal financial rewards. Moreover, the civil service has been largely dominated by in-

26. Pehrson, *op. cit.*, p. 26.

experienced young men desirous of moving up and out of the area as quickly as possible, or incompetent officers who are sent to the area as a form of punishment.[27] These practices, coupled with the ethnic and cultural gap existing between the power structure and the indigenous populace, provoked even broader discontent. The most immediate result of martial law in Makran in 1969 was the superimposition of military personnel on the civil administration. In the changed circumstances the bureaucracy became a target for renewed criticism. Accusations of *reshwat* (bribery) were common, and the martial-law administration terminated the activities of many officers who were believed to be especially flagrant in their abuse of office.

With the succession of Yahya Khan, Baluchistan administration was affected in two important areas. One was the abolition of the *jirga* system,[28] and the other was the dissolution of One Unit and the decision to delegate increased authority to regional, ethnic-interest spokesmen. Thus, in October 1969 the *sardari* system of the eastern Baluch tribes of the Marris and the Bugtis was restored, as was that of the Mengal Brahuis of Jhalawan. This was a reversal of the policy of the previous regime and aimed at placating these particularly politically dissident tribes.[29]

In December 1970 elections were held in Pakistan, marking the first time that Baluchistan had ever participated in the direct election of national and provincial legislators. The election results demonstrated that regional autonomy was important not only to East Pakistan, but to sectors of West Pakistan as well. The Pakistan People's Party under Zulfikar Ali Bhutto, relying on a theme of "change," won

27. Physical aspects of some of these local complaints were apparent on the oasis of Panjgur in 1968–69. A number of government-sponsored projects were either uncompleted and non-functioning (an X-ray facility, for example) or visually impressive but largely inefficient and wasteful (the meterological center, for instance). Meanwhile, the one hospital on the oasis, built by the British in the early part of the century, was antiquated, understaffed, and insufficiently supplied.

28. Herbert Feldman, *From Crisis to Crisis* (London: Oxford University Press, 1972), p. 201.

29. *Ibid.*, p. 195.

eighty-one seats in the National Assembly, but none were from either East Pakistan or Baluchistan. The National Awami Party (Wali faction) proved to be most vital in Baluchistan and Northwest Frontier. This faction of the NAP, stressing regional autonomy and socialism, won three out of four national seats and eight of twenty provincial seats from Baluchistan, although there "the unusually high number of candidates left the party with much less than wide support among the voters."[30] One major weakness in the Wali unit of the NAP in Baluchistan was its inability to win the support of Khan Abdus Samad Khan Achakzai ("The Baluch Gandhi"). He formed his own faction, which gained one provincial seat from Baluchistan.[31]

After the debacle of Bangladesh and the succession of Bhutto's government, the central administration attempted to continue a policy of greater regional self-determination. It was expected that Ghaus Baksh Bizanjo's appointment to the governorship of the newly recreated Baluchistan Province would co-opt the loyalties of this NAP leader, a long outspoken champion of Baluch nationalism. However, by the beginning of 1973 ethnic sectionalism had worsened. The Khan of Kalat forecast the danger of civil war in Baluchistan, and rumors circulated that a 20,000-man Baluch guerrilla force was being formed.[32] In February, Bizanjo was removed from office and his cabinet replaced by party sympathizers of Bhutto.[33] Troops under General Tikka Khan reportedly were dispatched to Baluchistan.[34] Akbar Khan, the Bugti Sardar who became the new governor of Baluchistan, noted that "open insurgency" appeared to be a real threat.[35] By August 1973 Bizanjo was in jail along with the Sardars of the

---

30. Craig Baxter, "Pakistan Votes – 1970," *Asian Survey*, XI, No. 3 (1971), 215.
31. *Ibid.*, p. 211.
32. Herbert Feldman, "Pakistan – 1973," *Asian Survey*, XIV, No. 2 (1974), 136–37.
33. G. W. Choudhury, "'New' Pakistan's Constitution, 1973," *The Middle East Journal*, XXVIII, No. 1 (1974), 17, maintains that this event "bode[s] ill for future stability and national integration. . . ."
34. *Newsweek*, March 5, 1973, p. 24.
35. Feldman, "Pakistan – 1973," *op. cit.*, p. 137.

Marris and the Mengals. Events in Baluchistan now moved very rapidly. Governor Bugti resigned in November but stayed on in office through December. In that same month A. S. K. Achakzai was assassinated in Quetta. By the beginning of 1974 the Khan of Kalat had taken over as governor of the province.

Constitutional issues as well as political events in 1973 pointed to the still pressing issue of national integration. In framing the new constitution (adopted in April 1973), "the most difficult and complicated issue" was that of the degree of regionalism to be provided for, since "the Baluch and the Pathans are anxious to protect their interests by demanding regional autonomy."[36] Despite government pledges to increase spending for social services and physical improvements in the area, sentiments for Baluch separatism reached such an extreme that by September 1974 Bhutto viewed the situation as urgent.

The problems facing the Pakistani government in dealing with Baluch secessionist agitation have been exacerbated by the active role played by foreign powers in fomenting such movements, either because of animosity toward Pakistan and/or because specific Baluch territories flank a zone of growing significance. A case in point, Makran lies in a strategic position with its western border on Iran and its coastal access to the oil-rich Persian Gulf.

The Kabul-based Pakhtunistan propaganda campaign is aimed at the Baluch as well as the Pathans, while Ulfat Nazim's World Baluchi Organization, influenced by Marxist ideology, works out of Baghdad with Ba'athist backing and seeks to organize the thousands of Baluch migrant laborers in Dubai and Oman. Iraq is particularly receptive to the operations of Baluch separatist propagandists because of its disputes with Iran, which harbors a large, potentially troublesome Baluch population. The Azad Baluchistan (Free

36. Choudhury, *op. cit.*, p. 16.

Baluchistan) movement is directed primarily to the Iranian Baluch,[37] while the Baluch Mutaheda Mahaz (United Baluch Front) is based in Sind and led by Mobashir Hassan Kesrani.

To a certain extent Baluch nationalism represents "something new under the sun" and is a departure from the traditional feudal social organization exemplified by Makran. One consequence of the emergence of Baluch nationalism is that on the local level there has been an erosion of traditional social cleavages within Baluch society. In Makran, for example, as of the period of our field work, people increasingly saw themselves less as *hakim, baluch,* or *hizmatkar,* and more as simply Baluch in opposition to a Punjabi-dominated central government. Another effect has been the emphasis on a new, if nominal, spirit of egalitarianism in leadership recruitment in the Marxist-oriented nationalist movements in contrast with the traditional social order of ascribed elites acting in explicit self-seeking collusion with central governments.

Such egalitarianism, however, should not be misconstrued. After the 1970 elections, it was suggested that "Traditional leadership in the former Baluchistan States Union has been rejected but it is too early to discern any pattern in the voting in the province."[38] Although we have no more detailed information than Baxter, on the basis of our experience we interpret this to mean that while specific individuals from traditional privileged sectors have been repudiated in the election, their replacements could well continue to come from these same social strata. In the Makran of 1969, for example, while there was dissatisfaction with the local old guard by the few educated and politically sophisticated "Young Turks," the critics generally came from these same

37. However, Salzman, "Continuity and Change in Baluchi Tribal Leadership," *International Journal of Middle East Studies*, No. 4 (1973), p. 439, notes that in the Sarhad region of Iranian Baluchistan (where the bulk of the population is pastoral nomadic), tribes act separately vis-à-vis the government, and there is "little sign, as yet, of the development of a Baluchi 'ethnic block' infrastructure there."

38. Baxter, *op. cit.*, p. 215.

old guard families. Thus, while the ideologies on which
leadership rests are changing and new faces are emerging
among Baluch leaders, the basic structure of the political
order remains conservative. Leadership still rests largely
on the predominance of traditional ascribed elites.

The above notwithstanding, there does appear to be
some erosion of the traditional pattern of state-supported
tribal chiefs' enjoying great prestige among their subordinate
followers. It would seem that central government backing of
the assorted Sardars who have recently succeeded one
another as governor of Baluchistan has been a sort of kiss of
death, undermining the chiefs' role as popular figureheads.
While we do not go so far as to suggest that the central
government has been totally Machiavellian in its manipulation of the situation, the outcome of the Bizanjo-Bugti-Khan
of Kalat succession manifests an almost axiomatic regu-
larity that has had the effect of seriously weakening the
whole Sardari system. The axiom goes as follows: A tribal
chief (e.g., Akbar Bugti), initially a spokesman for tribal
interests, is backed by the government as a provincial leader;
once in power he finds that his new role forces him to take
repressive measures against opposition tribal leaders (as
Bugti did with K. B. Marri and A. Mengal); this erodes his
support among the nascently nationalistic tribal populace —
his erstwhile supporters — and he is forced to resign, thus
having lost face both with the tribes and the state. As all
the recent governors of Baluchistan Province seem to have
gone through this cycle, will the future ones follow suit?

Conclusion

The vastness and isolation of Baluchistan, its small, dispersed population, and its extremely arid terrain have always
made it unamenable to political control. Nonetheless, its
strategic position on the crossroads between South Asia,
the Near East, and Central Asia has made such control vital

to ambitious political powers. Historically, Baluchistan has been a pawn, juggled between great and some not-so-great state systems. Makran has fully participated in the general history of Baluchistan, since there, as elsewhere, politics has been dominated by attempts on the part of external groups to stabilize frontiers and maintain viable corridors to other areas.

With the inclusion of Baluchistan into the nation of Pakistan, many of the same concerns and problems met by previous states have been encountered. The emphasis in this presentation has been on such continuities in Baluch adaptations to the states in which they have been enclaved. However, there is an important difference in this most recent attempt to integrate the southern Baluch into a state system. Unlike colonial administrations that derive their ultimate power from distant metropolitan sources, bolstered by the threat of military might, the authority of modern nationhood is ideally based on the support of the people. No matter how remote the region, it must in some way be included in the mainstream of a national political structure if national unity is to be achieved. Thus, Pakistan encounters a set of difficulties not entirely analogous to previous attempts at administration in Makran and the rest of Baluchistan. In the pursuit of this task, Pakistan must contend with local political structures molded in no small degree by previous state policies that were concerned more with the protection of Imperial Frontiers than with the incorporation of a population into the rights, privileges, and obligations of nationhood.

Editors' Note: The Sardari System in Baluchistan was abolished by an ordinance of the Bhutto government on April 8, 1976.

6

Economic Decision-making in Pakistan

Shahid Javed Burki

Economic rationality was a concept that not so very long ago could be defined with a fair degree of accuracy. In fact, economists had fashioned a large number of analytical tools to test rationality in economic policies at the formulation and implementation stages. In recent years the concept has become somewhat blurred. For instance, economic efficiency as understood in conventional terms resulted in regional or interpersonal distribution of resources that did not meet what have sometimes been called the non-economic demands of the society. Since the wide gap between the demand for resources and economic efficiency was first noticed by economists themselves,[1] it is not surprising that they have rushed to close it. They seek to fill the gap by broadening the definition of rationality to include non-economic considerations. Accordingly, society's welfare function as well as the constraints imposed on it for the purpose of attaining maximization now have important social and political elements. In view of this, can we be sure that economic de-

---

Editors' Note: This chapter represents the personal views and judgments of the author. It does not, therefore, reflect those of the International Bank for Reconstruction and Development where the author is employed. The IBRD is not responsible in any way for its accuracy or contents.

1. Mahbub ul Haq, chief economist in Pakistan's Planning Commission during the Ayub period, was the first to point out the adverse distributional impact of the model of growth pursued by the government during the sixties. According to him, some two dozen families had control over nearly two-thirds of the country's industrial wealth.

cision-making will be more rational now than it was some five or ten years ago? The answer to this question can only be provided if we know something more about another gap — that between economic and political rationality. Broad contours of economic policies are determined by politicians consumed by political considerations. These considerations may or may not stand the test of economic rationality. It is therefore useful to develop hypotheses that would explain the politics of economic decision-making. This subject has attracted some attention in the countries that have well-developed political institutions.[2] In most countries of Asia, Africa, and Latin America, political institutions are as underdeveloped as economic systems. To speculate about the interaction between them is not only difficult but can also be a hazardous undertaking.

The principal purpose of this chapter is to select cases from Pakistan's recent history to illustrate the way in which politics influences economic decision-making. The main conclusion reached here is not a surprising one: We find that in Pakistan, economic decision-making has been and continues to be a function of the political environment. In order to arrive at this conclusion, we will trace the way in which political forces have exercised influence over decision-making.

Since this chapter mainly focuses on the politics of economic decision-making, it is appropriate to define some of the terms and explain some of the concepts that will be used in this analysis. In Section I we present an overview of the main theme. In Sections II–VI, we apply the concepts developed in Section I to analyses of economic decision-making in Pakistan. The divisions of the chapter coincide with the five periods into which Pakistan's economic history

2. In this connection, see the pioneering work of Albert O. Hirschman, in particular his recent book, *Exit, Voice and Loyalty* (Cambridge: Harvard University Press, 1971).

can be conveniently divided. They are the Jinnah Period (1947–51), the Social Group Coalition Period (1951–58), the Ayub Khan Period (1958–69), the Military Period (1969–71), and the Bhutto Period (1971–   ). In the final section we present, for purposes of illustration, a more detailed analysis of economic decision-making under Bhutto.

I. *Politics of Economic Decision-making*

All political elites are concerned with the maintenance of their power, whether they adopt an active or passive approach. On the one hand, the elite attempts to enlarge its base of support; on the other hand, it attempts to meet the challenge of the opposition whenever or wherever it occurs. Economic policies, therefore, can be divided into two broad categories: the policies that seek to expand the political constituency of the elites, and the policies that are aimed at preventing any erosion of existing support. The first set are active policies, the second passive. The overall impact of the two sets can be very different. It is because of this difference in impact that passive elites seem to have longer political lives than active ones. Evidence will be provided from Pakistan's history to support this important conclusion. It is the author's contention that the present Pakistani elite, like those in the constitutional regimes which it followed, belongs to the passive category. It is therefore with the formulation of passive policies that this chapter is primarily concerned. This notwithstanding, it will be in order, if only to complete the picture, to discuss briefly the genesis of activist policies.

In formulating economic policies, activist elites are *not* responding to the new needs of their constituencies. By initiating new policies they hope to generate demand and hence build a constituency. Here is a political analogue of Say's Law. If these policies succeed in reaching their target groups, they will produce a state of political disequilibrium. The target groups or the new constituents of the political elites move ahead of other groups, causing frustration and resentment among the latter.[3] Most new nations do not have the institutions that can sustain the shock produced by the emergence of this kind of disequilibrium. In this respect, they are different from the countries of Western Europe that had centuries to solve the various problems posed by development, modernization, and nation-building.[4] Activist economic policies therefore can lead to extreme political instability[5] if they are not accompanied by the development of political institutions.

The passive approach to economic policy-making usually has the objective of restoring equilibrium rather than the creation of disequilibrium. The decision-making elites act because there is pressure on them to do so. Let us consider two somewhat different circumstances in which action may be taken. The first is a crisis produced by events over which the political elite has no control. The distress caused by such natural disasters as flood and drought is an example of this kind of situation. The elite is called upon to act, in part, because indifference to the crisis situation can prove to be politically costly. For instance, failure to act promptly after a devastating cyclone struck East Pakistan in the fall of 1970 is said to have contributed significantly to the strength of the separatist forces in what is now Bangladesh.[6] The other situation in which political elites are called upon to take action is produced by what may be called social group interaction. This latter phenomenon will be examined in some detail below.

3. This phenomenon has been described by Hirschman as the tunnel effect. See his "The Changing Tolerance for Income Inequality in the Cause of Economic Development," *World Development*, I, No. 12 (Dec. 1973), 29–36.

4. For a fuller elaboration of this point, see Samuel P. Huntington, *Political Order in Changing Societies* (New Haven: Yale University Press, 1968), chap. 2.

5. The impact of economic and political frustration has been traced in some detail by Tedd Gurr, *Why Men Rebel?* (Princeton: Princeton University Press, 1971). For an application of this concept to the case of Pakistan, see my article, "Ayub's Fall: A Socio-Economic Explanation," *Asian Survey*, XII, No. 3 (March 1972), 201–12.

6. Wayne A. Wilcox, *The Emergence of Bangladesh* (Washington, D.C.: American Enterprise Institute for Public Policy Research, 1973), *passim*.

To understand the politics of economic decision-making, it is helpful to adopt a view of society based on interest-group conflict.[7] Many of the groups we are concerned with in Pakistan are conventional economic interest groups, centered on the ownership of scarce resources. In the pre-Bhutto period, the controllers of scarce resources were powerfully represented in the political system. Other groups were important for their control of administrative institutions or for their monopoly of modern sector professional skills. Finally, we have the groups that wield or acquire power because of their size. Groups may therefore wield political power because of their economic strength or their domination over institutions or because of the size of their following. The nature of their power (quality) and the amount of support they can muster (quantity) would determine the type of role these groups play in the decision-making process. Those who derive power from their ownership of scarce resources (economic or administrative) are likely to play the role of decision-making elites, while those whose power is based on the size of their following are more likely to function as decision-influencers. If one can generalize, it could be said that those who have power in the qualitative sense get to be decision-makers, while those who have power in the quantitative sense get to be influencers of decisions.

In a less developed society such as Pakistan, decision-making is likely to be conducted at an early stage by one or more social groups (landowners, tribal chiefs, etc.). These groups not only provide national and regional leaders but are also represented in the civil and military bureaucracies. As a country begins to modernize, the dominant social group or groups will lose some of their decision-making power when new groups emerge. Thus, the social and economic back-

7. As I have argued elsewhere, motivation for the launching of a number of economic policies in a country such as Pakistan can be traced to conflict between social groups.

ground of the members of the civil and military bureaucracies in what is now Pakistan has changed considerably over the years. In the nineteenth century and the early part of the twentieth, the elitist Indian civil service was dominated by the landed aristocracy. The representation of this group was considerably diluted in later years.[8]

The decision-influencers are officially responsible for neither the planning nor execution of economic policies and programs. They are important, however, because they provide political and economic links between decision-makers and what may be described as the target population. In modernizing societies, groups move from the decision-influencing to the decision-making arena. In Pakistan merchant-industrialists, urban professionals, and some members of the middle classes joined the decision-makers after having functioned as influencers of decisions.

Before concluding this discussion of social groups, mention should be made of one other category, that of peripheral or target groups. These groups are the intended beneficiaries of political and economic reforms. They might typically include small farmers, tenants, landless labor, urban wage laborers, or workers in the service sector as well as those who influence and make decisions.

There are of course overlaps between all of these rather flexible groupings. Important landowners or employers of wage labor can function as decision-makers or decision-influencers. A large farmer who is elected or appointed to office occupies more than one category simultaneously, as does the bureaucrat or politician who is also an absentee landlord. The degree of differentiation between groups as to the role played by them in the decision-making process may have much to do with both the form of the policies and

8. For a discussion of the social and economic background of the civil servants in Pakistan, see Muneer Ahmad, *The Civil Servant in Pakistan* (Lahore: Oxford University Press, 1969), and my article, "Twenty Years of the Civil Service of Pakistan: A Reevaluation," *Asian Survey,* IX (April 1969), 239–54.

the probability of their alteration over time. A purpose in arranging social groups in this way is to suggest categories and levels of influence that are frequently important in both the formation and subsequent dynamics of economic policies.

What motivates economic decisions? How are they influenced and formulated? The foregoing analysis suggests at least a partial answer to the first question. Broad contours of economic decisions are determined for political reasons; in particular, for the reason that the important social groups in the society want to maintain their political power. Therefore, the groups who are to benefit from the decisions that are being taken are not restricted to those who formulate or influence the decisions but may include those who do not wield political power. When these peripheral groups become beneficiaries of economic policies it is usually because some important section of the politicized society sees non-action as ultimately constituting a political threat.

The second question concerns the way decision-influencers play their role in the decision-making process. There are two types of channels through which influence is exerted on the decision-makers. Established political, economic, and administrative institutions constitute formal channels. Political parties and legislatures, labor unions and chambers of industries and commerce, and civil and military bureaucracies are some institutions that link decision-influencers with those responsible for formulating economic policies. Informal channels for the flow of influence include the media, political meetings and demonstrations, and personal contacts. In Pakistan, very largely because of the absence of well-developed political and economic institutions, influence on the policy-makers was exercised in part by the civil and military bureaucracies and in part by those who had command over the informal channels.

The above are some of the concepts that will be used in describing the politics of economic decision-making in Pakistan. While emphasis is on the more recent period, it is necessary to briefly analyze the genesis of economic policies during the fifties and sixties.

II. *The Jinnah Period (1947–51)*

Before discussing the economic performance of the regimes during this four-year period, it would be appropriate to examine the social and political pressures that resulted in the creation of Pakistan. A fuller discussion of this important subject has been covered by Wayne Wilcox in chapter two.

My own treatment of the social genesis of the Pakistan movement is a highly unconventional one. It is based on an examination of the social and economic characteristics of the Muslim community that supported the Pakistan movement. This examination relies almost exclusively on demographic data that provide broad indications of the social characteristics of the Muslim community in pre-independence India.[9] A further justification of the view presented here will need a much more detailed investigation.

This notwithstanding, we can divide the Muslims in British India into three socio-economic groups. Economically, the most prosperous of these were the Muslims in the Muslim-majority provinces of the Punjab, Sind, Baluchistan, and the Northwest Frontier. Largely rural in character, this community wielded considerable political and economic power. There were two main reasons for their political strength. They remained loyal to the British during the 1857 Mutiny. In return, the British provided them with protection. The best example of the type of protection given to them was the Punjab Alienation of Land Act,[10] which in 1901 made it

9. Pre-independence India and British India are used interchangeably to refer to India before 1947. For a discussion of the demographic data on which this analysis is based, see Kingsley Davis, *The Population of India and Pakistan* (Princeton: Princeton University Press, 1968).

10. For a good discussion of the events that led to the formulation of the bill, see Norman G. Barrier, *The Punjab Alienation of Land Bill of 1900* (Durham, N.C.: Center for International Studies, Duke University, 1966).

illegal for the non-Muslim moneylender to foreclose mort-
gages in case of bad debts. Second, the very big landlords of
Central Punjab, with vast estates extending over hundreds of
villages, provided leadership and consequently lent political
strength to the entire community. These factors produced a
sense of confidence among the Muslims of this area and made
it difficult for them to fully comprehend the demand for
Pakistan. Accordingly, the Muslims of northwest British
India at first were reluctant to support the demand for a separate homeland for their coreligionists.

The second socio-economic group lived in northeast
India, in the provinces of Bengal and Assam. Though rural
in character, this community did not have the political and
economic strength of the Muslims in the northwest. The
Muslims of Bengal had stood against the British advance into
India in the eighteenth century, and for this they were
penalized, e.g., the Land Settlement System introduced by
the British reduced their economic and political power.
After two centuries of British rule, the Muslims of northeast
India were reduced to the status of sharecroppers and
agricultural laborers. It was from this rural proletariat that
the revival of Islam drew considerable fervor in the nineteenth century, and they also contributed to the 1857 Indian
Mutiny. The Mutiny was suppressed ruthlessly, and by the
beginning of the present century the Muslims of Bengal and
Assam found themselves largely landless. Most of the agricultural land they tilled was owned by Hindu landlords. The
sense of grievance against Hindu domination was strong and
was successfully diverted into political channels, first by
Fazlul Huq and then by the loyal followers of Mohammad Ali
Jinnah.

The third large group of Indian Muslims lived in the
Hindu-majority areas of Bihar, United and Central Provinces,
Rajputana, Gujarat, and Bombay. This community was more
urbanized and its members had a higher rate of literacy than
did the Muslims of northwest and northeast India. Led by

urban professionals (lawyers, teachers, doctors, engineers, and merchants), who found themselves competing in economic and political spheres with the non-Muslims, these Indian Muslims were early converts to the cause of Pakistan. It was in this community that the idea of a separate Muslim identity first took hold and was nurtured by leaders (Sayyid Ahmad Khan, Mohammad Iqbal, and Mohammad Ali Jinnah), all of whom had large followings in the urban areas.

The demand for Pakistan was a demand for a separate state for the Muslims of British India, and it was to be carved out of the Muslim-majority areas in northwest and northeast India. This meant the areas that provided most of the leaders for the Pakistan movement were not included in the territory being demanded for the new state. When the idea of Pakistan was accepted and an independent Islamic state was created in the subcontinent, some six to eight million Muslims moved in from across the Indian border. The early decision-makers in Pakistan came from among the refugees, particularly from the group that had migrated from the provinces of UP and Bombay.

The decision-making elite during this period of Pakistan's history did not have a large, natural political constituency. That constituency belonged to the landed aristocrats of the Punjab and Sind and the tribal leaders of the Frontier Province and Baluchistan. But these leaders could not immediately become decision-makers. The more important among them had opposed the idea of Pakistan. They could not now be entrusted with decision-making power in the new state. The decision-makers' constituency in this period was therefore confined to the urban areas where they faced two problems: settlement of millions of refugees and provision of basic consumer goods.

In handling the problem of refugee rehabilitation, the government showed sensitivity to the demands of its own constituency. Efforts were made to accommodate as rapidly as possible the refugees who had arrived from the urban areas of what was now independent India. The task of resettling rural refugees, however, received little attention. This policy had two important consequences. First, it alienated the more numerous rural refugees; second, it brought a large number of refugees to towns and cities.

The second important area of decision-making during this period was in the industrial sector. The territories that composed Pakistan were industrially among the poorest in British India. Both West and East Pakistan depended on the industries located in India for basic consumer goods. When these goods stopped flowing to Pakistan as a result of the 1949 trade war with India, the government announced an ambitious program of industrialization. In formulating the industrial plan, the decision-makers responded to the demands of a group that had gained considerable political power during the early forties. Mohammad Ali Jinnah's Pakistan movement had attracted most of the large Muslim merchant houses that operated in Bombay, Bengal, and South India.[11] It was to this class that the ruling elite turned when India applied economic pressure on Pakistan. Allocation of resources on a liberal scale and grants of protection from outside competition made it possible for the large merchant houses to quickly establish a number of textile and jute mills. Within a decade of Pakistan's first trade war with India, the country had become self-sufficient in a number of consumer items.[12] The successful outcome of the industrial plan not only provided additional wealth to the merchant-industrialists, it also bestowed upon them a great deal of prestige in domestic politics.

The industrial development plan serves as a good illustration of the way decision-makers synthesized the demands

11. Hanna Papanek, "Pakistan's Big Businessmen: Separatism, Entrepreneurship and Partial Modernization," *Economic Development and Cultural Change*, XXI, No. 1 (Oct. 1972), 1–32.

12. Steven Lewis, *Economic Policy and Industrial Growth in Pakistan* (London: George Allen and Unwin, 1969).

of decision-influencers (merchant houses) and peripheral groups (urban consumers). The refugee-rehabilitation policy, on the other hand, provides an example of decision-making in which synthesis was not achieved between the demands of decision-influencing (urban refugees) and some of the peripheral groups (rural refugees).

III. The Social Group Coalition Period (1951–58)

Mohammad Ali Jinnah, the founder of Pakistan and its first governor general, died in September 1948. Liaquat Ali Khan, his successor as national leader, was assassinated in October 1951. Liaquat's assassination brought to an end the curious period in Pakistan's political history in which power was wielded by a group that was essentially foreign to its polity. A major realignment of social groups took place in this period. The landed aristocracy was rehabilitated as an important element in the decision-making process. The rural refugees, mostly from the eastern part of the British province of the Punjab, emerged as an important influence on economic decision-making. Forging of a military alliance with the United States resulted in the emergence of the army as a powerful factor in domestic politics. The neglect of East Pakistan brought urban professionals of Dacca into the political arena. However, no single group and no single individual was able to dominate the political system. There were no political institutions that could synthesize group interests. It was a period of socio-political flux in which the task of economic decision-making was ultimately assumed by the bureaucracy, and within the civil bureaucracy a small group (the Civil Service of Pakistan) acquired a great deal of power.[13]

It was in this period that the country first became a food-deficit area. In the 1940s when the demand for the creation of Pakistan gathered momentum, the leadership of the Indian

13. Burki, "Twenty Years of the Civil Service of Pakistan," *op. cit.*

National Congress had described the call for Pakistan as an economically absurd idea.[14] The Congress argument was based not so much on the fact that the Muslim League demanded a country divided into two parts, separated by a thousand miles and related only through religion, but on the fact that the areas that were to be taken out of British India to form the new state were desperately poor. The provinces of the Punjab, Sind, Frontier, Baluchistan in the northwest, and Bengal in the northeast had no known mineral resources. They had no industrial base, and, largely because of Muslim suspicions of Western education, had also the least literate population of British India. The Muslim rejoinder to this argument was not formulated in pure economic terms. They pointed to the backwardness of the Muslim-majority provinces as sufficient reason for separating from "Hindu India."[15] Nevertheless, when confronted with their solution to the economic problems that an independent Pakistan would face, the Muslim leadership invariably pointed to the "enormous agricultural potential of the Punjab and Bengal."[16] If the Muslims had an economic plan, it must have been based on the ability of the Punjab to adequately feed the entire population and the ability of Bengal to earn, through jute exports, the foreign capital needed for economic growth.[17]

While there was considerable basis for the pessimism

14. The economic arguments against the creation of an independent Muslim state are best summarized in C. N. Vakil, *Economic Consequences of Divided India* (Bombay: Vora and Co., 1965). Also, see V. P. Mennon, *The Transfer of Power in India* (Princeton: Princeton University Press, 1957), *passim*, and Chaudhri Mohammad Ali, *The Emergence of Pakistan* (New York: Columbia University Press, 1967), pp. 332–55.

15. The same argument was to be used later by the Bengali national leadership against Pakistan. See the "Report of the Panel of Economists" in Government of Pakistan, *Reports of the Advisory Panels for the Fourth Five Year Plan 1970–1975* (Islamabad: Planning Commission, 1970), Vol. I.

16. The only systematic attempt to evaluate the economic potential of the future state of Pakistan was made by Professor Ashfaq Ali Khan who, writing under the pseudonym of Al Hamza, assembled some information and data to show the "enormous agricultural potential of the Punjab and Bengal." See his contributions to *Dawn* in 1946.

17. Ali, *op. cit.*

shown by the Congress leadership toward the economic future of Pakistan, there was some justification for the guarded optimism of the Muslims. After all, the western districts of the Punjab had been surplus in food ever since the British, with the help of an extensive system of perennial canals, opened up and "colonized" the rich alluvial *doabs* (land between two rivers) of Chaj and Rachna.[18] Also the eastern districts of Bengal produced the bulk of India's jute. Properly husbanded, the agricultural sector could sustain the development effort of the new state of Pakistan.

However, agriculture made little contribution to the growth of Pakistan's economy in the first post-independence decade. The agricultural output increased at a disappointing rate of 1.4 percent per annum, or nearly one-half of a percentage point less than the average for the years 1900 to 1947. For the first time in the history of the Punjab and Sind, per capita availability of food grains actually declined. It decreased from 0.17 ton in 1949–50 to 0.15 ton in 1959–60.[19] Consequently, in the early fifties, Pakistan became a net importer of foodgrains.

The neglect of the agricultural sector during the 1947–51 period was due largely to the absence of the rural classes from the decision-making arena, a situation that was rectified after 1951. However, agricultural output did not increase at any significant rate even when the landed aristocracy of the Punjab and Sind acquired power and influence. In the fifties the large landlords regained the political power they had lost during the previous decade, but the agricultural sector continued to perform poorly. The reason for this is to be found in the set of policies adopted in the period. These policies favored the large landlords and helped the

18. For a description of the introduction of irrigation in the provinces of the Punjab and Sind, see Aloys A. Michel, *The Indus River: A Study of the Effects of Partition* (New Haven: Yale University Press, 1967).

19. Government of Pakistan, *The Fourth Five Year Plan, 1970–1975, op. cit.,* Tables 3 and 6, pp. 3–5. Also, see Shahid Javed Burki, *Pakistan: A Demographic Report* (Washington, D.C.: Population Reference Bureau, 1973).

merchant-industrialists. They were accepted by the powerful civil service because its members felt comfortable with them.

The major government activity in the agricultural sector during this period aimed at bringing about rapid expansion in the area under cultivation. Large-scale investments were made in the public sector for expanding the Indus basin irrigation system. The principal beneficiaries of this investment were the very large landlords of the central Punjab and Sind, who saw hundreds of thousands of acres of their wasteland come to life with irrigation water. Moreover, increases in area under cultivation made it possible for the large landlords to sustain a deterioration in agriculture's terms of trade with other sectors. This could not be done by the middle and small farmers, who, for lack of investment funds, suffered a drop in total productivity. While the cultivated acreage in this period increased at the rate of 2.3 percent per annum,[20] the value of agricultural output grew at only 1.4 percent.

The bureaucracy went along with this approach because a number of civil servants had considerable experience in planning, implementing, and managing "colonization schemes." After the First World War, the British administration expanded the irrigation network in the Punjab and Sind. The Public Works Department designed the irrigation works and the Land Revenue Administration settled the newly irrigated land. These two branches of the civil administration used the experience to extend irrigation in the Indus plain during the fifties.

IV. *The Ayub Khan Period* (1958–69)

The process of indigenization of politics was still going on in Pakistan when Ayub Khan proclaimed martial law. As discussed above, the process of political indigenization involved the reentry of large landlords into the decision-

20. Government of Pakistan, *The Fourth Five Year Plan, op. cit.,* Table 2, p. 2.

making arena. By 1957 the landed aristocracy had organized the Republican Party and had taken over most of the important political positions in the country. The Republican Party sent Jinnah's Muslim League into opposition, and Firoz Khan Noon, a wealthy landlord from the district of Sargodah, became prime minister while Nawab Qizilbash, a Lahore-based member of the Punjab's landed aristocracy, came to dominate the political scene in West Pakistan.

Ayub Khan had little in common with the leadership that he displaced. He was a Pathan from the relatively backward district of Hazara. His family, although rural-based, did not own much land. Most members of his family were either in the army or in the professions. In other words, Ayub Khan's social and economic background prepared him to lead a new class into the decision-making arena. The rise of Ayub Khan therefore exemplified the emergence of the rural middle classes as a powerful social group in Pakistan's politics.

Using the cover of martial law (1958–62), Ayub Khan introduced economic reforms that were aimed at reducing the power of the landed aristocracy and merchant-industrialists. The not so very radical land reform of 1959 produced an important political and psychological impact: This was the first time that ceilings were introduced on the landlord's right to own rural property. But ceilings were liberal and loopholes many. Landlords could still own and cultivate about two thousand acres of irrigated land or four thousand acres of non-irrigated land if they transferred some of their property to their legal heirs and converted some other into orchards, nurseries, and game reserves. They could continue to evict tenants if the tenants failed to pay rent or cultivate land with a certain degree of efficiency. Nonetheless, the land reforms resulted ultimately in the transfer of a significant proportion of land from large owners to middle-sized farmers. Only 2.3 million acres were directly affected by the reforms, and of these 930,000 acres consisted of wastes, hills, and riverbeds.[21] The large landlords yielded another five to six million acres to small and middle farmers. According to one study, nearly one-fifth of the total land owned by the middle farmers in 1969 had been purchased in the previous ten years.[22]

In the urban sector of the economy the new regime sought to dilute the power of the Karachi-based merchant-industrial elites. During the first two months of martial law, the new regime operated strict price controls, according to which producers, wholesale merchants, and retailers were not allowed to make a profit of more than 10 percent on "reasonably determined costs." However, the cost for producing and selling goods was determined arbitrarily by local military commanders. The result was total anarchy in the marketplace.

This experience with hastily fashioned direct controls chastened the administration. Its next foray into industrial and commercial policy was a considerably more sophisticated one. It took the form of the Bonus Voucher Scheme (BVS), which allowed exporters to receive vouchers priced at a certain proportion of the value of goods and commodities they sold abroad. These vouchers could be sold at a premium in the market. They were bought by importers who could use them to obtain foreign exchange for purchasing from abroad the goods and commodities that were placed on the "bonus list" (a list which included both consumer durables and industrial raw materials). In appearance, BVS was an export promotion scheme; in actual practice it became a highly efficient tool for distributing economic benefits from one class of people to another.

The Bonus Voucher Scheme had an immediate impact

21. For a critique of Ayub Khan's land reforms, see Nimal Sanderatne, "Landowners and Land Reform in Pakistan," *South Asian Review*, VII, No. 2 (Jan. 1974), 123–36.

22. This role of the middle farmer has been described by me in considerable detail in *Agricultural Growth and Local Government in Punjab, Pakistan* (Ithaca: Cornell University Press, 1974).

on the Karachi-based merchant-industrialists who as a result of it lost their monopoly over scarce industrial imports. During the fifties industrial importers were licensed to restrict the sale of their imports to "legitimate users." This system discriminated against newcomers in the industrial sector. Many so-called legitimate users ran their industrial establishments considerably below capacity and sold surplus industrial raw materials in the highly profitable black market. The BVS, by allowing a number of raw materials to be imported against bonus vouchers, not only reduced profits in the black market but also made industrial imports available to new firms as well as to small unregistered ones. A result of this reform was the quick industrialization of the Punjab, made possible to a significant extent by the entry into the industrial sector of hundreds of small producers. By the end of the Ayub period, the Lahore-Lyallpur-Sialkot industrial triangle began to compete with Karachi-Hyderabad.

After reducing the economic and political power of the landed aristocracy and merchant-industrialists during the martial law period, Ayub Khan made it possible for them to return to the decision-making arena. Ayub had little to fear from these groups because the new constitution gave the executive control of the legislature. The new system assured Ayub total control over economic decision-making—the legislature could not even vote on government appropriations. Thus, the constitution of 1962 ushered in another period of coalition rule. There were, however, two significant differences between the 1951–58 and 1962–69 periods. In the latter, the political system was dominated by one individual and the groups functioned more as decision-influencers and less as decision-makers. Second, the ruling coalition was socially more broad-based. In addition to the military and civil bureaucracies, landed aristocracy, and large merchant-industrialists, it included middle farmers and small industrial producers. The objective of planned growth during the Second (1960–65) and Third (1965–70)

Five Year Plans reflected a synthesis between the economic interests of these powerful social groups.

The economic program during the Ayub period produced rapid growth but relatively little gain at the lower end of the income distribution scale.[23] The regime might have achieved a better distribution of national income had it continued those policies developed in the 1958–62 martial law period. Moreover, efforts aimed at increasing economic returns to the middle classes were somewhat offset by the incorporation of the large landlords and industrialists in the ruling coalition.

v. The Military Period (1969–71)

On March 25, 1969, Ayub Khan was forced out of office by the military. General Yahya Khan, after abrogating the 1962 constitution and dissolving the National Assembly, became Pakistan's second military president. This was not an ordinary coup d'etat. It was the end product of a prolonged movement of civil disobedience that started in mid-1967 and turned violent in the early months of 1969. The movement that forced Ayub Khan from power had some important economic causes. It surfaced when the economic slowdown of the late sixties began to be felt by those peripheral groups who had just entered the political system. The economic upswing of the early Ayub period had benefited middle farmers, small merchants, and minor industrialists. These small producers utilized labor-intensive, home-produced technology that benefited artisans and workers in unorganized industry and business. All this economic momentum had helped small-town professionals and given hope to the large and rapidly growing number of students in *mofussil* (towns and small cities) colleges. When the economy lost its

---

23. For a detailed treatment of the income distribution question, see Jawaid Azfar, "The Distribution of Income in Pakistan – 1966–67," and R. Khandekar, "Distribution of Income and Wealth in Pakistan," both in *Pakistan Economic and Social Review* II, No. 1 (Spring 1973), 1–39, 40–66.

momentum, these peripheral groups were the first to suffer. The anti-Ayub movement was in part the consequence of the economic stagnation of the late sixties.[24]

In the first few months following the imposition of martial law, the Yahya government concerned itself with economic reforms. These reforms were aimed at increasing the flow of benefits to the social groups who had acted against the Ayub government. Accordingly, labor and education reforms followed in quick succession. The former, for the first time in Pakistan's economic history, prescribed minimum wages for workers in large-scale industry (units using power or employing more than twenty workers). The latter sought to provide participation to the students in the management of educational institutions. Both policies were to have a significant impact on Pakistan's economic and social history.

While the anti-Ayub movement had originated in West Pakistan, it had a more lasting impact in the eastern wing. It brought to the surface Bengali grievances over the distribution of national resources. The dispute over the division of economic resources had started in the mid-fifties but became less acute during the period of rapid economic growth in the sixties. While the economic slow-down in the late sixties excited certain underprivileged groups in West Pakistan, it made East Pakistani political elements apprehensive about the future of their province. Given the distribution of political power, East Pakistan could increase its share of national wealth only when it did not cause a decrease in the flow of resources to the western province. This condition could not be fulfilled in the late sixties. In this period the rate of growth in national wealth was not sufficient to accommodate East Pakistan's aspirations without diminishing the resources available to the west wing.

24. See Burki, "Ayub's Fall," *op. cit.*

Conflict over the division of resources led to the popularity of the Awami League's Six Point Formula.[25] This formula sought economic independence for East Pakistan and was therefore immediately rejected by the leadership in the west. This rejection, however, strengthened the Awami League in Bengal. The party's unprecedented triumph in the 1970 elections and its claim to power in the early months of 1971 ended in bitter and bloody conflict. The result was the secession of East Pakistan and the emergence of Bangladesh as an independent state in December 1971.

VI. *The Bhutto Period (1971 to the Present)*

In December 1971 the military government of General Yahya Khan handed over power to Zulfikar Ali Bhutto, the chairman of the Pakistan People's Party (PPP). The elections of 1970 had provided Bhutto with a broad economic and political mandate in the Punjab and Sind. Eager to implement his program on a national scale, Bhutto considered the army less of an impediment than had his predecessor. The army's defeat in East Pakistan caused it to withdraw from the political mainstream, and the generals took a back seat in decision-making functions. The PPP represents a number of social and economic interests. It is essentially a coalition of forces sustained by Chairman Bhutto, its charismatic leader. Anwar Syed has analyzed the Chairman's role and personality in chapter four. This section relates that presentation to economic decision-making within the PPP government.

The first converts to the ranks of the PPP were the groups that had modernized rapidly during the early Ayub period. As noted above, in that period the national leadership pursued an activist program of social and economic reform. Moreover, Bhutto was an important member of the national

25. For an excellent summary of the debate on the division of national resources between East and West Pakistan, see "The Report of the Panel of Economists" in Government of Pakistan, *The Fourth Five Year Plan, op. cit.*

leadership; his departure from Ayub's cabinet in 1966 co-incided with a fundamental change in government policies. Traditional leadership groups once again entered the decision-making arena and brought their influence to bear on public programs. The groups that were economically and politically emancipated only in the first half of the sixties sensed a loss of influence, and they rallied behind Bhutto and his People's Party, interpreting his program as "moderately reformist."

The largest concentration of these groups resided in the cities of Sind (Karachi, Hyderabad, and Sukkur) and the rapidly urbanizing and industrializing parts of the Punjab. It was in these areas that the anti-Ayub movement of 1967–69 developed and gained momentum,[26] and it was this part of the Punjab that provided the PPP with its base of mass support during the elections of 1970. In what has elsewhere been described as modern Punjab, the PPP did not lose a single seat in the election to the National Assembly.[27]

As the PPP transformed itself from a movement into a party, it began to attract other groups that could not be absorbed in the more traditional political organizations. The most important among these were on the extreme left. For two decades they had wandered in search of a political home. Ever since the banning of the Communist Party in 1955, the left had drifted from one political arrangement to another. It finally found a haven in the PPP, attracted to it by Bhutto's aggressively pro-China foreign policy as well as by the loudly proclaimed Marxism of some of his followers. By and large the left's following was confined to two regions.

26. For an analysis of the anti-Ayub movement in the Punjab, see Shahid Javed Burki, "Social and Economic Determinants of Violence: A Case Study of the Punjab," *The Middle East Journal*, XXV, Nov. 4 (Autumn 1971), 465, 480.

27.   A recent article by Shahid Javed Burki and Craig Baxter contains an analysis of the PPP constituency in the modern Punjab. See "Socio-Economic Indicators of the People's Party Vote in the Punjab," presented at the Pakistan-Bangladesh Seminar, Southern Asian Institute, Columbia University, April 1974, and published subsequently in the *Journal of Asian Studies*, XXXIV, No. 4, pp. 913–30.

In the rural Northwest Frontier it had assisted the small peasants and sharecroppers in their long-standing disputes against the landed aristocracy. In the large urban centers of the Punjab, the left had assumed control over some of the large industrial and public utility labor unions. In the 1970 elections the support provided by radical labor leaders from the Punjab helped swell the PPP victory, while the peasants of the Frontier province gave the party a foothold in the northern areas.

The third element that was attracted to the party was from Sind and the adjoining areas of the Punjab. This group belonged to the large landed aristocracy that still dominated the social and political life of southwest Pakistan. Bhutto himself belonged to one faction of this landlord class. While members of the Bhutto faction joined the PPP, their traditional opponents remained with Ayub Khan's Conventionist Muslim League. Therefore, well before the PPP bandwagon started rolling, the party enjoyed a wide-based coalition. Eventually it extended from the geographic northeast to the southwest, and from the extreme right to the extreme left of the political spectrum. In designing its economic program the party, once in power, sought to satisfy all its major constituencies.

The most significant reform introduced by the Bhutto regime was in the area of economic management. In its *Election Manifesto* the PPP had promised "Islamic socialism," which meant using the public sector for redistributing some of the nation's wealth to the underprivileged sections of the society.[28] The first step toward the fulfillment of this promise was the enlargement of the public sector. This was brought about in a series of measures that started with the nationalization of ten "basic" industries in January 1972

28. The manifesto appeared in early 1970 as part of the PPP's *Foundation Documents*. For a discussion of this and the party's *Foundation Documents*, see chap. 4 in this volume.

and ended two years later with the government takeover of all private banks. In the interim, the government assumed control over life insurance companies, took possession of vegetable oil producing units, and nationalized rice and cotton export trades. These reforms have had a profound impact on the urban sector of the economy. For instance, there appears to have been a fairly significant transfer of income to consumers from the owners of industrial and commercial assets. Once the government had assumed control over the management of basic industries, it found itself in a position to influence wages as well as prices. It would therefore be appropriate to consider briefly the impact of the government wage and price policies.

It should be recalled that the merchant-industrial class had gathered considerable economic and political power during the fifties and sixties. One result of the power wielded by this group was the pronounced inequity in the distribution of wealth in the urban areas. According to one estimate, the share of wages in industrial output declined during the Ayub era;[29] according to another, two dozen industrial families owned the bulk of the industrial wealth in the country.[30] Given a vastly expanded industrial sector, the PPP regime has been able to devise the institutional means for increasing the income of urban workers. The government's share in manufacturing assets is now on the order of 18 percent. The "taken-over" industries[31] along with government-owned public utilities and transport services account for

29. Azizur Rahman Khan, "What Has Been Happening to Real Wages in Pakistan?," *The Pakistan Development Review*, VII (Autumn 1967), 316–47.

30. Mahbub ul Haq as quoted in Wayne Wilcox, "Pakistan: A Decade of Ayub," *Asian Survey*, IX, No. 2 (Feb. 1969), 72.

31. This paper was written long before the sweeping nationalization of the small-scale agro-industries in Pakistan. This nationalization was announced by Prime Minister Bhutto on Pakistan national television on July 17, 1976. It took the country by surprise. It had some immediate consequences, such as turning the investment climate sour. It is bound to leave a deep impact on Pakistan's economic, social, and political development.

an employment of 585,000 persons, or 11.7 percent of the total urban labor force.[32] By increasing the share of wages in industrial incomes, the government has used the position of leadership that it assumed in this sector. The wages of the workers employed by the public sector have been increased four times in the last three years. The real wages of unskilled workers in the government-controlled industries are now 60 percent higher than in 1969. Because of the lead given to the public sector and because of new labor legislation (introduced in two phases in 1972), there has been a pronounced increase in real industrial wages.

The government has been considerably less successful in using its price policy to redistribute income. In the first two years of its administration, the PPP government attempted to force the private sector into holding the price line. This brought the private sector into direct conflict with the administration, particularly after the devaluation of May 1972, when industrial producers found a sizable increase in the price of their inputs. The government's wage policy further eroded industrial profits. One consequence of this conflict was the nationalization of the important vegetable oil industry in the summer of 1973. This act of nationalization was important because it took the administration beyond its own program of public sector management of industries. With the takeover of the vegetable oil industry, the government found itself in possession of a number of small-scale enterprises producing an important item of everyday consumption. Although this industry was nationalized to hold the price line, public sector managers soon discerned that it was not possible to maintain the price of vegetable oil. By nationalizing the vegetable oil industry the government succeeded only in eroding its credibility with the industrialists and middle- and low-income urban consumers.

32. The data are from an official study done by me to examine the impact of labor reforms on industrial investment. This paper has not been released for publication.

The latter make up an important part of the PPP constituency.

In formulating its economic program for the rural sector, the regime has responded to the demands from three different constituencies. The long debate about mechanization seems over, with the decision in favor of large and progressive farmers of the central and southern regions, who, as was indicated above, form one of the three original constituencies of the PPP. The government's decision to introduce "controlled" mechanization has resulted in the establishment of a plant to assemble and then manufacture medium and large tractors. In addition to constituency pressure, the government was propelled toward this policy by two other developments. After taking over the "basic" industries, the government possessed a half-dozen small units engaged in tractor assembly. The modernization of these enterprises ultimately resulted in the decision to set up what is for Pakistan a fairly large-scale tractor assembly and manufacturing unit. Also, the floods in the summer of 1973 resulted in a loss of some $600 million, which the government sought to recoup by launching a program to increase the output of winter crops.[33] One part of this program involved the mechanized preparation of land for sowing of the wheat crop. The exact number of tractors made available for this purpose is not yet known, but it amounts to a sizable increase in the country's tractor population.

The second area of decision concerned terms of trade between the agricultural and nonagricultural sectors. The May 1972 devaluation of Pakistani currency, from a parity rate of Rs. 4.76 to one U.S. dollar to Rs. 11.00, was a major step in this direction. Although imposition of export duties (ranging between 10 and 40 percent on most agricultural exports) maintained a differential in price realized from the international market between agricultural and non-

33. The estimate of the losses incurred from floods in the summer of 1973 is from the finance minister's budget speech. See Mubashir Hasan, *Budget Speech for 1974–75* (Islamabad: Government of Pakistan, Finance Division, June 8, 1974).

agricultural commodities, the overall difference was now considerably narrower. The principal influence on this decision was exercised from abroad, particularly from the International Monetary Fund, which looked unfavorably on the multiple rate of exchange operated under the Bonus Voucher Scheme. To this pressure the surplus farmers of the Punjab added their weight. Export duties and the government's procurement policies prevented the farmer with marketable surplus from realizing the full benefit of devaluation. Following the devaluation decision, the government announced a number of revisions in its agricultural price policy. The new policy particularly benefited farmers producing wheat, rice, cotton, and sugar cane. The largest share in the value of the marketed output from these crops comes from the middle farmers of the Punjab. This class of landowners occupies an important place in the PPP, and its influence is clearly reflected in the government's economic program.

The land reform of March 1972 lowered the ceiling established by the Ayub regime in 1959. Instead of five hundred acres of irrigated land, the new ceiling was placed at 150 acres. The reforms also addressed themselves to owner-tenant relationships. A new code was prescribed under which the costs of current production as well as the costs of land development were to be met by the landowners. The PPP reforms, although considerably more radical in scope than those of 1959, nonetheless face a different situation in the rural areas. The 1959 measure reduced the economic power of the large landlords in the Punjab while preserving that of large owners in Sind. By choosing a land productivity index to measure ceilings and by applying the new standard to individuals rather than families, the new reforms have reinforced the change brought about in 1959. The major impact will be felt in those areas of the country in which land is cultivated under some kind of sharecropping arrangement. In other words, the reform is likely to have a far greater social impact in the Frontier Province than in the Punjab and Sind. As in the case of other economic measures adopted by the Bhutto regime, land reforms also serve to reward PPP supporters.

Another major area of economic reform under Bhutto is in the social sector. The largely private orientation of the Ayub period neglected this part of the economy. For instance, during the Third Five Year Plan, health and education received 3.8 and 4.7 percent, respectively, of total government development outlay. The new government has sought to repair this neglect. Under the new education policy, universalization of elementary education has been promised "within the shortest possible time." Of even greater importance is the government decision to nationalize privately managed colleges and schools in the Punjab and Sind. These institutions were the strong preserves of the classes (large landlords, merchant-industrialists, civil and military bureaucracies) that wielded enormous power during the pre-Bhutto period. They were, therefore, resented by the supporters of the new leadership. Once again Bhutto's reforms promised rewards to an important constituency. In the health sector the government adopted a policy equally supportive of its factionalized constituency. A number of new medical colleges are being set up in the cities that have been and remain in favor of the new ruling elite. The construction of these institutions in Larkana, Nawabshah, Quetta, Lyallpur, and Rawalpindi quiets a long-standing demand of the urban middle classes for health and medical training facilities.

VII. *An Evaluation of Economic Decision-making Under Bhutto*

In formulating its economic policies, Bhutto's administration has striven hard to accommodate each of the interests represented by the party. The landlords of Sind, the middle farmers of the Punjab, the sharecroppers of the Frontier,

all have benefited from his reforms. Industrial labor in large
urban centers, owners of small industrial establishments,
and petty merchants have been provided with suitable rewards. Somewhat more heterogenous groups such as college
and university students and middle-class urban consumers
have seen their not very well-articulated demands at least
partially fulfilled. In other words, Bhutto's administration
has made strenuous efforts to satisfy its constituents. All of
this notwithstanding, these reforms have yet to dispel a
sense of national frustration; it persists today as it did during
the latter part of the Ayub period. Given the hypotheses
presented in Section I of this chapter, an important question
can be posed: Why has Bhutto's passive approach failed to
achieve a social, political, and economic equilibrium in the
society?

Explanations for a great deal of the frustration that persists in Pakistan today are to be found in the content of the
regime's economic reforms[34] as well as in the manner in
which they were formulated. Given the model in Section
I, only regimes that synthesize articulated group interests
can expect to achieve political stability. Bhutto's administration, while responding to some group interests, has not
succeeded in fully synthesizing *all* economic demands in
the society.

A passive regime, responsive to *all* group interests, should
be able to establish a political equilibrium. The PPP-led
government has not been able to attain this state of equilibrium because it chose to be more selective in approaching
the economic demands of social groups. As described in
Section VI, the Bhutto regime has been responsive to the
pressure of the social groups that supported him before he
assumed power. However, the regime, at least during its
first thirty months in power, did not seem interested in

34. For a detailed discussion of the content of the PPP's economic program, see
chap. 7 by Gilbert Brown in this volume.

rewarding groups that ignored the PPP bandwagon in 1968. These groups, mostly belonging to the class of decision-influencers, have been largely neglected. In this respect, therefore, the Bhutto regime differs from the passive types that were identified in Section II. A passive regime, aiming at political longevity, will endeavor to bring about a synthesis of *all* social groups in the society. A regime showing the type of selectivity displayed by the new political leadership in Pakistan may not be able to bring about social equilibrium.

One reason for the difference in the *content* of the new regime's economic program is to be found in the *manner* in which it was devised. To appreciate more fully this aspect of decision-making, it is necessary to discuss the institutions used for synthesizing group interests.

Institutions such as political parties, legislatures, and bureaucracies assist the decision-makers in producing the desired synthesis. The decision-influencer groups described above are usually well represented in these institutions. Pakistan has yet to acquire viable political institutions, but it has had well-developed civil and military bureaucracies. It is interesting to note that the social composition of these bureaucracies changed with the development of Pakistan. At partition, the landlords and urban middle classes from the Muslim-minority provinces of British India had a powerful influence in the civil and military services. By the end of the Ayub period, these services had strong rural and urban middle-class representation. In other words, the bureaucracy, both civil and military, played a surrogate political role during much of Pakistan's history.

By reorganizing the military and civil services,[35] the present regime has ousted from the decision-influencing arena two institutions that are important in the synthesis

---

35. For a discussion of the administrative reforms undertaken by the PPP regime, see the contributions by Lawrence Ziring and Robert La Porte Jr. in the "Symposium on New Pakistan," *Asian Survey,* XIV, No. 12 (Dec. 1974), 1087–1103.

of group interests. In theory, these bureaucracies are being replaced by the Pakistan People's Party. But the party remains underdeveloped; its role in decision-making remains marginal at best. Indeed, factions within the PPP have raised serious problems that can only be resolved by the Prime Minister and his close political associates. This arrangement is clearly inadequate for synthesizing different socio-economic interests. For instance, the nationalization decisions reflected the wishes of an important constituency of the PPP, and so did the decision to restructure the bureaucracy. Having considerably weakened the bureaucratic structure, the government may find public management of an important part of the industrial sector enormously difficult.

The decision to devalue the currency and improve agriculture's terms of trade to some extent benefited an important segment of the landed aristocracy. In the last two years the large cotton producers of the south Punjab and north Sind have reaped large profits. However, the concomitant increase in the price of lint cotton produced serious disruptions in the small-scale textile weaving industry of Lyallpur and Gujranwala. The owners and workers in this industry constitute an important constituency for the PPP. The regime must strike a balance between the large cotton producers and the small-scale textile-weaving industry. The government's price policy with regard to some other agricultural products has also resulted in the generation of conflict between different groups. An increase in the price of sugar cane was demanded and obtained by the owners of large sugar estates in Sind. The increase in the price of refined sugar that resulted alienated a large number of consumers in the urban areas. The government's only response to this was the establishment of a dual market in sugar—an arrangement that meets a part of the urban demand for refined sugar at a subsidized price.

This catalogue of conflicts between different economic

interests is not unique to Pakistan. Simply put, the seesaw nature of policy-making in which different group interests are satisfied at different times may not produce social and political equilibrium. The PPP approach to economic decision-making is the product not so much of a lack of conviction but of the inability to resolve differences between elements within the ruling elite. The recent purge of the ultra-left from the central cabinet may mean that Bhutto intends to bring into the decision-making arena the social groups he previously ignored.[36] The first indication that this was happening occurred in June 1974 when the government presented a budget reflecting a departure from the previous two fiscal years. Does this mean that Bhutto is now in a position to achieve a working balance between various economic interests in the society, a balance that would result in the active participation of a number of groups hitherto neglected in the decision-making process?

The answer to this question lies in the regime's ability to structure institutions that would help in bringing about a synthesis of all powerful group interests. No regime, unless it is prepared to use its coercive power with great ruthlessness, can fully sanitize the society, and Bhutto is not likely to adopt a repressive course. The departure of the left and the possible reentry of the old merchant and industrial groups does not mean that the problem of synthesis has been solved. Unplacated, the left could still create problems for the regime. The option open to Bhutto's administration therefore is to develop institutions that can cope adequately with the demands of all social and political groups. With bureaucracies no longer performing this function, the burden is on the political parties.

36. Dr. Mubashir Hasan, the finance minister responsible for giving a "socialist direction" to Pakistan's economic development, was dropped from the cabinet on October 22, 1974. Dr. Hasan's portfolio went to Mohammed Hanif, a minister with a known center-of-the-road approach.

7

Pakistan's Economic Development After 1971

Gilbert T. Brown

The economic development of Pakistan after 1971 involves at least two subjects of great importance. One is the strength and performance of the former West Pakistan economy following the formation of Bangladesh; the other is the characteristics of its development policies and programs. The first subject can be discussed briefly as background for the complex issues of the second. Unless otherwise indicated, data for "Pakistan" prior to 1972 refer to former West Pakistan only.

Economic Performance

The economy of Pakistan (then West Pakistan) grew rapidly during the Second Plan (1960–65), with Gross Domestic Product (GDP) increasing at 6.7 percent per annum, compared with 5.6 percent for the entire country. This high growth was spearheaded by an industrial growth of 13.1 percent per annum. However, agriculture grew by only 3.7 percent per annum. West Pakistan's overall economic growth slowed somewhat during the Third Plan (1965–70) to about 6 percent per annum. The industrial growth rate fell to 7.6 percent, but agricultural output grew at 5.6 percent annually

Editors' note: Although the author is on the staff of the International Bank for Reconstruction and Development, the views expressed in this chapter are those of the author and should not be interpreted as reflecting the official views of the World Bank Group.

with the aid of new high-yielding wheat and rice varieties, reducing, but not eliminating, the food deficit (Tables 1, 2, 3, and 4).

Though it is hardly apparent in these figures, Pakistan's economic development began to encounter a number of difficulties after 1965. Import restrictions and other direct controls introduced at that time became permanent as the shortage of foreign exchange and budget resources persisted owing to higher defense expenditure, rising foreign debt service, and decreased foreign aid. Both net capital inflow and domestic savings declined, and investment fell from about 22 percent of GDP in 1964/65 to about 17 percent in 1969/70, and to only 11 percent in 1971/72.[1] The slowdown in industrial growth, along with urban population growth rates of more than 5 percent, led to a rapid rise in urban unemployment. In rural areas it was the larger farmers of West Pakistan who got most of the benefits from the new "green revolution."

The economy underwent severe strains during 1970/71 (FY 71) and 1971/72 (FY 72), reflecting both political events and prolonged drought that virtually halted the increase in agricultural output. While national income figures are better as indicators of trends rather than of precise amounts of change, GDP estimates show no change in FY 71, an increase of about 1 percent in FY 72, and increases of 6 percent in FY 73 and FY 74. For the two years FY 71 and 72, agriculture showed a net increase of less than 0.5 percent but increases of about 3.1 percent in both FY 73 and 74. Manufacturing value-added fell by more than 3 percent over the two years FY 71 and FY 72, but then rose about 5.5 percent in FY 73 and about 8 percent in FY 74.

The Pakistan economy has demonstrated its strength and resilience, both in its adjustment to the separation of the two

1. Most annual data on Pakistan are available only on a fiscal year basis. E.g., 1971/72 represents fiscal year 1972 (FY 72), running from July 1, 1971, to June 30, 1972.

Table 1. *Pakistan: Gross Domestic Product at Current Factor Cost 1959/60–1972/73 (Millions of Rupees)*

		Second plan period				
	1959/60	*1960/61*	*1961/62*	*1962/63*	*1963/64*	*1964/65*
1. Agriculture	7,711	8,184	8,216	8,565	9,499	10,438
i) Major crops	3,882	4,111	4,079	4,361	4,955	5,720
ii) Minor crops	893	900	911	864	1,150	1,346
iii) Livestock	2,837	3,064	3,110	3,203	3,238	3,199
iv) Fishing	71	79	83	98	116	127
v) Forestry	28	30	33	39	40	46
2. Mining/Quarrying	70	83	89	102	119	140
3. Manufacturing	2,018	2,258	2,602	3,024	3,414	3,759
i) Large-scale	1,159	1,383	1,688	2,043	2,390	2,704
ii) Small-scale	889	875	914	981	1,024	1,055
4. Construction	427	607	602	739	960	1,103
5. Electricity/Gas/Water Sanitary services	87	102	105	127	157	200
6. Transportation/Storage/ Communications[1]	921	1,061	1,065	1,140	1,240	1,737
7. Wholesale/Retail trade	2,105	2,320	2,505	2,706	3,159	3,690
8. Banking/Insurance[1]	—	—	—	—	—	—
9. Ownership of dwellings	837	875	924	593	1,000	1,083
10. Public administration/ Defense[1]	397	416	466	502	560	615
11. Services	1,411	1,505	1,600	1,640	1,756	1,926
Gross Domestic Product	15,984	17,411	18,174	19,498	21,864	24,691

1. The value added in PIA (included in Transportation and Communications Sector), Banking and Insurance, and Central Public Administration and Defense has not been included prior to 1969/70 because of difficulties in allocating them between former East and West Wings.

wings in 1971 and in its absorbing in the second half of 1973 the twin blows of the August flood and the October increase in international petroleum prices. The balance of payments crisis, precipitated in 1971 as a result of the loss of jute export earnings from East Pakistan, was much less severe than had been widely predicted. Pakistan was forced to stop payments on a substantial portion of its external debt for one year until a rescheduling could be arranged with creditors as well as to further curb imports. However, the

Table 1 (*cont.*)

	Third plan period						
1965/66	*1966/67*	*1967/68*	*1968/69*	*1969/70*	*1970/71*	*1971/72*	*1972/73*[2]
10,572	12,460	13,994	14,038	15,964	16,236	17,934	20,155
5,669	6,604	7,329	7,466	9,103	8,832	10,067	11,780
1,448	1,934	2,159	1,709	1,999	2,244	2,408	2,584
3,254	3,688	4,256	4,615	4,547	4,794	5,053	5,326
138	151	159	148	233	261	295	335
63	74	91	100	82	105	111	130
152	158	165	181	229	243	268	355
4,281	4,696	5,199	6,013	6,923	7,450	7,557	8,742
3,151	3,490	3,905	4,604	5,427	5,822	5,777	6,736
1,130	1,206	1,294	1,409	1,496	1,628	1,780	2,006
1,216	1,216	1,262	1,709	1,822	1,979	1,763	2,151
229	269	291	309	661	782	823	886
1,885	2,171	2,356	2,503	2,928[1]	3,000	3,228	3,759
4,100	4,786	5,116	5,538	6,475	6,781	7,085	8,333
—	—	—	—	771[1]	882	968	1,091
1,187	1,340	1,403	1,516	1,614	1,752	1,913	2,143
865	838	987	1,031	2,778[1]	2,967	3,450	4,238
2,118	2,395	2,528	2,673	3,134	3,475	3,894	4,454
26,605	30,329	33,301	35,511	43,299	45,547	48,883	56,307

2. Provisional
Source: Statistical Division, Ministry of Finance, Planning and Development.

value of exports to areas other than former East Pakistan rose by 41 percent in FY 72 and 39 percent in FY 73. This reflected both a sharp jump (about one-third) in the size of the cotton crop and in exports of cotton and cotton textiles, and the successful diversion to other markets of most of the flow of cotton, textiles, rice, and other goods with which West Pakistan had previously reimbursed East Pakistan for its flow of jute and jute earnings to West Pakistan. Between FY 70 and FY 72 Pakistan's exports to former East Pakistan

Table 2. *Pakistan: Gross Domestic Product at Constant Factor Cost 1959/60–1972/73 (Millions of Rupees; 1959–60 Prices)*

	1959/60	1960/61	Second plan period 1961/62	1962/63	1963/64	1964/65
1. Agriculture	7,711	7,695	8,171	8,597	8,813	9,276
i) Major crops	3,882	3,840	4,209	4,595	4,509	4,821
ii) Minor crops	893	869	818	891	1,129	1,130
iii) Livestock	2,837	2,887	2,940	2,996	3,048	3,121
iv) Fishing	71	67	70	77	85	91
v) Forestry	28	32	34	38	42	46
2. Mining/Quarrying	70	81	86	96	113	122
3. Manufacturing	2,018	2,276	2,576	2,863	3,186	3,501
i) Large-scale	1,159	1,394	1,671	1,934	2,233	2,523
ii) Small-scale	859	882	905	929	953	978
4. Construction	427	612	596	700	897	1,029
5. Electricity/Gas/Water/ Sanitary services	87	99	99	122	142	172
6. Transportation/Storage/ Communication[1]	921	1,023	987	1,086	1,124	1,490
7. Wholesale/Retail trade	2,105	2,251	2,427	2,665	2,935	3,166
8. Banking/Insurance[1]	–	–	–	–	–	–
9. Ownership of dwellings	837	853	888	916	943	976
10. Public administration/ Defense[1]	397	398	443	472	518	543
11. Services	1,411	1,478	1,537	1,601	1,665	1,732
Gross Domestic Product	15,984	16,771	17,810	19,118	20,336	22,007

1. The value added in PIA (included in Transportation and Communications Sector), Banking and Insurance, and Central Public Administration and Defense has not been included prior to 1969/70 because of difficulties in allocating them between former East and West Wings.

fell from $228 million to $56 million, while its exports to other countries increased from $338 million to $591 million. Devaluation in May 1972 gave a strong impetus to exports. Even though the government imposed substantial export duties on major agricultural exports, export earnings rose another 27 percent, to $823 million, in FY 73.[2]

2. On a custom clearance basis as reported by the Statistical Division, Ministry of Finance. In constant prices, the FY 73 increase was 14 percent (Table 6).

Table 2 (*cont.*)

	Third plan period						
1965/66	*1966/67*	*1967/68*	*1968/69*	*1969/70*	*1970/71*	*1971/72*	*1972/73*[2]
9,318	9,829	10,982	11,478	12,574	12,188	12,611	13,002
4,821	5,137	6,078	6,408	7,553	7,045	7,336	7,600
1,172	1,284	1,406	1,516	1,363	1,418	1,507	1,562
3,178	3,242	3,307	3,373	3,440	3,509	3,579	3,651
97	114	135	121	170	155	125	125
50	52	56	60	48	61	64	64
133	133	137	141	157	156	159	167
3,799	4,012	4,267	4,634	5,156	5,234	4,988	5,260
2,796	2,982	3,209	3,548	4,042	4,090	3,813	4,053
1,003	1,030	1,058	1,086	1,114	1,144	1,175	1,207
1,079	1,039	1,037	1,317	1,357	1,390	1,163	1,320
197	207	224	251	639	741	780	835
1,581	1,643	1,729	1,823	2,016[1]	1,970	2,011	2,164
3,440	3,621	3,754	4,020	4,457	4,453	4,414	4,797
–	–	–	–	597[1]	635	640	663
1,006	1,039	1,067	1,099	1,112	1,149	1,188	1,228
738	667	760	782	2,086[1]	2,137	2,282	2,573
1,801	1,878	1,954	2,031	2,169	2,276	2,391	2,516
23,092	24,068	25,911	27,576	32,302	32,329	32,627	34,525

2. Provisional.
Source: Statistical Division, Ministry of Finance, Planning and Development

Constant-price data show that the volume of Pakistan's merchandise exports in FY 73 was more than 40 percent above the FY 67–69 level of West Pakistan exports, including those to former East Pakistan (Table 5). The data indicate that the increase can be attributed entirely to growth in certain other exports, such as carpets, but unless the data are inaccurate, this has been offset by declines in other exports such as jute manufactures and some goods formerly sold to East Pakistan. Rising prices for rice, cotton, and cotton

Table 3. *Pakistan: Overall and Sectoral Growth Rates, 1960/61–1972/73* *(GDP at Constant Factor Cost)*

	Compound rates of growth	
	Second plan period	Third plan period
1. Agriculture	3.7	5.6
2. Mining/Quarrying	11.7	3.4
3. Manufacturing	11.6	8.0
4. Construction	22.0	5.7
5. Electricity/Gas/Water/Sanitary Services	14.6	9.9
6. Transportation/Storage/Communications[1]	10.1	4.7
7. Wholesale/Retail Trade	8.5	6.6
8. Banking/Insurance[1]	–	–
9. Ownership of Dwellings	3.1	2.9
10. Public Administration/Defense[1]	6.4	9.5
11. Services	4.1	4.0
Gross Domestic Product	6.6	6.0

1. The value added in PIA (included in Transport and Communications Sector), Banking and Insurance and Central Public Administration and Defense has not been included prior to 1969/70 because of difficulties in allocating them between former East and West Wings.

manufactures have further strengthened earnings, as the terms of trade moved in Pakistan's favor from 1971 until the petroleum "crisis" of late 1973.[3]

Pakistan's trade position received two severe blows in FY 74: extensive damage to standing rice and cotton crops and loss of stored wheat and other commodities as the result of the August 1973 floods, and the increased price of petroleum and other imports after the October 1973 and subsequent price increases by the major oil-exporting countries.

3. A Commerce Ministry study attributes 57 percent of the FY 1970–72 increase in exports to quantity increases, 25 percent to higher prices, and 18 percent to diversion from former East Pakistan.

Table 3 *(cont.)*

	Third plan period						
1965/66	*1966/67*	*1967/68*	*1968/69*	*1969/70*	*1970/71*	*1971/72*	*1972/73²*
0.5	5.5	11.7	4.5	6.4	−3.1	3.5	3.1
9.0	−	3.0	2.9	2.1	−0.6	1.9	5.0
8.5	5.6	6.4	8.6	11.3	1.5	−4.7	5.5
−4.9	−3.7	−0.2	27.0	3.0	2.4	−16.3	13.5
14.5	5.1	8.2	12.1	9.9	16.0	5.3	7.1
6.1	3.9	5.2	5.4	2.9	−2.3¹	2.1	7.6
8.7	5.3	3.7	7.1	8.6	−0.1	−0.9	8.7
−	−	−	−	−	9.7¹	0.8	3.6
3.1	3.3	2.7	3.0	2.6	3.3	3.4	3.4
35.9	−9.6	13.9	2.9	9.1	2.4¹	6.8	12.8
4.0	4.3	4.1	3.9	3.7	4.9	5.1	5.2
5.0	4.2	7.7	6.4	6.9	0.1	0.9	5.8

2. Provisional.
Source: Statistical Division, Ministry of Finance, Planning and Development

Reduced cotton and rice exports and increased wheat imports due to the floods are estimated to have cost Pakistan $300 million in foreign exchange in FY 74. Higher petroleum prices alone added perhaps a further $150 million to the trade deficit. Since the total trade deficit was only $445 million, this suggests that Pakistan's balance of payments position would have been very strong in FY 74 except for the floods and higher petroleum prices. Even though the volume of exports is expected to be substantially higher in FY 75, the trade deficit is expected to be larger than in FY 74 because of rising import demand for investment goods, sharply higher import prices, and stable or declining

Table 4. *Pakistan: Resources and Expenditures (Millions of Rupees: Current Market Prices)*

	1959/60*
1. *Gross Domestic Production, Factor Cost*	*16,733*
2. Net Factor Income from Abroad	−26
Receipts[1]	(41)
Payments[2]	(67)
3. *Gross National Product, Factor Cost* (1 + 2)	*16,707*
4. Indirect Taxes, Net of Subsidies	920
Plus Indirect Taxes	(928)
Minus Subsidies	(8)
5. *Gross National Product, Market Prices* (3 + 4)	*17,627*
6. *Gross Domestic Product, Market Prices*	
(1 + 4) = (7 + 8 + 9)	*17,653*
7. *Current Account Balance*	*−1,162*
Imports of Goods and NFS (Non-Factor Services)	*2,648*
Merchandise Imports, c.i.f.	(2,500)
From East Pakistan, c.i.f.[3]	362
From Rest of the World, c.i.f.[4]	2,138
Imports of Non-Factor Services[2]	(148)
Exports of Goods and NFS	*1,486*
Merchandise Exports, f.o.b.	(1,242)
To East Pakistan, f.o.b.[3]	512
To Rest of the World, f.o.b.[4]	730
Exports of Non-Factor Services	(244)
To Rest of the World[1]	175
Freight Receipts (Net) on Trade with	
East Pakistan[5]	69
8. *Gross Domestic Investment*	*2,040*
Fixed Capital Formation	(2,015)
Public Sector	990
Private Sector	1,025
Changes in Stocks	(25)
9. *Consumption*	*16,775*
Public Sector	1,869
Private Sector	14,906

1. West Pakistan's share of factor and non-factor service receipts (except freight and insurance receipts) is apportioned at 80% of all-Pakistan figures for 1969/70 and 1970/71, and at 90% for July-December 1971. Receipts from freight and insurance are allocated to West Pakistan on the basis of its share of total imports as mentioned in Footnote 4. Does not include inter-wing transactions in invisibles.

2. West Pakistan's share of factor and non-factor service payments (except freight and insurance payments) is apportioned at 66% of all-Pakistan figures for 1969/70 to July-December 1971. Freight and Insurance are excluded from this item and are included in imports, c.i.f. West Pakistan's share of freight and insurance is apportioned on the basis of its share of total imports as mentioned in Footnote 4. Does not include inter-wing transactions in invisibles.

3. Including inter-wing trade in foreign merchandise. CSO c.i.f. export data reduced by 10% to take into account freight and insurance charges from this source.

4. Imports and exports f.o.b. data are taken from the State Bank's balance of payments statements and are apportioned to West Pakistan in proportion to CSO data on West Pakistan's share of total imports and exports (including re-exports)

Table 4 *(cont.)*

1964/65*	1969/70	1970/71	1971/72[7]	1972/73[8] (provisional)	1973/74 (estimates)
26,033	43,299	45,547	48,883	56,307	64,754
−119	+186	−29	+218[6]	+638	+495
(76)	(547)	(332)	(599)	(1,728)	(1,634)
(195)	(361)	(361)	(381)	(1,090)	(1,139)
25,914	43,485	45,518	49,101	56,945	65,249
1,990	4,039	4,384	4,387	6,067	7,400
(2,150)	(4,218)	(4,533)	(4,612)	(6,455)	(8,300)
(160)	(179)	(149)	(225)	(388)	(900)
27,904	47,524	49,902	53,488	63,012	72,649
28,023	47,338	49,931	53,270	62,374	72,154
−2,337	−1,220	−1,747	−1,976[6]	−2,087	−3,417
4,710	4,863	5,652	6,064	11,513	15,791
(4,217)	(4,469)	(5,165)	(5,344)	(10,240)	(14,355)
537	923	804	431	−	−
3,680	3,546	4,361	4,913	10,240	14,355
(493)	(394)	(487)	(720)	(1,273)	(1,436)
2,373	3,643	3,905	4,088	9,426	12,375
(1,925)	(3,070)	(3,289)	(3,492)	(8,015)	(10,890)
787	1,499	1,240	427	−	−
1,138	1,571	2,049	3,065	8,015	10,890
(448)	(573)	(616)	(596)	(1,411)	(1,485)
342	379	452	528	1,411	1,485
106	194	164	68	−	−
6,016	7,520	7,892	7,731	8,847	11,250
(5,976)	(6,814)	(7,045)	(6,881)	(7,847)	(10,250)
2,746	3,321	3,514	3,335	4,020	5,700
3,230	3,493	3,531	3,546	3,827	4,550
(40)	(706)	(847)	(850)	(1,000)	(1,000)
24,344	41,038	43,786	47,515	55,614	64,321
3,017	4,846	5,270	6,310	7,213	8,690
21,327	36,192	38,516	41,205	48,401	55,631

respectively. Imports are apportioned to West Pakistan at 64% of total imports for 1969/70, 70% for 1970/71 and 72% for July-December 1971; exports are apportioned at 50% of total exports for 1969/70, 63% for 1970/71 and 72% for July-December 1971. Imports, c.i.f. are arrived at by including West Pakistan's assumed share of freight and insurance payments.

5. Ten percent of inter-wing exports and imports is assumed for freight and insurance charges of which 75% is allocated to West Pakistan as its net receipt from this source.

6. April-June 1972 US dollar figures are converted at Rs. 7.82 per US$1.00.

7. Pakistani rupee was devalued from Rs. 4.7619 to Rs 11.00 per US$1.00 on May 12, 1972.

8. Pakistani rupee was re-valued from Rs 11.00 to Rs 9.90 per US$1.00 on February 16, 1973.

* Staff Estimates

Source: Planning Commission, Statistical Division (Ministry of Finance, Planning and Development) and Staff Estimates.

Table 5. *Pakistan: Investment and Savings Rates, 1959/60–1973/74 (Percent of GDP at Current Market Prices)*

	1959/60	1964/65	1969/70	1970/71	1971/72	1972/73 (provisional)	1973/74 (estimates)
Gross Investment (Including changes in Stocks)	11.6	21.4	15.9	15.8	14.5	14.2	15.6
Financing							
Foreign Savings[1]	6.6	8.3	2.6	3.5	3.7	3.3	4.7
Domestic Savings	5.0	13.1	13.3	12.3	10.8	10.8	10.9
Public Savings	(−1.4)	(0.2)	(1.0)	(0.7)	(−0.4)	(...)	(1.8)
Private Savings	(6.4)	(12.9)	(12.3)	(11.6)	(11.2)	(10.8)	(9.1)
Gross Fixed Investment	11.4	21.3	14.4	14.1	12.9	12.5	14.2
Public Sector	(5.6)	(9.8)	(7.0)	(7.0)	(6.2)	(6.4)	(7.9)
Private Sector	(5.8)	(11.5)	(7.4)	(7.1)	(6.7)	(6.1)	(6.3)

1. Current account balance, excluding net factor income from abroad, and current transfers.
Source: Staff Estimates.

Table 6. *Exports[1] (in millions of U.S. dollars)*

	Average FY 1967–69[2]	FY 1972[3]	FY 1973	Estimated FY 1974
A. Constant 1967–69 Prices				
Raw cotton	97	117	89	22
Cotton yarn	46	119	168	144
Cotton cloth	72	5	103	84
Rice	50	89	145	114
Other primary agricultural commodities	–	–	70	74
Other manufactured goods	–	–	124	127
All other goods	228	213	–	–
Total goods f.o.b.	493	613	699	565
Non-factor services	90	79	96	91
Total goods and NFS	583	692	795	656
B. Price Indices (1967–69 – 100)[4]				
Raw cotton	100	147	125	269
Cotton yarn	100	90	112	194
Cotton cloth	100	108	114	179
Rice	100	62	78	175
Other primary agricultural commodities	100	119	150	202
Other manufactured goods	100	122	141	165
All other goods	100	122	141	165
Total goods f.o.b.	100	106	118	186
Non-factor services	100	122	141	165
Total goods and NFS	100	107	121	183
C. Current Prices				
Raw cotton	97	172	111	60
Cotton yarn	46	108	188	280
Cotton cloth	72	80	118	150
Rice	50	55	113	200
Other primary agricultural commodities	n.a.	n.a.	105	150
Other manufactured goods	n.a.	n.a.	189	210
All other goods	228	232	–	–
Total goods f.o.b.	493	647	823	1,050
Non-factor services	89	97	136	150
Total goods and NFS	582	744	959	1,200

1. Merchandise exports f.o.b. based on data of Statistical Division, Ministry of Finance, Planning and Development. These are based on customs records and vary somewhat from final balance of payment data.
2. Including merchandise trade with East Pakistan but excluding invisible transactions except freight.
3. Calendar year.
4. Variations of individual export prices in the past may vary from official price indices owing to quality changes and occasional "under-invoicing" (e.g., raw cotton in 1972/73).

Table 7. Balance of Payments *(in millions of U.S. dollars at current prices)*

	Average FY 1967–69[1]	FY 1972[1]	FY 1973	Estimated FY 1974
1. Imports (including NFS)[2]	1,007	1,050	1,092	1,645
2. Exports (including NFS)[2]	581	686	902	1,200
3. Balance of goods and NFS	−426	−364	−190	−445
4. Factor Services – total	−62	−56	−86	−100
a. Interest on public debt	(−40)	(−44)	(−83)	(−90)
b. Interest on other debt	..	..	..	..
c. Other factor services	(−22)	(−12)	(−3)	(−10)
5. Workers' remittances	23	92	147	130
6. Current transfers (net)	..	..	..	..
7. Balance on current account[3]	−465	−328	−130	−415
8. Private direct investment (net)	..	..	..	..
9. Official capital grants (net)	..	..	29	30
10. Public M & LT loans				
a. Disbursements	..	..	309	394
b. Repayments[4]	..	..	−103	−107
c. Net disbursements	..	..	206	287
11. Other M & LT (net)	..	..	..	..
12. IMF drawings	..	..	54	..
13. Other capital transactions (net) n.i.e.[5]	..	..	..	..
14. Use of reserves (−Increase)	17	−20	−159	98
15. Reserves (net) end period June[6]	257	192	370	272

1. Including merchandise trade with former East Pakistan but excluding invisible transactions except freight. Transactions with East Pakistan are converted to dollars at average effective export/import rates for all Pakistan. Data for 1967/69 and 1971/72 are staff estimates for West Pakistan.
2. Import and export totals for FY 1973 and prior years are taken from Pakistan's balance-of-payments accounts. Therefore, these figures differ somewhat from totals in the preceding two tables on imports and exports by commodities, which are based on customs clearing data that are subsequently adjusted to arrive at balance of payment totals.
3. Includes investment income (net) and private transfers (gross debits).   5. Includes errors and omissions.
4. Includes effects of debt relief from 1971/72 onward.   6. State Bank's gross reserves, net of IMF position.

agriculture export prices.[4] The current account deficit is
about the same size as (or slightly smaller than) the trade
deficit because receipts from workers' remittance nearly
offset the deficit on other invisibles.

The growth in production and exports that has occurred
is very impressive because it has taken place at a time when
the economy has had to adjust to the loss of markets and
sources of supply in the former east wing, and while something like an internal economic, political, and social revolution has been mounted. Recent and prospective growth —
and the fact that the deficits being incurred are within the
limits of credit availabilities to finance development projects
— indicates that Pakistan has an internationally viable economy. This is not to say, however, either that Pakistan is
safely launched on the high road to continuing rapid growth
or that any economic miracles have occurred. It is possible
to partially discount production growth in FY 73 and 74 as
recovery from a period of stagnation. Furthermore, an important part of growth has been obtained by a higher rate of
utilization of industrial and infrastructure capacity, as fixed
capital formation has been only about 12 to 14 percent of
GDP (Table 5). Unless investment rates and domestic
savings rates increase, future rates of growth may decline.
Private investment in other than small-scale manufacturing
has been quite limited because of fears of nationalization
and of government wage, price, and other policies. Government investment has also been modest, partly because of
limited resources, but also because of the need to rethink
investment and development plans after the administrative
disruptions caused by the return to a political-civilian government.

Domestic savings as a percentage of GDP are estimated

4. Wheat import requirements were less in FY 75 because of a record 1974
wheat crop, but they were still substantial in order to supply low-priced government ration shops in urban areas. Government procurement from farmers was only
about half of the requirement for ration shops, as farmers and dealers were unwilling to sell to the government at the offered price.

to have fallen by nearly one-fifth between FY 70 and FY 72 (Table 5). Since then the rate of private savings has continued to decline; public sector savings were negative in both FY 72 and FY 73, and though positive in FY 74 most public investment still had to be financed by domestic and foreign borrowing.

Inflation has been a serious problem. While prices were rising no more than 3 to 4 percent a year in the latter 1960s, between January 1972 and December 1973 prices rose about 20 percent annually. Partly because of strong fiscal and monetary actions from July 1973, however (and partly because of price controls that temporarily suppressed inflation), Pakistan has had a much slower rate of inflation in 1974. In fact, the wholesale price index shows average prices unchanged between December 1973 and May 1974 (a rather remarkable accomplishment in view of worldwide price trends), with higher petroleum and manufactured goods prices offset by declines in food and raw materials prices. The consumer price index shows a rise of about 5.5 percent over the same period. This period of stability was broken in June, however, as the government increased controlled prices of fertilizer, natural gas, vegetable ghee, sugar, kerosene, electricity, and railway fares to reflect increased costs of production. Moreover, the rate of expanding bank credit, which was only about 16 percent of FY 74, was more than 20 percent in FY 75.

Thus, the Pakistan economy is viable, but just how strong and how rapidly it will grow is still to be determined. The FY 75 Annual Development Plan called for a 7 percent growth rate, and the Fifth Plan is expected to call for at least a growth rate of 7 percent and possibly higher. Optimism about Pakistan's high growth potential, however, has been tempered by the continuing lag in savings and investment and overriding concerns about political problems that may limit economic initiatives. Most of the key economic policy issues of 1974 were also being discussed as major economic policy issues at the end of the 1960s. For example, most of the basic price distortion and tax structure problems of the 1960s remain, even though the export bonus system has been abolished and there have been great changes in many relative price relationships.

Economic Programs

The present government has adopted a large number of new programs (including some that resemble previous programs that had been abandoned prior to 1972) to carry out its program of "Islamic socialism" enunciated in the Pakistan People's Party *Election Manifesto* of 1970. These include the nationalization of all industries specifically cited in the *Manifesto* except textiles, extensive legislation to increase wages and improve job security and working conditions for private sector wage earners, programs to modernize the rural economy, and social service programs such as education, health, and housing. For many reasons, including lack of budget resources to dramatically increase expenditures, uncertainty about how to achieve the objectives of certain programs, and the inevitable social and cultural resistance to other changes, the impact of many of the programs to date has been limited. Some of the programs may never move much beyond the stage of concepts that affect the "style" in which a variety of activities are carried out. Nevertheless, their collective effect has already been substantial.

On January 2 and 16, 1972, the government nationalized thirty-one large firms in ten basic industries[5] and declared illegal the "managing agency" method of business organization under which owners with often less than 20 percent

5. Iron and steel, basic metals, heavy engineering, heavy chemicals, motor vehicle assembly and manufacture, tractor assembly and manufacture, heavy and basic chemicals, petrochemicals, cement, and public utilities.

of the equity had complete control of many enterprises.[6] Life Insurance firms also were nationalized. The vegetable ghee industry was nationalized in September 1973, and all commercial banks, retail petroleum distributors, and maritime shipping firms were nationalized on January 1, 1974.[7] That banks were not nationalized until two years after the present government assumed office reflected the judgment in early 1972 that the objectives of redirecting the flow of credit to small businessmen and farmers and other more "socially productive" purposes might better be achieved by regulation rather than by nationalization. Accordingly, under banking reforms announced in May 1972, the State Bank of Pakistan established rules reorienting the credit policy of banks in favor of wider dispersal of bank credit in respect to both size of accounts and sectors. The most striking result was a considerable flow of bank credit to small farmers in 1973. Similarly, bank loan officers went looking for small businessmen to whom they could make loans. At the same time, advances to large borrowers were curbed, and margin requirements against commodity loans were increased. In addition a People's Finance Corporation was established to serve craftsmen and extremely small businesses not likely to be reached by banks that had even the best of intentions.

A very large volume of labor legislation was passed in the first nine months of 1972. It included increased minimum wages; requirements that employers provide pension, education, health, and other benefits to workers and their families; job security provisions, including labor courts to which workers can appeal any dismissal; rights to form unions and

6. Strictly speaking, the thirty-one firms were not nationalized in January 1972, rather the government assumed management control and stockholders continued to own the companies and receive dividends. However, the government suspended stock market trading in the shares of these firms in September 1973 and is expected to reimburse their owners in fifteen-year negotiable bonds paying interest 1 percent above the Central Bank rate, or currently 10 percent.

7. Except for life insurance, foreign firms and shares were not nationalized in any of these actions.

engage in collective bargaining; and extensive safety provisions. Particularly in the Karachi area, the consequences for job security have been profound. Real wages of workers in many large establishments have been increased, although there are no adequate data to evaluate the effects on real wages of all employees.

The principal rural development programs to increase productivity and modernize the rural sector have been the People's Works Program (PWP), similar to the old Rural Works Program but including urban areas as well; an Integrated Rural Development Program (IRDP), with kinship to the former Village Aid Program, to mobilize farmers in local units to help bring adequate credit, inputs, know-how, and marketing opportunities to all farmers; an Agroville plan to develop small cities with close economic links to their agricultural hinterlands that would absorb excess rural labor and speed agricultural mechanization and modernization; and a relatively ineffective land reform that may have some long-run importance by improving the security and terms of farm tenancy.

A number of ambitious targets have been set for education, health, housing, transportation, and other social services and public utility programs that could play an important role in increasing the absolute and relative real incomes of lower-income groups. Because of limited financial capacity, however, most of these programs probably will either not meet their announced goals (for example, by 1980 to have all males and 70 percent of females of primary school age enrolled in schools) or will do so only by deterioration of the quality of the service. In health, the plans for clinics and hospitals proposed in the Third Plan have been revived, but neither the financial resources nor trained manpower are available to carry them out. Nevertheless, the resources flowing into these programs are increasing substantially in FY 75 and much is being accomplished. Importation of large numbers of buses and other measures have somewhat eased public transportation problems in Karachi and other urban areas. Water, electricity, and other public services have been improved in some urban slum areas, and plans are being made for such improvements in other locations. Rural electrification programs have been accelerated.

In an effort to help low-income regions, Annual Development Plan allocations for the two poorest provinces, Baluchistan and the Northwest Frontier, have been increased several fold and are now at least double the per capita level in the Punjab and Sind. Special efforts are also being made to speed development in the even poorer tribal areas and Azad Kashmir.

In another effort aimed at attacking the problems of low-income groups, the Bhutto government early focused its attention on consumption planning, particularly on eight essential items in low-income family budgets.[8] The government now has a list of eighteen key consumption items whose prices are surveyed and reported weekly in order to spot difficulties and to avoid or limit price increases by increasing supplies or taking whatever other actions are possible. Prices of wheat, flour, and sugar are controlled through government ration shops, and vegetable ghee and kerosene prices are controlled by law.

Economic Development Policy Issues

Some World Bank economists believe that Pakistan will be able to achieve an annual GDP growth of 7 to 8 percent and at the same time achieve a rapid expansion of social services and an improved distribution of income if it is successful in increasing savings and investment and can continue the expansion of its exports. Whether growth of

8. Wheat and flour, sugar, vegetable ghee, rice, cloth, kerosene, matches, and tea. The government estimated that in early 1973 these eight commodities accounted for 45 percent of the cost of living of those whose family incomes were less than Rs 300 per month. See Mubashir Hasan, *Budget Speech for 1973–74* (Islamabad: Government of Pakistan, 1973).

these key variables—savings, investment, and exports—is adequate to meet the government's growth and social objectives, however, will in turn depend upon the success of efforts to mobilize domestic budget and investment resources and to increase agricultural and industrial production. Going one step further, price distortions now discouraging production of such goods as cotton, livestock, and wheat, and resulting in open or hidden subsidies to urban consumers and producers of selected goods, may be the single most important factor in determining how much public sector savings and agricultural and industrial production can be increased. At the same time, additional tax revenue must come from agriculture and industry. For purposes of a reasonably brief and coherent presentation, in this chapter these questions are organized under the headings of domestic resource mobilization, technology, agricultural development, population and employment, and industrial development.

Domestic Resource Mobilization

The success of domestic resource mobilization programs will determine how rapidly investment can grow, how rapidly government programs such as health and education can expand, and how successfully inflation can be controlled. For former West Pakistan alone, savings have been estimated at 13.3 percent of GDP in 1969/70, but only 10.9 percent in 1973/74 (Table 5). Private savings in West Pakistan as a percentage of GDP are estimated to have fallen by about one-fourth, from 12.3 percent in 1969/70 to 9.1 percent in 1973/74. Public sector savings were negative in fiscal years 1972 and 1973, but positive in 1974.[9]

9. The absolute level and accuracy of these data are questionable, of course, but they are indicative of trends. As in most countries, domestic savings are derived as the difference between estimated investment and the current account deficit, excluding net factor income from abroad and current transfers. Public savings are estimated from government budgets, and private savings are estimated as the residual.

Problem of investment for growth

Future private sector savings will depend largely on the attractiveness of private investment and on the rates of interest available from deposits or securities of banks and other government-controlled organizations. The attractiveness of private investment in large-scale, highly visible enterprises has clearly been greatly reduced by the government's nationalization of many such enterprises as well as by legislation intended to raise real wages and strengthen the position of labor vis-à-vis management. A very limited and informal sampling of small manufacturing firms, on the other hand, suggests that this sector is doing quite well.

Bank interest rates were raised in March and again in August of 1973. Loan rates for large banks are now 11 percent and for small banks 12 percent, or 2 percent higher than previously. Interest rates on time and savings deposits have been increased by about the same or larger amounts, with savings deposits now paying 6 to 6.75 percent interest and time deposits 6.75 to 9 percent. The National Development Finance Corporation, established in 1973 as a development bank for public enterprises, offers 10 percent or more on deposits and securities, and the postal savings system pays 12 percent. Particularly with the slowing of inflation in recent months, these rates may prove increasingly attractive and maintain or increase the rate of private savings, or at least the rate of private savings as recorded in the national accounts and available to investors through financial intermediaries.[10]

Fiscal policy issues in domestic resource mobilization are most complex, but essentially they are the same as those of the previous decade. Central government revenues in FY 71 and FY 72 were lower than in FY 70. Current expenditures continued to rise without a pause, although capital ex-

---

10. Examples of unrecorded savings not available through financial intermediaries would include unrecorded investment in small industry and agriculture; capital flight through smuggling or underinvoicing of exports represents a loss of potential savings.

penditures dropped sharply.[11] The result was very large deficits in FY 71 through FY 73 that have played an important part in fueling inflation. In FY 74 a strenuous effort to control expenditures, plus taxation and appropriation by the government of much of the windfall profits of high international cotton and rice prices, sharply reduced the rate of increase in bank credit to the public sector. Unfortunately, the government appears headed for a renewal of bank borrowing this year, though not as great as in FY 1972 and 1973.

The only major change in the tax structure since the separation of the two wings has been the introduction of export duties. These were introduced at the time of the May 1972 devaluation when the export bonus scheme was abolished. Export duties were imposed on major agricultural exports both to limit the domestic increases in prices of such goods as cotton, cotton textiles, and rice, and to provide needed revenues to maintain levels of central government spending. The exporting of coarse rice and cotton became government monopolies in FY 74, giving the government additional means of controlling the margin between domestic and international prices. Export duties and monopoly profits on rice exports are estimated to have provided about 21 percent of the central government's net revenues in FY 74. In response to falling international prices and decreased exports of cotton yarn and cloth, however, export duties on these goods were eliminated in August 1974, and some other duties have been lowered. Consequently, export duties were a smaller portion of tax revenues in FY 75, and the government deficit rose.

The first post-separation budget, for FY 73, tried to make the income tax more meaningful by taxing non-wage employee benefits such as housing, abolishing the tax holiday,

11. Economic Advisor's Wing, Finance Division, *Pakistan Economic Survey 1973–74* (Islamabad: Government of Pakistan, 1973), Statistical Section, Tables 50, 51, and 52.

and abolishing the taxation distinction between registered and non-registered firms. The public outcry was so sharp, however, that the government retreated within a few weeks on all but the tax holiday. The income tax has now become even less effective either as a source of revenue or as a means of income distribution. The FY 75 budget was clearly aimed at tax relief for middle- and upper-income groups. The basic personal income exemption limit was raised from Rs 6,000 to Rs 9,000 per family in FY 74, and to Rs 12,000 in FY 75. When personal exemptions and earned income and other allowances are taken into account, no one with an income of less than Rs 16,000 to 18,000 (more than 98 percent of all families) will be subject to the tax, and by use of the investment allowance and exemptions on investment income those at much higher income levels need pay only very modest taxes. After some tightening in the FY 73 budget, tax concessions for inducing savings and investment have been retained or expanded in FY 74 and FY 75, probably more as a sop to middle- and upper-income groups than for any belief in their effectiveness.

Indirect taxes have increased steadily from 83 percent of tax revenues in FY 73 to 86 percent of FY 74. Aside from export duties, most of the rate increases have come in traditional areas such as tobacco and gasoline, with no significant change in degree of regressiveness. Indirect tax rates were not raised in FY 75 budget, but their share in tax revenues increased.

On the expenditure side, the government has been increasing Annual Development Plan (ADP) spending rapidly while trying to curb other expenditures. ADP expenditures in FY 70 were budgeted at Rs 5,305 million for all Pakistan, and actual expenditures in West Pakistan were estimated at Rs 3,350 million. FY 72 ADP budget expenditures for partitioned Pakistan amounted to only Rs 2,681 million, but by FY 74 they reached approximately Rs 6,113 million. For FY 75 the budget called for a further 39 percent increase, to Rs 8,500 million. After allowing for inflation, the real increase in ADP expenditures between FY 72 and FY 74 was probably about two-thirds. Between FY 73 (the first budget solely for present Pakistan) and FY 75, central government development expenditures were budgeted to more than double, while non-development expenditures were budgeted to rise only 50 percent. The present government has been saying that it will not repeat the old mistake of putting too much money into new capital expenditures at the expense of adequate operating funds, but the pressures and dangers are there.

Of total revenue expenditure (roughly current account expenditure), defense, internal security, interest payments, and subsidies amounted to 84 percent of FY 73 revenue expenditures and are budgeted at 85 percent of FY 75 totals. Of the remaining 15 percent of revenue expenditures, those for the so-called beneficent departments[12] have been rising faster than the total, but these departments accounted for only 2.4 percent of total revenue expenditures in FY 73 and 2.6 percent in the FY 75 budget. The balance went to general administration (5 percent of the FY 75 budget), grants to provinces (2.6 percent of thé FY 75 budget), civil works, pensions, and other uses.

When one looks for places to cut revenue expenditures, reductions in defense, internal security, and interest payment categories seem unlikely. The FY 75 budget already reflects a reduction in external interest payments as a result of agreements with foreign debtors about the transfer of some project debts to Bangladesh and a rescheduling of other debt. Internal interest payments, however, were budgeted to rise by more than 40 percent between FY 73 and FY 75. Defense expenditures are a favorite of economists for cutting, and their reduction would obviously be de-

12. Science, education, health, agriculture and fisheries, industries, aviation, broadcasting, and investment promotions and supplies.

Table 8. *Pakistan: Central Government Tax Revenues (Millions of Rupees)*

	1972/73 Actuals	1973/74 Revised estimates	1974/75 Without tax changes	1974/75 With tax changes*
Direct Taxes	**1,162.5**	**1,205.9**	**1,211.4**	**1,106.2**
Income Tax	(1,120.7)	(1,152.5)	(1,152.7)	(1,047.7)
Individual Income Tax	851.8	870.0	870.0	..
Corporation Tax	250.0	265.0	265.0	..
Income Taxes under MLRs	18.9	15.0	15.0	..
Workers' Welfare Tax	—	2.5	2.7	(58.5)
Property Tax	(41.8)	(53.4)	(58.7)	6.1
Estate Duty	..	6.0	6.2	44.9
Wealth Tax	..	40.0	45.0	7.5
Gift Tax	..	7.4	7.5	8,558.1
Indirect Taxes	**5,604.2**	**7,623.5**	**9,506.3**	
Customs Duties	(2,643.9)	(3,907.0)	(5,937.6)	(4,992.6)
Export Taxes	..	1,678.0	3,347.6	2,427.6
Import Taxes	..	2,199.0	2,550.0	2,525.0
Miscellaneous	(460.6)	30.0	40.0	40.0
Sales Tax		(650.0)	(700.0)	(696.8)
On Imports		450.0	480.0	..
On Domestic Production		200.0	220.0	

Central Excise Duties	(2,265.1)	(2,765.7)	(3,000.0)	(3,000.0)
Capacity Tax	..	727.4	850.0	..
Production Tax	..	2,038.3	2,150.0	..
Surcharges	(234.6)	(300.8)	(−131.3)	(−131.3)
Surcharge on Cement	15.8	17.6	18.4	..
Price Equilization Surcharge	18.5	20.0	20.0	..
Surcharge on Natural Gas	16.1	32.6	36.5	..
Surcharge on Petroleum	168.6	22.9	−531.1	..
Surcharge on Fertilizers	15.6	207.7	324.9	..
Total Tax Revenues (gross)	6,766.7	8,829.4	10,717.7	9,664.3
Less: Provincial Share	−873.6	−882.1	−1,254.5	−1,254.5
Less: Payments to Azad Kashmir Govt.	—	−25.0	−25.0	−25.0
Net Tax Revenues	5,893.1	7,922.3	9,438.2	8,384.8

* Effects of price adjustments on Government tax collections are not known. Increase in price of natural gas by 50 per cent for "domestic consumers" is expected to increase revenue receipts from excise duties on natural gas by Rs 100 million.

sirable on a number of grounds. Some reduction has been made in the proportion of resources going to defense, from 58 percent of revenue expenditures and 8 percent of GDP in FY 72 to 48 percent of revenue expenditures in FY 75 and 6.6 percent of GDP in FY 74.

The only other potential area for expenditure cuts is in budget subsidies. These are estimated to have been at least Rs 2,500 million in FY 74, or about 23 percent of total revenue expenditure (Table 9).[13] The FY 75 subsidy level was somewhat smaller, primarily because of a decline in wheat imports. The domestic price of fertilizer has been increased about 270 percent in the last two years in order to reduce the fertilizer subsidy, but the cost of this subsidy has continued to rise because of international fertilizer prices and increased consumption. Partly because of the rise in fertilizer prices, the government announced that procurement prices for the spring 1975 wheat crop would be nearly 50 percent higher than 1974, and about 120 percent higher than 1971. Budgetary and inflationary pressures required that ration shop wheat flour (*atta*) prices be raised correspondingly by the summer of 1975 in order to prevent the subsidy to consumers from increasing. This, in turn, was accompanied by a decree raising wages of both public and private sector employees sufficiently to offset the higher cost of wheat in low- and middle-income family budgets. This sequence was similar to the July–August 1973 price-wage adjustment package (discussed in the following section on agricultural development).

The only other fundamental direction for improvement of the budget position lies in higher revenues. Here the greatest potential lies in increased taxation of agriculture (including higher water charges) and in higher prices and profits for government enterprises. The quantitatively most

---

13. Table 4 includes only "non-developmental" or consumer subsidies, primarily on wheat and vegetable oil. "Developmental" revenue expenditure subsidies to producers apply to fertilizer, pesticides, tubewells, and seeds.

Table 9. *Pakistan: Central Government Non-development Revenue Expenditures (In millions of Rupees)*

	1972/73 actuals	1973/74 revised estimates	1974/75 budget estimates*	Change in 1974/75 over 1973/74
Defense	4,440	4,742	5,579	+ 837
Internal Security[1]	233	390	458	+ 68
Interest Payments	1,171	1,539	1,617	+ 78
Internal	(604)	(738)	(866)	(+ 128)
External	(567)	(801)	(751)	(− 50)
Subsidies	−[3]	2,185	1,191	− 994
Imported Wheat		(1,584)	(347)	(−1,237)
Domestic Wheat		(93)	(228)	(+ 135)
Edible Oil		(269)	(468)	(+ 199)
Others		(240)	(148)	(− 92)
Sub-total	*5,844*	*8,856*	*8,845*	*− 11*
General Administration[2]	458	498	578	+ 80
Beneficent Departments	178	273	309	+ 36
Scientific Departments	(65)	(136)	(120)	
Education	(19)	(40)	(59)	
Health	(34)	(49)	(65)	
Agriculture and Fisheries	(11)	(9)	(14)	
Industries	(4)	−[5]	(4)	
Aviation	(22)	(34)	(40)	
Broadcasting	(15)	−	−	
Investment Promotion & Supplies	(6)	(6)	(7)	
Civil Works	88	52	62	+ 10
Pensions	28	38	38	0
Grants to Provinces	50	254	304	+ 50
Miscellaneous	349	216	277	+ 61
Sub-total	*1,151*	*1,331*	*1,568*	*+ 237*
Non-Development Revenue Expenditure[4]	*6,995*	*10,187*	*10,413*	*+ 226*

1. Most of the expenditures are for maintaining security in remote areas.
2. Includes expenditures on 'direct demands on revenue' and administrative departments.
3. Figures not available.
4. Excluding appropriation for reduction and avoidance of debt (Rs. 128 million for 1972/73, Rs. 585 million for 1973/74 and Rs. 444 million for 1974/75).
5. Excluding expenditures of the Associated Cement, Rs. 120 million.
* These expenditure estimates do not take into account effects of the Government decisions to grant dearness allowances to employees at the rate of 10 percent of their annual salary and to increase their pension rates.

important problem has been the steady decline in the level of land revenue and water taxes. At current levels water is sold for much less than either its marginal cost or its marginal benefit to most farmers. The economically proper levels of water charges and land revenue taxes are complex questions, but clearly the fees are now too low. An agricultural income tax is also clearly desirable on economic grounds, probably on presumptive income as an adaptation of the land revenue tax. The greatest political obstacle to substantially higher taxation of agriculture, or reduction in subsidies to agricultural inputs, however, is that they must lead to higher prices for agricultural products, and therefore higher urban prices for foodstuffs, textiles, and other goods.

The pricing policy of public enterprises is of prime importance now that the government controls perhaps 20 percent of industrial assets plus most public utilities and major transport systems. Most government-owned industrial enterprises have been organized into ten or more major holding companies, each controlling a major industry or industrial sector, such as the Light Engineering Corporation, the Fertilizer Corporation, the Cement Corporation, the Automobile Corporation, etc. The proposal for establishing these enterprises calls for their operation on an efficient and commercially sound basis. This might well mean operating on some modest rate of return on equity, though probably substantially below the marginal value of capital. Pricing to yield returns closer to the economic value of capital could produce a substantially higher rate of public sector savings and investment, and of economic growth.

Technology

The desirability of intermediate technology has become almost a part of the conventional wisdom in Pakistan. One of the fundamental arguments in favor of devaluation was that it would permit development of Pakistan's capital goods industry. This, in turn, was expected to result in greater economic efficiency, increased employment, and improved income distribution—all as consequences of using equipment and production processes designed in Pakistan. Such designs would tend to take into account the relative availability and costs of labor, capital, and added inputs, along with maintenance, weather, and other considerations. The minister of finance, an engineer by training, has taken a special interest in this topic and has encouraged such diverse and productive directions as construction techniques, small hydroelectric units to harness mountain streams, and a "barefoot doctor" paramedical program. The Ministry of Production, in addition to various public enterprises, also have been working in this area. Many public enterprises have dealt with their own problems, but others have undertaken design of a wide variety of small-scale equipment, such as small tractors, improved raw-sugar-making equipment, small edible oil processing equipment, etc. The Pakistan Council for Scientific and Industrial Research has long done work in this area, although with relatively little commercial adoption to show for its efforts.

In February 1974 the National Assembly approved two new design and engineering organizations to increase Pakistan's design and engineering capacity. One, the National Design and Engineering Corporation, is planned as a design center both to develop indigenous technology and to advise on the purchase of appropriate foreign know-how. Its functions include converting older concepts and designs into modernized intermediate technology, and improving upon locally developed production processes. The other new organization is the National Engineering Laboratory, which is intended to be a hardware-oriented institution. It will design or produce individual pieces of equipment for manufacturers and assist existing capital-goods and other engineering firms in their engineering needs.

This emphasis on reexamining technology and on making efficient use of labor and capital is an environmental factor that has relevance to other developmental issues. As yet, it is still in the air rather than an embodied technology, but it is

having an effect on thinking and decision-making. One technological question that has attracted considerable attention
is whether Pakistan should seek to meet its needs for additional farm power primarily through standard (35–55 horse-
power) tractors, or through much smaller tillage and power
units. Other questions include the appropriate size and technological process for agricultural product processing mills
(rice, sugar, vegetable oil, flour, cotton ginning, and textile
mills). Smaller and more labor-intensive mills (relative to imported design and equipment) reduce transport costs and increase marketing opportunities for farmers, economize on
capital by utilizing redundant labor, and reduce migration to
the cities. It is not enough to reduce the scale of foreign-
designed equipment or to utilize insufficient older processes.
Traditional labor-intensive and small-scale oil-seed-pressing
equipment, for example, recovers between 60 and 70 percent
of the oil from the seeds. Modern large-scale solvent extraction processes are capital intensive, but extract more than 95
percent of the oil. Because of the social, transport, and other
costs of having only a few such mills imported, greater
benefits would be derived if a mill could be designed to get
an extraction rate close to those of large foreign mills but
costing far less in foreign exchange, employing more labor,
and small enough to be put in many locations. The same
applies to the extraction of the juice of sugar cane, and in
this case designs are under study for technically efficient mills
with crushing capacities as low as 100 tons of cane per day.

Agricultural Development

Agriculture contributes more than 35 percent of Pakistan's
GDP and employs more than 55 percent of the labor force,
and agricultural products and their manufactures account for
more than 80 percent of exports. The limited availability of
water and concomitant salinity problems (reflecting water
shortages in some instances and/or lack of drainage in others)
are probably the most serious limitations on agricultural

productivity. The other overriding problem is that of various government controls on prices of output, such as procurement prices, export duties, and export restrictions. Many of the other problems, such as untimely and poor cultivation practices, poor seed, and inadequate use of fertilizers and pesticides, would be helped by improvement of water and salinity conditions and by letting farm prices more nearly reflect free market levels. Increased availability of credit to small farmers to purchase fertilizer and other inputs, increased availability of needed inputs, and increased supplies of on-farm power (electricity, tractors, machinery, improved bullock instruments, etc.) are other frequently proposed means to increase farm output.

Investment in improved irrigation and drainage facilities and in combating salinity must be substantial. The government has proposed more than $1 billion (at 1973 prices) in irrigation, drainage, and flood control expenditures for FY 75–79, of which the waterlogging and salinity control components are about $320 million. Work on some obviously beneficial programs can begin quickly, but there are also policy questions to be answered as soon as possible. These include the balance to be struck between private and public tubewell development, the integration of tubewell and surface supplies, including decisions about the use of Tarbela water, and the relative emphasis between major works (drainage, canal rehabilitation, new canals) and programs for improvement of small water-course and on-farm water management.

Export duties and bans and the government monopoly of raw cotton and rice exports have kept domestic prices of many agricultural commodities far below world market levels. To use cotton as an example, in FY 71 cotton exports were transferred from the non-bonus to the 10 percent export bonus list, raising the exchange rate for its export from Rs 4.76 per dollar to about Rs 5.7 per dollar. At the time of the May 1972 devaluation, raw cotton was one of ten commodities on which export duties were imposed.[14] The export duty on raw cotton was set at 35 percent, giving exporters Rs 7.15 per dollar, rather than the official rate of Rs 11 per dollar. In September the export duty on raw cotton was raised to 40 percent (6.6 per dollar). Devaluation of the dollar in February 1973 lowered the exchange rate by 10 percent to Rs 9.9 per dollar, thereby lowering the price of cotton exports to about Rs 5.9 per dollar. In June 1973 the export duty on raw cotton was raised to 45 percent plus an additional 30 percent on any excess of the price over Rs 1,500 per bale. As a result, the average exchange rate on raw cotton exports in FY 74 was only about Rs 4.6 per dollar. Because of export duties on rice and its monopoly of rice exports, the government received about 75 percent of the price of Basmati rice exports and about 72 percent of the price of coarse rice exports in FY 74, implying an exchange rate of about Rs 2.7 per dollar.[15]

Despite these heavy rates of taxation, farm prices of cotton and rice have risen. The average price received by farmers per maund of seed cotton rose from about Rs 50 in FY 72 to Rs 60 in FY 73 and Rs 90 in FY 74. The government procurement price for Basmati rice was raised from Rs 46 per maund of rice in FY 73 to Rs 62 in FY 74, and has been set at Rs 90 in FY 75. Many farmers received lower prices for non-Basmati rice varieties in FY 74 than in FY 73 following the imposition of a government monopoly on the export of these other rice varieties. For FY 75, however, they will receive a 50 percent higher price for sales to the government.

Aside from its great need for revenues, the government's primary dilemma with agricultural prices is between letting farm prices rise higher to encourage production (which

14. Ad valorem or specific export duties were also imposed on cotton waste, cotton yarn, and gray cloth (at decreasing levels), raw hides and skins, semi-tanned and tanned hides and skins, rice, oil cakes, and raw wool. Relatively minor additions of similar products have subsequently been made.

15. Compared with an official rate since devaluation of the dollar in February 1973 of Rs 9.9 per dollar.

would increase both rural and urban production and employment) and limiting farm price increases in order to hold down increases in the cost of living. Lower farm prices also help reduce the government deficit by providing greater potential and actual government revenues from export duties (and monopoly profits on rice and cotton), and by reducing government expenditures to subsidize the sale of wheat through ration shops. The procurement price of wheat has risen from Rs 17 per maund in FY 72 to Rs 25.5 in FY 74. Retail ration shop *atta* prices are equal to the procurement price plus the fee paid for milling, with the government absorbing all handling and distribution costs. At Rs 25.5 per maund, farmers have been receiving the rupee equivalent of about $69 per ton, while nearly half of the FY 74 ration shop supply has been imported at prices near $200 per ton. Thus the government has been paying higher prices to American and Canadian wheat farmers than to Pakistani farmers. Moreover, that difference has been a drain on scarce budget resources, since all imported wheat has been bought for cash or on credits not exceeding three years and sold through ration shops at the same subsidized price as domestic wheat.

The government has taken action to raise controlled agricultural input and product prices closer to market levels, but with the exception of fertilizer most increases have brought them to a level much lower than world or free market prices. In July 1973, as part of a larger fiscal and monetary tightening effort, the government adopted a price-wage adjustment package that provided for increased prices of *atta* and sugar at government ration shops and set a ceiling on vegetable ghee prices that was about 20 percent higher than prices existing as recently as one month earlier (to prevent yet larger increases). Government procurement prices for wheat and rice were also raised at that time, and the price of fertilizer was increased for the third time in twelve months, to about double 1972 levels. The government also decreed that wages for all private as well as government employees earning less than Rs 700 per month were to be increased by Rs 35 per month in order to offset the cost-of-living increase for the average worker because of higher prices.

The government has also adopted a number of new programs and policies to help agriculture. Reference has already been made to the Integrated Rural Development Program (IRDP), the People's Works Program (PWP), and land reform. Another potentially important idea is for the expansion of numerous market towns or other centers into more truly urban centers (so-called Agrovilles) with manufacturing and other enterprises. To date, however, these programs have had no significant effect on development. Rather, they represent institutional initiatives that *may* eventually produce important changes.

The IRDP, along with the development of Agrovilles, is the vehicle by which the government hopes to create or modernize the countryside. The plan anticipates greatly increased productivity per farm worker and thriving local towns based on industrial and service activity. Much of the urban activity would center on the provision of agricultural production inputs, equipment repair and maintenance, consumer goods and services to farmers, and on processing and manufacturing based on local agricultural products. Implementation of both programs, however, is the responsibility of the provincial governments, with the central government developing guidelines and models and urging action. Thus, the character of the programs and the extent of their implementation vary between provinces.[16]

16. The two chief IRDP projects to date are at Shadab, near Lahore, and at Daudzai, near Peshawar. Shadab was planned by the central government and IRDP officials use it as a showplace to illustrate their ideas. As such, it serves an important function, but it suffers both from having been established without grassroots planning and over powerful opposition within other departments of the Punjab government. Daudzai, a pilot project of the Rural Academy at Peshawar, is following the Comilla pattern of putting emphasis first on those things the villagers feel they most want (often a road, a drainage ditch, or anti-erosion measures), organizing them into cooperative groups to do these things, while also introducing other elements of the rural development program.

The overall concept of the IRDP is a good one. Increasing agricultural productivity is the basic goal, but it is essentially concerned with achieving higher levels of education, health, and improving the general aspects of rural life. It is a system to integrate all productivity and income-raising service to agriculture, i.e., extension services, credit, inputs, and marketing; to integrate government programs at the local level, i.e., Agriculture, Public Works, Social Services, Water and Power Development Authority; and to organize the villagers into associations or cooperatives that will be integrated with the rest of the economy. Initially, the program also called for a system of elected local government below the district level, but this idea has been postponed with no early action likely.[17]

The People's Works Program is an employment and civil works program patterned after the Rural Works Program of the 1960s, although some urban projects are also being undertaken. Its economic objective is to mobilize unemployed labor for productive local work such as construction of rural roads, schools, housing, etc. Political and social goals involving government initiative and the building of morale and cooperative experience are equally important.

The March 1972 land reform has had only marginal impact on the pattern of landholding and little short-run effect on development. Under its provisions, irrigated holdings of more than 150 acres per owner, and dryland holdings of more than three hundred acres per owner, must be surrendered

17. The unit for implementation of the IRDP is the *markaz* (plural *marakaz*), a name applied both to the total area of each project, usually encompassing about fifty to sixty villages in an area of one hundred square miles or less, and to the *markaz* center where the government offices, marketing, credit, and other facilities are located. A tractor and equipment rental pool is also operating at Shadab and is planned for other *marakaz*. Each project has a project leader, and the central government model calls for officials of other government departments in that *markaz* to work at his direction. This has been a visible source of tension in the Punjab, but less so in other areas. Lack of cooperation between officials of different ministries was, of course, a major weakness and caused the failure of the Village Aid Program. Officials have studied that experience to avoid the development of such problems in the IRDP.

to the state without compensation for redistribution to land-less and small farmers. These reforms compare with limits of five hundred and one thousand acres per owner in the 1959 land reform. Since the limits are on an individual owner basis, however, effective household ownership of much larger areas is common. The parcelling out of land to wives, children, and other close relatives had already occurred in anticipation of such a reform, and much of the land taken over was of relatively little value. Perhaps more important, particularly for the long run, are provisions in the land reform requiring landlords to pay all taxes and water rents and half the costs of fertilizer, seeds, and other inputs. The landlord's share of the crop is limited to 50 percent, and tenants cannot be evicted as long as they till the land and pay their rents. Tenants are also given first rights to the purchase of the land they cultivate. Enforcement of these regulations has been difficult, however. Only a handful of formal actions against landlords have been brought to court, though complaints about continuing evictions, excessive rents, and other landlord violations of the reform's provisions are numerous. Nevertheless, the law has strengthened the psychological position of tenants and made many landlords more cautious about removing or exploiting them.

Population and Employment[18]

The census of September 1972 showed a raw annual population growth rate of 3.5 percent during the years since the 1961 census. Adjusted for estimated differences in degrees of underenumeration in the two censuses, the actual growth rate may have been no more than 3.2 percent annually. Still, this is one of the highest growth rates of any large country and has been accelerating as death rates have been falling while birth rates have shown no change. As a consequence,

18. This section draws heavily on unpublished memoranda and some of the writings of Ralph Hofmeister of the World Bank.

45 percent of the population is under fifteen years of age, and through 1990 the labor force growth rate will probably amount to 3.3 percent or more annually, with the chief variables in its fluctuation being the age of entry into the labor force (depending particularly upon levels of education) and how large a proportion of women join the work force.

Growth of the labor force at the present rate presents a serious challenge to a country in which gross underemployment is extensive. While open unemployment is estimated at only 2 percent, underemployment is estimated at perhaps 20 percent.[19] Given the magnitude of the problem, significant reductions in underemployment will require a labor-intensive growth strategy, i.e., one that provides rapidly rising levels of productive employment. Furthermore, between at least the middle years of the Third Plan (1967–69) and FY 72, it appears that the percentage of employment in agriculture rose substantially while that in industry fell, reversing previous trends. However, this may have been a temporary phenomenon reflecting industrial stagnation and political uncertainty during the period.

With the labor supply growing at more than 3 percent annually, it would appear that productive employment in agriculture will need to grow by at least 2 percent annually if underemployment is not to increase. To realize a 3 to 4 percent increase in output per worker, agricultural production must rise by 5 to 6 percent annually. Such a rate of growth seems possible, but calls for at least four policy actions. First, there is the need to increase the efficiency of use of existing water supplies and of the additional water made available by the Tarbela dam.[20] Second, export markets

19. This underemployment is obvious in the high proportion of self-employed and unpaid family workers in retail trades (over 80 percent) and in the numbers of tea pourers and door openers (*chaprasi*) in government and private offices; it is also obvious in at least seasonal underemployment in agriculture.

20. Damage occurring at the attempted closing of the dam in August 1974 was expected to delay the availability of significant additional water supplies from Tarbela at least until the end of 1975.

must be aggressively sought for fruits, vegetables, meat, and other high-value agricultural products. Third, cropping patterns need to be shifted toward more intensive cultivation, something which is consistent with trends in domestic demand. And fourth, a mechanization policy should be followed consistent with both cropping and labor intensity.

With per capita incomes expected to rise by perhaps 3 to 4 percent annually, demand for non-cereal foodstuffs will increase rapidly. Milk and milk products now comprise about one-fourth of household expenditures on food, and the income elasticity of demand is about one for all income groups.[21] Consumption of meat and eggs is at low levels, but the income elasticity of demand is extremely high. The elasticity of domestic demand for both cotton cloth and fruits and vegetables are likely to be at least near one, and each also has good export prospects. Each of these crops is more labor-intensive than cereal cultivation. Self-sufficiency in grains is a reasonable and rational goal for Pakistan, but once achieved further domestic growth is likely to be only about 4 percent annually. More rapid growth of these other agricultural products offers more rapid growth of value of output, while it is also more consistent with the growth of the agricultural labor force by 2 percent or more annually.

At a 2 percent growth rate the agricultural labor force would increase by two-thirds by the year 2000, or by 90 percent at a 2.5 percent growth rate. While some gradual tapering off in growth of agricultural employment may be likely, and some modest increase in agricultural land area may be possible, the intensity of labor to land use will have to rise much more rapidly than this rate in many areas because some low-rainfall areas will not be able to productively employ much additional labor. Thus a cotton-wheat double cropping pattern, the objective of much planning and ex-

21. Statistical Division, Ministry of Finance, Planning and Development, *Household Income and Expenditure Survey 1970–71* (Karachi: Government of Pakistan Press, n.d.).

pected to be achieved in much of the irrigated areas of the Punjab by additional tractors and other mechanization, is not an adequate solution to the demand for more labor-intensive and high-valued production.

Mechanization is also related to questions of ownership of the new equipment and to land-tenure issues as well as to the cropping pattern and labor-intensity. There is considerable evidence that the introduction of tractors (which now cultivate perhaps 10 percent of the annually cropped area) has led to increasing farm size and to the displacement of substantial numbers of tenants. Driving people off the land and into cities, or converting them into landless rural labor, adds to underemployment and social pressures. Yet most agriculturalists believe the number of tractors must be increased in order to make more efficient use of existing and prospective Tarbela water. The best answer to this dilemma lies in arrangements that place most of the new tractors in either government hire-rental pools or with private individuals who will use them for hire service. Efforts should be made to regulate their use by large landowners, and only under conditions in which tenants are not displaced. Granted, such provisions are likely to be difficult to establish initially or to police thereafter.

There are other avenues to explore in relieving the shortage of farm power at key periods (particularly at the spring wheat harvest and cotton planting). It should be possible to provide simple human or electric threshing equipment to free bullocks for cultivation. Electric or diesel power for other non-cultivation jobs is also possible. Improved bullock implements to reduce the time required and/or improve the quality of bullock cultivation is another avenue that holds considerable promise; it is probably the minimal capital-cost means of increasing effective farm power. Since bullocks now perform 90 percent of the cultivation, they are going to be in widespread use, particularly by small farmers, for many years to come. The "fractional-technology" approach to less capital-intensive mechanization for small farmers is another possibility on which extensive research is needed.[22]

In industry, provision for more rapid expansion of productive employment calls as much as possible for the development of labor-intensive small- and medium-scale production. Since enterprises of this size also appear to offer much of the potential for manufacturing employment in rural areas and small cities, they may also be the minimum capital-cost means of providing necessary housing and urban infrastructure for the growth of the non-farm population. This subject will be explored in the following analysis of industry.

Industrial Development

Reference has already been made to the nationalization of most large-scale manufacturing firms, labor legislation increasing worker job security and wages, and strengthening of the position of labor versus management. The three key developmental issues would appear to be the efficiency of operations and policies of nationalized industries, government policies toward the private sector, and policies to develop small industry. There are indications that the authorities want government enterprises operated efficiently and economically. One significant indication is the recruitment of much of the best private managerial talent to lead government enterprises. For example, the senior vice president of the Habib Bank at the time of its nationalization is now chairman of the Pakistan Banking Council (a policy committee made up primarily of the managers of the nationalized commercial banks). The former managing director of the same bank is now head of the public Mineral Development Corporation. The members of the Board of Industrial Management, (other than the minister of produc-

---

22. See, for example, Javed Hamid, "Agricultural Mechanization: A Case for Fractional Technology," *Pakistan Economic and Social Review.* X, No. 2 (Dec. 1972), 135–65; reprinted in *Teaching Forum.* No. 33 (New York: Agricultural Development Council, Inc., Sept. 1973).

tion) were all leading professional business managers. The chairman of the National Development Finance Corporation, which has been established as an investment bank for government enterprise, is the former manager of the First National City Bank's Lahore branch. The new National Design and Engineering Corporation is headed by Pakistan's leading chemical and industrial consultant. The Pakistan Fertilizer Corporation is headed by the former chairman of Packages Limited.

The reorganization of most government enterprises (both those recently nationalized and former government enterprises such as components of the Pakistan Industrial Development Corporation) into industry-wide holding companies with the objectives of increased efficiency, economic rationalization, and sound commercial operation bodes well for the efficient operation of these firms. An unanswered question, however, is whether outstanding management and good policies at the top can produce or maintain efficient operation of large enterprises when all employees have the high degree of job security of government employees.

Those in the remaining large- and medium-scale private sector enterprises continue to be hesitant about government intentions and policies. Though public assurances were given by the minister of finance that the program of nationalization was completed on January 1, 1974, small agro-industries were nationalized in July 1976. A more widespread fear is that the government will skim off much of the potential profit of remaining private enterprise through wage and labor policies, taxes, price controls, or other means.

Informal and random contacts with small-scale manufacturers, on the other hand, suggest that at least this portion of the private sector is healthy. This is a sector over which the government has very little statistical or other surveillance. For this reason, such industry is undoubtedly attractive for investment because it is least likely to attract attention for nationalization or other official intervention. In fact, the government has credit and other programs to help support such firms.

Pakistan already has an extensive and able small-scale engineering goods and metal-fabricating industry. The most extensive and best-known center is a triangular area including Lahore, Daska, Gujranwala, and Sialkot. However, similar firms may be found in Lyallpur (now the textile loom manufacturing center), Multan, Karachi, and elsewhere, including the famous rifle factories in the Northwest Frontier. These firms have the advantage of being self-generating and self-sufficient, serving local needs with local skills (often developed through generations) that might not otherwise be utilized. The skill of the craftsmen is superb. Their biggest problems are lack of knowledge of alternative designs, the rudimentary nature of quality control and material standards, and the lack of standardization of components and end products.

Two aspects of industrial development appear to be of special importance and potential for Pakistan at this time. One is the development of indigenous technology, the other the development of small- and medium-scale private manufacturing, particularly but not exclusively outside the major cities. Mention has already been made of the boost given to domestic capital equipment production by devaluation and of the psychologically favorable environment for development of domestic designs and production processes. Now that devaluation has removed the tremendous price advantage of imported equipment under the previous multiple exchange-rate system, local producers are providing looms, farm implements, and many other types of capital equipment at prices one-half or less than those of similar imported items.

To multiply the successful number of small manufacturing firms, and to upgrade small firms through the development of more sophisticated products and techniques, it is important that present rural artisans and small manufacturers have access to credit, raw materials and equipment, electricity, training in managerial and technical skills, and knowledge of design and more modern engineering. This is not to suggest that every artisan evolve into a small-factory producer, or that every small factory should become large. However, labor force survey data show that 55 percent of manufacturing employment, or about 1.3 million persons so employed, live in rural areas, or towns and villages of less than five thousand persons. About 80 percent of this force are self-employed or unpaid family workers, i.e., carpenters, blacksmiths, weavers, potters, and shoemakers. The remaining 20 percent are employed in generally small enterprises. These people represent an invaluable pool of skilled producers who (with technical, financial, or other assistance) can become the basis for widely dispersed local manufacturing, auto and tractor servicing, and other industries.

Economic Prospects

Pakistan has the potential for rapid expansion of agricultural and industrial production. Human resources are the nation's greatest asset. It has a hard-working and talented population, widespread entrepreneurial talent, and highly educated and sophisticated elite groups. Since Pakistani industry (other than metals and engineering goods) is largely based on domestic raw materials, success in raising agricultural productivity will largely determine success in raising national income levels. Export potential of both industry and agriculture appear to be substantial. Factors limiting growth include the high cost of required water and drainage investments, the fears of the private sector, internal political and social tensions, the inelasticity of government revenues, the low levels of savings and investment, and the high level of defense expenditures. Translating these factors into a global estimate, a 7 percent GDP growth rate is a reasonable forecast.

Political and social factors appear to be the fundamental restraints on growth. They tend to limit the amount of private and public savings as well as investment. Incentives to private savings and investment, the ability to collect government revenues, and the organizational capacity to carry out initiatives for increasing agricultural productivity and exports are economic reflections of political and social factors.*

* *Editors' Note:* An important illustration of how socio-political factors influence economic development was Bhutto's signing of a "Peasant's Charter" on December 18, 1976, which supposedly grants all state lands to their cultivators.

8

Labor Force Structure and Change in Pakistan: A Demographic Interpretation

Lee L. Bean

A difficult problem with far reaching economic, social and human consequences confronting the country [Pakistan] at present is that of unemployment. Unemployment represents a wastage of productive power which adversely affects the whole gamut of human life and outlook creating a sense of frustration. The magnitude of the present unemployment is to a considerable extent the consequence of capital intensive mode of development in the past. To overcome the shortcomings of past planning it has been decided to treat employment as the primary goal of economic development and an essential criterion in assessing the viability of projects and programmes.[1]

The introductory statement from the Government of Pakistan's 1972–73 economic survey continues and strengthens a verbal commitment to a program supported in principle from the earliest stages of formal economic planning in Pakistan. The commitment to full employment has been an explicit goal and remains so, but the ideal and reality remain far apart.

Provision of full employment for a growing labor force is a difficult and complex task that will not yield to simple solutions. Any successful program is more likely to emerge

1. Government of Pakistant, *Pakistan Economic Survey 1972–73* (Islamabad: Finance Division, Economic Advisor's Wing, 197?), pp. 119–20.

from a full rather than from an incomplete understanding of the scope of the problem at hand. It can be argued, for example, that the lack of success in providing full employment for a growing labor force in Pakistan partially arises from piecemeal planning efforts based upon incomplete and inaccurate data related to the scope of the problem.[2] It can also be argued that attributing the unemployment problem to a particular mode of economic planning or a particular mode of social and economic organization leads to oversimplified perceptions of the causes underlying the problem. The quotation above, for example, gives too much emphasis to the "consequences of capital intensive mode of development" relative to other factors. Bhagwat's argument in his paper, "Main Features of the Employment Problem in Developing Countries," illustrates the point:

> Our survey of the employment problem in the developing countries indicates that it can be thought of, from the point of view of devising ameliorative policies, as having three aspects, which concern population growth, open unemployment, and widespread low-productivity utilization of labor in the traditional sector. Usually the population issue is posed as a Malthusian food scarcity issue, or more recently as an ecological issue at the global level. In fact, it is no less important as an employment issue. The prevailing high rates of growth of the labor force in the developing countries are historically unprecedented and create the difficult challenge of productively absorbing this labor into the economic system.[3]

Even with the limited data available on the labor force and employment in Pakistan, it is important to consider approaches to the problem that in conjunction with other studies

2. For a comprehensive statement of the issues involved in employment planning in Pakistan, see F. G. Seib, "Manpower Planning in Pakistan," unpublished paper presented at the seminar on "Population Problems in the Economic Development of Pakistan," Pakistan Institute of Development Economics, Karachi, 1967. This statement was prepared by Seib, then director of the ILO manpower planning group in Pakistan, as a proposal involving a number of agencies in the collection and analysis of materials related to the overall program. The plan, however, was never implemented.

3. Avinash Bhagwat, "Main Features of the Employment Problem in Developing Countries," *International Monetary Fund Staff Papers*, XX, No. 1 (1973), 97.

may result in a somewhat more comprehensive assessment of the employment problems in Pakistan. Therefore, in this chapter, we approach the study of employment problems in Pakistan from a point of view designed to specify at the broadest level the basic structure of the potential labor force relative to the total population of Pakistan. The chapter focuses on the demographic characteristics and conditions that influence the growth and structure of the actual and "potential labor force."[4] In part, this analysis must be historical because the demographic conditions underlying the employment generation problem in Pakistan are conditions that existed roughly ten to fifteen years previously. Events prior to that time shape and structure the crude demographic parameters of the labor force. The chapter also deals with the future, because over the next ten to fifteen years current demographic conditions in Pakistan will set the framework within which are identified the dimensions of the "potential labor force" for which employment must be provided if the goal of full employment is to be met.

Whether dealing with historical conditions or future trends as they affect the labor force in Pakistan, we face a problem of speculation. The quality of population data were and are less accurate than one would like. Employment data are particularly meager and somewhat suspect. Indeed, the quality of labor force data is such that one may be led to suspect the sincerity of the government regarding the importance of employment problems. Only limited resources are invested in improving labor force data relative to resources invested in collecting, analyzing, and publishing other forms of economic data.[5]

4. The term "potential labor force" is used in this chapter to refer to the gross numbers of individuals one could anticipate available for employment should sex, age, and specific labor force participation rates remain relatively constant.

5. Wouter Tims, who served as a Ford Foundation adviser to the Planning Commission, argues that because of the poor quality of data available on the labor force, employment, and underemployment, "The Third Five Year Plan . . . pays little attention to employment effects of the development programme." This would appear to be in conflict with the expressed perspective plan goals outlined in the

Finally, we will deal briefly with the issue of employment planning in Pakistan as it relates to shaping the occupational structure, and as it relates to programs designed to improve the unemployment and underemployment situation in Pakistan.

Population and Labor Force Data

The major source of labor force data for Pakistan remains, as it has been for several years, the 1951 and the 1961 population censuses for Pakistan. Labor force statistics are not available from the 1972 population census nor from the planned follow-up surveys.

As originally scheduled, the 1971 population census, which was actually carried out in the third quarter of 1972, was to have been a closely coordinated three-part operation. The "Big Count" was to be a complete enumeration of the population with a few items of information collected for each individual: relationship to head of the household, age, sex, marital status, religion. The second phase of the census was planned as a post-enumeration check to establish the quality of the complete enumeration and to generate more accurate household listings that would serve as a sampling frame for the Housing, Economic, and Demographic (HED) Survey. The HED Survey was designed to provide detailed information on employment, industrial and occupational distributions, and other population characteristics. Because of political events, other statistical priorities, and natural disasters (the floods of 1973), the completion of the post-enumeration check was delayed, and the HED Survey that should have been undertaken in the spring of 1973 was postponed until the fall of that year.

With limited skilled manpower available and priorities

Third Five Year Plan, but Tims further notes that these provided only *guidelines* for long-term planning, while the *central objective* of the Third Five Year Plan was to increase per capita income. *Analytical Techniques for Development Planning* (Karachi: PIDE, 1968), pp. 23–24.

allocated to other statistical procedures—including President Bhutto's 1973 mandate to the census organization to register all voters—unanticipated and unwanted delays have been encountered in the tabulation of even the most basic census data. For example, demographic evaluation of the accuracy of the 1972 census requires, at a minimum, age-sex distributions of the population. Such tabulations have been scheduled and rescheduled with the best recent estimate suggesting that such tabulations would be available in the not-too-distant future.

At this stage, therefore, major reliance must be placed on the 1951 and 1961 population censuses, even though these two censuses differ to some degree in the concepts utilized in the collection of labor force data.[6] (It is, of course, incorrect to state that the 1951 and 1961 population censuses are the sole sources of employment and unemployment data in Pakistan. Several additional sources of information are available, including employment surveys, industrial surveys, and special purpose surveys.)

Although the above forms of demographic-labor force surveys are conceptually distinct, often various forms were combined in a single operation. For example, the first major labor force survey in Pakistan independent of the census operation was undertaken by the International Labor Organization (ILO) on invitation of the Pakistan government. The invitation was tendered early in 1954 with the proviso that the findings be available for the development of the First Five Year Plan. Some data for the plan were available from initial phases of the operation, but the full survey took place between November 2, 1954, and April 17, 1956. The first phase of the operation was largely an industrial survey

6. See Lee L. Bean, "The Labour Force of Pakistan: A Note on the 1961 Census," *Pakistan Development Review*, VI, No. 4 (1966), 587–91; Ghazi Mumtaz Farooq, "Economic Growth and Changes in the Industrial Structure of Income and Labor Forces in Pakistan," *Economic Development and Cultural Change*, XXI, No. 2 (1973), 294, and "An Aggregate Model of Labor Force Participation in Pakistan," *The Developing Economies*, X, No. 3, 267–89.

covering organizations with twenty or more workers – defined as large-scale employers. The second phase consisted of a household sample survey covering approximately 21,000 households in the two provinces. The ILO Survey was continued during the period from October 1956 through July 1957, although during this phase of the project the study was restricted solely to the urban population. A third manpower survey was carried out in 1959, but in this case it was restricted once again to a survey of industrial firms employing twenty or more workers.[7]

Little can be gleaned from these surveys regarding changes in the structure of the labor force in Pakistan subsequent to the 1951 census. The crude rates of labor force participation diverge so greatly from the census rates that the data cannot be compared. Coverage in the household sample is suspiciously high – four refusals out of a total of 21,000 households covered in all three phases of this survey. Age-specific labor force participation rates are excessively high – 100 percent for males between the ages of 36–45. Finally, the industrial surveys were based upon inadequate sampling frames. Interviewers were employment exchange workers and they were instructed simply to find and to interview personnel in industrial firms with twenty or more workers or twenty or fewer workers. Thus, there is no means of determining how exhaustive the interview procedures were. And, of course, since employment exchange workers were used, given the limited budget for the survey, the studies were carried out only in those urban areas where employment exchanges were located.

A more recent source of labor force data for Pakistan is derived from the "Quarterly Survey of Current Economic Conditions," which includes statistics regarding employ-

7. During the latter stages of the study, efforts were made to extend the survey to cover establishments with fewer than twenty employees. For a full review of these surveys, see S. Rahmat Ali, "Definitions and Concepts Used in Labour Force Statistics in Pakistan," unpublished paper, Karachi, PIDE, 1967.

ment, unemployment, and hours worked. These surveys were started in 1963 with a pre-test, and the full survey initially covered the 1963 fiscal year. The series has continued with periodic, serious disruptions. While reports from the earlier surveys have been published, many of the survey results from the latter part of the last decade remain unpublished. Typically, however, manpower planners have found the accuracy of the data on the labor force in these surveys suspect, ignoring these more current results for data from the 1961 population census.[8]

In general, given the limitations of the above sources of non-census labor force data, including employment and unemployment data, the scholar interested in analyzing the demographic aspects of the labor force in Pakistan is severely restricted. The lack of adequate data, however, is due to at least three factors. First, there is the basic problem of collecting any demographic data of high quality in a country such as Pakistan. Second, there is a problem of applying labor force concepts that have been developed traditionally in modern, urbanized, industrial societies to developing countries.[9] Third, there is the apparent, but implicit, order of priority assigned to various forms of statistics collected, analyzed, and published by the Government of Pakistan.

In spite of the expressed commitment to deal with the problems of employment generation, little attention has been devoted to the development of adequate statistical systems focusing on employment and the labor force. Such

8. K. Rudd, for example, notes: "Besides the population census there are a number of other statistical sources relating to manpower. None, however, seem yet to be sufficiently coordinated with the population census to give a reliable picture of intercensal development. The household sample survey, 1963–64 was comprehensive enough . . . but the results were so divergent from those of the population census that the two cannot be taken as comparable." "Programme for Projecting Manpower Requirements of the Fourth Plan," unpublished paper, Government of Pakistan, Planning Division, 1966, p. 3.

9. Nural Islam, "Concepts and Measurements of Unemployment and Underemployment in Developing Economics," *International Labour Review*, LXXXIX, No. 3 (1964), 240–56.

a statistical posture reflects, to some degree, a more general attitude toward economic planning and development. Specifically, it may be argued that direct intervention into the problem of employment generation may be less beneficial than other more indirect modes of intervention. Such a position was implicit during the latter part of the last decade in Pakistan, but one should note that such a position is found in most developing countries.[10]

Labor Force Participation: Demographic Parameters

The proportion of the population involved in economic activities is a function of a set of complex and interacting conditions including employment demand and the supply of actual or potential labor, in part determined by social institutions and value systems.[11] The availability of universal and extensive educational systems often required by the structure of particular occupational systems results in moderate or lengthy postponements of entrance into the labor market. Governmental and private social welfare programs lower the age of withdrawal from the labor supply. Values with respect to certain categories of individuals also influence

10. Lieserson, for example, writing on Indonesia, notes: "The point is simply that labor legislation may not be, and in Indonesia's case probably is not, of as great significance for employment as other types of government regulations and intervention in areas that may seem far removed from the labor market. The economic issues raised by labor regulations are, in fundamental ways, tied up with the whole question of appropriate pricing of factors and ought not to be considered in isolation; policies with respect to interest rates, investment, exchange rates, tariffs and imports are likely to exert much more important influences on employment. As far as labor market policy itself is concerned, however, it would seem better to emphasize 'positive' measures to improve relevant institutions, such as vocational training and guidance, better information flows, and programmes to facilitate labor market adjustments to economic change." Mark W. Lieserson, "Employment Perspectives and Policy Approaches in Indonesia," *International Labour Review*, CIX, No. 4 (1974), 353.

11. The effect of values influencing labor participation rates is most evident in terms of the employment of selected identifiable groups in a variety of societies and over a variety of time periods: the employment of blacks and other minorities in the United States, employment of Jews in Nazi Germany on the free labor market, the employment of Indians in certain Castilian-dominated Latin American countries, or the employment of women in Pakistan.

levels of labor force participation, as in the case of female employment in Pakistan and other Islamic societies.[12] The interaction of supply and demand operating within a system of institutional and normative constraints, however, takes place within the framework of a potential supply of labor that is broadly determined by demographic factors.

The demographic parameters establishing this potential supply of labor are explicit in the age and sex distribution of the population, that is, the *population structure.* The relative distribution of the population in the societally defined potentially productive years of life sets the outside limits of the number of individuals in a society who can (under existing market and value structures) be drawn into the labor force.

The simplicity of this notion is expressed in a ratio to identify the relative strength of the potentially productive population vis-à-vis the nonproductive or dependent population. For comparative purposes, this dependency ratio has traditionally been computed as the ratio of the population between the ages of 15–64 to the sum of the individuals under 15 plus those 65 and older. Here we will use the age groups 0–14, 15–59, 60 and over.[13]

For Pakistan, the dependency ratios were 96 in 1951 and 98 in 1961. The ratios, however, are not as greatly different from countries with entirely different demographic characteristics as one might expect. For example, using the above age categories, the ratio for the United States was 82 in 1966.

The similarity of the dependency ratio among countries with greatly different population structures is due, partially, to the relative distribution of the young and old population as defined by the dependency ratios. Typically, countries

---

12. See Lee L. Bean, "Labour Force of Pakistan," *op. cit.*, and Nadia Haggag Youssef, *Women and Work in Developing Societies* (Berkeley: Institute of International Studies, University of California, 1974).

13. These age ranges are used because 1951 and 1961 census data were reported in this form. Government of Pakistan, *Census of Pakistan*, 1961.

such as Pakistan with high rates of population growth due largely to high fertility levels are characterized as young populations because of the broad-based age structure. Countries with moderately long histories of low fertility have a much higher relative proportion of older individuals. It is thus useful to compute a youth dependency ratio (population 0–14 divided by the population 15–59) that suggests the relative number of individuals in the productive years of life who must bear the economic responsibility for the support of the young non-working population. Using this index, the youth dependency ratios for Pakistan in 1951 and 1961 were 70 and 85, respectively. In contrast, the youth dependency ratios of the United States (1966) was only 55.

It is, of course, more meaningful to specify the actual proportion of the population in the labor force, insofar as data are available. Aside from the economic and social determinants of labor force participation, this proportion is heavily influenced by previous demographic trends — fertility, primarily, and mortality to a limited degree. If fertility and mortality rates have remained constant over long periods of time, then the crude activity rate tends to remain stable. Ghazi Mumtaz Farooq, for example, notes:

The overall stability can partly be explained in terms of age structure of the population. It has been observed that unless there are unusual changes in the cultural and socio-economic structure, (absent in case of India or Pakistan) the age structure remains the basic factor determining the crude activity rate. As a result of continuing high levels of fertility, with no appreciable migration into or out of the Indo-Pakistan subcontinent, the age structure has been relatively stable.[14]

When population growth rates and fertility in particular change, then the shape of the basic population structure

14. Ghazi Mumtaz Farooq, "Labour Force Participation Rates in Pakistan, 1901–1961." *The Pakistan Development Review*, VII, No. 1 (1968), 86.

changes, hence, the crude activity rates of the population also change. For example, if fertility rates decline, the relative proportion of the potentially economically active population increases, and if the age-sex specific labor force participation rates remain constant, the crude activity rate increases. In contrast, if fertility remains high and constant while mortality rates decrease substantially, then the population becomes increasingly younger—an increasing proportion of the population falls in the young age categories. With constant age-sex labor force participation rates, the crude activity rates will decrease, thus also paralleling an increase in the dependency ratio, or "burden," on the population.

Given these expected relationships, considerable effort has been made to identify the patterns of change in crude labor force participation rates as a preliminary to the examination of those conditions that might account for non-demographic fluctuations in such rates. Undertaking such an exercise, however, is made more difficult in Pakistan because of the poor quality of population data in general and labor force data in particular.

Farooq's "Labor Force Participation Rates in Pakistan: 1901–1961" provides the longest series of estimates of the crude labor force participation rates in Pakistan. Using the 1951 and 1961 census along with district census reports for the pre-partition areas of Pakistan,[15] Farooq notes that the proportion of the population in the labor force in Pakistan declined from 1901–51, but increased from 1951–61.[16] (See table.) The patterns are less clear, however, if one examines labor force participation rates by sex. Indeed, the general pattern is strongly influenced by changes in female labor force participation rates.

15. The time series is discontinuous because the 1941 census reports for such data are unavailable.
16. See Farooq, "Labor Force Participation Rates," *op. cit.*

Crude Labor Force Participation Rates by Sex, 1901–61

Year	Sexes	Male	Female
1901	34.8	57.0	8.4
1911	34.1	57.0	6.2
1921	33.3	56.1	5.4
1931	31.8	53.8	4.8
1951	30.7	55.2	2.2
1961	31.8	54.1	6.0

Source: Ghazi Mumtaz Farooq, "Labour Force Participation Rates in Pakistan, 1901–1961," *The Pakistan Development Review*, VII, No. 1 (1968), 85.

The changes in the crude participation rates for males (1901–11 through 1931) could be attributed solely to demographic changes. Given the continuation and the extension of previous trends (moderately constant high fertility associated with declining mortality resulting in increasing growth rates), one should also anticipate that the crude male labor force participation rates would continue to decline. The increase between 1951 and 1961, therefore, would suggest increased employment opportunities absorbing unemployed and underemployed males into the labor force.

A more recent article by M. Afzal Beg, "A Review of Labor Force Participation Rates in Pakistan," reports the same data and notes that the increase may be a *statistical artifact*.[17] In this respect, Beg confirms one conclusion reached by Farooq and Bean in earlier studies of the 1951 and 1961 Pakistan census data.

Since the same demographic trends have continued from 1951 to 1961 it is unusual to find an increase in the level of labor force participation for this period. The trend is even more remarkable given the continuing expansion of educational opportunities and

17. See M. Afzal Beg, "A Review of Labour Force Participation Rates in Pakistan," *The Pakistan Development Review*, XII, No. 4 (1973), 392–406.

the increase in the level of urbanization, particularly in West Pakistan . . . the increase . . . seems to be a statistical artifact. As Bean has shown in an earlier article, the increase can be attributed to a change in labor force concepts between 1951 and 1961 so that unpaid family labor, particularly female, was excluded from the 1951 census but included in the 1961 census. Thus, the evidence suggests that an increasingly smaller proportion of the population provided the labor for a rapidly growing population.[18]

Beg, however, has supplemented his study of the 1951 and 1961 census data by utilization of the data from various labor force surveys and ultimately rejects the statistical artifact argument. These alternate data suggest somewhat higher participation rates from 1961 through 1972 than noted in the 1951 census. Therefore, Beg argues that the rise in labor force participation rates between 1951 and 1961 may be real.

Significantly, the labor force participation rates reported in these surveys are also higher than the rates reported in the 1961 census. Retrospective surveys in Pakistan, however, have been noticeably deficient in correctly identifying population, particularly in the youngest age categories. That type of systematic error alone would account for the somewhat higher crude participation rates accepted by Beg.

Data errors, however, are more clearly evident in the female labor force participation rates. Certainly the significant increase between 1951 and 1961 is due to variations in data collection procedures. As noted in an earlier article on the collection of employment data in Pakistan:

In 1951, a female must have been self-supporting or partially self-supporting to be included in the labor force. Given the patriarchal organization of the Pakistani family, it would be very difficult to secure acquiescence to this question. In 1961, it was only necessary to be *helping* a member of the family in order to be included in the labor force.[19]

18. Farooq, "Labour Force Participation Rates," *op. cit.*, p. 91.
19. Lee L. Bean, *Population Projections for Pakistan: 1960–2000* (Karachi: Pakistan Institute of Development Economics, 1967), p. 590.

The evidence is relatively strong supporting the argument that the increase in total crude labor force participation rates significantly reflects the increase in female labor force participation rates (1951 to 1961) and that this increase may be largely a statistical artifact. What is less evident are the reasons for the apparent increase in the crude male labor force participation rates in the 1951 and 1961 population censuses, thereby halting the trend developing between 1901–31. Because this change runs contrary to what one would expect under the current demographic conditions, the data suggest that some expansions of employment opportunities occurred during the last two decades.

Population Projections and Labor Force Projections

During the last decade several attempts have been made to estimate future employment requirements in Pakistan necessary to achieve targets of full employment. The question has been addressed in slightly different ways. On the one hand, studies have been undertaken to determine the degree to which governmental projections are realistic insofar as selective targets for development have been established. On the other hand, some projections have been generated to determine the extent to which specific forms of development, industrialization in particular, would influence the absorption of the growing potential labor force. Thus, the first type of study treats the labor force as a single aggregate, while the second type depends upon a two-sector — agriculture and nonagriculture — model.

As an illustration of the first form of study, based upon a series of population projections prepared by the Pakistan Institute of Development Economics in 1966, Bean estimated the size of the potential labor force through 1985, the end of the Perspective Plan as outlined in the Third Five Year Plan. Assuming constant age-specific labor force participation rates, it was estimated that the Planning Commission underestimated the labor supply by 8 to 12 million for the country as then constituted.[20] For Pakistan as currently constituted, the projected labor force in 1985 would be underestimated by 4.6 to 7 million potential workers. The margin of error between government projections and those of Bean and others arises from the unwillingness to accept, for planning purposes, actual rates of population increase. For example, the Third Five Year Plan was based upon an assumed rate of population growth of 2.6 percent per annum when it was generally accepted—even on an individual basis by members of the Planning Commission—that the population was growing at a rate of 3 percent.

Bose, using slightly different population data, projected the potential labor force in Pakistan through 1985 with results similar to those subsequently reported by Bean.[21] Bose, however, was more concerned with specific employment generation possibilities during the 1961–71 period, because at the time of his study the government had not published or made available employment generation targets for the Third Five Year Plan or the Perspective Plan period. Given the concentration of the labor supply in the rural sector, Bose's model explored the degree to which planned industrialization could absorb surplus agricultural labor and he concluded:

Since agriculture is already heavily burdened with surplus labor, it has been argued that significant employment opportunities would grow mainly in the non-agricultural sector as it increases in size and improves its productivity. Rough estimates have been made about such employment prospects during the decade 1961–1971. Even on very liberal assumptions, it appears that, during the period 1961–71, out of this labor force increase of 8.71 million, the non-agricultural sector would absorb only about 4.94 million,

20. See Lee L. Bean et al., "Demographic Aspects of Potential Labour Force Growth in Pakistan," in *Proceedings: Sydney Conference, International Union for the Scientific Study of Population* (Sydney, Australia: IUSSP, 1967), p. 94.

21. See Swadesh R. Bose, "Labour Force and Employment in Pakistan, 1961–86: A Preliminary Analysis," *The Pakistan Development Review*, III, No. 3 (1963), 371–98.

and about 3.77 million would be added to the agricultural labor force, which would increase from 24.36 million to 28.13 million. Meaningful employment opportunities will fail to keep pace with the increasing labor force.[22]

Regardless of the analytic model utilized, studies concerned with employment generation in Pakistan have uniformly concluded that the programs of development planned during the 1960s could not effectively provide employment for the increasing labor supply because of the high rate of population growth.[23] The conclusions reached from employment generation estimation studies carried out prior to 1971, however, should be viewed with caution because the particularly adverse conditions prevalent in East Pakistan influence any findings that would relate to the country as then constituted. With a much higher proportion of agricultural labor and a slower rate of industrial growth anticipated, employment-generation possibilities in Bangladesh would be expected to be less than in Pakistan. Given the growing proportion of the population employed in nonagricultural activities in Pakistan, it would appear that there are reasons to be somewhat optimistic, as Brown notes in chapter six.

There are factors that would mitigate the assumptions utilized in the labor force projections of both Bean and Bose.

22. *Ibid.*, p. 387.
23. Azizur Rahman Khan's study of East Pakistan provides additional evidence. He analyzed the development strategy developed by the Pakistan Planning Commission for the Fourth Five Year Plan, and he notes that under the most optimistic assumptions the nonagricultural sector in East Pakistan might absorb between 75 to 78 percent of the additional labor supply. More realistically, he states, "Once we allow for the facts that . . . a) the projected increase in labor supply is almost certainly an understatement and that . . . b) the use of the labor-coefficients of nearly a decade ago leads to an overestimate in employment since some increase in labor productivity would be inevitable particularly in the service sectors, it would appear that the additional non-agricultural employment during the Fourth Five Year Plan would be a much smaller proportion of the increased labor supply—perhaps between a half and two-thirds." "The Possibilities of the East Pakistan Economy During the Fourth Five Year Plan," in Azizur Rahman Khan, ed., *Studies on the Strategy and Technique of Development Planning* (Karachi: PIDE, 1969), pp. 208–9.

The proportion of the population working or seeking work may be influenced by moderate amounts of outmigration, stimulated more recently by the decision of the government to encourage labor migration. It has been reported, for example, that, "The President [Bhutto] issued orders for the creation of a new division to be called the 'Manpower Division' within the Ministry of Labor and Works to look after the problems relating to the manpower and to take measures for encouraging emigration to other countries."[24]

A program encouraging emigration, if successful, will have both negative and positive consequences, but will probably have little statistical effect on the total number of individuals in the entire labor force available for and in need of employment. The negative effect of the policy will flow from the fact that those who are most likely to be in a position to find employment outside of the country will be the skilled or high-level manpower, thus constricting the supply of individuals in precisely those categories that are essential for successful development planning and operations.[25]

The positive consequences are twofold: generation of foreign exchange arising from funds returned to families by Pakistani citizens working abroad, and generation of employment for selected highly trained individuals who are unable to find satisfactory employment in Pakistan. In terms of the issues raised in this chapter, however, the migration stimulation policy will have little impact on the total numbers

24. *Pakistan Exports*, XXIV, No. 5 (1973), 29.
25. A minor illustration of the point is that between 1950 and 1974, sixteen Pakistan citizens were awarded Ph.D.s in demography or other social science fields with specialization in demography. By mid-1974 only two were employed in Pakistan. All others were working for international agencies (the World Bank, and various agencies of the United Nations) or Australian, Canadian, Iranian, and U.S. universities and colleges. Consequently, after fifteen years of providing funds for training and providing funds for expatriate advisers in demography, donor agencies were still seeking qualified expatriates for positions as advisers and providing funds to train individuals up through the Ph.D. for specifically those agencies that have proved to be incapable of maintaining trained staff.

for whom employment must be generated because of the specialized skills involved among those who can find employment outside of the country.

Other factors that might reduce the actual number of individuals for whom employment must be provided include the governmental policy of encouraging earlier retirement, thus creating some additional employment vacancies for younger members of the potential labor force. Finally, the government policy of increasing educational facilities will have some effect by increasing the age of entry into the labor force for some proportion of the population (largely male). This "saving" will be short run and will be offset by potentially adverse effects of having increasing demands placed on selected job categories that may not be expanding at a sufficiently high rate of growth to provide employment for the more educated entrants into the labor market.

One must also recognize that there are factors which may serve to compound the employment generation problem. First, in spite of the cultural constraints on employment of women in Pakistan, the increasing educational levels of females will typically result in some increase in rates of female employment. Second, increasing mechanization of agriculture may result in increasing numbers of permanent (non-family) farm laborers being displaced from the agricultural sector.[26] Third, the growth of capital-intensive industries in Pakistan will negatively affect the labor market picture, which has been developed on the basis of older, less positive productivity ratios.

In short, without more recent and more accurate data on

26. See S. R. Bose and E. H. Clark, "Some Basic Considerations in Agricultural Mechanization in West Pakistan," *The Pakistan Development Review*, IX, No. 3 (1969), 273–308; Carl H. Gotsch, "Tractor Mechanization and Rural Development in Pakistan," *International Labour Review*, CVII, No. 2 (1973), 133–66 and Bashir Ahmed, "Field Survey of Large Farmers in the Pakistan Punjab," Working Paper No. 7, Project on Rural Development in Pakistan (Cambridge: Harvard University, 1972), mimeographed.

the labor situation in Pakistan, one must conclude that on balance the earlier projections of labor growth and employment demand are reasonable. Employment targets have been set too high: employment-generation programs are deficient, and because the basic structure of the potential labor force has been established by extremely unfavorable population dynamics, the possibility of full employment in the short or medium run is low. To provide full employment, the government must provide for far more employment opportunities than it has projected, because the labor force will be growing more rapidly than previously anticipated.

Planning for Employment Generation

There now appears to be consistent evidence that the Pakistan government recognizes the failure of previous development plans to provide sufficient employment opportunities for the labor force, which continues to grow rapidly because of the country's previous demographic dynamics. The quotation beginning this chapter is representative of that position.

To deal with employment generation, a series of new programs was outlined in the *Pakistan Economic Survey* for 1972–73. One program is primarily concerned with development of employment opportunities for the highly educated.

Aside from the formulation of a long-term employment strategy, the government decided to launch programmes to increase work opportunities for the educated unemployed by making fuller use of the existing facilities and organizations both in the private and the public sectors. An important link in the chain of the employment policy was the launching of an ambitious National Development Volunteer Programme (N.D.V.P.). This programme aims at providing job opportunities to scientists, engineers and technicians. To be employed as probationers in the public and private sector organizations these persons will be imparted on-the-job-training. . . . Stipends for the training period in public sector organizations will be paid by the government in full. In the case of private sector, 50 percent of stipend money will be paid by the government and the remaining 50 percent by the employers.[27]

Other programs include the "hiring" of one thousand engineers in the Construction Engineering Corporation, which essentially will provide financial assistance to the engineers to establish their own business ventures. It has also been reported, "At the village and city levels enrollment of unemployed persons has already started under the name of Education and Social Services Corps. The educated and skilled persons will be enrolled as volunteers, trained and deputed to motivate the people to undertake projects on self-help basis."[28]

In the rural sectors three programs are planned. A People's Works Program is designed to provide employment on short-duration projects covering housing, roads, playgrounds, adult education, and forestation. Each of the subsequent two programs cited are likely to have little employment generation impact. The Integrated Rural Development Program has four specific goals, but an overriding goal of increasing agricultural productivity will depend upon development of machinery pools and encouragement of mechanized farming. The end result is likely to be negative rather than positive, insofar as the underlying function is the generation of employment.[29] The development of Agrovilles, small towns designed to be self-contained settlements, is assumed to have an unemployment reducing effect: "By providing employment opportunities to people near their places of abode, the Agrovilles would help in checking the present large-scale migration to cities, which, in turn create conditions of over-crowding with concomitant social problems in the cities."[30] The idea is an old one,

27. *Pakistan Economic Survey, op. cit.*, p. 120.
28. *Ibid.*
29. See Bose and Clark, *op. cit.*, and Ahmad, *op. cit.*
30. *Pakistan Economic Survey, op. cit.*

having been suggested by Karol Krotki in an unpublished paper prepared at the Institute of Development Economics early in the last decade. It is, however, too early to predict how many individuals would be involved in such projects.

It is questionable whether any of these programs are likely to have major impacts. Since partition, several programs have been supported by the Pakistan government, most of which were designed to have an indirect if not direct effect on the generation of employment or the utilization of the unemployed to achieve some development goal.[31] In comparing the operation and results of various development programs, Burki has argued that most social development programs in Pakistan have had limited success. Of the six programs reviewed by Burki, three may be viewed as having moderately direct employment considerations as part of the overall objectives: the Village Aid Program, the Rural Works Program, and the Refugee Rehabilitation Program. According to Burki, the first was stopped; the second was revised but eventually stopped; and only the third could be viewed as being "partially successful."[32]

Certain of the new programs proposed to deal with employment generation bear a striking similarity to earlier, now defunct programs. A cavalier view of the future would suggest that the projected programs are likely to be as unsuccessful as the previous ones. But clearly with the right commitment and the right leadership, these programs might prove successful. It would appear, for example, that the Moroccan "Promotion Nationale" (a form of a V-AID or

31. See Richard V. Gilbert, "The Rural Works Programme in East Pakistan," *International Labour Review*, LXXXIX, No. 3 (1964), 213–26.

32. The social development programs reviewed by Burki represent a broad mixture of multi-purpose programs. The three cited above are those which in my opinion contained a significant "employment" generation consideration. Three others had more limited direct functions that did not include considerations of employment generation: nutrition, malaria, and family planning. In practice, however, the family planning program has generated more employment than any of the other social development programs. See Shahid Javed Burki, "Population Pressure and Public Policy," *Pakistan Economist*, April 14, 20, 1973, pp. 14–18.

Rural Works Program) has proved to be particularly successful in dealing partially with the problem of rural underemployment and unemployment.[33] Perhaps a careful review
of the conditions that led to the termination of earlier employment generation programs in Pakistan, and a review of
moderately successful programs utilized in other countries,
might provide more effective guidelines to the strengthening of such programs in Pakistan.

Conclusions

There are few specific statements regarding the structure
of the labor force in Pakistan that can be made with any
conviction. As noted above, the absence of 1972 census
HED data compounds our increasing ignorance after the
1961 census because of limited and unpublished intercensal
survey data. If one is content to allow the specifics to await
more detailed data, there are several useful conclusions
that can be stated.

First, because of the continuing high rate of population
growth in Pakistan,[34] producing a continuing young population, the labor force remains less than one-third of the total
population. As a consequence of the same demographic
trends, unemployment and/or underemployment have probably not been lessened. This conclusion is based upon the assumptions that continuing investments in capital-intensive
development and increasing mechanization of agriculture

33. See D. Jackson and H. A. Turner, "How to Provide More Employment in a
Labour-Surplus Economy," *International Labour Review*, CVII, No. 3 (1973),
315–18.

34. I have avoided the interesting exercise of "estimating" the current labor
force in Pakistan, even roughly. One could do so by applying crude labor force
participation rates (1961 census) to the 1972 census. That exercise would suggest
a 1972 labor force of 20 million, or an increase of 62 percent. I have not included
this calculation because I believe the census count is too high and because we have
no way of estimating the current crude labor force participation rate. Lee L. Bean,
"The Population of Pakistan: An Evaluation of Recent Statistical Data," *The Middle
East Journal*, XXVIII, No. 2 (1974), 177–84.

have offset the effects of any significant economic growth. Furthermore, no major government programs of a labor-intensive nature have been mounted that would offset those negative influences.

Second, because of the mechanization of agriculture and because of the industrial and service expansion in Pakistan, one may anticipate that the country will become predominately nonagricultural in terms of its industrial distribution. That may well mean, however, that the locus of under-employment shifts from rural to urban communities.

Third, with the increasing educational opportunities for males and females, there are likely to be increasing pressures on selected sections of the employment market.

Fourth, because of the limited success of the family planning program, there is little reason to assume that fertility and thus the rate of population growth has declined substantially since the middle of the last decade. And, of course, any reductions in fertility during that period would not begin to effect the labor supply until the end of this decade.

In combination, these conditions suggest continuing high levels of unemployment and underemployment. And these levels may increase, thus compounding critical social and political issues related to employment.

In the medium and long run, continued support of an aggressive anti-natalist policy will have a significant effect on the growth of the potential labor supply. But in the short run, the possible demographic policies that might be supported are likely to have little effect. The new entrants to the labor force ten to fifteen years from now have been born. Significant savings in numbers for whom employment must be provided will not appear until ten to fifteen years after a reduction in fertility.

Therefore, while the very unfavorable population problems of Pakistan partially account for the current labor problem, the amelioration of that problem in the short run quires government policies other than demographic olicies. But failure to actively support programs that may reduce fertility in the future is a shortsighted approach to a complex problem that cannot be solved by any single governmental program.

9

Political Leadership and Institution-building Under Jinnah, Ayub, and Bhutto

Khalid B. Sayeed

Political leadership is defined here as the exercise of power or influence in a social collectivity, both in terms of discerning, defining, and shaping the goals, purposes, or objectives of that collectivity and in terms of creating appropriate structures through which the leadership's purposes may be fulfilled or attained. In a developing society, leadership has to take a dynamic view of goals and values and of the structures necessary to attain these goals. This appreciative art, as characterized by Sir Geoffrey Vickers,[1] has to be understood at two levels. There is first of all the broader comprehension of the direction and thrust of historical forces. Zulfikar Ali Bhutto claims that the great failing of his predecessors was their inability to comprehend the flow of history and to adjust their policies to historic changes.[2] The second and equally important level of leadership is the capacity to understand one's own society in all its historical and cultural complexity. Rather simplistically, the late President Mohammad Ayub Khan described this capability as one of understanding "the book of Pakistan," an understanding "based on my knowledge of the people

---

1. Sir Geoffrey Vickers, *The Art of Judgment* (London: Methuen, 1965), pp. 73–74.
2. Zulfikar Ali Bhutto, President of Pakistan, *Speeches and Statements, July 1, 1972–September 30, 1972* (Karachi: Department of Films and Publications, Government of Pakistan, 1973), pp. 219–20.

and the soil of Pakistan."[3] When analyzing this kind of leadership, we move away from the elitist kind of leadership to that leadership under which social and political development becomes possible because the leaders have been able to evoke mass support and cooperation by touching certain cultural and primordial chords in the public mind. Mao characterizes this kind of leadership as "from the masses to the masses," which means "take the ideas of the masses (scattered and unsystematic ideas), then go to the masses to propagate and explain these ideas until the masses embrace them as their own, hold fast to them and translate them into action, and test the correctness of these ideas in such action."[4] Thus, it may be argued that Pakistan's leaders, besides sometimes not fully comprehending the ebb and flow of historical currents, have so far failed to understand the genius and traditions of their multi-cultural, multi-lingual, and predominantly rural society.

Political scientists also tend to oversimplify the art of leadership when they describe it as the art of institution-building. This art is usually conceived of in terms of power as a resource through which a polity may be built or developmental changes promoted. Samuel Huntington extols Ayub Khan as coming close "to filling the role of a Solon or Lycurgus or 'Great Legislator' on the Platonic or Rousseauian model"[5] because he was successful in concentrating power to a greater degree than that available in the American or French constitutions and expanding his power base through the institution of Basic Democracies.[6] Similarly, Huntington rates Lenin's achievement in establishing the supremacy of the party over all other social forces as much more impressive than that of Marx as the formulator of the

3. Mohammad Ayub Khan, *Friends Not Masters* (London: Oxford University Press, 1967), p. 207.
4. Jerome Ch'en, *Mao: Great Lives Observed* (Englewood Cliffs, N.J.: Prentice-Hall, 1969), p. 169.
5. Samuel P. Huntington, *Political Order in Changing Societies* (New Haven: Yale University Press, 1968), p. 251.
6. *Ibid.*, pp. 252–55.

theory of social revolution.[7] But this overemphasis on power misses the key and crucial element of ideology in the institution-building of Lenin and particularly in the leadership of Mao in sinocizing Marxism-Leninism and bringing about the social transformation of China. Ideological leadership, as J. W. Lewis points out, cannot be conceived of in terms of power but in terms of the relationship between the leader and the led.[8]

In addition to an understanding of the historical and social reality and devising appropriate structures or institutions to achieve certain social objectives, leadership also has to be looked at in terms of the personality of the leader, his life experiences, and how his judgment has been colored by both life and professional experiences. "Political Science without biography," says Lasswell, "is a form of taxidermy."[9] Jinnah's leadership in the creation of Pakistan can be understood not only in terms of his legal background or his political strategy but also in terms of how he sought and mobilized political power, both for social purposes and as a means of seeking compensation for certain deprivations he had suffered.[10]

Jinnah's Leadership

A common explanation of Jinnah's unparalleled success in achieving Pakistan within seven years of the passing of the Pakistan Resolution was his charismatic leadership.

7. *Ibid.*, p. 337.

8. John Wilson Lewis, *Leadership in Communist China* (Ithaca: Cornell University Press, 1963), p. 75.

9. Harold D. Lasswell, *Psychopathology and Politics* (New York: Viking Press, 1960), p. 1.

10. I have tried to show how the failure of this marriage is a key factor in explaining Jinnah's single-minded pursuit of social and power objectives in the creation of Pakistan. Khalid B. Sayeed, "The Personality of Jinnah and His Political Strategy," in C. H. Philips and Mary Doreen Wainwright, *The Partition of India: Policies and Perspectives 1935-1947* (London: George Allen and Unwin, 1970), pp. 276–82.

Muslims were both awed and stirred and felt that he was a heroic leader endowed with a political shrewdness and sagacity that could overwhelm Hindu and British opposition to Pakistan. His critics, particularly Lord Attlee, the prime minister who transferred power to both India and Pakistan, have suggested that even though he himself was not a good Muslim, he deliberately exploited Islam in mobilizing Muslim support and in overwhelming the opposition to Pakistan. Both these explanations are unsatisfactory. President Nasser has referred to a "wandering role that seeks an actor to perform it."[11] Muslims in India ever since the demise of Mughul power have yearned for the creation of a separate political entity that would ensure their Islamic identity in India. When Jinnah raised his cry for Pakistan, he was responding to this long-felt urge for political power. Their poet Iqbal had also looked for a leader who would preside over their renaissance.

> Appear, O rider of destiny.
> Appear, O light of the dark realm of Change . . .
> Silence the noise of the nations . . .
> Arise and tune the harp of brotherhood,
> Give us back the cup of the wine of love.[12]

Therefore, one could argue that in this sense more charisma was conferred on Jinnah than he actually had. It must be remembered that he was a powerful orator in English, but not in Urdu, that he often appeared in Western clothes, and that a number of his political opponents were much better versed in Islamic law and theology.

Another prominent trait in his leadership was his skillful and judicious exercise of power. He was convinced that in politics only those who had power would be respected and

11. Gamal Abdel Nasser, *The Philosophy of the Revolution* (n.p., n.d.), p. 72.

12. Dr. Sir Muhammad Iqbal. *The Secrets of the Self*, trans. Reynolds A. Nicholson (London: Macmillan, 1920, and Lahore: Sh. Muhammad Ashraf, 1960), pp. 83–84. Reprinted by permission of Macmillan, London and Basingstoke and of Sh. Muhammad Ashraf.

feared. "Appeals to patriotism, justice and fair-play and for goodwill fall flat. It does not require political wisdom to realize that all safeguards and settlements would be a scrap of paper, unless they are backed up by power."[13] He was often derisive toward Gandhi's excessive or ill-planned use of power. It was only when he realized that the mere organizational backing of the Muslim League would not enable him to extract what he considered a fair settlement from the British and the Congress that he asked his followers to organize themselves for direct and militant action.

> If there is not sufficient power, create that power. If we do that, the Mission and the British Government may be rescued, released and freed from being cowed down by the threats of the Congress that they would launch a struggle and start non-cooperation. Let us also say that.[14]

It has also been argued that the secret of Jinnah's rapid and spectacular success lay in the fact that by raising the cry of Pakistan and organizing the Muslim League with the help of the middle classes and the enlightened landed gentry, he raised the expectations of the Muslim middle classes that Pakistan would create enormous job and commercial opportunities for them. The Muslim League in Hindu-majority provinces (India) was also a champion of Muslim middle classes who wanted to hang on to their privileged positions in provinces like the United Provinces and Bihar or to claim their proportional share in terms of population in other provinces. It has been suggested that Jinnah, through his charisma and with the help of the nascent middle classes, displaced the traditional landowning Muslim leadership in Muslim-majority provinces like Bengal and the Punjab. This analysis, besides being simple, is not quite accurate. Let us see how the Muslim League during 1945–46 was able to over-

13. Sir Maurice Gwyer and A. Appadorai, eds., *Speeches and Documents on the Indian Constitution 1921–47* (London: Oxford University Press, 1957), II, 620–21.
14. M. Ashraf, ed., *Cabinet Mission and After* (Lahore: Ashraf, 1946), p. 291.

come the Unionist-cum-District Commissioner-landlord-
caste/baradari opposition. First of all, it must be borne in
mind that the latter coalition had emerged so dominant in
1937 that the Muslim League obtained no more than two out
of eighty-six Muslim seats in the election. Muslim, Hindu,
and Sikh landlords, drawing their support from their castes
or baradaris based on a patron-client relationship, had been
working amicably with the deputy commissioners as rep-
representatives of the provincial and the central British
government. They had also captured local government institutions. With the support or goodwill of the deputy commissioner and the coercive powers that their economic sources
could command through *rassagirs* (cattle lifters) and other
armed elements, their dominance in the rural social structure
could not be easily challenged.

In addition, their own membership in the baradaris or
their alliances with others provided so much political power
and influence that their support of the Unionist Party was
decisive in enabling the latter to capture majority support
and establish its dominance in the Punjab in 1937. It was
because of this objective political reality that Jinnah reached
an understanding with Sikander Hyat Khan and through
such a pact tried to penetrate the Muslim supporters of the
Unionists and establish the presence of the Muslim League
in the Punjab. By 1943 he had achieved only a modest
degree of success, but particularly after 1944, when the
Unionist–Muslim League understanding broke down, the
Muslim League launched a massive campaign against the
Unionists. There are no records that spell out or document
the superb political strategy that Jinnah and the Muslim
League followed during the elections of 1945–46. However,
what can be pieced together from newspaper reports, and
particularly from a first-rate graduate paper by David Gilmartin, is that mass meetings organized by the Muslim
League with the help of students were successful in de-

stroying the Unionist ascendancy in Muslim constituencies.[15] The Unionists used all their resources. It was clear that their candidates would be supported by the deputy commissioner. Firoz Khan Noon revealed that even the Viceroy, Lord Wavell, in a speech to the Viceroy's Durbar of notables in Rawalpindi, clearly hinted that votes in the forthcoming elections should be cast in favor of the trusted leaders.[16] It was true that in one critical two-week period before the election some 1,500 students addressed an estimated number of 700,000 Punjabis. It was also true that the Muslim League not only used Islam as a rallying cry but resorted to the questionable tactic of manufacturing Muslim divines, or *pirs*, out of some of the city-dwelling but landowning elite members of the Lahore gymkhana club. The Munir Report, commenting on how the Muslim League enlisted the support of the masses through a Mashaikh committee, pointed out that some members of this committee were the Nawab of Mamdot, Shaukat Hayat Khan, Firoz Khan Noon, and Nawab Mohammad Hayat Qureshi. Religious designations had to be invented for these notables.

Khan Iftikhar Husain Khan of Mamdot was described as Pir Mamdot Sharif, Sirdar Shaukat Hayat Khan as Sajjada Nashin of Wah Sharif, Malik Feroz Khan Noon of Darbar Sargodha Sharif, and Nawab Muhammad Hayat Qureshi as Sajjada Nashin of Sargodha Sharif, and to top all, the Secretary of this Committee, Mr. Ibrahim Ali Chishti, was designated Fazil-i-Hind Sajjada Nashin of Paisa Akhbar Sharif.[17]

The Unionist leaders countered this campaign by seeking public support through their well-established institutions

15. David Gilmartin, "The Rise of the Muslim League in the Punjab and the Destruction of the Unionist System," a term paper presented to the History Department, University of California, Berkeley, June 15, 1973, pp. 28–36.

16. Firoz Khan Noon, *From Memory* (Lahore: A Hameed Khan, n.d.), p. 192.

17. *Report of the Court of Inquiry Constituted Under Punjab Act II of 1954 to Enquire into the Punjab Disturbances of 1953* (Lahore: Government Printing Office, 1954), p. 255. Commonly known as the Munir Report.

like the district boards and the Zamindara League. They did not address mass meetings but gatherings of local notables or baradari leaders. The appeal to Muslim unity was countered by the appeal to caste or baradari solidarity. Both Hindu and Muslim landowning classes were members of such baradaris. One Unionist MLA remarked, "I am a Jat first and a Mussalman afterwards. Our ancestors were Jat Hindus, and now we are Jat Muslims." Khizr Hayat tried to rally support through the Anjuman-e-Muslim Rajputani.[18]

The Unionists could also claim that, given the communal composition of the Punjab in which the Muslims did not have a predominant majority, the Unionist approach of building and maintaining intercommunal harmony was the only solution because Muslims by themselves could not govern the Punjab. But the heady wine of Muslim power was so intoxicating that Muslims were being persuaded that they were not merely after power in the Punjab, but that they wanted Muslim power in Pakistan. If Muslims in India could believe that somehow they would also stand to gain through Muslim power in Pakistan by taking a stand against the Hindu majority in their own provinces, one can see how effective must have been the Muslim League invocation of Islamic unity and power.

Was the political and organizational character of the Muslim League changing? Infusion of students and younger elements from the urban and landowning classes brought about an impressive radicalization of Muslim League politics and programs at the surface level.[19] The Punjab Muslim League manifesto was probably drafted under the influence of Danial Latifi, who turned out to be a member of the Communist party, and included planks like village uplift and the nationalization of key industries. Probably students and the younger elements by themselves could not have

18. Gilmartin, *op. cit.*, p. 30.
19. *Ibid.*, p. 35.

made much of an impact had it not been for other economic and social factors that were working against Unionist control of the Muslim electorate. First of all, the Unionists had never been able to win over the urban Muslims of the Punjab. Between 1921 and 1941 the number of urban Muslims doubled, and in the central plains districts of the Punjab urban Muslims constituted almost 25 percent of the Muslim population. Growing conflict between the Ahrars and the Khaksars in the urban areas meant that the Muslim League emerged as the only viable alternative to the Unionist Party for the Muslim electorate. But the Muslim League could not have built its strength purely on an urban basis. Its real strength came when a number of landlords started drifting from the Unionist Party to the Muslim League. This happened because some of these landlords had acquired Western educations. A number of successful rural candidates from the Muslim League in 1946 were lawyers. High prices during the war meant that even the smaller- and medium-sized landlords could assert their independence. Since the Unionist Party, alleged to be in league with Hindu businessmen, finally agreed to impose price controls, it lost much of its appeal to the Muslim landlords.[20] It was not only the young, Oxford-educated Daultana who became a prominent leader of the Muslim League; the older, Oxford-educated Unionist landlord-cum-former member of the Viceroy's Executive Council, Firoz Khan Noon, was also swept up by the winds of change. The result was that the Muslim League, which was being led by the younger urban and some progressive elements, was soon to be infected by the influence of older landowning classes. Thus, many felt that the Muslim League in Pakistan was a new version of the old Unionist Party with these differences: it was being led by younger landlords and only by Muslim landlords unlike the old Unionist Party, which was ruled by a Muslim-Hindu-Sikh

20. *Ibid.*, pp. 38–39.

landlord alliance. This suggests that the dominant objective of the Quaid-i-Azam was to get together that coalition of rural-urban elements that could win the elections. Probably there was no time to develop organizational strength in the Muslim League that could contain the so-called conservative or reactionary elements. "We shall have time for domestic programme and policies, but first get the Government. This is a nation without any territory or any government."[21]

In addition to the influence of landlords and the factional politics generated during the 1940s and 1950s, the Muslim League in the Punjab was also riddled by baradari factions that cut across rural-urban lines. A publication of the Awans gives detailed figures on the candidates belonging to various baradaris — Jat, Rajput, Arain, Awan, Baluch, Pathan, Gujar, Syed Qureshi, Khoja Sheikh, Kashmiri, Kakazai, Noon, Tiwana, and Khatar — who received Muslim League tickets in the 1945–46 election in the Punjab. While giving detailed figures of the population of each of these baradari members, based on the census of 1941, the publication points out that even though seven Awan candidates were entitled to Muslim League tickets, not one was given such a ticket. Jats were entitled to twenty, but they got eighteen. Rajputs were entitled to twenty-one, but they received ten. Commenting on the injustice done to the Awans, it said that the Awans had been treated by the Muslim League in a worse fashion than the Scheduled Caste had been treated by the Hindus. The Awans were "kept out of the bounties that were available from the politics of Punjab as one would keep the dirty flies from milk." Among the illustrious Awans who could have been given such a ticket, the publication lists the name of Nawab Amir Mohammad Khan Kalabagh, who became Governor of West Pakistan under Ayub Khan.[22]

21. Jamil-ud-Din Ahmad, *Speeches and Writings of Mr. Jinnah* (Lahore: Ashraf, 1964), II, 199.
22. Lal Khan, *A Moment of Thought for the Awan Baradari* (n.p., n.d.), pp. 2–5. Other pamphlets and constitutions of various baradaris stress promotion of solidarity

Does this suggest that Jinnah was a brilliant founder of a state but not as great as an institution-builder? He used the Muslim League as a means to achieve Pakistan and did not seem to regard party organization as an integral and essential part of the political system of a free people. The Muslim League, particularly in the Punjab, was supposed to have freed the people from bureaucratic and landlord domination. After Pakistan was established, the Muslim League cabinets and the political machinery were handed over to the control of governors and bureaucrats. It was a Mudie or a Cunningham who sent detailed reports about cabinet and party factions. The kind of advice that Jinnah was receiving can be seen in the letters of these British governors.

The main tenor of these letters was that the politicians were not allowing the government machinery to function with its pre-independence bureaucratic efficiency. Jinnah could have drawn two conclusions from this: one, to place the politicians under bureaucratic tutelage; and two, to improve the party machinery to eliminate some of the factions and accommodate others. He was, after all, a dying man and could think of only immediate short-term remedies. In settling for the first alternative, he not only took care of the immediate problem but laid the foundations for future actions and policies of his successor governments, which, as we know, outdid him in establishing bureaucratic control over politicians. Again, Jinnah and the ruling elites in Pakistan seemed to be completely convinced that just as the state of Pakistan had been won through centralized control of the Muslim League and Islamic unity, unitarian strategies were the only ways of keeping the state intact. Jinnah was one of the first few who had questioned the

within the community and protection and furtherance of educational and economic interests. *Objectives and Rules and Regulations of the Jat Association of Pakistan* (Urdu), July 1956; *Constitution of Central Awan Conference, Punjab* (Urdu) (Lahore: Chaudhri Muhammad Husain, n.d.); *Rules and Regulations of the Pakistan Awan Conference* (Urdu) (Lahore: n.p., n.d.).

suitability of British parliamentary institutions to a heterogeneous society like that of India. But he and his successors
often seemed to forget that Pakistan was also physically
and culturally heterogeneous. Therefore, a new constitutional and political machinery had to be devised. Instead,
Jinnah grafted or imposed a highly centralized constitutional
system like that of the adapted Government of India Act,
1935, onto this heterogeneous reality. Chaudhri Mohammad
Ali, the first secretary-general of the Government of Pakistan who also became a prime minister, in his book deplores
the fact that the Muslim League, instead of following the
centralist and unitarian traditions of the pre-partition era,
discarded them in favor of a more federalized machinery.[23]
But he draws immense satisfaction from the fact that the civil
service of Pakistan discarded the provincial cadres and set
itself up as an even more centralized bureaucracy than its
predecessor, the Indian civil service.[24]

Ayub's Leadership

In order to understand Ayub's leadership and the institutions that he tried to develop, one should know Ayub, the
man, both his personality and the profession that to some extent molded his personality. Ayub had sprung from a fairly
humble background, but he never admitted this. He claimed
that his father was not only an important officer in the
British Indian army but also a notable in Hazara in the Northwest Frontier. His detractors would point out that this was
more than an exaggerated claim, for the total land revenue
that his father paid was pitifully low. When one talked to
Ayub, one came away with two distinct impressions. First,
there was much more glitter than substance in his personality.
He looked big and powerful, but no one so far has credited

23. Chaudhri Muhammad Ali, *The Emergence of Pakistan* (New York: Columbia
University Press, 1967), p. 374.
24. *Ibid.*, p. 357.

him with military brilliance. One felt at ease talking with him because he did not have too many ideas and therefore gave a willing ear to others who seemed intelligent to him. Nevertheless, there was an immense amount of common sense and homespun wisdom in the man. He knew that he owed almost everything to the military commission he had gained in 1928 and to his service in the British Indian army. Therefore, the army had left a profound impact on his personality, his living habits, and his thinking. We have been told again and again that the basic army approach to everything is to reduce a complex problem to its bare essentials and then establish a clear chain of command with authority flowing downward. To an army man, the basic failing of an academic person, or even of many politicians, is that he is impressed by the complexity of human problems and correspondingly unwilling to make up his mind. Addressing the cadets at the Kakul Academy, Ayub exhorted them to hang this motto on their walls: "I may be right, I may be wrong, but I have no doubts."[25]

The first title of Ayub's book, *Friends Not Masters: A Political Autobiography*, was announced as *Endure and Prosper*. Oxford University Press was prevailed upon to change the title, even though the proof copy of the book was in hand, because in the coffee houses of Karachi and Lahore one could hear such remarks as, "Of course, we endure and you prosper." It is said that even after the title was changed to *Friends Not Masters*, the intelligentsia continued to draw some mischievous pleasure by inserting a comma after Friends Not, so that the new title would read *Friends Not, Masters*. In this book Ayub published the famous master plan, "A Short Appreciation of Present and Future Problems of Pakistan," outlining the One Unit plan and the plan for Basic Democracies. Ayub had prepared this plan as early as October 4, 1954, when he was staying at a hotel in London on his way to the United States. There were ominous por-

25. *Dawn*, Oct. 13, 1963.

tents on the Pakistan horizon as Ghulam Mohammad was planning to dismiss Mohammad Ali Bogra. Ayub says that ideas rushed to his mind and the moving finger wrote. Both Von Vorys and Huntington have paid glowing tributes to Ayub for this exercise in political planning under which Ayub formulated a plan in 1954 and carried it out almost to the letter during his regime. Without disagreeing with this assessment, we would emphasize that in a very significant way the publication of this plan caused considerable damage to Ayub's image in East Pakistan and above all contributed to the worsening of relations between West Pakistanis and Bengalis. Ayub's views regarding East Bengalis in this plan would obviously hurt Bengali susceptibilities. The thinly concealed contempt (at least the Bengalis would see it that way) is combined with racial arrogance.

It would be no exaggeration to say that up to the creation of Pakistan, they had not known any real freedom or sovereignty. They have been in turn ruled either by the caste Hindus, Moghuls, Pathans, or the British. In addition, they have been and still are under considerable Hindu cultural and linguistic influence. As such they have all the inhibitions of down-trodden races and have not yet found it possible to adjust psychologically to the requirements of the new-born freedom. Their popular complexes, exclusiveness, suspicion, and a sort of defensive aggressiveness probably emerged from this historical background.[26]

One may go so far as to say that in Ayub one detects not only a lack of sympathy toward or appreciation of the political and economic aspirations of Bengalis, but, as a military officer who had spent all his life in British India in the 1930s and 1940s, he shared the failing of most British and some Indian officers that General Auchinleck called an unawareness or lack of understanding of the political currents that had swept the urban areas in India. This explains why Ayub never had a feel for what urban aspirations or frustrations were all about. He tended to dismiss the intel-

26. Ayub Khan, *op. cit.*, p. 187.

lectuals as impractical bookworms and the urban politicians as either selfish or irresponsible. To these views is linked his broader view of urban malcontents, reinforced by the military approach that even malcontents could be managed through a combination of patience and coercion with occasional persuasion. Otherwise how can one explain passages such as the following:

On the introduction of the Constitution the country started behaving like a wild horse that had been captured but not yet tamed. Every time you try to stroke it affectionately or feed it, it bites you and kicks you.

To my knowledge there has never been so much freedom in this country as there is today. On a number of occasions I have been accused, abused, and vilified, subjected to all kinds of rumours and slanders, all thoroughly unjustified and untrue, by some of the biggest blackguards in the country, and I have swallowed it. I have put up with it for the simple reason that I want to nurse and protect the system. I will not allow it to be demolished.[27]

One may argue that, however exaggerated or distorted his dissatisfaction might have been with the previous political system, this dissatisfaction turned out to be a creative force in Ayub because he was the first Pakistani leader who realized that no political system could strike deep roots in Pakistan and bring about social transformation unless it provided for institutional links between the government and the rural sector where the great majority of Pakistanis lived. As was suggested earlier, military officers, having sprung from the rural martial races, had greater sympathy for rural people than they had for urban interests. But the innate conservatism of Ayub, and of advisers like the Nawab of Kalabagh with whom he surrounded himself, never allowed his vision to soar above the Unionist horizons. Thus, one could see that the sympathetic dispositions of Ayub toward the rural areas worked hand in hand with his power interests. There was no question that he wanted to improve their

27. *Ibid.*, pp. 217 and 218.

economic lot, and the economic development that took place along with the Rural Works Program and the emergence of the newly affluent middle farmers bore testimony to that. His detractors have poked fun at the limited or simplistic perspectives with which he pursued his objective of rural economic development. Douglas Ashford thinks that the Ayub regime looked upon the Basic Democrats "as Boy Scouts." When once asked on his return from East Pakistan what the conditions of the people were, Ayub replied they were "cheerful and have clean clothes."[28]

Can one therefore characterize Ayub's approach to rural areas, the main sources of his political support, as basically Unionist? The regime retreated from all further attempts to introduce any more land reforms, even though suggestions had been made in earlier drafts of the Third Five Year Plan that ceilings on landholdings would be further reduced to levels below those of 1959. This was a clear concession to the landlords. Ayub Khuhro in an interview in 1967 pointed out how much wiser and sounder Ayub's approach had become over the years on agricultural matters. As regards the abolition of the Village Agriculture and Industrial Development Program (Village AID) and the handing over of the agricultural development functions to the Provincial Agricultural Department, a civil servant, Masihuzzaman, writes: "We may hypothesize that programmes with a large content of socio-economic development face greater prospects of elimination than those with heavier emphasis on mere economic development, specially if—and that is more likely—this tends to support the existing power structure."[29]

As we look downward, below the landlords and the deputy commissioners, one comes across the same pathetic resignation of the rural masses toward repression that has

28. Douglas Ashford, *National Development and Local Reform: Political Participation in Morocco and Tunisia and Pakistan* (Princeton: Princeton University Press, 1967), pp. 129 and 132.
29. Masihuzzaman, "Community Development," typescript, pp. 147–48.

been going on almost since time immemorial. The alliance between the landlords and the *rassagirs* (cattle rustlers), and the insecurity that the peasant experienced both in terms of his property and his women (referred to by Sir Malcolm Darling in his books written more than forty years ago[30]), seem to have continued even as late as the 1965 elections when the son of Firoz Khan Noon, the former Prime Minister, described to me the following conditions in the district of Sargodha:

In our society, the arm of the law is removed from where you live. It may be twenty or thirty miles away. I may be dead before I get to law. The tendency, therefore, is to gang up. . . . If somebody stole my friend's cattle, my friend is right when he bashes him up. I support my friend irrespective of whether he is right or wrong. This is a sort of insurance policy for the whole group. And you vote for a leader who helps in getting one's nephew released from police lock-up.

Thus, one begins to wonder how the Ayub regime can be applauded for forging the so-called grandiose links between the government and the countryside through the institutions of Basic Democracies when the changes he brought about did not significantly alter the repression that continued almost unabated.

The question that needs to be raised is this: Does institution-building have a social purpose and social benefits, or is it designed purely for expansion of the power of the state with no social purposes at all? It is significant that Huntington was content to extol Ayub for having instituted Basic Democracies and thus expanded his power. Huntington probably assumed that this expansion of power would serve certain social purposes without caring to tell us what they precisely were. When one looks at Ayub's constitution, which was designed to remove the obstacles that hampered executive decision-making both at the center and in the

30. Malcolm Darling, *Punjab Peasant in Prosperity and Debt* (London: Oxford University Press, 1930), p. 227.

provinces, one is struck by the fact that Ayub, by trans-
forming the government into a government of the President,
by the President, and for the President, stripped himself of
a considerable sense of legitimacy and at the same time
alienated a host of urban forces. Thus, the social costs that
he incurred, whether for personal or social benefits, were so
high that a few massive uprisings in the urban centers shook
his regime to its foundations, and when the social unrest
spread in both wings his regime collapsed like a house of
cards.

Bhutto's Leadership

Ayub represents a watershed in the history of Pakistan.
It is in his regime that we see a clear unfolding of certain
trends and developments that represent what may be described as an ideological change in Pakistan. Under him we
see economic change through industrialization, improved
agriculture, and modest land reforms spreading to areas
other than Karachi, particularly to the Punjab and to a few
urban centers in Sind and the Frontier. Can one suggest
that as a result of these changes the masses in many parts
of West Pakistan can no longer be aroused by appeals to
vague and emotional notions of Islamic unity? The role of
an ideology in the last resort is to justify or explain the
existence of a particular social order. If the ruling elites in
Pakistan are not very religious and at the same time have
created an economic and social system that is inegalitarian,
and the knowledge of such social and economic inequities
is spreading, there arises a serious credibility gap if the ruling elites continue to preach that Pakistan's polity is Islamic.
This explains why Bhutto's Pakistan People's Party made
such serious inroads in the semi-prosperous areas of Lahore
division, eastern Multan division, and all along the Grand
Trunk Road where lie areas of industrial development and

agricultural prosperity. The PPP offered a new but vague ideological program under the name of Islamic socialism, or Masawat. Ayub, by not being able to satisfy the Bengali expectations he had aroused through his constitutional assurances that disparity would soon be removed and by his policies of coercion of urban elements in East Bengal, laid the foundations for the dismemberment of Pakistan in 1971. It was during Ayub's regime that in both East and West Pakistan there was a growing skepticism as to whether the appeal of Islam could continue to keep the two disparate wings together. This represents the other side of ideological change; that is to say, Islam could neither be used to justify or explain the increasing inegalitarian society that had emerged in West Pakistan nor could the Islamic factor serve any longer as the only cementing force between the two disparate wings of the country. How does one encapsulate this ideological change that took place during the Ayub era? We have suggested that the existential base had changed, creating in its wake certain social conflicts. The GNP went up, but inequitable distribution of these increases in the GNP stared in the people's faces. Expectations had been aroused both in the urban and rural areas. Islam as the cementing force between the two wings did not seem to be working, and it was clear that Bengali aspirations could never be satisfied within the existing framework if the economy had to satisfy the increasing expectations of the West Pakistanis as well. There were regional conflicts in West Pakistan itself. Class conflict in the urban areas of the Punjab and Sind were increasing. Bhutto interpreted and tried to channel such changes and the accompanying social conflicts through the legitimizing cultural framework of Islam.[31] The way to resolve these conflicts and at the same

31. I have adapted Lane's paradigm of ideological change. Robert E. Lane, *Political Ideology* (New Haven: Yale University Press, 1962), pp. 415–19.

time move the country ahead was through Islamic socialism. It was a masterly move designed to give him short-term advantages, but it was fraught with ominous consequences.

Bhutto had received his training in political science and law, and in the portfolio of foreign affairs he seemed to have found the full flowering of his talents and training. Both his schooling and his contacts with the world's statesmen had aroused in him an intense desire to play a dominant role in the politics of his country. He was an astute observer of events and a master tactician. But he was mostly at home in international affairs and diplomacy, and one often felt that he tended to look at domestic affairs from international and diplomatic perspectives. His social background was that of a Sindhi landlord. His feudal origins provided sources of material comfort and he was not altogether ashamed of his social background and upbringing. An extract from Selig Harrison's article was reproduced by an Embassy of Pakistan publication in which it was stated: "Bhutto carries his wealth easily, observing matter-of-factly that he would find it difficult 'to indulge in all of my weaknesses' if he did not have the income from his 110,000-acre family estates along the Arabian Sea and the Baluchistan border."[32] There is no doubt that Bhutto feels genuinely about the poverty that exists in his society. Those who have watched him deciding petty cases of theft, cattle-lifting, kidnapping, or police brutality in the open *kucheries* (offices where decisions are announced) cannot but be impressed by his concern for the plight of the common man. But not having suffered the deprivations that he is trying to remedy, he can only think in terms of remedial actions and not quantum leaps. Therefore, one cannot expect him to produce a blueprint for the next decade because he is at his best in making short-term, but rapid, advances and outwitting his opponents.

32 Zulfikar Ali Bhutto, *A South Asian View* (Washington, D.C.: Embassy of Pakistan, n.d.), p. iv.

Progressive De-radicalization of the PPP

1. *Cleavages and conflicts*

Immediately after his election victory Bhutto is reported to have remarked to a foreign correspondent that the people who were most unhappy with his election victory were the Communists. At the party convention in November 1972, probably referring to radical impatience with the pace of change, he made it clear that his party's program stood for socialism and not for communism. So far as socialist ideas were concerned, resumption of three million acres of land without compensation, nationalization of insurance, and the takeover of twenty categories of industries were steps designed to establish socialism in the country.[33] One of the MPAs in the Punjab pointed out that Bhutto could not take a radical stand against the landlords. In addition to the kind of political support they provided for winning elections, Bhutto felt that the land reforms under Ayub had gone far enough and that the party should take a stand against the industrialists and capitalists who exploited the resources of the country in a monopolistic fashion. This was also borne out by the *Foundation and Policy* document of the party, which states:

In the rural areas, in relation to agriculture, *the cultivator may suffer under a feudal system of land tenure* and be exploited through the process by which his produce is brought to the market or the consumer. *It is, however, in the industrial sector of production, which is principally urban, that the problem of capitalist exploitation presents itself in its typical form.* [My italics.][34]

The radical leader, Meraj Mohammad Khan, disclosed in an interview that his differences with Bhutto started at the Hala

33. Zulfikar Ali Bhutto, President of Pakistan, *Speeches and Statements, October 1, 1972–December 31, 1972* (Karachi: Department of Films and Publications, Government of Pakistan, 1973), p. 170.

34. *Foundation and Policy: Pakistan People's Party* (Lahore: Printed privately by Dr. Mubashar Hassan, n.d.), pp. 34–35.

conference in 1970 when he advocated that in its fight against imperialism the PPP should take a stand against the capitalists, but the party should also try to liquidate the feudal system. Thus, Meraj Mohammad Khan argued that he and his group wanted to place primary emphasis on the liquidation of feudalism, whereas Bhutto was opposed to this and wanted primary emphasis placed on controlling or fighting capitalism because imperialism depended upon capitalism and not feudalism.[35]

We are not so much concerned with describing or explaining the political or ideological conflicts in the Pakistan People's party as we are in exploring what impact such conflicts have on the party organization and above all on its viability as an instrument to mobilize political support. Bhutto seems to think that as the supreme builder and arbitrator of the party he should be able to keep divergent or conflicting elements within the party and keep the party intact if these elements would follow his leadership. He is politically flexible enough not to commit himself too rigidly but to keep his options open. When pressure for the party to take a stand in favor of lower land ceilings and radical land reforms became too strong, he made the necessary concessions. Could it be that he has always been in favor of the more moderate type of socialism, that is, the democratic or Islamic variety, but he wanted to enlist the support of the radicals, some of whom were Communists? Without such support, he could not have organized his party against his former landlord rivals, old politicians, and particularly the Jamaat-i-Islami.

2. *The Party at the Worker or Polling Station Level*

Political parties have often been studied in terms of the interests they aggregate. Political parties in developing societies have also been studied as grand national move-

---

35. Interview in *Al-Fatah* (Karachi), Sept. 6–13, 1973, p. 20.

ments. There are not too many studies that bring out the characteristics, the social background, and political skills of party workers. In societies where elections have been fought on the basis of adult franchise, the role of party workers as transmitting agents or opinion leaders or as controllers of voting banks (in the case of baradari leaders in Pakistan and jati leaders in India) is important. A study entitled *Pakistan People's Party: Past, Present and Future*,[36] written before the general elections of 1970, suggested that even though the key positions in the party were occupied by members of the upper middle class, landlords, and small capitalists, nevertheless farmers, students, laborers, small shopkeepers, and merchants from cities and villages were the active party workers. They occupied lower positions at the constituency and polling station level. Thus, we interviewed party workers in the constituencies of Mubashir Hasan, that is, Baghbanpura, Moghalpura, Dhenapura, or polling stations 73, 85, 87, 88, and 89; Z. A. Bhutto's constituency, which later became the constituency of Mahmud Ali Kasuri, that is, the cantonment area; Sheikh Rashid's constituency, Ichhra, Ward No. 19; and finally, the constituency of Malik Akhtar, namely, parts of Walled City and Gwalmandi. These interviews were carried out during January-February 1971. The professions of party workers ranged from such middle-class ones as those of doctors, insurance managers, and agents to such lower middle-class and working-class professions as tea stall owners, foodgrain agents, railway clerks, fruit sellers, electricians, fitters, and workers from the mint, railways, and Water and Power Development Authority.

In between the MNA and MPA and the lower-level polling station workers there stood the active party organizers, most of them experienced party organizers either from the Muslim League or even from the Communist Party. In some

36. *Pakistan People's Party: Mazi, Hal, aur Mustaqbil* [Past, Present, and Future] (Rawalpindi: Javid Iqbal, n.d.).

cases, their views were the same as those of the MNA, but in a few cases one noticed that the party organizers were more militant than either the MNA or the MPA. One party organizer who worked in the Mint area and the adjoining areas of Baghbanpura was a former Communist Party worker who constantly stressed that his workers were so militant they often felt like encircling the house of the MPA who was a small capitalist. The MNA seemed to think that neither the Chinese nor the Russian social model was applicable to Pakistan's condition, whereas his party organizer held just the opposite view.

It is essential for political scientists to go to the grass-roots level and get a full flavor of the politics of poverty, despair, and rising militancy. It is difficult to get this flavor through survey research. One has to go inside the dark, dingy huts in the Mint area to see how eight or ten people live in a room no more than twelve feet by ten feet. The phrases one comes across, the manner of speech, are all different. When you refer to socialism, they talk about Masawat (equality) because that is how they understand the term socialism. It is not just Masawat, it is Masawat-i-Muhammadi. The upper middle-class leaders may be concerned about the *fatwas* (religious decrees) that the *ulama* may have issued against them, but to be called an anti-Islamicist in the press or in public speeches by one's opponents does not endanger the personal safety of the upper middle-class leaders. But these workers are on the firing line. They are being attacked in the sermons in mosques. Some of their neighbors may have stopped speaking to them. How do they go about counteracting this kind of propaganda and the personal discomforts it may entail? They have to meet the propaganda by constantly stressing that the Prophet established equality, that Bilal, who was a Negro, was asked by the Prophet to summon the faithful to the prayers in the Kaba itself. Since God's own place did not come in danger or become impure when Bilal, the Negro, came into the Kaba, how can Islam come in danger if the common people's rule is established? The standard of living and the social status of the barber, of the laundryman, are being raised in the same way that the Prophet raised the status of inferior persons. The workers might say that the *maulvi* who was giving the sermons against the PPP was in the pay of the rich.

In July 1974, nearly three and a half years after the first interviews were carried out, we interviewed some of the same party workers in Baghbanpura. This time we detected a distinct overtone of pessimism and disappointment. They said that just as the Muslim League cadres had been infiltrated by Unionist Party workers, the PPP was suffering the same fate. They tended to be guarded in their remarks in the sense that they would not support extreme radicals like Mukhtar Rana because he wanted to take over factories in Lyallpur in haste. The party had become unpopular because it had been infiltrated by corrupt people. As many as 155 workers in the area had left the party and joined the Pakistan Kisan Mazdoor Party. As a former member of the Communist party, one of the principal interviewees complained that workers were given party offices without going through a probationary period. He was in favor of establishing a school to train party workers. Socialism had almost become a bad word. The movement against the Ahmadis had strengthened the Islamicists. In addition, the party workers complained that the party had been factionalized by ministers and MNAs trying to rally their respective bands of followers. This suggests that the links between the upper echelons and the grass roots have become increasingly tenuous. The fact that the anti-Ahmadi riots erupted and took the government by surprise indicates that the party was not providing timely intelligence, a defect readily admitted by Mr. Bhutto when his attention was drawn to it.

3. The Role of the Party and the System of Political and Administrative Management in the Punjab

For as long as people in the Punjab can remember, they say that the province has needed an iron hand to maintain

order and political stability. Thus, it may be said that Mustafa
Khar was placed in charge of the Punjab by Bhutto for two
purposes: first, to provide strong government; second, to
keep the radicals under control and allow the middle-of-the-
road or moderate sections in the party to come to the top.
According to various reports, Khar and Mubashir were successful in destroying the party structure that Rashid had
built. Even in Lahore, with the exception of Baghbanpura,
the party structure had been completely overhauled in such
a way that radicals were eliminated. Hanif Ramay, the
former chief minister of the Punjab, has disclosed in an
interview that during Khar's time, central ministers could
not visit the Punjab without Khar's permission.[37] When it
was obvious that Khar was unleashing so much terror and
oppression and thus had caused irreparable damage to the
party organization, Bhutto acted much too slowly, not removing him until March 1974. This again indicates that the
party is not often regarded as an essential part of the machinery of government. It is somewhat strange that Bhutto,
who has so recently won political support and office through
the PPP organization, would let the party disintegrate and
intervene only when the rot had gone too far. One clue to
this puzzle is that the administrative and police machinery
of the government is so strong that a political leader can often
afford to dispense with the party machinery. We have pointed
out that this kind of weakness had emerged under Jinnah as
well. In this tradition of political management of the province
by the administrators, the party, if necessary, can be used as
a docile instrument not so much by party officers as by
bureaucratic officials. When a meeting has to be organized,
it is the police officials who assemble the required crowd,
and in this task the party officials may be called upon to help
them. Under Ayub, it was usually the police officials who
were thanked by the President and the governor for having
organized the political meeting peacefully.

37. Interview in *Akhbar-e-Jehan* (Karachi), June 5, 1974, p. 12.

4. Reorganization of the Party

It has been announced with considerable fanfare that the party is being reorganized, particularly in the Punjab and Sind. The chief organizer in the Punjab is Meraj Khalid, and in Sind, Syed Qaim Ali Shah. In the Punjab, Meraj Khalid has issued an elaborate party document, *The New Reorganization of the Party: Objectives, Rules and Methods.* One of the central doctrines of party organization that he expounds is democratic centralism. He points out that the principle of majority rule should be accepted. The lower echelons would have to follow the directives and decisions coming from the top. However, every worker would have the right to express his views freely. It is not stated how this doctrine is going to be made operational in the party organization. The document is full of platitudes. Party workers are exhorted to be of unimpeachable character, and all those party workers who have been dishonest, corrupt, oppressive, and have thus tarnished the reputation of the party and the leader should be summarily removed from the party. How inconsequential this attempt is likely to be is partly indicated by the fact that the secretary-general and the deputy secretary-general are almost poles apart in their political views. The deputy secretary-general, Taj Mohammad Langa, described himself as a scientific socialist. In an interview he has cited numerous instances of how poor peasants are being evicted from their lands, and when they protest, the police, instead of helping them, oppresses them.[38] Mr. Rizvi, who is secretary-general of the party, when interviewed complained that radicals were creating rifts within the party. "They claim to be Socialists. Maybe they are Communists. They do not believe in Islamic Socialism."

When we interviewed party MPAs to find out how the party was being reorganized at the district level, we were told that the basic strategy of the president of the PPP in the Punjab, Meraj Khalid, was to prevent the conflicts and cleav-

38. *Al-Fatah,* July 19–26, 1974, pp. 33–34.

ages from tearing the party apart and somehow keep the conflicting elements within the same fold. One MPA remarked:

On the reorganizing committee of Jhang, _____ and myself have been appointed. I thought the dispute should be first settled. We were told that the two of us should sort out our differences. Since his way of party organization is different from mine, there were going to be two reports. We were told we should submit one report. The decision was that he takes 50 percent of offices, and I take 50 percent of offices. The result—the party will not get the best people.

Huntington suggests a series of dichotomous criteria for testing the level of institution-building in a society: one of them is autonomy-subordination. The Pakistan People's Party has not yet emerged as an autonomous institution conducting some or a number of its activities on its own without being rigorously supervised or directed by the Chairman, nor has it become a totally pliable instrument in the hands of the Chairman or other upper-echelon officials. Increasing radicalism in Pakistan's politics has become a fact. There are trade union strongholds where the police run the risk of being assaulted or brutalized. Even in the political backwater of Sind, radical rebelliousness may be detected. Party workers openly talk about how *haris* (peasants) are being evicted from their lands, and some of them at personal risk to themselves have disclosed the names of individual *wadiras* (Sindhi landlords) who have oppressed the *haris*. They are even resentful toward the Chairman for having allowed the party's power structure to be infiltrated by unpopular *wadiras*. Not only does the party's chief organizer, Syed Qaim Ali Shah, constantly refer to the way *haris* are being evicted on a large scale and how *wadiras* are becoming powerful, but even Mumtaz Ali Bhutto, who until 1974 was chief minister of Sind and is himself one of the biggest landlords, talks of the eviction of *haris* and the growing influence of certain *wadiras* with bad records. Seemingly, these are two of the most popular issues in Sind politics. What is even more striking is the emergence of left-right cleavages at the highest level, namely, in the cabinet of the PPP government. Fourteen PPP MNAs have signed a statement criticizing Mr. Khurshid Hasan Meer, the minister of communications. They accuse him and his followers of functioning as tools of persons with Communist ideas and of having launched a campaign against Maulana Kausar Niazi, the minister for information and broadcasting.

The party as an organization is in considerable disarry. One visits party headquarters in Rawalpindi or its main office in Karachi only to find that apart from a few posters and menial servants, not a single party worker or an officeholder is present. No other person in Pakistan deserves as much credit as Bhutto for having aroused political consciousness in the country. Bhutto should welcome the emergence of ideological rifts within the party and should have improved the organizational machinery to provide a forum for accommodating or resolving such conflicts.

The party even in its heyday was basically an urban phenomenon. Whatever activity emerged at the rural level was largely the creation of urban party workers. Impressed by Mao's ideas, the *Foundation Document* proudly proclaimed:

We will go to the people in humility to learn as much as to teach. Once the people are mobilized we can march forward together, hand in hand, towards our destined goal. You members of the Party must study the problems of the common man and carry the Party's message to the masses. In this way they will be brought to the right path and we shall correct our mistakes.[39]

Nothing has come of these attempts to make the mass line an organizing principle of the party. This is where the building of the party can become institution-building at its creative best. Cattle-lifting, land disputes, and even low agricultural productivity exemplify what Banfield has described as the main characteristic of a backward society,

39. *Foundation and Policy: PPP*, op. cit., p. 6.

namely, the inability to conduct economic or social activities through concerted action and teamwork. It is here that the party can learn and teach, but before it teaches it has much to learn at the grass-roots level. Meraj Mohammad Khan in an interview pointed out what enormously challenging tasks awaited party workers in infiltrating the feudal structures of Sind and Baluchistan. "We have no idea how the sardari system in Baluchistan works in all its details and complexity and how can we dismantle or replace it before we know its intricate working."

10

Nationalism and the Quest for Ideology in Pakistan

Hafeez Malik

A consensus has emerged among modern historians that defines nationalism as a "corporate will" of the people to live together in one state under a government of their own making.[1] This corporate will may be produced by any of the following factors: common geography, economy, language, ethnic background, history (reflecting not merely a sharing of common experiences, but reacting to them with more or less similar sentiments),[2] and religion. Crystallizing in the century prior to the advent of Pakistan, Muslim nationalism in India reflected the dynamics of historical, economic, and religious forces.

This century of nationalism also awakened the Hindus, who developed several religious and social reform movements.[3] The All-India National Congress channeled the Hindu awakening into self-determination by emphasizing concepts of India's territorial and cultural unity. Dialectically opposed to these concepts of "Indian" nationalism, Muslim nationalism developed its own character and it steadily grew more exclusive and separatist. Acceptance of the Muslim nationalists' claims by the Congress would amount to

---

1. Hans Kohn, *The Idea of Nationalism: A Study of Its Origins and Background* (New York: Macmillan, 1944), pp. 10–13. See also Louis L. Snyder, *The Dynamics of Nationalism* (Princeton: D. Van Nostrand, 1964), pp. 1–2.

2. For example, foes of one people should not be the heroes of the other.

3. For the role of social reform movements in awakening Hindu cultural as well as political consciousness, see Charles Heimsath, *Indian National and Hindu Social Reform* (Princeton: Princeton University Press, 1964).

abandoning the view of India's territorial unity and accepting a blow to the self-identity of the Indian nationalists.

In the century preceding partition, Indian and Muslim nationalists strenuously endeavored to disprove each other's cherished theories of nationalism. For purposes of analysis, this historical debate can be divided into two unequal periods: (*a*) 1857–1947 and (*b*) 1947–72.

Indian View of Indian Nationalism and Culture: 1857–1947

The Muslim claim to a separate cultural identity was rejected by Indian scholars and ridiculed by the Congress leaders. Hindus considered Muslims "indianized" because of their cultural contacts with the Hindus. To support this contention, a four-stage process of Indian history was invoked: (1) foreign races regularly invaded India, especially after the Indo-Aryan invasion around 1500 B.C.; (2) they were amalgamated with the "native" Indian population; (3) the foreign and indigenous cultures were synthesized; and (4) the invaders eventually disappeared as a separate entity. Just as the pre-Muslim invaders of India, i.e., Persians, Greeks, Scythians, Kushanas, and White Huns had been assimilated into the Hindu culture, so too the Muslims had lost their cultural distinctiveness.[4] Rabindranath Tagore expressed the theory of Muslim assimilation in his famous "Hymn to India."

> Here I stand with arms outstretched to hail man,
> Man divine in his own image,
> And sing to his glory in notes glad and free.
>   .   .   .   .

---

4. For the most recent exposition of this theory, see Romila Thapar, *A History of India* (Baltimore: The Johns Hopkins University Press, 1966), I, 303. Thaper maintains that Muslims were assimilated into the Hindu social order during the period of the Delhi Sultanate, especially during the sixteenth century.

No one knows whence and at whose call came pouring
Endless inundations of men
Rushing madly along, to lose themselves in the sea;
Aryans and non-Aryans, Dravidians and Chinese,
Scythians, Huns, Pathans and Mughals —
All are mixed, merged and lost in one body.

Among Congress leaders, the more vigorous exponents of this theory were Mahatma Gandhi and Jawaharlal Nehru. Gandhi combined two contrasting strands of thought. In his personal tolerance and sympathy for other faiths he was progressive; on the other hand, traditional Hinduism with its rigid caste rules was decisive in developing his religious and cultural orientations. To Gandhi, Muslims were an additional caste that should be reclaimed in forging Indian unity. He believed that "every Muslim is merely a Hindu who has accepted Islam, and every Muslim will have a Hindu name if he goes far enough in his family history."[5]

Gandhi insisted Hindu converts to Islam could not be considered a separate nationality, because even in outward appearance they could not be distinguished from the parent stock. "The vast majority of Muslims in India are converts to Islam or are descendants of converts," stated Gandhi.

They did not become a separate nation as soon as they became converts. I have often found it difficult to distinguish by outward sign between a Bengali Hindu and a Bengali Muslim. The same phenomenon is observable more or less in the South among the poor who constitute the masses of India. When I first met the late Sir Ali Imam I did not know that he was not a Hindu. His speech, his dress, his manners, his food were the same as that of the majority of the Hindus in whose midst I found him. His name alone betrayed him. Not even that with Quide-Azam [Mohammad Ali] Jinnah. For his name could be that of any Hindu. The reader will be surprised to know that for days, if not for months, I used to think of the late Vallabbhai Patel as a Muslim as he used to sport a beard and a Turkish cap. Sir Muhammad Iqbal used to speak with pride of his

5. Mahatma Gandhi, *To the Protagonists of Pakistan* (Ahmadabad: Navajivan, 1949), p. 65.

Brahminical descent. Iqbal and Kitchlu are names common to Hindus and Muslims. The Hindus and Muslims of India are not two nations. Those whom God has made one, man will never be able to divide.[6]

In analyzing the impact of history and religion on the Muslims of India, Gandhi tacitly implied the existence of a "Muslim mind" or "Muslim character." But this was all he would concede to the Pakistan national movement. On the other hand, Nehru recognized the existence of a "narrow communal mentality" seeking political power and patronage for India's Muslims. Like Gandhi, Nehru displayed a dialectical clash of orientations. He had a lifelong commitment to bourgeois institutions of parliamentary democracy, but Nehru thought like a Marxist when analyzing India's history and cultural development. For Nehru, Hindu-Muslim conflict was only an economic conflict that future prosperity would eliminate. "Politically," says Nehru, "the idea [of a Muslim nation and Muslim culture] is absurd, economically it is fantastic; it is hardly worth considering."[7]

While Marxist in orientation, Nehru's analysis reflected an unusual metaphysical approach to Indian culture: "Some kind of a dream of unity has occupied the mind of India since the dawn of civilization." Muslims were an essential element of that unity around which Emperor Akbar (1556–1605) hoped to build his empire; Hindus and Muslims were to be "organically fused into one people." Thus the Mughal rulers were strong so long as they identified themselves with "the genius of the nation" and endeavored to work for a common nationality. When Aurangzeb (1658–1707) began to suppress this unity movement and to behave more like a Muslim than an Indian, the Mughal Empire began to disintegrate. The Maratha and Sikh movements, contesting Aurangzeb's policies, represented "resurgent nationalism."

6. Mahatma Gandhi, *Communal Unity* (Ahmadabad: Navajivan, 1949), pp. 294–95.
7. Jawaharlal Nehru, *An Autobiography* (New York: John Day, 1941), p. 469.

According to Nehru, the political and religious strife made Shivaji (1630–80) "the symbol of a resurgent Hindu nationalism, drawing inspiration from the old [Hindu] classics."[8]

Nehru insisted the emergence of eighteenth-century Hindu nationalism was a reaction to Aurangzeb's policies, but he failed to admit the development of a corresponding sentiment among the Muslims and the Sikhs. This author has compared elsewhere Aurangzeb's fifty years of warfare against the Sikhs and Hindus in northern and southern India to the Napoleonic wars in Europe inasmuch as both succeeded in unleashing a nationalistic upsurge among the combatants.[9] While Muslim nationalism was confined to the northern Indian Muslim elites, it was not until after 1857 that Muslim middle and working classes began to feel its impact. However, during the eighteenth century Shah Wali-u'llah (1703–62) and his followers were instrumental in promulgating a separate political destiny for the Muslims of India.

The Muslim View of Muslim Nationalism and Culture

Nationalist Muslim Interpretations

The Muslim interpretations of nationalism were by no means monolithic since they were divided in their allegiance between several political parties. For convenience, the Muslims can be divided into two broad categories—*Nationalist Muslims* and *Muslim Nationalists*. Not merely semantic, the differences between them were of basic orientation toward the future of India and the Muslims' position in its political system. Nationalist Muslims were

8. Jawaharlal Nehru, *The Discovery of India* (Calcutta: Signet Press, 1946), p. 319.

9. Hafeez Malik, *Muslim Nationalism in India and Pakistan* (Washington, D.C.: Public Affairs Press, 1963), chap. 3.

committed to the territorial unity of India and sought to maximize Muslim "influence" in its future polity. In the five Muslim-majority provinces and the large Muslim-majority states of Jammu and Kashmir (which in a United India would have become the sixth Muslim province), the Nationalist Muslims saw an automatic solution to the problem of Muslim cultural autonomy. Fair treatment of the Hindu minority in these "six" provinces would, in their eyes, ensure fair treatment to the Muslims in the more numerous Hindu-majority provinces. Although Indian "socialism" in a framework of federalism might ensure an equitable distribution of resources, partition would only split the Muslims into three units, with none enjoying the power or prestige to compete with a Hindu-dominated India.

While the Nationalist Muslims opted for the territorial nationalism of India, they differed radically with each other over the concept of Muslim culture. The "composite Indian culture" became the slogan of the modernized secularists, who were led by Abul Kalam Azad, and in the 1960s by his protégés, Hamayun Kabir, M. C. Chagla, and Dr. Zakir Husain. Lifelong members of the Congress party, they were individually influential in the Congress hierarchy but distant from the Muslim masses. Religious traditional political parties, including Jamiat Ulama-i-Hind, Jamaat-i-Islami, and Majlis-i-Ahrar in the Punjab, also remained loyal to the concept of a united India, and with the exception of Jamaat-i-Islami accepted the leadership of the Congress in political matters. Culturally, however, they remained united with the Muslim League and shared its conviction that the Muslims remained an exception to the "assimilative churn" of Indian cultural history. Like the League, they believed the Muslims not only had a separate cultural identity, but that it ought to be strengthened to prevent Muslim assimilation into the Hindu culture. Unwittingly these Islam-oriented political parties, though loyal to the Congress party, generated frequent tension and violence in Hindu-Muslim relations by undertaking campaigns to purify the mores of the Muslims if they reflected Hindu culture; or by attempting to Islamize the Hindus, especially in the Muslim-majority provinces. No one undermined the position of the modernized secularist Nationalist Muslims more than the religious Nationalist Muslims who charged the former with being a culturally alienated elite. Strange bedfellows in their support of the Congress party, the Nationalist Muslims failed to realize how their dialectical positions kept the majority of the Muslims alienated from the Congress.

Among the modernized secular Nationalist Muslims, Badruddin Tyabji (1844–1906) did not subscribe to the view that India was one nation and that Muslims had ceased to have a cultural identity of their own. Writing a letter to Sir Sayyid Ahmad Khan on February 18, 1888, Tyabji stated:

Your objection to the Congress is that "it regards India as one Nation." Now I am not aware of anyone regarding the whole of India as one Nation, and if you read my inaugural address[10] [of December 26, 1887] you will find it distinctly stated that there are numerous communities or nations in India which had peculiar problems of their own to solve. . . .[11]

Sir Sayyid failed to convince Tyabji of the Congress party's irrelevance to Muslim political aspirations, and Tyabji could not persuade Sir Sayyid that the Congress was an appropriate forum to articulate common Indian demands or grievances. Tyabji, however, remained close to Sir Sayyid's conception of the cultural issue by actively involving himself in the affairs of the Muhammadan Educational Conference, which Sir Sayyid had established in 1886. Tyabji and his family discarded Gujrati and adopted Urdu as their spoken tongue. He also presided over the seventeenth session of the Muhammadan Educational Conference in Bombay on December

10. For the text of Tyabji's address, see A. G. Noorani, *Badruddin Tyabji* (New Delhi: Publications Division, Ministry of Information, 1969), Appendix II.

11. *Ibid.*, p. 178.

28, 1903. He used the occasion to defend his support of the Congress, maintaining that Muslims should cooperate with each other to promote social reforms, modern education, and common Muslim culture.[12]

Tyabji was consistent in his political life; consequently his pronouncements never caused any confusion in the minds of his followers or critics. Not so with Abul Kalam Azad (1888–1958) who became an enigma for his admirers and an object of disdain for his opponents. A Muslim Nationalist from 1906 to 1920, Azad first rejected political cooperation with the Hindus. However, he ended his life as a secular Nationalist Muslim who would have no part of Pakistan. As a Muslim Nationalist, Azad rejected the concept of territorial nationalism and disapproved of those Muslims who wanted to collaborate with the Hindus. Discussing the Muslim problem of identity and self-awareness, Azad stated in *Al-Hilal* on September 8, 1912:

Hindus can, like other nations, revive their self-awareness and national consciousness on the basis of secular Nationalism, but it is indeed not possible for the Muslims. Their nationality is not inspired by racial or geographical exclusivity; it transcends all manmade barriers. . . . Europe may be inspired by the concepts of "Nation," and "homeland," Muslims can seek inspiration for self-awareness only from God and Islam.[13]

The Caliphate movement in India during the 1920s forced some of the reluctant Muslim Nationalists, including Azad, to forge an alliance with Mahatma Gandhi and the Congress. Azad had the task of convincing his followers that in the struggle for the Caliphate, cooperation with the Hindus was permissible according to Islamic law. From Sura LX (i,9) of

---

12. For the text of his presidential address to the Muhammadan Educational Conference, see Maulvi Anwar Ahmad Zubairi, *Khutab-i Aliya: Chahel Sala Khutbat-i Sadarat ka Majmu'a.* Vol. I (Aligarh: Aligarh Muslim University Press, 1927), 223–36.

13. Abul Kalam Azad, *Madamin-i Abul Kalam Azad* (Delhi: Hindustani Publishing House, 1944), p. 87.

the Quran, legitimacy was derived for a political alliance with the National Congress:

God forbids you not, as regards those who have not fought you in religion's cause, nor expelled you from habitations, that you should be kindly to them. . . . God only forbids you as to those who have fought you in religion's cause and expelled you from your habitations, and have supported you in your expulsion, that you should take them for friends.

Azad interpreted the Quran to mean that the Hindus had never invaded a Muslim land, nor killed Muslims for their religious faith, nor supported their expulsion from any country. Despite this interpretation, Azad's alliance with the Congress was not based on an acceptance of a common Indian Hindu-Muslim nationality. Congress support was welcomed by Azad because it aided in the struggle for the Caliphate. After the First World War, however, Mustafa Kamal Ataturk abolished the Caliphate. Arab nationalism, appealing to all Arabs on the basis of language, common history, and culture regardless of racial and denominational affiliations, asserted itself. These events greatly impressed Azad, and his concept of nationality radically changed. In the post-1920 period Azad ceased to be a Muslim Nationalist; he accepted the fundamental principles of Arab and Turkish secular and territorial nationalism and applied them to the Hindu-Muslim relationship in India.

Addressing a provincial assembly of the Caliphate movement in Agra on October 25, 1921, Azad carried the point of Hindu-Muslim cooperation to its extreme. He referred to the Prophet Muhammad's covenant between the Muslim inhabitants of Medina and the Jews. The covenant was negotiated by the parties some time after the entrance (A.D. 622) of the Prophet into Medina. Its purpose was to establish an alliance for the common defense of the Prophet's followers and Jews against the hostile Quraysh (Mecca's pre-Islamic keepers) who had persecuted the Prophet in Mecca and forced him to emigrate to Medina. The preamble

of the covenant stated: *"Bism Allah al-rahmān al-rahım.
Hadha Kitāb min Muhammad al-Nabīy bayn al-muminīn
wa-al-muslimīn min Quraysh wa-Yathrib wa-man tab hum
falhaq bham wa-jahad ma ham al-naham ummat wahidat
min dūn al-nūs."*[14]

In the name of God, the Compassionate, the Merciful. This is a
document from Muhammad the Prophet [governing the relations]
between the believers and Muslims of Quraysh and Yathrib [al-
Medina] and those who followed them and joined them and
labored with them. They are one community [*Ummā wahidā*]
to the exclusion of all men.[15]

Azad's rendition of the key phrase *Ummā wahidā* gives it a
connotation different from any that are generally accepted.
He rendered the translation as follows: "We enter into an
agreement and truce with all tribes inhabiting the suburbs
of Medina, and we together want to constitute a nation."[16]
The application of this covenant, as a historical precedent,
to the political situation between the Hindus and the Muslims was analogous to Muslim cooperation with the Hindus
in the Caliphate movement. Azad's translation could not
provide a justification for a joint Hindu-Muslim nation in
India. However, by the 1930s he was expounding the
Congress view of Indian nationality. While the Muslim
League under the leadership of Jinnah was passing the
"Pakistan Resolution" in 1940, Azad, in his presidential
address to the Ramgarh Session of the All-India National
Congress in the same year, reiterated his commitment to
the concept of Hindu-Muslim nationality. "I am a part of

14. Abd al-Malik Ibn Hisham, *Kitab Sirat Rasul Allah*, (Gottingen: Dieterichsche
Universitäts-Buchhandlung, 1858), p. 341.
15. Alfred Guillaume, *The Life of Muhammad*, a translation of Hisham's *Kitab
Sirat Rasul Allah* (London: Oxford University Press, 1955), pp. 231–32. Muir, however, offers the following translation as part of this document: "The Jewish clans in
alliance with the several tribes of Medina are one people with the unbelievers."
Sir William Muir, *The Life of Muhammad* (Edinburgh: John Grant, 1912), p. 184.
16. Abul Kalam Azad, *Khutbat-i Abul Kalam Azad* (Lahore: Al-Manara Academy,
n.d.), p. 42.

the indivisible unity that is Indian nationality," declared Azad. "I am indispensable to this noble edifice and without me this splendid structure of India is incomplete. I am an essential element which has worked to build India. I can never surrender this claim."[17]

To what extent did the Nationalist Muslims succeed in achieving acceptance for their ideas? Not very much! After the abolition of the Caliphate by Ataturk in 1925, traditionalist Ulema who stood for a united India lost credibility with the Muslim masses, and the Muslim middle classes turned toward the Muslim League and Pakistan. Consequently, secular Nationalist Muslims lost their natural constituency and became an anathema in India for the masses; this was especially so after 1947 when the masses perceived them as "agents" of the ruling Congress party. Among the traditionalists, Jamaat-i-Islami's Maududi was a maverick who opposed the Congress' concept of "composite Indian culture and nationalism," while he rejected simultaneously the ideology of Muslim nationalism as un-Islamic. He opposed Pakistan because it territorially confined Islam. He called for the rise of a new "nationality of all believers so that a world nationality of Islam might take place."[18] On a lesser scale, Maududi hoped to transform the whole of India into Dar-ul-Islam (Land of Islam), and the Jamaat-i-Islami was founded in Lahore on August 25, 1941, to bring this about. Although Maududi had little influence in Indian politics before 1947, he became a significant politico-religious force after Pakistan gained its independence.

Muslim Nationalist Interpretations

The political genealogy of the Muslim Nationalists has been traced by Ishtiaq Husain Qureshi, Aziz Ahmad, and

17. *Ibid.*, p. 317.
18. Abul Ala Maududi, *Masla-i Qawmiat* (Pathankot: Maktaba Jama't-i Islami, 1947), p. 117; *Jama't-i Islami: Us ka Maqsad, Tarikh Awr Lahya-i Aml* (Pathankot: Maktaba Jama't-i Islami, 1943), p. 90.

Hafeez Malik to Shah Wali-u'llah, and even to Mujadid Alf Thani (b. 1564) who was instrumental in eliminating the socio-religious implications of Emperor Akbar's Din-i-Ilahi (Religion of God). Modern Muslim nationalists include in their ranks Sir Sayyid Ahmad Khan, Ameer Ali, Mohammad Ali and his older brother Shaukat Ali, the poet-philosopher Sir Mohammad Iqbal, and finally Mohammad Ali Jinnah. The majority of Muslim Nationalists were Western-educated and came from the middle and upper classes. Somewhat paradoxically, the Muslim Nationalists were closer to the secular Hindu leaders in their cultural and political orientations than to the traditionally religious Nationalist Muslims on whom the Congress relied to win Muslim support for a united India. Not to have won them over to the cause of a united India by sharing power with them was the greatest failure of the Congress. One can, however, just as forcefully argue that Muslim Nationalists were determined to achieve sovereignty in a smaller state and were not content with political influence in a larger Indian state. That might have been the Muslim Nationalists' state of mind during the 1940s; however, as late as 1946 in describing the League's acceptance of the Cabinet Mission Plan, Jinnah stated: "The League, throughout the negotiations, was moved by a sense of fair play and sacrificed the full State of Pakistan at the altar of the Congress for securing the independence of the whole of India."[19]

Exactly ten years earlier the Muslim League's fourteen-point program (of June 9, 1936) reflected nothing but the Muslim Nationalist desire to have "some influence" in the Indian political system. Of the fourteen points, only three related to the Muslims' religious rights, i.e., "promotion and protection" of the Urdu language and script and "the amelioration of the general conditions of Muslims." The remaining

19. Jamil-ud-Din Ahmad, *Speeches and Writings of Mr. Jinnah*, Vol. II (Lahore: Shaikh Muhammad Ashraf, 1964), 309.

points related to the general political conditions of India. This is not to suggest that the Muslim Nationalists did not take Pakistan seriously; tactically the separate Muslim state was a last resort if the political modus vivendi with the Congress could not be achieved. Political autonomy, which would ensure Muslim cultural identity, was the real aim of the Muslim Nationalists.

Among the Muslim Nationalists Sir Sayyid Ahmad Khan (1817–98) made a distinction between the love of land and nation. In the first issue of the *Tahdhib al-Akhlaq: The Muslim National Reformer* (December 24, 1870), while discussing Tunisian-Arab nationalism, Sir Sayyid acknowledges that he adopted for the *Tahdhib* the modified motto of the Tunisian newspaper *al-Rai'd al-Tanusi:* "*Hubbal-qawm min al-iman faman yas y fi izaz qawmat anama Yas y fi izaz dinah.* Love of the Nation is the essence of faith. Whosoever strives for the progress of his Nation really endeavors to raise the honor of his religion." (al-Rai'd al-Tanusi's motto had started with the love of the native land, and then equated it with "the honor of one's own religion.")

Sir Sayyid discussed the concept of Muslim nationalism in the terminology of nineteenth-century Europe, and like Henry St. John Bolingbroke (1678–1751) enunciated the concept of aristocratic nationalism. Sir Sayyid, despite the democratic consequences of his Aligarh movement, was an aristocratic democrat, and his Muslim nationalism was essentially based upon an enlighted conception of noblesse oblige. He encouraged understanding and solidarity between the lower and upper strata of Muslim society but by no means desired to eliminate class differentiation. An enlightened bourgeoisie, in his view, created the political and intellectual climate in the society, enabling the lower classes to lead a relatively prosperous and contented national life and to make their contribution to the national progress. This hierarchical view of society, which was the hallmark of eighteenth- and nineteenth-century capitalist Europe, blended harmoniously with the aristocratic background of Sir Sayyid.

Like Bolingbroke, Sir Sayyid regarded nationalism as the most natural and reasonable means not only for safeguarding Muslim national interests but also for achieving amiable relations with the Hindus. During the first phase (1857–84) of his public life, relations with the Hindus were generally cooperative; in the second phase (1885–98), these relations broke down when Sir Sayyid advised the Muslims not to join the Congress.[20] Sir Sayyid emphasized a negative and a positive policy, and both were espoused subsequently by the Muslim Nationalists. They included (1) opposition to the introduction of the one-man, one-vote principle of elections in the Viceroy's Legislative Council; and (2) support for the principle of separate and proportional representation of Muslims in the legislatures. Examined from the Hindu viewpoint, these two positions appear retrograde, but Sir Sayyid viewed them with the orientation of a Muslim Nationalist — whether or not the Congress was conducive to furthering Muslim Nationalist interests. Moreover, Iqbal and Jinnah remained true to Sir Sayyid's position.

Mohammad Iqbal (1877–1938) deserves to be called the poet-philosopher of Pakistan. First, his conception of *Khudi* (ego, self-affirmation), expressed through his poetry, led him to oppose the syncretic doctrine of *wahdat al-wujud* (unitarian monism). The pantheistic road, in Iqbal's eyes, would lead the Muslims to cultural assimilation with the Hindus. The ecological theories of Darwin and Wallace[21] helped evolve the concept of collective ego, which found an

20. For a detailed discussion of these two phases, see Hafeez Malik, "Sir Sayyid Ahmad Khan's Doctrines of Muslim Nationalism and National Progress," *Modern Asian Studies* (Oxford), II, No. 3 (1968), 221–44, and "Sir Sayyid Ahmad Khan's Contribution to the Development of Muslim Nationalism," *ibid.*, IV, No. 2 (1970), 129–47.

21. For a detailed discussion of these ideas, see Hafeez Malik, "The Impact of Ecology on Iqbal's Thought," *Iqbal Review* (Oct. 1968), pp. 47–67; *Iqbal: Poet-Philosopher of Pakistan* (New York: Columbia University Press, 1972).

eloquent expression in Iqbal's *Asrar-i Khudi*. *Khudi*, or self-preservation, became the frame of reference for Iqbal's analysis of Indian history. Political forces or persons were positive insofar as they strengthened the collective Muslim *Khudi*. Hence, Iqbal could not appreciate Emperor Akbar's assimilative *Din-i-Ilahi*. But he approved the work of Mujadid Alf Thani and extolls his virtues. Iqbal says in *Bal-i Jibril*:

> I stood by the Reformer's tomb: that dust
> Whence here below an orient splendour breaks,
> Dust before whose least speck stars hang their heads,
> Dust shrouding that high knower of things unknown
> Who to Jahangir would not bend his neck,
> Whose ardent breath fans every free heart's ardour,
> Whom Allah sent in Season to keep watch
> In India on the treasure of Islam.[22]

By the same token, Aurangzeb reinforced the collective Muslim ego. According to Iqbal, Aurangzeb understood the reality of the ideological and cultural as well as the ecological struggle in India. Discussing in *Ramuz-i Bekhudi* (the mysteries of selflessness) the personal fulfillment of the individual in society, Iqbal described Aurangzeb as:

> He the last arrow to our quiver left
> In the affray of Faith with Unbelief;
> Then God chose from India
> That humble-minded warrior [Aurangzeb] Alamgir
> Religion to revive, faith to renew.
>
> . . . .
>
> He was a moth that ever beat its wings
> About the candle-flame of Unity,
> An Abraham in India's idol-house.[23]

In summing up Iqbal's role in the development of Muslim nationalism, it is necessary to emphasize his three major

---

22. Iqbal, *Bal-i Jibril* (Lahore: Shaikh Mubarak Ali, 1946), pp. 211–22; V. G. Kiernan, *Poems from Iqbal* (London: John Murray, 1935), p. 58.

23. A. J. Arberry, *The Mysteries of Selflessness* (London: John Murray, 1953), p. 17.

contributions. First, given the doctrine of *Khudi*, Iqbal's interpretation of Indian history enabled him to develop the "Two Nation Theory" in his presidential address to the Muslim League at Allahabad in 1930, which the League adopted in 1940 in the form of the "Pakistan Resolution." Second, Iqbal persuaded Mohammad Ali Jinnah, the founder of Pakistan, to demand a separate Muslim state. In a letter to Jinnah on June 21, 1937, he stated unequivocally: "A separate federation of Muslim provinces . . . is the only course by which we can secure a peaceful India and save Muslims from the domination of non-Muslims. Why should not the Muslims of north-west and Bengal be considered a nation, entitled to self-determination just as other nations of India and outside India are?" Third, his philosophy of *Khudi*, expressed in elegant Urdu and Persian poetry, provided a frame of reference not only for the individual Muslim but also for the Muslim national identity.

Iqbal did not coin the name Pakistan nor did he include Bengal as an integral part of the "Northwestern Muslim State." Deriving the name from the first letters of the provinces to be included in Pakistan — *P* standing for the Punjab, *A* for Afghania, i.e., Northwest Frontier Province, *K* for Kashmir, *S* for Sindh, and *tan* for Baluchistan — Chaudhary Rahmat Ali thus developed the name for the future Muslim state.

Considerably influenced by Iqbal, Rahmat Ali started the Pakistan National Movement in Britain in 1930 to "transform the cult of Indianism into the creed of Islamism, the course of minority communalism into the call of Muslim nationalism," and to safeguard "the perilous position of Muslim territories as provinces of India, into the status of the Muslim fatherland of Pakistan, of Bang-i Islam [Bengal] and Usmanistan [State of Hyderabad], in South Asia."[24]

---

24. C. Rahmat Ali, *What Does the Pakistan National Movement Stand For?* (Cambridge: W. Heffer & Sons, 1933), p. 4; *The Millat of Islam and the Menace of Indianism* (Cambridge: W. Heffer & Sons, 1940), pp. 7 ff.

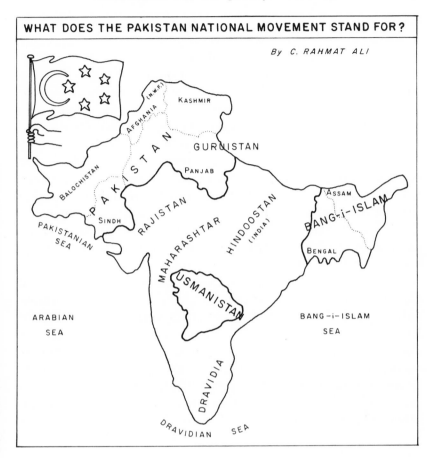

WHAT DOES THE PAKISTAN NATIONAL MOVEMENT STAND FOR?

Post-Independence Evaluation of Nationalism:
1947–70

None of the ideologists of Pakistan (not even those of the "Pakistan Resolution" of 1940) included Bengal in the future state of Pakistan. Indeed, the eastern province had long been given separate status. That Jinnah, the most pragmatic states-man of all Muslims, should have accepted in 1946 Bengali politicians' suggestion to make Bengal an integral part of Pakistan is an inexplicable feature of his shrewdness. Commenting on Jinnah's contribution to Muslim nationalism, Aziz Ahmad remarked: "He did not lead, but was led by the Muslim consensus. His role was that of a sincere and clear-headed lawyer who could formulate and articulate in precise constitutional terms what his client really wanted."[25]

Facts of history, created by the success of Muslim nationalism in India, started to have a profound impact on Indian as well as foreign scholars regarding the nature of Indian nationalism. Finally, they shared a general understanding that "India in fact experienced many nationalisms, as many as there were generally accepted ideas of the nation. As developments in the twentieth century proved, some of those nationalisms worked in opposition to others."[26] With the disappearance of British imperial rule after 1947, primordial forces of race, caste, and regional loyalties reasserted themselves in India. Now the Indian government was forced to ask the question: Was Hindu India a nation, and was not the Congress party's vision of secular Indian nationalism an ideal rather than a reality? The Indian government's States Reorganization Commission (established in December 1953) acknowledged that "the culture-based regionalism, centering around the idea of linguistic homogeneity represents to the average Indian values easily intelligible to him. Indian nationalism, on the other hand, has still to develop into a positive concept."[27]

While Indian nationalism was still being questioned in

25. Aziz Ahmad, *Studies in Islamic Culture in the Indian Environment* (Oxford: Clarendon Press, 1964), p. 276.

26. Cf. Charles H. Heimsath, *Indian Nationalism and Hindu Social Reforms* (Princeton: Princeton University Press, 1964), pp. 132–33; J. Kennedy, *Asian Nationalism in the Twentieth Century* (New York: Macmillan, 1968), pp. 84, 179 ff.

27. Government of India, *The Report of the States Reorganization Commission* (New Delhi: Government of India Publications Division, n.d.), p. 43; also, B. R. Ambedkar, *Maharashtra as a Linguistic Province* (Bombay: Thacker & Co., 1948); Dhirendranath Sen, *A Case for Linguistic States* (Calcutta: Uttarayan, Ltd., 1954); Krishna P. Mukerji and Suhasini Ramaswamy, *Reorganization of Indian States* (Bombay: The Popular Book Depot, 1955), contain balanced analyses of the states reorganization debate.

the 1950s, the successful expression of Muslim nationalism in the form of Pakistan compelled a reassessment of its nature in India. Discussing the Muslim period of Indian history, leading Indian historians, including K. M. Munshi, R. C. Majumdar, and A. D. Pusalkar, stated: "Unlike the previous invaders, the Muslims did not merge themselves with the Hindus, and thus for the first time the population of India was divided into two separate units with marked distinctions. This was the historic beginning of the Hindu-Muslim problem that led after more than six hundred years to the creation of Pakistan."[28] It is noteworthy that a grudging but private acknowledgment of the "Two Nation Theory" had already taken place in the highest ranks of the Congress leadership. Abul Kalam Azad revealed in 1960 that after the collapse of the Cabinet Mission Plan in 1946 Sardar Vallabhbhai Patel had admitted to him: "Whether we [the Congress leadership] like it or not, there were two nations in India." According to Azad, Patel maintained that "Muslims and Hindus could not be united into one nation. There was no alternative except to recognize this fact."[29]

What Pakistan's ideologists avoided recommending in their theoretical formulations, the Muslim League leaders unwisely adopted. Yoking East Bengal to the western four provinces made Pakistan a house divided against itself—not only geographically but ethnically, culturally, economically, and linguistically. Ignoring these differences in the flush of victory, the League leaders formulated a new ideology that they thought would overcome the geographic anomaly of the new nation-state. The salient features of this ideology were repeated in policy pronouncements such as: (1) Pakistanis (hailing from east and west) were a nation; (2) Pakistan was a homeland of all Muslims who might migrate from India; (3) Urdu would be the national language of Pakistan;

---

28. R. C. Majumdar et al., *The Delhi Sultanate* (Bombay: Bharatiya Vidya Bhavan, 1960), pp. xxix, 616–17.
29. Abul Kalam Azad, *India Wins Freedom* (New York: Longmans, Green, 1960), p. 217.

and (4) Islam would provide the understructure for the cultural and political life of Pakistanis. The fact of geography, more than any other factor, prevented the successful Muslim nationalism from evolving into this "new" Pakistani nationalism. Qualitatively, the nationalisms of East and West Pakistan were destined to differ because the ideological conceptions and symbols in the divided state failed to generate mutual appeal.

Migrating from Urdu-speaking areas of India, the Muslims who settled in East Pakistan became a suspect minority. Instead of becoming a means of communication between East and West Pakistan, Urdu, to the Bengalis, was a symbol of West Pakistan's claims that they represented a legacy of several thousand years of unified history. Especially in August–September 1955 during the National Assembly debates over the creation of one province in West Pakistan, Urdu was deeply resented by the Bengalis. In 1955 the Muslim League leader, Mumtaz Mohammad Khan Daultana, painted West Pakistan's picture of linguistic and cultural homogeneity in exceptionally bright colors:

Historically the region had been one from times immemorial. The excavations at Mohenjo Daro [in Sind] point out that a great civilization had flourished there in the centuries past with its off-shoots at Harapa [the south Punjab], Taxila [the north Punjab], and Machha [Baluchistan]. Here from the beginnings of time, the people have acted in unison and close cooperation with each other . . . the people of West Pakistan had the same mental direction since ages. Even before the glorious advent of Islam in the region, people of this part fought together, struggled together and developed together. The first mystic of India, the author of Rig-Veda[,] gave his spiritual message from the region . . . in accepting Buddhism the whole region responded as one people. Then came Gandhara culture, which also originated from here. When Islam came this area reacted as one whole and embraced it.[30]

Reacting to Daultana's image of West Pakistan, Nur-ur-Rahman, an East Pakistani legislator, retorted: "Your exist-

---

30. *Pakistan Times*, Aug. 27, 1955.

ence may have resulted from the Indus Valley culture, but I wonder where does East Pakistan stand after the exposition of this theory."[31] One year later, on January 16, 1956, another East Pakistani leader reiterated the same dilemma in even more forceful language: "It is a country [Pakistan] which in reality is not one country. We are going to form one state out of two countries. We are going to form one nation out of two peoples."[32] During the 1960s, however, Bengali political thought was no longer ambivalent regarding Pakistan's unity. In his *Social History of East Pakistan*, Kamruddin Ahmad suggested that the Muslim League had abandoned the "Two Nation Theory" when it accepted the Cabinet Mission Plan in 1946. Moreover, he suggested the Lahore Resolution of 1940 could not be scrapped by the resolution of the less representative convention of the legislators who met in 1946 under Jinnah's leadership. Taking pride in the Dravidian origin of East Pakistanis, Ahmad expounded the theory that Bengalis were always unjustly treated by the pre-Islamic Aryans of northern India, and this pattern of history had repeated itself during the rule of the Mughal Empire and Pakistan. "In a sense the unjust treatment given to the Bengalis by the Mughal Emperors helped the former in unfolding their genius." Ahmad implied that the Bengali involvement in Pakistan was sharpening their national consciousness.

Viewed against this background, increasing Bengali self-awareness provided fertile ground for Sheikh Mujibur Rahman's movement for an independent Bangladesh. Outbidding the Muslim League, Mujib enunciated a "Three Nation Theory," especially after his electoral victory in December 1970. Speaking at a Bengali Academy meeting on February 15, 1971, Mujib stated: "after years of struggle and sacrifice, Bengali nationalism was now a reality and Bengalis were a nation. 'Joy Bangla' was not merely a politi-

31. *Dawn*, Aug. 27, 1955.
32. *Constituent Assembly of Pakistan Debates*, I (Jan. 16, 1956), 1815-6.

cal slogan, but it embodied all aspects of Bengal's life —
politics, economy, culture and language." On March 24,
1971, Mujib greeted the Students Volunteer Corps marching
in front of his Dhanmandi residence by waving the new
Bangladesh flag and raising the slogan: *"Ebarere sangra
muktir sangram, ebarere sangram sewadhinatar sangram"*
(the struggle is for emancipation and freedom).[33]

Even before the breakdown of the Yahya-Mujib negotiations in March 1971, it had become obvious that East and
West Pakistan could coexist only in a confederation with a
minimum of mutual obligations. East Bengal's separation
from Pakistan established the fact that Muslim nationalism
was an abiding influence in South Asia but that Pakistani
nationalism had failed to develop a new national identity.

Since the emergence of Bangladesh, regionalism in Pakistan has shown renewed vigor. Five factors are instrumental
in generating regional tensions: (1) the capitalist mode of
economy that encouraged an uneven distribution of economic resources; (2) linguistic diversity; (3) the transnational distribution of some ethnic groups, i.e., the Baluchi and
Pathans, in the two neighboring states of Iran and Afghanistan; (4) Muhajir (immigrant) Muslim settlements in Pakistan since 1947, particularly in Sind; and finally, (5) Punjabi
"domination," which is reflected in the Punjabis' constituting 60 percent of Pakistan's population and providing a
substantial percentage of the personnel in the civil services
and armed forces.

Before 1972 Pakistan not only repudiated socialism but
in the process of her economic and political development
created an intellectual climate conducive to the growth of
capitalism. Liberal and Western-oriented political leaders
as well as the *ulema*, the traditional religious leaders, developed economic paradigms, i.e., "Islamic socialism" and
"Islamic economy," while adducing from Islam essential

33. *Dawn*, Feb. 16, 1971.

support for the development of capitalism in Pakistan. Pakistan's establishment provided the private sector with maximum opportunities for growth.

In 1950, in order to develop heavy industries in the country, the Pakistan government created an autonomous investment body, the Pakistan Industrial Development Corporation. By 1959 the PIDC held an interest in twenty industrial enterprises with a capital of $170 million. In the early 1960s the government sold both the successful and un-promising plants to private entrepreneurs. Most of these industrial complexes came into the hands of a small number of Muhajir capitalists in Karachi and well-established Punjabis. Some Muslim communities, largely migrant from India and representing under 1 percent of the population, controlled more than half the industrial assets by 1959:

Approximate Percentage of Industrial Assets by Community[34]
1959

Community	Private Muslim firms only	All firms	Share of population
Minor Muslim communities	74.5	50.5	0.5
Pathans, Bengalis, and other Muslims	25.5	16.5	87.5
Bengali Hindu	—	8.5	10.0
British	—	7.5	—
Other private non-Muslims	—	5.0	2.0
Public enterprises	—	12.0	—
Total	100.0	100.0	100.0

34. The most important community was that of the Memons. In 1959 members of this community controlled one-quarter of investment in privately owned Muslim firms. This community is defined by its origin in a few small towns in the area of Kathiawar (between Karachi and Bombay). The second important group, the Chiniotis, came from a small town in the Punjab. Both of these groups belong to the Sunni majority in Islam. Three other important communities (Bohra, Khoja Ithna Ashari, and Khoja Ismaili) are members of the minority Shia Islam. Most of their members originated in Gujrat and Kathiawar. Stephen R. Lewis, Jr., *Pakistan: Industrialization and Trade Policies* (London: Oxford University Press, 1970), pp. 47–48; G. F. Papanek, *Pakistan's Development: Social Goals and Private Incentives* (Cambridge: Harvard University Press, 1967), pp. 41–43.

Writing a foreword to the *Third Five Year Plan* (1969), President Ayub openly admitted that "the Government has gradually removed most of the administrative and bureaucratic controls which hampered progress of the private sector. The result of this approach has been the rapid growth of private capitalism in Pakistan." Thus, an impression developed that the government promoted economic deprivation, especially among the Baluchis, Sindhis, and Pathans. Baluchistan was the most neglected province, with the landowning Sardars perpetuating a feudal economy. The current political unrest in Baluchistan can be traced to political and economic inequities (as the Pastners have noted in their chapter in this volume.) Moreover, sociopolitical tensions in Pakistan largely reflect the economic contradictions created by the Ayub regime between 1958 and 1969.

Twenty-two languages are spoken in Pakistan, while the Punjab, Sind, Baluchistan, and the Frontier Province generally represent the Punjabi, Sindhi, Baluchi, and Pashto languages. Punjabi and Baluchi are spoken tongues without scripts of their own. (The Punjabi Gurmukhi script used by the Sikhs in the Punjabi Subah of India is unknown in Pakistan.) Sindhi and Pashto employ an Arabic-Persian script and a vocabulary like Urdu. While Punjabi is the mother tongue of the Punjab, before 1947 it was never used as the medium of instruction, even at the elementary level. By learning Urdu in their schools, the Punjabis have become bilingual and are strong supporters of Urdu as the national language. Urdu is also dominant in Sind; and long-range trends suggest the eventual shift from Baluchi and Pashto to Urdu, not as a language of daily discourse, but as a vehicle of educational and scientific expression.

Only Sind, however, has gone through a traumatic linguistic shock. With the advent of Pakistan, large numbers of Urdu-speaking muhajirs poured into Sind from India. Sind also lured to its new industries many Urdu-committed non-Sindhis from other provinces. Seven large Sindhi cities and towns have been turned into Urdu-speaking towns. In 1951, out of the total urban population of 699,751 in Sind and Khairpur state, some 351,941 were muhajirs. Currently, the best available estimate of muhajir strength in Sindhi towns is as follows:

City and town*	Total population	Percentage Muhajir
Karachi		80–85
Hyderabad, including Latifabad	400,000	60–65
Sukhar	200,000	50–60
Larkana	60,000	50
Mirpukhas	50,000	50–55
Nawabshah	40,000	45–50
Dadu	30,000	40–45
Shikarpur	20,000	35–40
Thatta	10,000	35–40

Before 1947 Sindhi was the only spoken language in these cities; after 1947, especially in Karachi, Hyderabad, Sukhar, Larkana, and Mirpurkhas, "to speak Urdu is the rule, to converse in Sindhi the exception." In other towns as well, Urdu is now the spoken language. In addition to changing the language of Sind, the muhajirs filled the professional vacuum created by the emigrant Hindus while the Sindhi Muslims lagged behind. Although in 1951 the muhajir community was only 11.17 percent of the total Sind population, they made up more than 51 percent of the educated class. For example, of 13,000 high school graduates, 6,273 were muhajirs; of 2,758 college degree holders, 1,434 were muhajirs; and of 1,002 possessing higher degrees, 572 were muhajirs.[35] Therefore, Sindhi regionalism derives its combustible elements from linguistic tensions as well as from

35. Gul Hasan M. I. Abbasi, ed., *Census of Pakistan, 1951: Sindh and Khairpur State* (Karachi: Government Publications), VI, 88–89.

the economic contradictions of Pakistani capitalism. (Since 1972 the governments of Pakistan and Sind have encouraged the native Sindhi bourgeoisie to invest in industrial enterprises, but it will take time for the Sindhi bourgeoisie to catch up with the Muhajirs.)

A trilingual situation prevails in the Frontier Province. In 1960 Peshawar Division reported 2,240,500 persons (or 67.97 percent of the population) using Pashto as their mother tongue, while 79,229 could speak Pashto as an additional language. Moreover, 33.7 percent could speak Punjabi and 10.33 percent Urdu. In Dara Ismail Khan Division 63.23 percent spoke Pashto and 51.7 percent Punjabi. In Baluchistan also, Urdu and Punjabi speakers have increased considerably since 1951. In 1961 Pashto, instead of Baluchi, was reported to be the mother tongue of 54 percent of the population, followed by 18 percent Baluchi, 14.7 percent Punjabi, 6.2 percent Brahui, with Urdu occupying the fourth position—3.3 percent. However, in Kalat Division, 52 percent of the people claimed Baluchi rather than Pashto as the mother tongue, 16.3 percent Sindhi, 28.2 percent Brahui, and only 1.9 percent Pashto.[36] In view of this linguistic diversity, all the provincial governments after the East Pakistan secession declared Urdu to be the official language of their provincial administrations. While the Government of Sind made Sindhi the second official language of the province, the National Awami Party governments in the Frontier and Baluchistan did not do the same for Pashto or Baluchi.

With Urdu the lingua franca of Pakistan, the language problem is politically manageable; but the transnational dispersion of the Baluchis, and particularly the Pathans across the Afghan border, has encouraged the Afghanistan government to press irredentist claims against Pakistan. Afghanistan has some support from the former Red Shirt

36. *Ibid.*, pp. 89–90.

leaders of the Frontier Province (now organized in Wali Khan's National Awami Party). This group also was the one that collaborated with the All-India National Congress against the Muslim League before 1947. In denouncing the Durand Line (the international boundary), the Afghanistan government has made the following demands of Pakistan: (1) Pakhtunistan should be the name of the Frontier Province along with certain areas of Baluchistan; and (2) the tribal areas of Pakistan's side of the Durand Line should be declared the sovereign state of Pakhtunistan with the Frontier Province and Baluchistan being incorporated in this new state.[37]

Since 1947 Pakistan-Afghanistan relations have remained in a state of low normality or cold war. Moreover, with the overthrow of King Zahir Shah in 1973, the Afghan government appeared to accept the Soviet call for an Asian Collective Security System, which is designed to "contain" China. Thus, the Soviet Union has accelerated military aid to Afghanistan, and in July–October 1974 Afghanistan moved its troops to the Pakistan border. Afghanistan also sent diplomatic notes to the United Nations recommending self-determination for the Frontier Province. Armed confrontation between Pakistan and Afghanistan would put a great burden on the national loyalty and political consciousness of the Pathans in Pakistan.

Constituting 60 percent of Pakistan's population, the Punjabis have a significant responsibility in holding the country together. Pakistan's first twenty-five years have demonstrated that Islam was not strong or cohesive enough to prevent East Pakistan's secession. And the central government's recent display of economic generosity toward Baluchistan and the NWFP may not be adequate to maintain their national loyalties. (Until 1970 Baluchistan's annual develop-

37. *Pushtoonistan: Prime Minister's Statement in the Constituent Assembly on January 9, 1950* (Karachi: 1950), p. 6.

mental allocation never exceeded Rs 30 million, but this was increased to Rs 220 million in 1973–74.) Political unrest in both provinces underlines the validity of this judgment. In order to develop a "consensus of sentiment," Ralph Braibanti has suggested Pakistan must learn to accord a "parity of esteem" to the cultural traditions of various non-Punjabi groups.[38] The comparatively more educated and "modernized" Punjabis tend to be too narrowly chauvinistic, and hence disrespectful of non-Urdu cultural traditions. Moreover, they still dominate the civil and armed services, even though Prime Minister Bhutto's government has endeavored to increase the representation of Pathans, Sindhis, and Baluchis. A Sindhi himself, Bhutto is sensitive to this ethnic and regional problem; but (as others have noted in this volume) his political opposition must also be accorded more recognition in order to "free" the smaller provinces from the complex of Punjabi domination.

In the face of these major impediments, what are the prospects for the development of Pakistani nationalism? In order to establish its identity, Pakistan needs internal as well as external peace. India is still perceived to be the main threat to Pakistan's territorial integrity. Pakistan's defeat in 1971 has proved the worst fears of Pakistanis regarding Indian intentions. However, another war with India, instead of solving any of Pakistan's problems, would produce new unpalatable realities for Pakistan.

In order to secure a stable peace, Pakistan must settle the Kashmir problem with India. This could mean compromising on the Pakistani demand for self-determination for the Kashmiris. It might also result in the acceptance of an international boundary somewhere along the present ceasefire line. Hopefully, the elimination of this territorial dispute

38. For further analysis, see his chapter, "The Research Potential of Pakistan's Development," in the present volume. Illustrations of failure to accord parity of esteem can be found in Ralph Braibanti, "Pakistan's Experience in Political Development," ASIA, *Supplement No. 1* (Fall 1974), pp. 25–43.

can establish peaceful relations between the two countries, and would dissuade India, with Afghanistan's collaboration, from hemming Pakistan in. Pakistan, nevertheless, would need to maintain a creditable defensive posture toward India (and Afghanistan) in order to make the cost of Indian hegemony over South Asia prohibitive. Also, India's internal economic problems can be counted on to help establish at least a generation of unbroken peace in the subcontinent.

Pakistan needs tranquility to maintain internal cohesion and to minimize its economic contradictions. In order to foster Pakistani nationalism, Bhutto has suggested (to this author and others) that Pakistan base its policies on the four principles of: (1) distributive justice, (2) political participation, (3) Islamic solidarity, (4) and the promotion of Urdu as the true lingua franca of Pakistan. Indeed, demographic shifts in the social structure of Pakistan are causing a melting-pot situation to develop that can be strengthened by the widespread diffusion of Urdu.

From Torkham on the Durand Line, to the outer limit of Swat at Kalam where the peaks of Sinkiang and Gilgit converge, to the flatlands of Sind around Larkana and Mohenjo Daro, Urdu has become an effective means of communication. Furthermore, all the provincial governments accept Urdu's nation-building role. Pakistan's new culture—one can see its outlines on the social canvas—would be an Urdu culture, which will be determined not by the Punjabi language or culture of the majority province, or for that matter by any other regional tongue. Based on the religious and cultural traditions of the Middle East and Central Asia (the regions where people in successive migrations settled in "Pakistan" from the eighth to the sixteenth centuries), this new Urdu culture of Pakistan would lean heavily on the native traditions of the Indus Valley and draw closer to the Middle East states for greater cultural harmony and political support. Committed to the concept of "distributive justice," the new culture would carry forward the Aligarh

legacy of social reform and modernization. Until the blend-
ing of these traditions is harmoniously accomplished, the
phenomenon of Pakistan nationalism will remain an ideal
rather than a living reality. Finally, the development of an
Urdu culture would establish Pakistan's identity vis-à-vis
India, Afghanistan, and Iran. Pakistan has just begun to
create its brand of Pakistani nationalism.

11

The Balancing Process in Pakistan's Foreign Policy

W. Howard Wriggins

There are two very different approaches to understanding Pakistan's foreign policy. Stressing its uniqueness, one can focus on how its foreign policy differs from that of all other states. This leads to identifying the peculiarities of its original geographical structure; the quite unparalleled influence during the early period of refugees whose former homes were within the territory of the country's larger neighbor; the unusual concentration of foreign policy authority in the hands of a few men, mainly drawn from only one part of the country—the Punjab; the weakness of civilian representative institutions; and the increasingly important role of "the military" in shaping the concepts and determining the size and nature of resources devoted to foreign policy problems. The real afficionados with inside information can, like King Lear, "talk of court news . . . who loses and who wins, who's in and who's out," and how these changes affect the pace, direction, and scope of shifts in foreign policy.

Alternatively, one can look at Pakistan as simply yet another state in a system of states, as a representative of a variegated but still distinguishable type of political community—a state. This state, like others, has territory, boundaries, a government usually capable of making decisions consequential to most who live within its frontiers, and possessing during most of its history a monopoly or near-monopoly of the legitimate use of force. In this view, if there are generalizations about interstate relations, they should apply to Pakistan as well.

Since most of the chapters in this volume concentrate their attention on the uniqueness of Pakistan, this discussion climbs the abstraction ladder and looks at Pakistan as if it were one example within a largish category of political entities called states. It will argue that given one premise, there is little in Pakistan's foreign policy behavior since independence that could not be adequately understood from the perspective of the state-to-state model familiar to students of international politics.[1]

The Balancing Process

From this intellectually rather conservative perspective, two major themes will be explored. The first concerns the process engaged in by the smaller, weaker state of balancing the power of its larger neighbor.[2] It is not so much "the balance of power" as a static equilibrium, but rather a balancing process, an endless effort of the weaker state to find ways of counterbalancing the greater power of its much larger neighbor, in this case India. To be sure, sometimes the notion of balance of power is used so loosely that it loses meaning. But in this instance the common usage is helpful and provides one key to understanding Pakistan's foreign policy behavior. The second theme concerns a different aspect of the balancing process, namely the effort of

1. For much of the chronological sequence, I am indebted to S. M. Burke's *Pakistan's Foreign Policy: An Historical Analysis* (London: Oxford University Press, 1973).

2. For an essay that stimulated this approach, see Martin Wight, "The Balance of Power and International Order," in Alan James, ed, *The Bases of International Order, Essays in Honour of C. A. W. Manning* (London: Oxford University Press, 1973), pp. 85–116.

a smaller, weaker state to improve its bargaining position vis-à-vis Major Powers. Again, it will be argued that Pakistan undertook rather typical policies in efforts to improve its bargaining position vis-à-vis a Major Power with which it became allied, the United States.

Pakistan's Central Preoccupation: *Fear and Ambition Toward India*

The single premise that has underlain Pakistan's foreign policy derives from India's centrality in nearly every calculation of Pakistan's foreign policy makers. A detailed explanation of why India played such a central, one might even say "obsessive," role in Pakistan's foreign policy would lead us into a fascinating, and complex, field of subcontinental political, constitutional, and religious history, which shall be left for the most part to the specialists. But another more general element in Indo-Pakistani relations derives from the simple fact of size and strategic and economic asymmetry.

Typically, smaller states next to larger ones are rendered anxious by that larger neighbor. Thucydides held that statesmen were driven by a number of motivations, of which fear was central.[3] However unjustified Indian leaders may have thought it, Pakistan's overriding concern vis-à-vis India was fear, fear of India's sheer size, the size of its army (never less than two times larger than Pakistan's) and fear of the effects of the hard fact that a large, contiguous India with internal lines of communication separated Pakistan's comparatively small two parts by over a thousand miles. At certain points, West Pakistan, for instance, was scarcely 250 miles across,

3. In his *History of the Peloponnesian War,* Thucydides explains Athens' behavior toward its neighbors by pointing out that "acting as human nature always will, . . . [Athens' leaders were] . . . constrained by three all-powerful motives: ambition, fear, interest." F. R. B. Godolphin, ed., *The Greek Historians,* Vol. I (New York: Random House, 1942), 600.

while its major city, Lahore, lay less than ten miles from the Indian frontier in the flat and easily traversed Punjab plain. Fear, too, was compounded out of not infrequent public statements by prominent Indians regretting the tragedy of partition and reiterating the inherent unity of the subcontinent. These statements, sometimes said more in sorrow than in anger, seemed to intensify a conviction that India had never, as the saying went, "reconciled itself to the existence of Pakistan." As a small candle can throw a large shadow that may scare whoever sees it with a mind prepared by fear, every event in India of possible pertinence was read so as to increase the sense of Pakistan's vulnerability to its larger neighbor.[4]

European statesmen of the fifteenth and sixteenth centuries would have understood Pakistan's security problem better than did most statesmen of the 1950s. In those days it was characteristic that a ruler's realm could be widely scattered. The art of statesmanship, among other things, was to evoke sufficient sinews of statehood to ensure that out of this fragmented realm a viable polity could be marshaled.[5] Connections between the different parts were often tenuous, demands made upon the scattered provinces were often few and typically only periodic, when external dangers threatened or princely ambition required a special collective effort. In those centuries Pakistan's problems would have been familiar; in the mid-twentieth century such a state was unheard of, only intensifying the sense of Pakistan's vulnerability.

There were more specific vulnerabilities, too. Though the army's manpower had a high reputation for martial prowess,

4. For a detailed discussion from the Pakistan perspective, see G. W. Choudhury, *Pakistan's Relations with India — 1947–1966* (London: Pall Mall Press, 1968), intro. and chaps. 1, 2, and 3. For a thoughtful and more recent essay, see Anwar H. Syed, "Pakistan's Security Problem: A Bill of Constraints," *Orbis* (Winter 1973), pp. 952–74.

5. For a vivid discussion of such problems, see J. H. Elliott's *Imperial Spain, 1469–1716* (London: Arnold, 1963), esp. chap. 5.

the army was an ill-equipped structure with aging, obsolescent equipment clearly not comparable to India's larger and better-equipped force. The Sterling balances inherited at partition from wartime British India were briefly reinforced during the Korean War, but that boom soon collapsed. As prices for Pakistan's cotton and jute slipped badly on world markets, import requirements for simple maintenance and urgent development expenditures became more insistent. A severe drought in the early 1950s dramatized the need for concessional imports of foodgrains. Together these manifest vulnerabilities made the sense of anxiety and fear more palpable.

But it would make the analytical—and policy—task too simple if fear alone were to have illuminated Pakistan's policy. As Thucydides also noted, statesmen were moved by interest and ambition in addition to fear. With all these sources of weakness vis-à-vis India, Pakistan also had ambitions toward India. Its leaders had undertaken a commitment to ensure that the Muslims in Kashmir had an opportunity to express a choice about their future. Pakistan was unready to reconcile itself to the "Indian solution" to the Kashmir problem. Legally, the ruler had acceded to India, and the Indians had proceeded to occupy the best parts. But there had never been a plebiscite to which both parties had agreed at the United Nations; and each claimed the other had refused to fulfill the prerequisites for that reference to the people. In any event, since India held the most important areas of that lovely but poverty-stricken area, it was India's unwillingness to hold an internationally neutral plebiscite that remained decisive in Pakistan's eyes.

While the details of the Kashmir dispute are unique to the subcontinent, and a major uniqueness was the attachment of each to contradictory principles of statehood leading to opposite positions on the future of Kashmir, there was nevertheless nothing startlingly unusual about the fact that two neighboring states had ambitions to control the same territory. Western European, Middle Eastern, and Asian history are full of territorially based quarrels.

Nor is it unique to Pakistan that the weaker neighbor persists in attempts to change the local situation in its favor at the cost of its more powerful neighbor. A quite typical consequence is a persisting gap between foreign policy goals and insufficient foreign policy means. The effort to fill that gap by the weaker party requires a ceaseless experimentation and adroit maneuvering. The difficulty of this task goes far to explain much of Pakistan's foreign policy behavior.

The Search for Outside Backing

The United Nations and Middle Eastern States

Shortly after partition, as already noted, the smaller and larger subcontinental neighbors fought a small war over the disputed valley. The advantage of surprise gained by tribes and auxiliaries from the smaller country was counterbalanced by the indiscipline of the infiltrators and by better materiel, less inhibited generalship, and larger numbers on the Indian side. It was the larger power that originally called in the United Nations because the area it conceived of as its own had been the "victim of international aggression." Now well-established in the more advanced military positions, India soon considered the United Nations as an interloper, for the United Nations showed itself progressively more interested in organizing a plebiscite to record public sentiment in the valley than in directly repudiating the steps that forces from Pakistan had taken. In consequence, understandably enough, India became less and less cooperative.

In contrast, the weaker country, Pakistan, increasingly sought to strengthen its position by efforts to enlist the United Nations, particularly the larger countries in the

Security Council, on its behalf in an effort to redress the local balance that was then working to its disadvantage. Again, it is quite characteristic policy for smaller states in contention with a more powerful neighbor to seek outside support to counterbalance their own weakness.[6]

A certain success was registered at the United Nations and among a number of countries outside, which expressed their support for a plebiscite. In the end, however, the effective position of an India determined to avoid an internationally supervised plebiscite blocked that avenue for change.

Parallel efforts by Pakistan to enlist support from fellow-Muslim countries in the Middle East bore little fruit. Each state was beset by acute internal problems, or, as in the case of Egypt, was dealing with the remnants of the European presence. Most were stressing secular, not religious, values, and few found Pakistan's effort to establish an Islamic state relevant to their problems. President Nasser may have seen in Pakistan's talk of "Islamic unity" competition with his own conception of Arab unity under his leadership.

Support from the Commonwealth relationship, particularly Pakistan's expected backing from Great Britain, did not materialize as Karachi had hoped, since Great Britain was as determined to maintain relationships with India as with Pakistan, and undue partisanship on behalf of one side in the subcontinent would mean hostility from the other. Indeed, it was the outsiders' unwillingness to side with Pakistan against its larger neighbor that bedeviled Pakistan's foreign policy from the start.

6. For useful discussions, see George Liska, *Nations in Alliance: The Limits of Interdependence* (Baltimore: Johns Hopkins University Press, 1962); David Vital, *The Survival of Small States* (London: Oxford University Press, 1971); Robert Rothstein, *Alliances and Small Powers* (New York: Columbia University Press, 1968). Throughout, we designate Pakistan as a "Small Power," not because of its actual size, but by virtue of its relative size and power compared with India. It also fits Rothstein's definition: "A small power is a state which recognizes that it cannot obtain security primarily by use of its own capabilities, and that it must rely fundamentally on the aid of other states, institutions, processes or developments to do so" (p. 29).

A Major Power as an Ally?

Given, then, a substantial amount of fear, a goodly dose of ambition to "redress the injustice in Kashmir," and a failure of efforts to provide either security or satisfaction through the international community broadly conceived, through Islamic solidarity, or through the Commonwealth link, Pakistan not surprisingly sought an alliance with an outside Major Power.

The following account will suggest that much that has happened is not entirely atypical of state system behavior. The main Major Power candidate to act as an ally (the United States) was at the time building a system of alliances designed to block the expansion of its major opponent (the Soviet Union). Pakistan responded favorably to American soundings regarding a possible close association.

One finds striking parallels in the actions, say, of Czechoslovakia and Poland in the 1920s, perceiving themselves weak in relation to both Weimar Germany and Bolshevik Russia, readily accepting alliance arrangements with victorious France; or at the turn of the century, when Austria's leaders calculated that their country's position vis-à-vis Italy and Tsarist Russia would be improved by alliance with the larger Germany.

The American Connection: Advantages and Liabilities

By 1951–52, like Barkis, the United States was certainly willin' to develop a close working relationship with Pakistan. It had but recently found dealing with a limited war in Korea a good deal more demanding than it had anticipated; its leadership, particularly Secretary of State Dulles, feared a repetition in South Asia of what it conceived of in Korea as a Soviet-inspired initiative. Washington recalled what had been revealed in the Nazi-Soviet documents and considered these reflected a long-run Russian interest "in the area of the Persian Gulf." And it was at the time seeking, with British assistance, to find a way of developing mutual defense arrangements with Middle Eastern countries. President Nasser had rejected the concept of a Middle East Defense Organization requiring Arab cooperation with Western Europe and America, but there was then emerging a concept of the "northern tier," involving Turkey and Iran.[7]

From the American point of view, if Pakistan's manpower could be added to the combination, Pakistan's interest in defending itself against Soviet encroachment through Afghanistan would strengthen Middle East defenses and block a historic route from central Russia into South Asia. The Americans were impressed by Pathan and Punjabi reputations as "martial races." The fact that Pakistan was an Islamic country and had made consistent efforts to reach out to the Islamic Middle East made it all the more attractive to the Americans.[8]

For a number of responsible figures in the Pakistan government, the United States appeared to be the logical – indeed, the only plausible – Major Power for Pakistan to turn to. Moscow was still not yet free from the thrall of Stalin's harsh rule, and it had no military equipment or economic resources to spare. China's new regime had hardly yet mastered its dissident areas. By the early 1950s the United States was actively pursuing in Asia a policy, begun in Europe and in Greece and Turkey, of developing alliances and supporting aid relationships. Washington was already releasing badly needed agricultural "surpluses" to Pakistan. It seemed ready to commit large economic resources to assist its friends in Asia. Above all, it appeared ready to provide up-to-date military equipment and training.

Moreover, the United States filled another requisite of prudent statesmanship – it was far away. Machiavelli warned his Prince against the risk of associating too closely with a

---

7. For accounts, see *The Memoirs of the Rt. Hon. Sir Anthony Eden: Full Circle* (London: Cassell, 1960), *passim;* Dwight D. Eisenhower, *The White House Years, Waging Peace: 1956–61* (London: Heineman, 1965), pp. 133, 145; and Townsend Hoopes, *The Devil and John Foster Dulles* (Boston: Little, Brown, 1973).

8. See, e.g., editorials in *New York Times*, Jan. 24, 1953; Nov. 5, 1953.

bigger power close to one's borders, for there have been many examples, Machiavelli argued, when a large neighboring ally had come to help and remained to rule. America, some 12,000 miles away, could hardly pose such a threat.

One liability of a major associate so far away was the probability that it would have many other preoccupations apart from those of its small ally halfway around the world. In distance also lay the risk that when an issue arose of Pakistan security, the major ally's attention might be diverted by developments elsewhere. There were also risks in too much intimacy with such a power. Given the asymmetry between the Major Power and the Small Ally, no matter how far away he might be, would involvement with him unduly inhibit one's freedom of foreign policy maneuver? How often would one have to publicly side with the Major Power Ally on issues of little direct interest to oneself but in ways that might cost one the friendship of potentially important third parties? Would his weight become unduly influential in one's own internal affairs? These typical questions were expolored within segments of the Pakistan government and, on balance, the alliance relationship seemed to be worth the risk.

The main framework for the alliance arrangement was a network of multilateral treaties (SEATO and CENTO) in each of which the casus belli was specifically defined as "Communist aggression." This was not Pakistan's main worry, but the substance of the "special relationship" with the Major Power was built on bilateral military and economic assistance agreements that brought resources badly needed by the military and civilian segments of government. This too was quite characteristic, and finds close parallels with the British coalition system during the Napoleonic wars and with inter-war alliances between France and members of the Little Entente.[9]

9. For a discussion of the latter, see Rothstein, *op. cit.*, chap. 10.

At the core of the arrangement, however, was a fundamental difference between the two countries in focus and sense of priority. For the Major Power, the main concern was the Soviet problem and its ally China, and a possible thrust southward by one or both, analogous to the invasion of South Korea by North Korea several years earlier. To the Smaller Ally, by contrast, the main problem was its much larger subcontinental neighbor, India.[10] To be sure, Afghanistan posed a problem among Pakistan's tribal peoples, and its relations with the Soviet Union were periodically troublesome. But by comparison, Afghanistan was small worry; India was the overriding concern. The ambiguity in the relationship came early, for soon the United States sought working relations with both its Small Ally, Pakistan, and the latter's source of principal anxiety, India, at the same time.

There is nothing remarkable in such differences. Rarely do two states, separated by such distances, experience of statehood, and of such unequal power see eye to eye. As Rothstein put it,

An alliance between a Great Power and a Small Power may also involve an inherent difficulty arising from the extent of their interests. The Great Power tends to ally in terms of a threat to the balance of the whole system; the Small Power in terms of a threat to its local balance. Inevitably conflicts of perspective emerge.[11]

But what the two states did share was clear. They agreed that if Pakistan's military capability could be improved by injections of military equipment and training, and its political capabilities consolidated by substantial economic assistance, the leaders of Pakistan would be better able to cope should an external threat materialize.

10. For an illuminating discussion of this ambiguity as it affected Pakistan's approach to SEATO, see George Modelski, *SEATO — Six Studies* (Melbourne: F. W. Cheshire, 1962), pp. 137–138, 155, *passim.*
11. Rothstein, *op. cit.*, p. 62.

Quite typically, the alliance brought a sharp increase in military equipment and in economic resources devoted to bolstering local military expenditures of the Smaller Ally. Over $900 million worth of military equipment was transferred to Pakistan, although the exact figure is not known. Transport, mobile equipment, and tanks were delivered in substantial numbers, as were B-57 bombers and more sophisticated aircraft including numerous F-86s and, in the early 1960s, twelve jet fighter F-104s. The latter could outfly anything in the Indian armory, though the latter had many more if less sophisticated aircraft. Large economic assistance transfers were also made, and foodgrain shipments tided over bad seasons. Indeed, economic assistance trebled after 1954 in comparison with the years preceding the alliance, grants coming to nearly $900 million and concessional loans and PL 480 foodgrains together totaling another $1.5 billion.[12]

Moreover, also typical of many alliance arrangements, the mutual interchanges became so close and detailed between the Major Power and its Small Ally that at least within the Washington government a substantial group of international security officials emerged who were deeply committed to protecting the alliance arrangement with their Smaller Ally.

There also developed a potential bargaining asset that proved useful later on—the electronic installations at Peshawar.[13] Originally these had not been planned when the alliance was first bruited, but it turned out that the electronic characteristics of the Peshawar valley were ideally suited to tuning in on the Soviet Union's major missile-testing range. Peshawar also proved to be a useful jump-off point from which, on occasion, the Major Power Ally

12. Shaheen Irshad Khan, *Rejection Alliance? A Case Study of U.S.–Pakistan Relations (1947–1967)* (Lahore: Ferozsons, 1972), p. 186.

13. For a discussion, see Selig Harrison, "America, India and Pakistan — A Chance for a Fresh Start," *Harper's*, CCXXXIII (July 1966), 56–68.

sent reconnaissance planes at some 80,000 feet across Russia to the territory of another ally, Norway.

In addition to providing the location for electronic surveillance, which became in itself a source of policy leverage to the Pakistan government, the Small Ally supported its Major Power Ally's position at the United Nations on many (though not all) issues.[14] At meetings of the "non-aligned" statesmen, such as at Bandung and Colombo, it argued on behalf of the legitimacy of alliance relationships undertaken in self-defense and criticized the Soviet Union's form of "colonialism in Asia" and "neo-colonialism." Such statements were all the more acceptable to the Pakistan authorities since they were not only highly regarded by representatives of the Major Power Ally, but they also ran counter to the arguments made by Pakistan's large neighbor, India.

Though subsequently these arrangements and policy lines came to be seen as very mixed blessings, and some stressed their net liability all along, it could be argued that for five or six years the Small Ally prospered within the alliance. Particularly in relation to its larger neighbor, Pakistan's defense and diplomatic position had markedly improved by comparison with 1954. As Wayne Wilcox put it,

The alliance with America offset India's military preponderance and changed the diplomatic weightings of the Indian and Pakistani cases on Kashmir. The army's own "tools" were not only expanded, but much enhanced in quality and sophistication. U.S. military advisers brought new techniques of command and communication to what was, in fact, an obsolete light infantry formation.[15]

To be sure, Pakistan did not gain enough diplomatic clout to solve the Kashmir problem its own way. But its sense of anxiety about the ability of its larger neighbor to overrun

14. It differed on China policy, for example, from 1959 onward.
15. "Political Role of Army in Pakistan: Some Reflections," *South Asian Studies* (Jaipur), VII, No. 1 (Jan. 1972), 30–44, quoted on 36.

it sharply diminished; the original sense of acute fragility was markedly reduced. On the economic side, its irrigation infrastructure, transport, and industrial facilities improved sharply, and urban food prices were held down, allowing city payrolls to remain stable and the cost of exports to be competitive.

At the same time, however, the substantial improvement in Pakistan's position had its effects on developments in India. It was not an intended by-product of the military assistance program, but that did induce the Indians to increase their defense budget. The competition hardly became an "arms race" as the super-powers experience them, but in terms of local resources it came close to that as each party increased defense expenditures in rather close relation to the other.

The Alliance Loses Its Charm

The alliance arrangement, however, was far from perfect, and it came to be seen by prominent Pakistanis as less and less satisfactory.

In the first place, the rate of military deliveries leveled off after a rapid surge during the first years of the alliance. The military services were naturally disappointed that the early pace was not maintained. Second, the Small Ally found that its Major Power Ally did not wholeheartedly support its case against India on the disputed territory, but sought to maintain working diplomatic and economic relations with both countries. Third, because of the United States' desire to block Soviet expansion and the very size and possible consequential character of India in the future Asian balance, the Major Power sought to strengthen the Small Ally's opponent by a substantial economic assistance program. To be sure, on a per capita basis, economic aid to India never reached more than half as much, but since the country was four times as large, the non-ally often received nearly twice

16. For a discussion, see Rothstein, *op. cit.*, pp. 251–59.

as much in real terms as the Small Ally. "What kind of a 'special relationship' was this?" it could be and was argued in Pakistan.

Fourth, a new element in the state system became increasingly obvious, promoted in part by the energetic activities of the large neighbor—namely, the mystique of nonalignment and the effort to undermine the reputation of statesmen who sought to solve their diplomatic and security problem by allying with a "neo-colonialist" Major Power.[16] It may have been coincidence, but apart from Yugoslavia, whose position was unique, and Ghana in Africa, the principal proponents of nonalignment just happened to be by far the largest countries in their respective areas and were not experiencing the sense of local threat from larger neighbors that troubled Pakistanis. But diplomatic costs became associated with the alliance relationship at the United Nations, at "Third World" conferences, and in other multilateral forums where diplomats confabulated and reputations were upheld or undermined.[17]

Moreover, the relationships developed as part of the alliance affected the domestic balance of political forces within the Smaller Ally. The army was receiving large flows of military supplies and the central bureaucracy was receiving and allocating substantial economic assistance transfers. Accordingly, these elements in the political system were gaining in preeminence at the expense of civilian political forces and institutions and domestic regional interests. Bengali opposition against Ayub Khan, the leader of Pakistan who had earlier been welcomed as the architect of the alliance, became focused on the alliance as the source of domestic political distortions. Growing domestic resentment against both the army and the bureaucracy built up hostility

17. Godfrey Jansen, *Non-Alignment and Afro-Asian States* (New York: Praeger, 1966); Alvin Z. Rubinstein, *Yugoslavia and the Non-aligned World* (Princeton: Princeton University Press, 1970).

against those alliance arrangements that were seen to be consolidating the latter's position at home.

In 1960 the downing of the U-2 dramatized the Major Power's activities on Pakistan's soil directed against the Soviet Union. The Russian threat to retaliate against Peshawar by releasing nuclear missiles sharply inflated the apparent cost of the alliance arrangement. It raised widespread questions about the advantages of the alliance that had not been raised before.[18]

In 1962 the Small Ally's principal opponent became embroiled in military conflict with China, Asia's largest country. Instead of standing by, as Pakistan would have preferred, Pakistan's Major Power Ally promptly come to India's assistance. United States' military assistance was never "massive" as alleged. Nevertheless, the Major Power's military aid to the Small Ally's major opponent came as a shock. It underlined the hard fact that the so-called special relationship had not been nearly as special as had been touted. This proved particularly vivid when the Major Power was not prepared to make its limited military assistance to India contingent on a settlement of the disputed territory in a way favorable to its Smaller Ally, as the latter insisted.

Such developments are not unusual in alliances. As Modelski points out, when a Great Power provides a security guarantee, it "has the right to expect that such support will not be called for except in defense of the most vital interests. [Nevertheless,] the small countries have a propensity for using the Great Power for their own . . . interests and . . . local preoccupations."[19] Pakistan, he argued, consistently sought to draw SEATO into its quarrel with India over Kashmir, an endeavor that distracted the countries of Southeast Asia from what had presumably brought them together in the first place, i.e., the perceived threat from China.

18. For a brief discussion, see Burke, *op. cit.*, p. 266. See also Z. A. Bhutto, *The Myth of Independence* (Lahore: Oxford University Press, 1969).
19. Modelski, *op. cit.*, p. 155.

More Varied Options in Asia

It is characteristic of alliance relationships in a highly dynamic area and period that they do not last. Two elements contributed to changing Pakistani views of the utility of the American alliance. As pointed out, at the core of the arrangement were the very different weights Washington and Karachi/Islamabad attached to the Russian and Indian threats. Whenever this difference became apparent, the alliance was brought into question in both capitals. Second, China's rise from the ashes of civil war and revolution meant that a new and major element in the Asian state system, just on India's northern border, might also play a useful role in balancing the power of India.

As early as 1959 Pakistan had begun to broaden its relationships with its Asian neighbors to the north in a search for additional ways of dealing with its Indian problem. Negotiations with Russia led to oil-exploration agreements — on the assumption that such arrangements might induce Russia to be less wholehearted in its support of India's case at the United Nations, quite in addition to the intrinisic value of having additional explorations for oil under way. In 1959 President Ayub offered "joint defense" to India and spoke of the "danger from the north," meaning China, a ploy that pleased Washington and put New Delhi in a bad light. When it rejected Ayub's initiative in late 1959–60, however, Pakistan approached China regarding a possible frontier delimitation in the area of the Karakorams. Nothing came of this latter step until after the Sino-Indian border war had begun, but these initiatives showed Pakistan's interest in broadening its Asian relationships. Its Major Power Ally did not welcome these initiatives, since both Russia and China were then considered by Washington as its foremost opponents. But the Small Ally persisted all the same.

In 1962 the success of China in ignominiously defeating India opened a major alternative for Pakistan in its effort to balance the power of India. Machiavelli had urged his Prince to develop friendly relations with the neighbors of his larger neighbor. Kautiliya, Chandragupta's adviser, had elaborated this principle as early as 300 B.C. He had sketched a typical checkerboard pattern, where one's immediate neighbor was an enemy and the country on the other side of one's neighboring enemy was one's natural ally. The simplified apothegm for this theorem is the familiar, "The enemy of my enemy is my friend."[20] Following 1962, China, for Pakistan, fitted this recommendation perfectly; it was clearly India's enemy and it had now demonstrated its proven capacity to preoccupy India and to distract it from ambitions it might harbor toward Pakistan. Pakistan's Major Power Ally, acting on the same principle, saw India as its principal "friend" on the subcontinent, since it was directly opposing Washington's enemy, China. Accordingly, it was not prepared to press India hard on behalf of a "Pakistan solution" in Kashmir. Perhaps, some Pakistani officials argued, India's enemy — China — might be persuaded to oblige on Kashmir, since the Americans clearly would not.

This new opening posed a diplomatic conundrum, however, since the Major Power with whom Pakistan was allied was acutely hostile to Pakistan's Kautilyan "friend." Following 1962, therefore, Pakistan developed further a more complex policy. President Ayub called it the "triangular tightrope." It sought to retain whatever advantages the alliance with its Major Power Ally might still provide, while simultaneously reaching specific agreements with one of the Ally's major Asian opponents. The trick was to find issues of such manifestly reasonable substance that its Ally's objections could not be too sharp. Yet the issues had to be of sufficient import to dramatize to Pakistan's subcontinental opponent — India — its new flexibility and its potential for

20. For a discussion, see George Modelski, "Kautiliya's Foreign Policy and International System in the Ancient Hindu World," *American Political Science Review* LVIII, No. 33 (Sept. 1964), 549–60, quoted on 555.

bringing new sources of pressure to bear. Within most alliances at one time or another, particularly when important shifts are taking place, such conundrums present themselves and often take some years to solve.

Another question typical of alliances is the matter of how domestic politics affect alliance relationships. To go very far in this direction takes us away from the state-to-state model we are working with, but a few words would be in order. We have already seen the alliance's effect on strengthening the hand of the army and the bureaucracy and noted that criticism of the regime was in part taking the form of criticism of the alliance. Now the flow of influence ran the other way, as criticism of the alliance began to cost the regime further domestic support. Younger political leaders with an eye to the future began to dramatize their own differences with the regime by stressing the constraints imposed on their country by the alliance. They publicly urged the merits of closer relationships with their large Asian neighbors to the north.[21] Elements of the professional military establishment and the foreign policy community, frustrated by the declining rate of military aid transfers and anxious to make the most of their larger neighbor's embarrassment, pressed for a closer Chinese connection. Any improvement in relations with Russia might loosen the Delhi-Moscow connection and would tend thereby to further weaken external backing for the larger neighbor.

Accordingly, despite criticism from the Major Power Ally, a border settlement was finally worked out with China in 1962. Some military assistance arrangements were also defined and a series of state visits arranged. These steps signaled to the larger neighbor that Pakistan had additional ways of countervailing against the latter's dominant position; to its domestic critics it showed that it was not bound

21. See e.g., Bhutto, *op. cit.*, where he develops the arguments he and others began to use a good many years before the publication in 1969, even when he was still in the government.

hand and foot by the alliance with the Major Power, as the critics alleged.

It was noted earlier that within the alliance arrangements the Smaller Ally sought to improve its own bargaining position in relation to the Major Power. These symbolic steps served also to dramatize to the Major Power Ally that Pakistan ought not to be taken for granted, and that although Pakistan had stood out in support of its Major Power Ally's positions on many occasions in the past, there were limits to its acquiescing to everything the Major Power might want to do. Indeed, some observers believed the Government of Pakistan welcomed, and may even have encouraged, sharp public criticism of American policy. The public protests demonstrated that domestic pressures on the Pakistan government were so severe, it might have to withdraw from the alliance if American policy did not change. This may have strengthened Pakistan's hand in dealing with the United States, though it might as likely provoke equally compelling impatience on the part of the Major Power Ally.[22] These steps did not answer Pakistan's aspirations for the disputed territory, nor did they slow down the growth of India's military strength.

Just as its larger neighbor (India) had protested loudly against any transfers of military equipment from the Major Power (the United States) to its Smaller Ally (Pakistan) in 1954, now the Smaller Ally reacted vigorously to any military transfers to its larger neighbor. The sharp objections against the limited American transfers to India in 1962 have been mentioned. These so aroused the anxieties of the Smaller Ally that its representatives appeared to be, as someone said, "almost out of their minds with worry."[23] Gradually, the close personal collaboration between the military services of Pakistan and the United States was restricted;

22. See, e.g., *New York Times*, April 29, 1963, from Karachi.
23. Personal interviews.

the training role and mobility of the American mission were pared down. American officials were often put on the defensive in what seemed to be well-orchestrated personal encounters.

In an effort to reassure the Small Ally, in the spring of 1963 a number of high-level envoys from Washington visited the subcontinent, including Secretary of State Rusk and President Kennedy's personal military adviser, General Maxwell Taylor. About this time, it is reported that the American Embassy in Rawalpindi indicated to the Government of Pakistan, in a letter from President Kennedy, that the "United States commitment to Pakistan was not limited to Communist countries, but specifically includes India" as well.[24]

Moreover, in 1963 the Indian government sought a major modernization program from the United States. An impressive military mission went to Washington and sought military assistance reported to be valued at between $500 million and $1.5 billion over a three- to five-year period. If the latter figure was nearer the mark, the contemplated transfers would have been well beyond those already made to the Smaller Ally.[25] Debate within the American foreign policy community was intense and protracted. In the end, the Major Power proposed to provide much of what was asked for, with the exception of the supersonic, high-performance aircraft similar to what had already been transferred to Pakistan. From the Indian point of view, this downgrading of the assistance package was so serious that they rejected most of it

24. Unpublished memorandum by B. H. Oehlert, Jr., "How to Lose Allies," dated May 19, 1970, reported by G. W. Choudhury, "The Emergence of Bangladesh and the South Asian Triangle," *The Yearbook of World Affairs 1973* (London: Institute of World Affairs, 1973), p. 81.

25. The lower figure is from Chester Bowles, *Promises to Keep* (New York: Harper & Row, 1971), p. 475; the higher from the *New York Times*, May 21, 1963. The actual value of military assistance at that time, of course, varied greatly, depending upon the pricing policies of the supplier and the opportunity costs actually attributed to financing loans at different interest rates, "grace periods," and years to repay.

except for some radar defense installations to be located across the northern frontier and a used munitions plant to be moved from St. Louis.[26] There is little doubt that the leading officials of the Smaller Ally were greatly relieved.

It can be fairly argued that an important implicit consideration in Washington's deliberations was the likely effects such a program as proposed by India would have on relations between the United States and its Smaller Ally. The Pakistanis were at pains to make clear their acute anxiety. And by now the Smaller Ally had some bargaining power in dealing with its Major Ally. The professional proponents of the Pakistan connection in the United States, particularly within the military establishment, argued strongly on behalf of the interests of the Smaller Ally. Its growing Chinese relationship strengthened their hand, as they could argue the importance of not "driving Pakistan into the arms of the Chinese," a point the Pakistani officials were actively pressing as well. To what extent the electronic installations at Peshawar were a bargaining chip thrown into the scale is not known, but they probably played a part.[27] The prospective transfer of supersonic aircraft was particularly disturbing to the Pakistani authorities, for at a stroke their only technical military advantage would have been checkmated. It seemed likely that there was a hard bargain on that specific issue – which proved to be decisive in leading the Indians to turn down the package offered.

In the end, of course, Pakistan's large neighbor found the Russians more willing than the Americans, as Ambassador Bowles had warned all along, and a large build-up, begun before 1962, accelerated after the lukewarm Washington offer in 1963. Just as China had seen Pakistan as a useful counter-

26. For contemporary published reports, see *New York Times*, March 25, May 21, May 31, June 20, and June 30, 1963.

27. Certainly Grand Harbor's naval facilities played a crucial part in the hard bargaining Malta engaged in vis-à-vis Great Britain in 1971. For this fascinating encounter, see my "Up for Auction: Malta Bargains with Great Britain" in I. William Zartman's *The 50% Solution* (New York: Anchor Books, 1976), pp. 208–34.

weight to India on the latter's western flank, so the Soviet Union must have seen India as a convenient counterweight to China on the latter's southern flank.

The 1965 Gamble

Direct Challenge to the Large Neighbor

There are times in a state's history when the tide of events appears to be turning against it, when a formerly precariously held but just tolerable position is visibly eroding. The difficulties may be domestic, they may be foreign, or a combination of both. At such times, statesmen are tempted to stake a good deal on a bold initiative. Once even a minor resort to violence is accepted, a gage is thrown down to *fortuna;* the outcome must in some measure depend on chance. In 1965 Pakistan's leaders gambled heavily — and lost.

By then, Pakistani officials could not help but notice that the military strength of their larger neighbor was improving, thanks to Soviet equipment transfers and a growing arms industry that Pakistan could not hope to match. Politically, India was progressively drawing the disputed territory of Kashmir into India's constitutional system. In contrast, the Small Ally was receiving fewer military supplies than it had before, for its Major Power Ally's strategic orientation was downgrading South Asia generally as a result of ICBM technology, some measure of detente with Russia, and a growing concern with Southeast Asia. In 1962 and the early spring of 1963, many Pakistanis came to believe that the United States had not been a reliable ally, for it had refused to make arms shipments to India contingent on Indian concessions on Kashmir. Having let that opportunity pass, Pakistan officials must have reasoned, Washington was not likely to press Pakistan's larger neighbor further. The United Nations was moribund on the issue of Kashmir. Domestic opposition in West Pakistan was increasingly critical of the regime for its inaction. In East Pakistan, however, critics of Islamabad focused more on lack of economic growth and insufficient political representation of Bengali interests, for they cared little for the Kashmir issue that so exercised opinion in the west.

In retrospect, one can see that the Pakistan initiative of 1965 was a turning point. Again, details would take us too far into the particularities of India's, Pakistan's, and subcontinental history, but certain key points can be quickly made.[28]

There developed a growing conviction among a number of key Pakistani leaders that a policy of doing nothing would mean that the disputed territory of Kashmir would be irrevocably surrendered to India. Such an approach was not only seen as dishonorable desertion of Muslim brethren left under Hindu rule, but would be politically risky at home, particularly in the Punjab where sentiment in regard to Kashmir was most exercised.

Portents of short-run Indian weakness could be seen in the succession to Nehru's mantle of the unprepossessing and reputedly Gandhist Shastri and the unimpressive performance of Indian troops in the Rann of Kutch combat in the spring of 1965.

Already in late 1963 discontent in Kashmir was dramatized when the theft of a hair from the Prophet's beard held as a sacred relic in the principal mosque of Srinagar precipitated severe rioting and police shootings. A situation ripe for rebellion might be at hand, some thought, if only Pakistan could show determined support for its Muslim brothers in the valley.

Part of the effort may have been designed to forcefully drag the attention of the international community back to Kashmir. It is credible, though admittedly speculative, that there was

28. For a critical, analytical discussion, see Herbert Feldman, *From Crisis to Crisis, Pakistan from 1962–1969* (London: Oxford University Press, 1972), chap. 9.

a belief among a number of Pakistani officials that only if there was an outbreak of violent (though limited) international conflict would the international community, including the Major Powers, bring sufficient weight to bear on Pakistan's larger neighbor to force a mutually acceptable settlement. Nasser, perhaps, had tried such a maneuver in 1967 and failed, but Sadat had been bolder in 1973 and had gained a measure of success. In 1965 some Pakistani policymakers may have calculated in a similar vein.[29]

It may be that they believed others shared their view regarding the sharp distinction they saw between the "line of demarcation" in Kashmir separating the two parts of the disputed territory and the "international boundary" separating Pakistan and India in the Punjab. Seen from this perspective, an intrusion of "irregulars" into the valley from Azad Kashmir could remain quite distinct from any action India might take elsewhere in retaliation. If India did move across the international frontier, some may have argued, this would represent Indian aggression and the specific American assurances mentioned earlier, reportedly given in 1962–63, might bring Pakistan's Major Power Ally to the support of Pakistan.

There may have been a further expectation. If the adventure did go so far as to bring war between the two South Asian countries, the Kautiliyan formula would prove correct and Pakistan's friend China, the enemy of its enemy, would again drive southward – or at least threaten to do so – to confound Pakistan's larger neighbor.

In the early months of 1965, India took further steps to integrate Kashmir into the Indian political and administrative system. Local political groups desirous of cooperating

29. On Nasser's presumed calculations, see Miles Copeland, *The Game of Nations* (New York: Simon & Shuster, 1969), pp. 144–46, 253–58; Yair Evron, *The Middle East: Nations, Super-Powers and Wars* (London: Elek, 1973), p. 185, citing article by Heikal; and Insight Team, *The Middle East War* (London: Sunday Times and Andre Deutsch, 1974), pp. 42 and 228.

with India were made parts of the Indian National Congress party; titles of key officials were made identical with similar officials in India; provisions of the Indian constitution relating to the application of emergency powers were, for the first time, made operational in Kashmir. The worst suspicions of Pakistanis seemed to be about to be fulfilled in such a Fabian way that outsiders were scarcely aware of what was happening; or if they were aware, they did not seem to care.

A classic example of reciprocal escalation got under way. Activity across the Kashmir cease-fire line intensified. Claiming that Pakistani armed men were trying to interrupt traffic on the precarious road from Srinagar to Leh, in mid-May the Indian government ordered its troops to cross the cease-fire line where they occupied three posts in the Kargil area. Pakistan protested to the United Nations, and the Indian troops were withdrawn on the guarantee that the United Nations supervisory corps would occupy the evacuated posts and ensure that there were no repetitions of the alleged actions by Pakistani troops. Incidents (border crossings, firings, etc.) became more frequent all along the line; the United Nations reported over two thousand during the first six months of 1965. Unrest in Kashmir was said in Pakistan to be rising sharply with the political changes; Indian officials claimed that all was calm and peaceful as usual. Officials in Azad Kashmir reportedly organized guerrilla training units, the Indians arguing these were really elements of the regular Pakistan army training under leadership based in Murree. In early August substantial numbers of infiltrators penetrated the Indian-held parts of Kashmir.[30]

30. For a long time Pakistan officially denied the fact of infiltrators from its side of the line. Perhaps the most objective and informed testimony comes from General Nimmo, chief of the United Nations Military Observer Group, who reported "that the series of violations that began on 5 August were to a considerable extent in subsequent days in the form of armed men, generally not in uniform, crossing the cease-fire line from the Pakistan side for the purpose of armed action on the Indian side." United Nations, *Report of the Secretary General on the Current Situation in Kashmir* (Doc S/6651), Sept. 3, 1965.

They appear to have hoped to evoke a popular uprising or to give heart to those Kashmiris who wanted to oppose the valley's integration with India.

In response to the infiltration, the Indian army again crossed the cease-fire line "to eliminate the source of the infiltrators." The Pakistan army retaliated on September 1 by sending a regular force against the Indian army units defending the road from Jammu to Srinagar near Akhnur. A week later, the Indians eventually replied, as they had always said they would, by attacking Pakistan across the international frontier in the Punjab and pressed toward Sialkot and Lahore. Two days later, Washington announced a stop to all military assistance to both India and Pakistan. After some seventeen days of combat between regular army units of both sides, the indecisive war ground to a stop.

Each side claimed military victory, since each had gained some territory at the expense of the other. The net assessment concludes that the Pakistan army was effectively brought to a halt, while the Indians had many uncommitted troops and much more materiel than their opponent when the cease-fire came, though these forces were scattered and would have required some time to be brought to bear. It is probable that President Ayub and his immediate military advisers knew the position, but the newspaper reporting had been so exaggerated that the populace was bewildered. They could not understand how such a series of "victories" would end with such a miserable, indecisive peace. The terms of the peace were confirmed at Tashkent, when the Russians mediated the settlement, with the inconspicuous involvement of the American President, Lyndon Johnson.[31]

We now know that this adventure was a disaster for Pakistan and for its regime. China did threaten, but it did not move. Politically, the gambit did not succeed because the

31. W. W. Rostow, *The Diffusion of Power: An Essay in Recent History* (New York: Macmillan, 1972), p. 410.

inhabitants of the disputed territory did not rise, and most of the infiltrators were turned in and killed or imprisoned. Militarily, it showed an early success, but Indian numbers and the inherent vulnerability of Lahore left Pakistan with no alternative but to accept a cease-fire once it became clear that replenishments from the United States were not forthcoming.

These actions dramatically underlined the outer limits of the alliance with the Major Power. Not only did the Major Power Ally refuse to come to the rescue of its Smaller Ally; in an effort to bring the conflict to a prompt halt it stopped all arms shipments to both belligerents. This policy hurt its Ally more than its Ally's opponent, since the latter had its own armaments industry and the flow of supplies from the Soviet Union was hardly affected. In its own defense, the Major Power Ally argued, not without logic, that it had never offered to guarantee Pakistan against the consequences of any high-risk initiative it might be tempted to take, particularly against other than the assumed Communist threat. Even the specific bilateral commitment made in 1962 in the aftermath of military aid to India did not apply when Pakistan itself had by its infiltration gambit in effect pulled the main trigger first.

Understandably enough, the Pakistanis looked on this as near treachery on the part of Washington, since India had been the first to cross the international boundary. In any event, as the Pakistanis saw it, India had precipitated the situation by its political moves in changing the constitutional status of Kashmir. As Washington saw it, however, the sending of irregulars into the valley was the real precipitant of the conflict and that initiative absolved the United States of the obligation to fulfill its guarantee in this instance. That Pakistan's tactics were precisely the ones the Americans were grappling with in Vietnam only served to further weaken sympathy for Pakistan in Washington.

As a result of this conflict, the predominant mood in the

capital of Pakistan's Major Power Ally became "a plague on both your houses." In Pakistan, this change of attitude called for an urgent search for alternatives to the now virtually inoperative American connection.

The Chinese Option Becomes All the More Important

Problems within the alliance intensified. Efforts of Pakistani spokesmen to improve relations with China and the Soviet Union by criticizing the Major Power Ally's policy in Asia made collaboration within the alliance all the more difficult. Eventually, the American President became so annoyed by these differences, vigorously aired in public, that on indecently short notice he abruptly postponed visits of both the Pakistan President and the Indian Prime Minister; a critical meeting of the international consortium on aid to Pakistan was not held on time because, it was said, the American representative was not given clear instructions, certain "political problems" having to be clarified first. It is reported that the foreign minister, a strong critic of American policy, was fired at American insistence. To placate the supporters of the first and to protect the regime from being criticized for being too pro-American, the finance minister, a strong proponent of the alliance, was also dropped.

In short, instead of eliciting a response that furthered the interest of the Smaller Ally, as had occurred in 1962 when Pakistani officials made clear their acute anxiety over American aid to India, the public criticisms and risky military initiative had only weakened Pakistan's supporters in the capital of the Major Power Ally. Such protests might have been good domestic politics, however, for the Pakistani public was understandably as bitter against Washington as were the officials who had advised on the decisions leading to the outbreak of war. But from the foreign policy point of view, they were, as the saying goes, counterproductive.

On the other hand, Pakistan's relationships with its Kautiliyan friend China were improving. Arms flows increased, some MIG fighters were delivered, and the ever-present possibility of renewed Chinese activity on India's northern border was thought to inhibit Indian activities.

The Government of Pakistan also sought to affect the balance between itself and India by seeking constructive relationships with the Soviet Union. While differences with the United States were intensifying, Pakistan began to receive limited military assistance from the Soviet Union. Moscow reportedly also urged India to try to stabilize relationships with Pakistan by moderating its position on Kashmir. As part of its bargain with the Soviet Union, Pakistan finally closed the American listening post in Peshawar at the expiration of the original agreement.[32] Satellite technology had apparently rendered it less crucial to the United States by then. But as it had served Pakistan well in bargaining with the United States in 1962, so it was useful as a chip in bargaining with the Soviet Union in 1968. But it was a one-shot asset then, for once it had been closed in exchange for some Soviet military equipment, Pakistan could no longer use it in dealing with either Major Power.

So long as the Johnson Administration grappled with the North Vietnamese in Vietnam, these Pakistan relationships with the Asian Communist giants complicated Pakistan's relationship with Washington. But once the Nixon Administration sought to bring an end to American participation in the Vietnam war by improving relations with both China and Russia, Pakistan's position became more acceptable in Washington. The "triangular tightrope," of which President

32. International Institute of Strategic Studies, *Strategic Survey 1968* (London: IISS, 1969), pp. 33–34.

Ayub spoke in explaining his efforts to have simultaneous relationships with the United States, China, and the Soviet Union, was developed further by his successor. It was through Islamabad that the Americans and Chinese arranged their first steps toward direct discussions between the American and Chinese heads of state.

By now it was clear that instead of coping with its major problem—India—through its close association with a Major Power Ally, as between 1954 and, say, 1965, Pakistan had broadened its options and was dealing directly with its two larger Asian neighbors to the north, with a much looser relationship with the United States. It had not been successful in isolating India from its Soviet backer, but since the Tashkent settlement following the 1965 war the Soviet Union had been steering a less one-sided course in South Asia than it had before—or than it resumed following the treaty arrangement with India in 1971.

The 1971 Debacle

The next major shift in the subcontinent's balance of power came as a result of the follow-on events after President Yahya had opened Pakistan's domestic political system to the freest elections the country had ever had. This led to a geographical polarization of political support for two civilian leaders who were unable to bury their differences in common effort to ensure a continuation of civilian rule encompassing both wings. Acute linguistic, economic, and political grievances, a total misreading by Pakistani officials at the center of the intensity of resentment in the Bengal region, and a misplaced confidence in the efficacy of large-scale military action to suppress agitational regional politics led the Islamabad authorities to concentrate nearly a third of their forces in the eastern province. A savage repressive effort backfired hideously and intensified the determination of Bengali political leaders to accomplish the separation that the army's action had been intended to prevent.

From India's point of view, the opportunity to "finally" deal with its Pakistan problem, the flood of millions of refugees, and the disorders likely to move across the frontier into its own most disturbed state of West Bengal led it to receive, train, and equip guerrillas to fight the army-imposed regime in East Pakistan. Its own military preparations, begun in April and May 1971, and its Treaty of Mutual Friendship, concluded in the summer of 1971 with the Soviet Union, were contingent preparations for a highly skillful and well-executed Indian military penetration of East Pakistan in December.

The repressive action of the Pakistan army had lost Pakistan most of its friends abroad, quite as much as within East Pakistan. Although China stood at the ready on the frontiers, any initiative it might have been tempted to take was inhibited by Soviet power, now committed to India's defense by Article (9) of the new Treaty of Mutual Friendship.[33] The United States attempted to mediate a political settlement between authorities in East and West Pakistan, but the timing of Indian moves preempted whatever slight chances of success that diplomatic initiative might have had. The Americans made gestures of support for Pakistan when the Indian armies crossed East Pakistan frontiers, and it sent units of the Seventh Fleet to the Bay of Bengal, though they were not in the area until the conflict was virtually over. Once again, the Major Power Ally appears to have been inhibited by the steps the Pakistan authorities had taken to precipitate the new conflict and by the Ally's unwillingness

33. For a detailed discussion of the military planning, actual preparations, and course of the Indian campaign, see the excellent study by Pran Chopra, *India's Second Liberation* (Delhi: Vikas Publishing, 1973); also International Institute of Strategic Studies, *Strategic Survey 1971* (London: IISS, 1972), pp. 46–54.

to involve itself in a direct military engagement against Pakistan's larger subcontinental neighbor.

In the end, Pakistan saw over half the country's population splitting off to form the new state of Bangladesh, over one-third of its army taken prisoner, and its larger subcontinental neighbor virtually in command over its former eastern province. As the International Institute of Strategic Studies put it, Pakistan now had only one-tenth the size of India, with "about an equivalent proportion of its diplomatic and political leverage."[34] The refugees returned, and within five months the Indian army had gone home in a neatly managed military victory, brief occupation, and prompt withdrawal. Pakistan's prisoners of war were taken in tow to India, to remain in camps for over a year and a half.

Indian preponderance on the subcontinent could not now be doubted. Whether this state of affairs would persist depended more on India's domestic capacity for coping with intractable economic and political difficulties at home than on India's unambiguous numerical superiority in military strength, population, and economic potential.

Prime Minister Bhutto's Predicament

Since taking over his shattered country, much that Prime Minister Bhutto has done can be seen as concerned with this persisting foreign policy problem. His early fast-paced travels to the Middle East, to Peking, Moscow, and Washington can be understood as continuing episodes in the search for economic and military resources from abroad and foreign political support.

Quiet special relationships with and the assignment of technicians to the Gulf sheikdoms provide badly needed

34. *Ibid.*, p. 46.

foreign exchange and may have been designed to assure adequate representation of Pakistani interests in the councils of the OAPEC. But undue preference for Saudi Arabia and the neighboring sheikdoms could run counter to Iran's conception of its future role in the area and complicate relations with Iran. Even though both may have shared concerns regarding Afghanistan, Pakistan's policy toward Baluchistan can have a direct effect on Iran's conception of Pakistan's intentions. A loan of some $500 million from Teheran in the summer of 1974 suggests that the Shah, however, sees a considerable parallel interest with Pakistan's.

The Simla accord in July 1972 opened the way for a process of accommodation between India and Pakistan on such problems as the return of the prisoners of war, trade relations, collaboration on river valley development, etc. If success could be achieved on specific issues, the level of mutual suspicion might decline and a number of cooperative enterprises of mutual benefit be begun. But India's nuclear explosion could only intensify Pakistan's anxieties once more and would require substantial Indian diplomatic art to assuage.

The Islamic Summit in the winter of 1974 sought to dramatize the breadth of Pakistan's support among Muslim states stretching all the way from Morocco to Indonesia. It permitted subtle political steps toward recognizing Bangladesh, a prelude to renewing ties with the former east wing. And since the conference followed the Yom Kippur War and the quadrupling of oil prices in November and December 1973, it may have been designed to gain for Pakistan assured oil supplies at preferential prices from the Muslim Middle East.

Looked at from another angle, Mr. Bhutto's foreign policy predicament was severe. On the one hand, he could not expect major military assistance from the United States. What equipment Pakistan required had to be purchased, on whatever lending terms could be obtained, in the open arms market, further enlarging Pakistan's already very substantial foreign indebtedness. Some degree of detente with the Soviet Union was desirable to minimize the risk of Soviet pressure on the Northwest Frontier. And an easing of tension with India could reduce military expenditures and turn more attention in both countries to domestic development. But in the absence of a solid civilian political party structure and established political institutions, any regime had to depend on either popular enthusiasm or the substained goodwill of the military. Since popular enthusiasm was likely to be fickle and the military tended to be both conservative and still committed on Kashmir, they were not likely, separately or together, to provide the domestic base for such unpopular but probably prudent policies.

Conclusion

In sum, we can see four major periods, each marked by a different Pakistani approach to balancing the power of its larger neighbor. During the first period, from independence to roughly 1954, Pakistan sought to accomplish this end by turning to the international community in the form of the United Nations to bolster its position and by seeking support of countries in the Arab Muslim Middle East.

By 1952 this course seemed inadequate, and Pakistan turned toward developing close relations with a distant Major Power, the United States. By 1954 this relationship was institutionalized in a series of alliances and military and economic assistance arrangements. This second effort to alter in Pakistan's favor the balance of power between Pakistan and its larger neighbor brought a considerable improvement. However, it fell short of Pakistan's highest aspiration since the disputed territory of Kashmir was not successfully obtained.

The state system is always in flux, however. Arrangements

useful in one period may become inadequate in another. The relative position of Pakistan via-à-vis India began to slip in 1960–61. In part, this is attributable to the Indian response to Pakistan's improved arms position in the mid-1950s as a result of the American alliance. But India's concern with China had an independent dynamic influence on India's military position. The two together, however, and Indian interests in a general improvement in her own defense position, particularly after the 1962 debacle, led to a rapid step-up in India's defense after 1962.

As a result of these changes and Pakistan's changing perception of the utility of the American connection, Pakistan sought to correct its weakening position by developing broader options within Asia itself. China's success in humiliating Pakistan's rival and its readiness to play a direct role in balancing India improved Pakistan's position after 1962. But the gain was limited and proved only temporary. Soviet military assistance to India increased following the war with China. The politico-military debacle of the 1965 Indo-Pakistan war and its side-effects on America's commitment to Pakistan, changes in American perceptions of the politico-strategic importance of the subcontinent, and the somewhat dramatic style of political spokesmen in demonstrating their independence from the Major Power Ally, all weakened the utility of the American connection. Growing contention within China resulting in the Cultural Revolution made the China connection temporarily less useful. Nevertheless, while there was a net loss in the military balance, there was some diplomatic and political gain, for Pakistan now had more variegated options, no longer depending solely on decisions made in any one capital for whatever outside backing it might obtain.

Finally, the way the regime dealt with the crisis in East Pakistan in 1971 and the Indian military success thereafter left the remaining half of Pakistan in a far weaker position than it had been at any time since, perhaps, the early 1950s.

The futility of attempting to fill the gap between foreign policy goals as set in the 1950s and the foreign policy means available in 1970 was dramatically revealed. One result could be that the aim of gaining control over the disputed territory can now be abandoned with honor. It may also lead to a new quality of relationship between the two countries on the subcontinent. The outcome would depend as much on the style and objectives of Indian diplomacy toward Pakistan and the backing available to either from outside Major Powers as on internal dynamics with Pakistan itself.

How Useful a Model?

This account of Pakistan's efforts to balance the power of India provides one reasonably efficient interpretation of Pakistan's foreign policy behavior. It does not, however, account for a number of important aspects of Pakistan's approach to foreign policy.

It does not explain the costly Pakistan commitment to regain Kashmir, a commitment that has contributed so much to the heavy emphasis on military preparations and the intensity of hostility toward India. Nor does it explain India's reluctance to either make concessions in Kashmir or to take other steps to reduce Pakistan's anxieties. This approach does not explore long-standing Muslim-Hindu antagonism, nor the incompatible principles of statehood that provided a sense of moral self-righteousness to both parties to the Kashmir dispute. It does not consider the domestic political pressures that sustained the interest in the struggle in both countries. Accordingly, it does not provide an adequate reflection of the inwardness of this antagonism to policy-makers in both countries. But the logic of arms-race theory and of Kautilyan perspectives provides a good deal of understanding of this competitive hostility.

Many interesting and important questions have not been looked at. Most states are not monoliths in fact, but a congeries of competing and collaborating interests. What were the bureaucratic, professional, or economic interest groups within Pakistan that have been most important in shaping the concept of "national interest" and the making of foreign policy in Pakistan? Did domestic political support at any one time depend as heavily upon a high degree of hostility toward India as many Indians argue? How did the institutional structures of the Foreign Affairs and Finance ministries affect foreign policy choices?[35] Were economic interests as important in supporting the alliance relationship as is often alleged? Were there serious debates regarding the possible advantages (or disadvantages) to the economy as a whole, particularly of East Pakistan, if more constructive economic relations with India had been instituted, even at the cost of some reduction in hostility toward India?

Certain turning points were not inevitable, although the state-to-state model suggests they were. The gradual movement from close alliance with a distant Major Power to the "triangular tightrope" was to be expected at some point. The exact timing, however, may owe something to domestic politics in both Pakistan and the United States and to the styles and preoccupations of their respective leaders.

While the 1965 gamble that proved so consequential was in itself understandable enough, another leader or the same one in other administrative or political contexts might have weighed the chances differently and sidestepped that particular risk. This would surely have produced a different set of succeeding events. Nor was the separation of Bangladesh inevitable; or if it had to come, it did not have to be such a tragic and destructive affair. The competition between

---

35. For an interesting discussion of aspects of Pakistan's institutionalizing efforts, as they relate to other aspects of Pakistan's political development, see Ralph Braibanti, "Pakistan's Experiment in Political Development," ASIA *Supplement No. 1* (Fall 1974) pp. 25–42.

the two subcontinental states no doubt eased the advances of the Soviet Union into a position of influence on the sub-continent, but it would be wrong to argue that Indo-Pakistan contention is sufficient explanation for Soviet interest in South Asia, and that had the two been able to avoid conflict, Moscow would have had no opening. Kautiliyan logic would have led Moscow to seek an opening into the subcontinent as soon as the Sino-Soviet split became obvious, from the early 1960s forward at least. Nevertheless, India's concern about Pakistani irredentism in regard to Kashmir and Paki-stan's military support from Washington no doubt made it easier for Moscow to follow the advice of Chandragupta's adviser.

State systems often set narrow limits to what statesmen can do. Scholars and observers tend to exaggerate statesmen's room for maneuver. But within these margins, there is nearly always a range of human choice. Close observation of the uniqueness of each state, the specific settings of statesmen and how they grapple with successive difficulties is neces-sary before one can presume to define more narrowly the range of their choice and how parsimonious or extrava-gant they were in the use of what foreign policy resources lay to hand. The detailed examination of the changing con-tours of the state system and the shifting flow of power within it can help us see these limits more clearly.

It is, however, only by careful and repeated observation of the linkages between the state system and the domestic setting, as mediated by political elites, that we are likely to improve our ability to generalize. And for that, we need a combination of the area specialist and the student of state systems.

12

The Management of Pakistan's Foreign Policy

S. M. Burke

"I shall never forget," recalls Vincent Sheean, "that when I first visited the new establishment [Karachi, 1947] there was only one typewriter in the whole Foreign Office."[1] This impossible situation of having to conduct relations with all the world with just one writing machine well illustrates the crushing difficulties the infant state of Pakistan faced at the time of her birth on August 15, 1947. In fact, that there would be a state called Pakistan was not definitely known till His Majesty's Government announced on June 3, 1947, that British India would be partitioned into two sovereign states. The Muslim League leaders decided to make Karachi the provisional capital of their new country and hastily established a Construction Circle within the Sind Public Works Department to perform the stupendous task of finding accommodations for the coming flood of central government officials and departments. The authorities, at the same time, had to cope with millions of refugees from India, rich and poor, who were clamoring for assistance in their freshly adopted motherland. But even the members of the Construction Circle had nowhere to stay, and they finally found shelter within the precincts of the Indian Military Hospital!

The Ministry of Foreign Affairs and Commonwealth Relations, as it was then called,[2] was alloted two residential villas

---

1. Vincent Sheean, *Nehru: The Years of Power* (London: Gollancz, 1960), p. 93.
2. Now simply known as the Ministry of Foreign Affairs. Pakistan left the Commonwealth when Britain recognized Bangladesh in January 1972.

across the road from each other, Mohatta Palace and Bhopal House. Their location near the beach of Clifton, a suburb of Karachi, was pleasant enough, but the foreign office was the only arm of the government in that locality. All the other ministries had been housed in the city of Karachi some miles away and were scattered over several buildings. Continuous personal consultation between officers belonging to the different branches of the government, so necessary for the smooth conduct of any administration, was therefore difficult and time-consuming. Nor was it any easier to communicate by telephone. The existing lines could not satisfactorily cope with the tremendous extra load suddenly cast upon them.

Pakistan, moreover, started with a woefully small number of officers and clerical staff, and while there were individuals with experience in departments such as defense, finance, law, education, and commerce, there were none who had been involved in the foreign policy process of an independent nation because external relations had been the monopoly of the British government in London.

Upon its establishment the Pakistan Foreign Office was headed by Mohammad Ikramullah, a member of the old Indian Civil Service. He was assisted by about a dozen officers who had escaped the scramble for personnel by other central ministries and provincial governments. There was no full-time foreign minister. Prime Minister Liaquat Ali Khan, already burdened with duties as head of government and as defense minister, also carried the portfolio of external affairs. It was not till December 1947 that Pakistan got its first foreign minister in the person of Chaudhri Zafrulla Khan. However, within a few days of Zafrulla's appointment, India took the Kashmir dispute to the Security Council and he was compelled to spend long spells abroad debating the question with Indian spokesmen.

Pakistani missions were equally shorthanded. Even important embassies at London and Washington had but one diplomatic officer to assist the ambassador until the trickle of service officers began in the early 1950s. The first batch of young recruits to that service was selected in 1948, but these thirteen freshmen required training and after that could join only as third secretaries.[3] It was decided to fill eighty-five positions from different age groups on an ad hoc basis, but the vacancies were not advertised till November 1948 and it took considerable time to complete the formalities and basic orientation. Also, owing to the general paucity of qualified persons in the country, the successful applicants were of uneven quality.

The earliest step toward establishing a regular foreign service was taken by a press note issued by the Ministry of Foreign Affairs and Commonwealth Relations on November 18, 1948. The note revealed it had been decided to create a new service to be known as the Pakistan Foreign Service, consisting initially of 120 persons of the following categories: (1) fourteen already chosen by a competitive examination held before partition (actually thirteen seem to have been taken); (2) twenty-two between the ages of twenty-one and twenty-six, to be recruited by competitive examination in January 1949; and (3) eighty-five, belonging to various age groups (from twenty-seven to fifty) to be selected on an ad hoc basis.[4] In 1952 the strength of the service was raised to 160, in 1960 to 172, in 1965 to 210, and in 1972 to 323. Since several officers defected during the East Pakistan secession, 121 candidates ranging in rank from third secretary to minister were enlisted in 1973. This contingent, for the first time, included women. By July 1974 the strength of the service stood at 438. Of this number, 239 (including 105 probationers) were posted at headquarters; the remaining 199 (including ten probationers) were serving abroad. Thirty-one heads of

3. It was in April 1966, after a period of eighteen years, that a member of this group first reached the rank of ambassador.
4. See *Three Years of Pakistan, August 1947–August 1950* (Karachi: Pakistan Publications, n.d.), p. 2.

mission were career officers, and thirty were non-career appointees.

The total number of missions and sub-missions is approximately seventy-nine. Those established in recent years have all been in developing countries, i.e., Mauritania, Somalia, Ethiopia, Abu Dhabi, Dubai, Muscat, Qatar, Guinea, North Korea, India, and Bangladesh. The strongest representation is in Asia, especially in the Middle East; the weakest is in South America.

At first the grades in the foreign office followed the nomenclature that had been in vogue in the pre-partition Government of India, i.e., secretary, joint secretary, and deputy secretary. In 1959 these ranks were redesignated secretary, director-general, and director. A research wing under a director-general was added to the foreign office in the same year. In 1972 an additional post of secretary for administration was created to enable the foreign secretary to devote all his attention to diplomatic duties. External publicity, which previously was the responsibility of the Ministry of Information and Broadcasting, was turned over to the Ministry of Foreign Affairs in April 1973.

The young entrants to the foreign service originally were sent abroad for a two-year training program. They started in the Fletcher School of Law and Diplomacy in the United States for theoretical instruction and moved to the Department of State in Washington and the Foreign Office in London for practical training. Finally, they spent six months in France learning the French language. This system was abandoned in 1960, and the entire schooling since then has been done in Pakistan. This includes a three-month attachment to different ministries at headquarters. Since 1968 the trainees have been sent abroad to learn foreign languages. They are attached to local Pakistan missions as third secretaries for the duration of their courses.

In November 1965 the foreign office was shifted to Islamabad and temporarily occupied the Capital Development Authority Municipal Building. On June 1, 1973, it moved into its permanent location, previously the Hotel Shahrazad.

I. 1947–51

In the beginning all chiefs of missions were public men, some very good and others quite poor. Prime Minister H. S. Suhrawardy once asked the author whether politicians or career men made better ambassadors. The response was as follows:

The best of the politicians make better ambassadors than the best of the officers because the outlook of the former is less cramped by addiction to precedents and red tape, but the average foreign service officer is better than the average non-career appointee. The reason is that an official would never reach the rank of ambassador unless he was a man of requisite ability and experience. He is, therefore, less likely to make himself ridiculous than an eager politician occupying a glamorous official position for the first time.

Suhrawardy smiled broadly and said, "I accept your view because I am a top politician myself."

A serious impediment in Pakistan's dialogue with other countries was that it was born in a totally unsympathetic world. The Hindu-Muslim problem, being peculiar to India, was not accepted by outsiders as a rational ground for demanding a separate state in the secular twentieth century. Even the British, who knew the conditions firsthand, wished to leave behind a united India. They had been condemned for having despoiled a rich and teeming land by the age-old colonial strategy of divide and rule. Had they been able to leave behind a politically united subcontinent, their honor would have been considerably redeemed. During the debate on the Indian Independence Bill, Prime Minister Attlee said, "For myself, I earnestly hope that this severance may not endure, and that the two new Dominions which we now propose to set up may, in course of time, come together again to form one great member State of the British Commonwealth of Nations."[5] Since Islam was not a factor in their own politics, other Muslim countries too found it easier to admire the Indian National Congress, which, like themselves, was struggling to overthrow Western domination. To these states it appeared the Muslim League was acting as the tool of Britain in the continuing game of "Divide and Rule." "In the first appraisal of her position among the community of self-governing nations," summed up Keith Callard, "Pakistan could find no single country which could be counted as an unfailing friend and ally willing to lend aid and comfort in time of need."[6]

And what about India with whom Pakistan had so many grave disputes and who desired an early extinction of Pakistan's separate identity? Gandhi and Nehru were world figures, respected everywhere for their sustained and doughty fight against British imperialism, while Jinnah and his colleagues were little known beyond the confines of their own native land. Jawaharlal Nehru, moreover, since the inauguration of the Interim Government in September 1946, had held the portfolio of external affairs in the Viceroy's Executive Council and had begun to advance the interests of India even before it was decided that there would be a country named Pakistan. India became a sovereign state on August 15, 1947, but Nehru even earlier had been allowed by the British government to behave as if he were the foreign minister of an independent country. "We shall take full part in international conferences," he had asserted, "as a free nation with our own policy and not merely as a satellite of another nation."[7] Brit-

5. *House of Commons Official Report*, July 10, 1947, col. 2445.

6. Keith Callard, *Pakistan, A Political Study* (London: George Allen and Unwin, 1957), p. 303.

7. Quoted by K. P. Karunakaran, *India in World Affairs (August 1947–January 1950)* (London: Oxford University Press, 1952), p. 3.

ish India had been an original signatory to the Charter of the United Nations at San Francisco, and new India was allowed to continue this membership while Pakistan had to apply for membership to the world organization. Nehru deputed an Indian delegation to the fall 1946 session of the General Assembly under the leadership of his own sister, Vijaya Lakshmi Pandit. Pakistan could not appear at the U.N. until a year afterward. Membership in all other international bodies also automatically devolved on India; Pakistan had to seek entrance everywhere as a newcomer.

Indian ambassadors to the more important countries got accredited before India became legally free. The Indian high commissioner in the United Kingdom, hitherto principally concerned with trade and administrative matters, assumed full diplomatic functions in September 1946. Asaf Ali presented his letter of credence to Truman in Washington on March 1, 1947, K. P. S. Menon to Chiang Kai-shek in Nanking[8] on March 29, 1947, and Mrs. Pandit to Shvernik in Moscow on August 13, 1947. For Pakistan, Habib Rahimtoola did not arrive in London until the middle of August 1947; M. A. H. Ispahani presented his credentials in Washington on October 8, 1947, Shoaib Qureshi in Moscow on December 31, 1949, and General Raza in Peking on November 12, 1951.

When the actual date for transfer of power arrived, the Indian Ministry for External Affairs simply continued to function as it already had done for nearly a year. Nehru literally kept sitting in the same chair as foreign minister that he had occupied as a member of the Viceroy's Council. All the existing diplomatic representatives, who had been formally selected by the then united India but in fact by Nehru for the new Union of India, continued to represent India. The premises of the diplomatic and trade missions abroad were also

8. Chiang Kai-shek had transferred his capital to Nanking. The People's Republic moved it back to Peking when it installed itself there on October 1, 1949.

taken over by India as running concerns. Pakistan had to buy or build new embassies and offices everywhere. This substantial head start enabled India to exploit the already existing conception of itself as potentially one of the world's leading powers and that of Pakistan as an unnatural temporary growth in the international field.

In March 1947, while the protagonists of Pakistan were still immersed in the struggle for their dreamland, Nehru's India attracted worldwide attention by calling an Asian Relations Conference, which was attended by twenty-four Asian countries and Egypt. Its formal host was the Indian Council of World Affairs, but it was lost on no one that the moving spirit behind all the activity was Jawaharlal Nehru, who, as already mentioned, was functioning virtually as India's foreign minister. After independence, India convened a Conference on Indonesia (January 1949) to condemn the renewed Dutch military action in the East Indies. These conferences and the Indian Prime Minister's confident role in world affairs were read by the international community as evidence that India was seizing the leadership of Asia. Mrs. Pandit averred in parliament: "Whether the Prime Minister wishes to assume leadership or not, India has assumed leadership."[9]

If a country cannot hope to obtain at the negotiating table what it is not expected to win on the battlefield, Pakistan's position in her numerous disputes with India was well-nigh hopeless. Though Muslims traditionally had formed the backbone of the celebrated British Indian army, the organization of that army had been such that it created special problems for Pakistan when the armed forces were split into two. Muslim intransigence toward British rule in the early period, especially the role of the Muslims in the great Mutiny of 1857, had left a lasting impression on the British mind. Consequently, while they had formed several purely Hindu, Sikh, and Gurkha regiments in the pre-partition Indian army,

9. *Parliamentary Debates of India*, Dec. 23, 1953, col. 3013.

the British never developed a combatant all-Muslim unit. The Pakistani army, therefore, had to be formed out of "bits and pieces like a gigantic jig-saw puzzle with some of the bits missing." The men "came from different units and different areas and they had all to be welded into fighting and ancillary units, divisions, and corps."[10]

During the Second World War most of the bases for operations against Japanese-occupied Southeast Asia had been set up in eastern and southern India. The military stores had been concentrated at these bases and at the major ports. All these areas fell within India upon partition and the supplies went with them. "The position was so bad," recalled Ayub Khan, "that for the first few years we could only allow five rounds of practice ammunition to each man a year."[11]

While the means at the disposal of the defenders of Pakistan were almost nonexistent—making them little better than "tin soldiers," to borrow Prime Minister Liaquat Ali Khan's expression—the area to be shielded was extremely difficult to protect. One of the main reasons advanced by the Cabinet Mission in its statement of May 16, 1946, for rejecting the demand for Pakistan was that "the two sections of the suggested Pakistan contain the two most vulnerable frontiers in India and for a successful defense in depth the area of Pakistan would be insufficient." East Pakistan, surrounded as she was by India on three sides, was especially hard to hold. Ayub Khan, who was the general officer commanding there for two years from January 1948, has stated he had only six hundred soldiers at his disposal[12] and practically no equipment: "At Headquarters there was no table, no chair, no stationery—we had virtually nothing at all; not even any maps of East Pakistan."[13] As Mountbatten put it during the

10. M. Ayub Khan, *Friends Not Masters* (London: Oxford University Press, 1967), p. 20.
11. *Ibid.*, p. 21.
12. *Dawn*, Dec. 9, 1964.
13. Ayub Khan, *op. cit.*, p. 22.

Indo-Pakistan tension over the question of Junagadh, war between India and Pakistan "might be the end of Pakistan altogether."[14] He could very well have expanded the context and stated that war between India and Pakistan over any issue might have been the end of Pakistan.

Luckily for Pakistan, at its disposal during those perilous early years were a handful of highly determined and dedicated men. Prime Minister Liaquat Ali Khan carried a cool head on his shoulders and was a man of strong common sense; Foreign Minister Zafrulla Khan more than matched anyone India could depute to the United Nations; Secretary-General of the Cabinet Chaudhri Mohammad Ali was a civil servant of considerable intelligence,[15] and Foreign Secretary Ikramullah was a man of great charm and compassion who knew how to get the best out of those who worked for him. The portfolio of finance, which can affect the working of any and all government departments, was in the competent hands of Ghulam Mohammad.[16]

All these persons had worked in the Government of (pre-partition) India at New Delhi and knew and respected one another. Liaquat and Zafrulla had been fellow members of the Central Legislative Assembly for a number of years; Ikramullah and Ghulam Mohammad had been officials in departments that were presided over by Zafrulla as a member of the Viceroy's Council; and Chaudhri Mohammad Ali had been additional finance secretary and Liaquat's principal confidant when Liaquat was finance minister in the Interim Government. In the new Government of Pakistan, Secretary-General Mohammad Ali worked closely with Foreign Secretary Ikramullah and this ensured the foreign office continuing liaison with the Prime Minister and the rest of the government departments.

14. Quoted by V. P. Menon, *The Story of the Integration of the Indian States* (Bombay: Orient Longmans, 1961), p. 132.
15. Previously a member of the Indian Audit and Accounts Service.
16. Another former member of the Indian Audit and Accounts Service.

Important foreign policy decisions were made by the cabinet over which Liaquat presided with aplomb and skill. The Prime Minister listened to his colleagues and sought consensus in decision-making.[17] Occasionally, if the situation demanded, the Prime Minister would make personal decisions, but he always referred the question to the cabinet afterward.[18] Of course, during the lifetime of the Quaid-i-Azam every decision of policy, including foreign policy, was subject to his approval. This supremacy did not originate from the statute book but flowed automatically from the Quaid's unique position as the father of the nation.

The main elements of Pakistani foreign policy were clear enough: utter mistrust of India and the fear that she was bent upon undoing partition and reabsorbing Pakistan within the Indian union; an emotional urge to cultivate brotherly ties with every Muslim country and to work for the unity of the Islamic world; a tilt in favor of the Western democracies and wariness of the communist states.[19] This unambiguity in important matters greatly mitigated the difficulties resulting from Zafrulla's prolonged absences from headquarters. The foreign office at Karachi and Zafrulla in the United Nations in fact operated as two almost independent units. Zafrulla knew full well what line to take in the Kashmir dispute, in the Arab-Israel question, and in other topics that came up in

17. Liaquat was an aristocrat by birth and upbringing. He had turned out to be an unexpectedly shrewd finance minister in the Interim Government, but on the whole he had been overshadowed by his more illustrious chief, Mohammad Ali Jinnah. After Jinnah's death Liaquat rose to the occasion admirably and proved to be an impressive prime minister.

I attended several sessions where the Prime Minister discussed foreign policy matters with the foreign secretary and other government officials. As a result of this experience I came to know Liaquat Ali Khan's style first-hand.

18. The system of taking important questions to the cabinet is still in vogue. It remained in suspension during periods of martial law.

19. For a fuller discussion of this aspect of Pakistan's policy, see S. M. Burke, *Pakistan's Foreign Policy: An Historical Analysis* (London: Oxford University Press, 1973), pp. 91–95, 123–35, 147–49, and S. M. Burke, *Mainsprings of Indian and Pakistani Foreign Policies* (Minneapolis: University of Minnesota Press, 1974), pp. 50–53.

the world organization. He had no need for a day-by-day briefing by the cabinet. In Karachi the store was minded by the secretary-general and the foreign secretary under the control of the Prime Minister. Of course, a constant flow of coded telegrams between Karachi and New York enabled both sides to maintain contact with each other and seek advice on specific points. Fortunately, there was complete trust between Liaquat and Zafrulla.

Thanks to the unceasing efforts of this well-integrated team, Pakistan acquitted itself surprisingly well in the arena of international politics. Zafrulla was able to turn the tables on India in the Kashmir case, and he won the esteem of the Arab states for his brilliant espousal of their causes in the United Nations. Back home Liaquat rode out several crises with India and managed to avert full-scale war without loss of dignity.[20] The world at large began to have some misgivings about the self-proclaimed moral greatness of India and no longer unquestioningly accepted her assertion that the creation of Pakistan was a blunder that history soon would rectify.

II. 1952–57

The opening years of Pakistan's independence were a unique period in its life. The country lacked the normal resources for the management of foreign policy and faced impossible odds. But a handful of remarkable men working closely together were able to avert disaster. Their success in no small measure was due to the fact that the people of Pakistan, still full of zeal for the promised land, were united behind Quaid-i-Azam Mohammad Ali Jinnah and, after his

20. An undeclared war limited to Kashmir was fought by India and Pakistan from May 1948 until January 1, 1949. All-out war nearly broke out between them in the spring of 1950 and in the summer of 1951. See Burke, *Pakistan's Foreign Policy, op. cit.*, pp. 57–60.

death in September 1948, behind his political heir, Prime
Minister Liaquat Ali Khan. By 1951 conditions had begun to
look up. Older members of the foreign service, who had been
recruited on an ad hoc basis, as well as the younger men,
who had completed their training, had begun to relieve the
personnel shortage in the foreign office as well as in the field.
Partition problems, such as the flood of refugees, were becoming less intense. However, just as the situation was beginning to ease off, the ship of state suddenly lost its captain:
Liaquat Ali Khan was felled by an assassin's bullet as he rose
to address a public meeting at Rawalpindi on October 16,
1951.

The outstanding feature of the years that immediately
followed was utter political confusion. In the absence of any
leader of national stature to hold it together, the ruling Muslim League party fragmented into querulous factions. A re-
lentless scramble for power ensued. During the seven years,
from Liaquat's assassination in October 1951 till Ayub's
revolution of October 1958, Pakistan had six prime ministers.
In the short space of four years preceding Ayub's takeover,
East Pakistan witnessed a procession of eight governors and
seven ministries.[21] Relations between East and West Pakistan went from bad to worse. During the March 1954 provincial elections the purely regional parties of the eastern
wing constituted themselves into a United Front and won
223 seats to the Muslim League's ten. When the various
units of the western part of Pakistan were constituted into a
single province in 1955, many Bengalis felt the measure was
the West Pakistani response to East Pakistan's resounding
election victory of the preceding year. West Pakistan, having
tasted the bitterness of defeat, it was surmised, was consolidating itself to be able to talk to its eastern counterpart

---

21. *Dawn*, Dec. 20, 1964. The seven ministries were headed by the following
persons: Fazlul Huq (56 days), Abu Hussain Sarkar (450 days), Ataur Rahman Khan
(550 days), Abu Hussain Sarkar (1 day), Ataur Rahman Khan (78 days), Abu Hussain
Sarkar (4 days), Ataur Rahman Khan (42 days).

with one voice. Pakistan's two-commodity economy,[22] after a spurt of prosperity during the Korean War, began to slide downhill. Food shortages added to the existing gloom. The country, in Zafrulla's words, now was "even more vulnerable internally than it already was externally."[23] The gap between the people and those who sought office only for personal aggrandizement progressively widened. In this state of turmoil, power gravitated toward two institutions that, under the parliamentary system which Pakistan professed, were expected to remain above the rough-and-tumble of everyday politics: the governor-general (renamed president when the new constitution came into force in 1956) and the commander-in-chief of the armed forces.

After Liaquat's demise, Khwaja Nazimuddin, who had succeeded Jinnah as governor-general, became prime minister, and Finance Minister Ghulam Mohammad was elevated to the position of governor-general. In 1955 Iskander Mirza[24] succeeded Ghulam Mohammad. According to the letter of the law, the governor-general had the authority to dismiss a prime minister and his cabinet but the spirit required that he should do so only if the prime minister had lost the confidence of the majority in the legislature. Taking advantage of the utter disarray in the ranks of the politicians, the governor-general began to exercise the power of dismissal arbitrarily, thus becoming the controlling political force in the land. Both Ghulam Mohammad and Iskander Mirza[25] took a

22. East Pakistani jute and West Pakistani cotton.
23. Muhammad Zafrulla Khan, *The Agony of Pakistan* (Lahore: published by the author, 1974), p. 105.
24. An army officer who had joined the Indian Political Service. After independence he was defense secretary, governor of East Pakistan, and interior minister before becoming head of state.
25. President Mirza was a good administrator, but his grasp of international affairs was not particularly profound. His outlook was colored by years of service in the Northwest Frontier region where over generations tribesmen are friends or enemies for personal reasons. Once I happened to discuss the nature of Pakistani–United States relations with him. He seemed to think America had become Pakistan's eternal "friend." I said the Americans had never ceased to believe that India

dominant part in all national affairs, including the formulation and direction of foreign policy that by right fell within the jurisdiction of the prime minister and the foreign minister.

The fear of India under which Pakistan perpetually labored was bound to magnify the importance of the armed forces in Pakistan in any case. General Douglas Gracey, the first commander-in-chief, being a non-Pakistani and having contracted to serve for a limited time only, had no reason to become involved in politics, but Ayub Khan, who succeeded him in January 1951, immediately became a key component of the national power structure. In his own account of the Indo-Pakistani crisis in the summer of 1951, he states that Liaquat and the other politicians as well as Pakistani troops seemed disposed to accept India's challenge to fight, but "it was my job to hold them back which, thank Heavens, I did."[26] After Liaquat's death the political fragility of the country further enhanced the importance of the armed forces and their commander. The author of *My Chief* tells us that Ayub's influence was so pervasive that "his counsel was obtained before any big or vital decision was taken by the Government and it did not matter whether that action was connected with commerce or education, foreign affairs or the interior, industrial development or social welfare."[27] In 1954 Ghulam Mohammad invited Ayub to take over the reins of government, but the latter declined the offer.

The following extracts from *My Chief* further illustrate the Commander-in-Chief's major role in external relations:

The United States Military Aid . . . was made possible through the initiative and efforts of General Ayub. The idea was born in his

---

is the real answer to Communist China and they would turn toward India if they ever got an opening to do so. He peremptorily terminated the argument with the curt remark that I knew nothing. On the other hand, Ghulam Mohammad was a sick man during most of the time he was governor-general.

26. Ayub Khan, *op. cit.*, p. 40.

27. Colonel Mohammad Ahmed, *My Chief* (Lahore: Longmans, Green, 1960), p. 50. *My Chief* is an authorized biography of Ayub Khan.

mind and it was through his negotiations with American political and military leaders that the United States Government invited Pakistan to enter into a Mutual Defense Pact. . . .[28]

In October 1953, General Ayub visited the States. . . . In the meantime the late Mr. Ghulam Muhammad, who was then Governor-General of Pakistan, arrived in Washington and wanted to negotiate personally with President Eisenhower regarding military aid. There was embarrassment all around the State Department, because constitutionally the Governor-General could not negotiate about such matters. . . .[29]

General Ayub and Major-General Iskander Mirza went to Turkey and broached the subject of the [Baghdad] Pact with the Turkish Prime Minister. I am convinced that it was because of Mr. Menderes' appreciation of General Ayub's breadth of vision and sincerity of purpose that they came to agreement with each other so readily. . . .[30]

On 17 November 1956, he [Ayub] accompanied the Prime Minister, Mr. Suhrawardy, and Mr. Iskander Mirza to Iran, Iraq and Saudi Arabia on a semi-official visit. There again I found that the presence of General Ayub proved to be of vital importance for the interest of Pakistan. He was only the C.-in-C. of the Pakistan Army, and not a member of the Cabinet and yet I could see that the one person who attracted the greater attention of the Iraqi, Saudi and Iranian authorities, Kings and Ministers alike, was General Ayub.[31]

The foreign policy of the government, for obvious reasons, lacked the general backing it had enjoyed prior to Liaquat's death. First, except during one year of Suhrawardy's premiership (1956–57), power was exercised by persons who were not public men and had little rapport with the masses. Second, the most important Arab states, Egypt and Saudi Arabia, bitterly criticized Pakistan for joining the Baghdad Pact. To the people of Pakistan, who passionately desired a special relationship with these countries, this meant a trau-

28. *Ibid.*, pp. 73–74.
29. *Ibid.*, pp. 74–76.
30. *Ibid.*, p. 68.
31. *Ibid.*, p. 69.

matic failure in foreign policy. During the Anglo-French invasion of Suez, in particular, the masses were bitterly angry with their government for not siding with Egypt unreservedly. Third, due to their estrangement from the West Pakistani–dominated central government, the East Pakistanis were critical of all federal policies as a matter of course. Soon after the 1954 election, 162 members of the East Pakistan legislature issued a statement calling upon the people of Pakistan to protest against the pact with the United States.

Suhrawardy was the only prime minister during this period who had the courage directly to invite a vote of confidence on foreign policy in parliament and to defend it in public,[32] but even during the term of office of this politician of high caliber, President Mirza continued to play an active role in external affairs.[33] The reason, of course, was that the President had the backing of the army and his will, therefore, was supreme in the land. When differences arose between the two men (October 1957), Mirza compelled Suhrawardy to resign. The latter asked the President to summon the National Assembly to test whether he, the Prime Minister, still enjoyed a majority in the house, but to no purpose.[34]

Gone were the days when foreign policy was in the hands of a few like-minded persons working as a team. The original group had quickly dispersed after Liaquat's death. Mohammad Ali became the finance minister,[35] and Ikramullah left for an ambassadorial position. Zafrulla lingered on until

32. See Burke, *Pakistan's Foreign Policy, op. cit.,* pp. 251–53.

33. For example, see the telegram he sent to President Eisenhower jointly with the President of Turkey and the Shah of Iran expressing appreciation for sending American marines to Lebanon (*United States Department of State Bulletin,* Aug. 4, 1958); and the joint communique to which he subscribed along with the same dignitaries (*Dawn,* July 18, 1958). Mirza's activities were criticized in the National Assembly of Pakistan by Sardar Fazlul Karim, an East Pakistani, in these terms: "There was a Conference held at Ankara and the President went to attend it. May I know why our Prime Minister did not go there to attend it. I do not know what Article of the Constitution allows this." (*Official Report,* Sept. 3, 1958, p. 235.)

34. G. W. Choudhury, *Democracy in Pakistan* (Dacca: Green Book House, 1963), p. 114.

35. He also became prime minister from August 1955 to September 1956.

1954. By 1958 conditions inside Pakistan had become so chaotic that Nehru complained India did not quite know whom to address in that country.[36] During these uncertain years even Pakistan's well-wishers doubted her viability as an independent state.

Why did not India use this opportunity to destroy Pakistan? India did not even threaten war against her smaller neighbor as it had done earlier in 1950 and 1951. Paradoxically, it was Indian foreign policy that proved to be Pakistan's salvation. As soon as it became evident that the Maoists would emerge victorious in the civil war in China, the Americans concluded that the only country big enough to offset the new Communist giant was India, "the world's largest democracy." Nehru was invited to the United States in October 1949 and given a hero's welcome. An article in the *New York Times Magazine* greeted him as "the world's most popular individual," and the same newspaper in a daily issue said, "Washington wants India to be a bulwark against Communism." Secretary of State Dean Acheson ranked the Indian leader with Thomas Jefferson, Abraham Lincoln, and Woodrow Wilson.[37] But these and other blandishments failed to enlist Nehru in the cold war against Communism. As a matter of fact, in the main concrete issues of the day — the Korean War, the Japanese Peace Treaty, and the seating of Communist China in the United Nations — Indian policy was pronouncedly closer to that of the communist powers.[38] The Indian Prime Minister was also an untiring critic of the chain of Western military pacts of which the United States was the leading champion. By the latter part of 1951 Americans had begun to despair of Jawaharlal Nehru. The *New York Times,* which had striven so hard to win over the Indian

36. *Hindu,* June 5, 1958, quoted by Karunakar Gupta in *India in World Politics: A Period of Transition, Fall 1956 to Spring 1960* (Calcutta: Scientific Book Agency, 1969), p. 219.

37. *Jawaharlal's Discovery of America* (Delhi: East and West Publishers, 1950), p. 10.

38. Burke, *Pakistan's Foreign Policy, op. cit.,* pp. 126–35 and 149–52.

leader, expressed its utter disappointment by dubbing him the "Lost Leader."[39]

Not surprisingly, the United States began to edge toward Pakistan, though the formal agreement that brought Pakistan massive military assistance on a grant basis was not signed until 1954. The influx of American arms quickly transformed the picture. Early in 1957 Commander-in-Chief Ayub Khan, who in the past had deplored Pakistan's military weakness, declared confidently: "We are no more short of men and material. . . . If we are to hit a target today, it will not be the same tomorrow."[40] Prime Minister Suhrawardy stated later in the same year that Pakistan was now in a position to repel aggression and was living "in an atmosphere free from dread."[41] A gift of 700,000 tons of American wheat in 1953 saved Pakistan from a threatened famine,[42] and the sharp increase in economic assistance from the same year bolstered her sagging economy. As an Indian writer has commented: "India held the pistol at the head of Pakistan until, in 1954, the American alliance delivered the country from that nightmare."[43]

III. 1958–71

From October 1958 until December 1971, Pakistan was successively ruled by two military dictators, Ayub Khan

39. See editorial, "Lost Leader," in *New York Times*, Aug. 28, 1951.

40. *Dawn*, Jan. 31, 1957, quoted by Aslam Siddiqi, *Pakistan Seeks Security* (Lahore: Longmans, Green, 1960), p. 118.

41. *Dawn*, Oct. 6, 1957.

42. In June 1953 the United States agreed to supply 1 million tons of wheat to Pakistan. While 700,000 tons were to be an outright gift, the terms of the balance, if required, were to be settled later. Pakistan actually used only 606,000 tons and decided that further shipments were not required.

43. Niran C. Chaudhuri, *The Continent of Circe* (London: Chatto and Windus, 1965), p. 244. In his speech in the National Assembly of Pakistan on December 21, 1973, Prime Minister Bhutto said that American military assistance to Pakistan had been "colossal." "It maintained a balance of power in the subcontinent, it prevented India from daring to pursue an adventurist policy towards Pakistan." For the text of this address see *Dawn*, Jan. 14, 1974.

(October 1958–March 1969) and Yahya Khan (March 1969–December 1971). Due to his close involvement in the administrative and political affairs of the country ever since his appointment as the army chief, Ayub was well prepared to fill the office of president; Yahya had done little beyond soldiering. Ayub, moreover, had assumed power when the people of Pakistan were tired of political intrigues and welcomed a strong hand. Yahya took office when the country already had had its fill of military leaders. Ayub's early years, in fact, were the most promising Pakistan has ever experienced. Governmental machinery was toned up and the economy assumed an upward trend. The President had a striking personality and created a good impression wherever he went;[44] and he was ably assisted by Foreign Minister Zulfikar Ali Bhutto who articulated the administration's position with considerable effectiveness.

The first serious test of Ayub's foreign policy came in the wake of the Sino-Indian border conflict in October 1962 when Pakistan's principal Western allies, the United States and the United Kingdom, disregarded Pakistani protestations that continuing military assistance to India be made conditional upon a settlement of the Kashmir issue so that India and Pakistan no longer would have any cause to fight each other and the threat to Pakistan from a more powerful India would be eliminated. Ayub and Bhutto displayed considerable resourcefulness in turning China into a friend of Pakistan and "normalizing" relations with the Soviet Union to the extent that it abandoned an earlier posture of siding with India. The Soviet Union remained neutral when India and Pakistan went to war in September 1965, and played the broker afterward at Tashkent. Because of the decline in

44. For example, Mrs. John F. Kennedy said, "Ayub is like Jack — tough and brave and wants things done in a hurry. . . . Wasn't he magnificent in his uniform?" Joan Braden, "An Exclusive Chat with Jackie Kennedy," *The Saturday Evening Post*, May 12, 1962. The Duke of Edinburgh stated that the good work, ideas, and influence of President Ayub Khan had given a new life to Pakistan (*Dawn*, July 16, 1961).

India's prestige after the 1962 war with China and the visible progress of Pakistan under Ayub, Pakistan was also able to overhaul her influential neighbor in the Afro-Asian world, especially in the Muslim countries. However, the cordiality with China was not achieved without causing annoyance to the United States. The U.S. suspended military supplies to both sides during the Indo-Pakistani war. This seemingly evenhanded step declaredly was taken to expedite a cease-fire, but in fact it hurt Pakistan more because she was entirely dependent for such materials on the U.S., while India had other sources of supply. Ayub tried to recapture American goodwill by a personal visit to Lyndon Johnson in the middle of December 1965, but Pakistani–United States ties did not improve perceptibly until Richard Nixon took up residence in the White House.[45]

Though Pakistan had captured more territory and suffered fewer casualties than India, inside Pakistan the inconclusive war was viewed as a failure of foreign policy. East Pakistan had been entirely cut off from West Pakistan during the hostilities and was stated to have been saved from an Indian conquest only because China had threatened direct intervention. East Pakistanis who were less emotionally involved in the Kashmir issue than West Pakistanis thought it a mistake to risk the lives of more than 100 million Muslims of Pakistan and 40 million Muslims of India for only 4 million Muslims of Kashmir. West Pakistanis favored the war against India but, having been led to believe that decisive victory over India was just around the corner, were confounded when their government accepted a cease-fire. They burst into anger when the negotiations at Tashkent failed to produce a concrete plan for a solution of the Kashmir problem. Ayub's hold over the country after Tashkent weakened significantly. His basic weakness was that he failed to live

45. Nixon as vice president had favored an alliance with Pakistan and had been consistently friendly toward her thereafter.

by his own maxim: "You must carry the people with you."[46]
His economic policies had benefited only the small number
of already wealthy businessmen and industrialists. He had
antagonized the politicians, the lawyers, and the intellectuals
in various ways. They had all been biding their time and
now saw a chance to destroy him. He had been receptive
to objective advice at first but began to resent it in later
years if it did not conform to his own preconceived notions.[47]
The law-and-order situation having grown impossible, Ayub,
in March 1969, was compelled to step down in favor of
Commander-in-Chief General Yahya Khan.

Yahya lacked the finesse to navigate the tricky shoals
of external affairs successfully. His closest advisers were an
inner circle of army colleagues; the foreign office was not
taken into confidence to any large extent. His boorish
references to Mrs. Indira Gandhi as "that woman" show that
he was deficient in even the elementary norms of diplomatic
deportment. At a time when Pakistan was in desperate need
of international support, he affronted the Soviet Union, a
superpower, by reminding it of its own atrocities in Czechoslovakia and the Central Asian Republics in order to justify
the onslaught of the predominantly West Pakistani army on
East Pakistan.[48]

Yahya's decision to use military force in East Pakistan
was not only a disastrous error domestically but was also a
foreign policy blunder of the first magnitude because, given

46. Ayub Khan, *op. cit.*, p. 225.

47. When Ayub first took over the presidency, the foreign secretary told me that
he could always dial the President direct at a given telephone number and freely
speak his mind. By 1966 Ayub had lost the faculty of paying heed to others. In that
year I visited Kabul and had useful discussions there with the Prime Minister of
Afghanistan and the Pakistani ambassador. Both of them made certain suggestions
for improving the relations between Pakistan and Afghanistan ("Pakhtunistan"
was not at all mentioned by anybody). Subsequently when I called on Ayub I found
him quite courteous, but the moment I broached the topic of Afghanistan he cut me
short. His mind on that subject seemed utterly closed.

48. G. W. Choudhury, "The Emergence of Bangladesh and the South Asian
Triangle," *The Yearbook of World Affairs 1973* (London: Institute of World Affairs,
1973), p. 71.

all the circumstances, war with India was a distinct probability and Pakistan was in no position to fight its much larger adversary. His order for the removal of all foreign correspondents from Dacca — yet another ill-considered move — lost Pakistan the sympathy of the powerful world press and enabled India to paint a one-sided picture of all the grisly happenings.

The only assignment Yahya completed with the requisite amount of discretion was that of preparing the ground for the opening of a dialogue between the United States and China that Nixon had asked him to undertake.[49] But his utter failure at home overshadowed his good turn to others. Pakistan lost her more populous half forever and at the same time suffered a humiliating military defeat at the hands of India. Never before had the country's fortunes fallen so low.

IV. 1972–76

For the last several years Pakistan's destiny has been guided by Zulfikar Ali Bhutto. The country for the first time in history has a leader who can efficiently manage foreign policy at all levels — public, parliament, press, and international.[50] And he has summoned to headquarters, to assist him, Pakistan's two outstanding diplomatists, Minister of State for Defense and Foreign Affairs Aziz Ahmed and Foreign Secretary Agha Shahi.

Pakistan's earliest rulers had assumed national stewardship automatically as the founding fathers of the new state, and after Nazimuddin's dismissal (April 1953) the final word lay with those who had the indirect or direct support of the army.

49. Nixon had made this request when he visited Pakistan in August 1969. *Ibid.*, p. 66.

50. Suhrawardy was a competent politician but he labored under two handicaps: (1) the governor-general was the dominant official in the country at that time, and (2) Suhrawardy's popular following was confined almost wholly to the eastern half of the country.

Bhutto is the first head of government in Pakistan who owes his position directly to success at the polls.[51] It can be scarcely lost on him that Pakistan's public men potentially are his rivals and that the officers of the armed forces, like those of most less-developed countries, are apt at any time to take it into their heads that they can run the government much better than any politician. While not neglecting any of the other instruments of power, Bhutto, therefore, places the greatest reliance on the common man in Pakistan.

In his very first broadcast to the people on December 20, 1971, he said: "I am no magician. I am a fallible individual and without your co-operation, I simply cannot succeed. But with your co-operation and with your support, I am taller than the Himalayas. . . . Under no circumstances will I move one step in any direction without your approval."[52] Again, at a public meeting in Lahore on March 19, 1972: "I belong to the people and love them. They have created me. As fish cannot live out of water, I cannot do without my people."[53] Elected assemblies, he says, are necessary because "the wishes of the people can be properly manifested only through institutions."[54] At difficult moments he consults the legislators because it amounts to taking into confidence their electorates also.[55] Politicians, whether in government or in opposition, are guided by the "rules of politics." The poor people on the other hand have no vested interests except the self-respect, survival, dignity, and progress of the nation; "therefore, correct decisions always come from the general

51. Following the East Pakistani debacle, Yahya no longer could remain in office. Nor would the country have tolerated another army officer as head of government after the stunning military reverse. By dint of his election victory in West Pakistan in December 1970, Bhutto was the obvious person to form a civilian government in the remaining part of the state.
52. Zulfikar Ali Bhutto, President of Pakistan, *Speeches and Statements, December 20, 1971–March 31, 1972* (Karachi: Department of Films and Publications, Government of Pakistan, 1972), pp. 1, 2.
53. *Ibid.*, p. 137.
54. *Ibid.*, p. 59.
55. *Dawn*, Feb. 23, 1974.

mass of the people."[56] During the debate on the Simla agreement he plainly told the members of the National Assembly:

The people are the final arbiters; the people are finally sovereign. They have a sixth sense which none of us is endowed with. That is why the people have accepted it [the Simla agreement]. Now whatever you may say against it, eloquently or otherwise, they are not going to refuse this agreement. It does not betray their interests; it has not been against them. So the debate here is really superfluous.[57]

Perhaps the most difficult problems that Bhutto has faced so far have been the Simla agreement, to which he subscribed jointly with Prime Minister Indira Gandhi on July 2, 1972, and the recognition of Bangladesh by Pakistan on February 22, 1974. A resumé of his careful handling of these delicate questions would provide a good illustration of his style of diplomacy.

On the eve of his departure for Simla, Bhutto himself summarized in a broadcast the thorough preparations he had made, for the forthcoming summit conference:

In the last two weeks I have talked to leaders in every field, to elected representatives, politicians of every shade of opinion, *Ulema*, intellectuals, editors and journalists, lawyers, teachers, students, and labourers. I have also met the commanders of our Armed Forces. For the first time in the history of Pakistan, representatives of all sections have been involved in matters of vital national concern at the highest level. . . .

Apart from the people of our country, I have also consulted our friends and neighbors abroad. As part of this process, I have also visited Peking and Moscow, and recently sent a Special Envoy to these two capitals.

As you all know, my last Mission took me to 14 countries in the Middle East and Africa. This was in continuation of my earlier visit to eight Muslim countries in January.[58]

56. Zulfikar Ali Bhutto, President of Pakistan, *Speeches and Statements, April 1, 1972–June 30, 1972* (Karachi: Department of Films and Publications, Government of Pakistan, 1972), p. 224.

57. *National Assembly of Pakistan Debates, Official Report*, July 14, 1972, p. 699.

58. Bhutto, *Speeches and Statements, April 1, 1972–June 30, 1972, op. cit.*, p. 221.

Bhutto addressed a joint meeting of the central and Punjab legislators and made a public speech at the Lahore airport before enplaning for India. He held a press conference in Simla and on his return home addressed the public at the Lahore and Islamabad airports, broadcast to the nation on July 8. Finally he explained and defended his policy at a specially convened session of the National Assembly and obtained from it a verdict in favor of what he had accomplished. During the debate he pointed out that because of its victory over Pakistan, India held all the cards during the negotiations, "and India is not a generous negotiator"; he also acknowledged that he had been able to acquit himself creditably only because "the common man of Pakistan, the poor man of Pakistan, the nameless man of Pakistan, the faceless man of Pakistan was with us."[59]

The question of recognizing Bangladesh was a highly emotional one in Pakistan. Many felt that the secession, if endorsed, would mean a positive repudiation of the "Two Nation Theory," on the basis of which the state of Pakistan had come into being. It also would give a decided fillip to the already discernible movements for separation in the smaller provinces of what is left of the country. Though India exerted pressure for an early recognition by holding on to the Pakistani prisoners of war in contravention of international law, and most other countries extended recognition and exhorted Pakistan to do the same, Bhutto tenaciously refused to give in. He personally was in favor of accepting the inevitable, but he patiently waited for an opportune moment in order to make the move acceptable to public opinion in Pakistan. He addressed gatherings all over the land recommending recognition but pledged also that he would not compromise national honor in the process, in particular that he would insist upon the release of all Pakistani prisoners of war, including the 195 whom Bangladesh wished to try for

59. *National Assembly Debates, op. cit.,* July 14, 1972, p. 698.

war crimes. To forestall damaging criticism after the event from any important quarter, he first obtained the advisory opinion of the Supreme Court of Pakistan that the National Assembly of Pakistan was constitutionally competent to adopt a resolution authorizing the Government of Pakistan to accord recognition to Bangladesh when such a step would be in the best national interests of Pakistan. Only then did he obtain such an authorization from the Assembly.[60] At the same time he made Bangladesh realize that it could not become a full-fledged member of the international community without Pakistan's concurrence. When the newborn state requested membership of the United Nations, its application was vetoed by the People's Republic of China at Pakistan's request. The moment eventually chosen for recognition was psychologically perfect, February 22, 1974, the day of the opening of the Muslim Summit Conference of thirty-seven states at Lahore. In announcing recognition Bhutto said he had taken the step on the advice of the leaders of the Muslim world, who are "certainly the well-wishers of Pakistan." Characteristically, he broke the news at a nationally televised gathering of the provincial governors, chief ministers, federal ministers, provincial ministers, and legislators, explaining that he was addressing the people at large through their representatives. Mujibur Rahman flew from Dacca to Lahore on the following day.[61] Those still against accepting Bangladesh as an established fact could not strike a strident note in an atmosphere so highly charged with feelings of the universal brotherhood of Islam. Mujib did not immediately renounce his government's intention to try

60. For extracts from the opinion of the Supreme Court (July 6, 1973) and text of the Assembly resolution (July 10, 1973), see *Pakistan Horizon*, No. 3 (1973), pp. 108 and 113.

61. Mujib had been arrested for treason in Dacca on March 25, 1971, under Yahya's orders and flown to a West Pakistan prison. Bhutto had released him unconditionally soon after becoming president.

the 195 Pakistani prisoners of war,[62] but there can be little doubt but that the leaders of other Muslim countries, through whose good offices the reconciliation had been brought about, had privately obtained his assurance and conveyed it to Bhutto.[63] When the representatives of India, Pakistan, and Bangladesh met in New Delhi in April 1974 it was duly agreed that all Pakistani prisoners, including the 195, would be repatriated.

After recognition Bhutto has continued his policy of not taking any significant step until he has won the backing of popular opinion in Pakistan. During his visit to Bangladesh in July 1974, Mujib pressed him to make a declaration on financial and other matters outstanding between Pakistan and Bangladesh, but he declined to do so on the ground that Pakistan is a democracy and he could not decide such matters without the advice and consent of the democratic institutions of his country.[64]

Bhutto's continual consultations with the people, however, should not be taken to mean that there is any doubt as to who is at the controls of the decision-making mechanism in Pakistan. When the editor of the Indian newspaper *Blitz* observed that Indians had begun to wonder who runs Pakistan, the Pakistani leader expounded his philosophy in these terms:

In a democracy everyone has to put in his weight. . . . But essentially when it comes to the real decision, I am in charge of affairs and I have been no one's tool so far. . . . Our people know that I am not to be led by anyone. At the same time no one should expect

62. In fact, he could not have done so because the prisoners were held by India and the Indo-Pakistani bilateral agreement of August 28, 1973, had stipulated that the fate of the 195 prisoners would be decided trilaterally by India, Pakistan, and Bangladesh.

63. For instance, President Anwar Sadat of Egypt said in Lahore that he felt sure Mujib would respond to Pakistan's gesture of recognition by a similar gesture on the question of the 195 prisoners. *Dawn*, Feb. 25, 1974.

64. *Pakistan Affairs*, July 16, 1974.

me to ride roughshod over the raw feelings and sentiments of the people. That is not possible. It is not in my political temperament. It is necessary to carry the people.[65]

Both at home and abroad Bhutto is also Pakistan's most assiduous and effective publicist. He is an indefatigable traveler abroad, welcomes an unceasing stream of foreign dignitaries at home, and finds time to grant innumerable interviews to foreign correspondents and to maintain close personal contact with the envoys who reside in the Pakistani capital. In the changed circumstances, following Pakistan's dismemberment and defeat in the East Pakistani war, Bhutto has not hesitated to go back on some of his own past utterances.[66] For instance, he stands for conciliation and negotiation with India instead of one thousand years of confrontation that was previously his stand. He is striving for closer relations with the United States, although he was critical of such ties in the past. He has kept Pakistan in CENTO contrary to statements made during the 1970 election campaign that Pakistan would withdraw from all Western military pacts. He disarms his critics by frankly stating that these decisions have been deliberately taken to further the interests of Pakistan. It is impossible not to admire his skill or his boundless energy.

65. Zulfikar Ali Bhutto, President of Pakistan, *Speeches and Statements, October 1, 1972–December 31, 1972* (Karachi: Department of Films and Publications, Government of Pakistan, 1973), p. 55.
66. For Bhutto's explanation for these modifications, see, respectively: (1) *National Assembly Debates, op. cit.,* July 14, 1972, pp. 714–15, as well as Bhutto, *Speeches and Statements, April 1, 1972–June 30, 1972, op. cit.,* pp. 56–57, (2) his speech in the National Assembly of Pakistan on December 21, 1973, and (3) *National Assembly Debates, op. cit.,* July 14, 1972, pp. 686–89.

13

Pakistan's Foreign Policy:
Shifting Opportunities and Constraints

William J. Barnds

The Pakistan that emerged from the traumatic experiences of 1971 is, in certain obvious respects, quite different from the country that existed for the previous quarter-century. Its shrunken size and greatly reduced population are the most dramatic elements of difference. Its former claim to be the homeland of the Muslims of the subcontinent is no longer tenable, which poses serious if nebulous psychological and political problems. Its political system is now democratic in form and, to a decreasing extent, in substance as well.[1]

At the same time, there are certain similarities to the Pakistan of the past—particularly Ayub's Pakistan. The West Pakistani elite that controlled the country in the past retains great power. Control of the government is largely in the hands of one man. There is a certain vigor in the economy despite the many obstacles apparent to any observer. A strong, if somewhat subdued, military establishment remains on the scene. And the present government has scored many tactical successes in the field of foreign policy without resolving the crucial issue of the nature of its relations with India. Given the centrality of this issue, a look backward

---

1. Martial law was in force until late 1971, and the National Assembly and Senate approved a six-month extension of the state of emergency and the President's order suspending certain fundamental rights on March 4, 1974. Karachi Domestic Service, March 4, 1974; reported in *Foreign Broadcast Information Service, Middle East and Africa*, March 5, 1974.

is necessary before recent events can be appraised and future developments considered.

The Legacy of Success and Failure

When Pakistan was born amid the upheavals of partition in 1947, it faced a series of monumental tasks. It had to establish a functioning national government where none had existed before, and to instill a sense of nationhood among its disparate peoples. The government had to establish an administrative structure that would enable it to extend its writ across its widely dispersed territories, and do this in the face of an acute shortage of senior civil servants. It had to create effective military forces out of the scattered elements of the British Indian forces it inherited. The country also faced the awesome task of reorienting and developing its economy — or rather its *two* economies, for there existed few economic links of any consequence between East and West Pakistan. And it had to fashion a foreign policy that would advance the interests and enhance the security of the whole country.

From today's vantage point, Pakistan's failures are so much more obvious than its successes that it is worth enumerating the latter as well as the former. A functioning government was created. An administrative system that, whatever its deficiencies, enabled the government to enforce its laws, was established.[2] A strong — perhaps too strong — military establishment was developed. The economies were reoriented and integrated at least as much as was practical. After a slow start, considerable economic development took place — although it was spread very unevenly among the various areas and classes.[3] Given the circumstances of

2. For a discussion of the administrative strengths and weaknesses, see Lawrence Ziring, *The Ayub Khan Era: Politics in Pakistan, 1958–1969* (Syracuse, N.Y.: Syracuse University Press, 1971).

3. Joseph J. Stern and Walter P. Falcon, *Growth and Development in Pakistan: 1955–1969* (Cambridge: Center for International Affairs, Harvard University, April 1970, Occasional Paper No. 26).

Pakistan's birth and the obstacles in its path, these were no mean achievements.

Where Pakistan failed was in the political and foreign policy arenas. The political failure is obvious. The country never developed a political system that provided the measure of participation for different areas and different classes that might have allowed a sense of nationhood to develop. (Nor did any charismatic leader appear who, through his personal appeal and tactics, might have bridged the gap between east and west and rich and poor for a time.) The reasons for this failure are outside the scope of this chapter, but it is important to note that this failure — or at least the extent of the failure — was *not* obvious to many scholars or informed observers (Pakistani or foreign) as late as the country's twentieth birthday in 1967. True, few regarded the political system as a success, but it was not until the 1969–71 period that the extent of the failure became widely apparent.[4]

If the political failure is widely recognized today, the judgment that the country's foreign policy was not successful might still be challenged by many. As late as 1972 Wayne Wilcox, the most perceptive U.S. scholar writing on Pakistan, concluded that its foreign policy had been "creative and successful" — although by no means so successful as to enable it to realize all its objectives.[5] Did not Pakistan attract extensive great power support? Did it not attain a status in the world that was remarkable for a country in its circumstances? Did not such achievements — particularly the maintenance of good relations with the United States, the Soviet Union, and China in the mid- and late 1960s — reflect considerable diplomatic skill? Did not Pakistan's ability

4. See W. H. Morris-Jones, "Pakistan Post-Mortem and the Roots of Bangladesh," *Political Quarterly* (April–June 1972), 187–200.

5. Wayne A. Wilcox, "Pakistan," in Wayne A. Wilcox, Leo E. Rose, and Gavin Boyd, eds., *Asia and the International System* (Cambridge, Mass.: Winthrop, 1972), p. 113.

to secure extensive foreign aid demonstrate an impressive ability to convince the international community that its economic prospects and policies were such as to merit widespread support? One can answer all of these questions affirmatively but still conclude that Pakistan's foreign policy was a failure — a failure because of the simple but oft-forgotten maxim that success or failure must be measured in relation to the needs and objectives of a country. When one looks at the fundamental issue of bringing ends and means into harmony or balance, the luster of Pakistan's tactical successes is dimmed by its strategic failure — its inability either to accommodate itself to India's superior position or to secure external support sufficient to force India to yield to it.

How did this come about, and, more importantly, is it likely to recur? The men who guided Pakistan's foreign relations, while inexperienced, and subject to normal human shortcomings, were not idiots or megalomaniacs. There did exist, as many observers have noted, a complex mixture of contempt for the Indians as individuals and fear of India as a larger nation, which led the country to be at once assertive and insecure.[6] Yet the most striking aspect of Pakistan's foreign policy was its extremely ambitious goals. From the beginning, two unorganized and impoverished pieces of territory, as yet a nation in name only, not only sought to gain security through strength rather than accommodation but also set forth to wrest a sizable piece of territory (Kashmir) away from a neighbor several times its size. Moreover, it should be borne in mind that this "policy" was adopted long before Pakistan had any valid reason to believe it could secure significant great-power support. Indeed, Pakistan's initial efforts to secure external support — from other Muslim states and from the Commonwealth — ended in frustration. It was only in 1954, when the U.S.-

6. Keith Callard, *Pakistan's Foreign Policy: An Interpretation* (New York: Institute of Pacific Relations, rev. ed., 1959).

Pakistan alliance was formed, that Pakistan secured meaningful external backing.

In part, of course, the policy grew out of the same Hindu-
Muslim hostility that led to partition. The accidents of history
also played a role, for the turmoil of partition, the quarrels
over the disposition of the assets of British India, and
particularly the Kashmir dispute all pushed both governments into hostile postures before they had the opportunity
calmly to weigh the various alternatives. Indeed, it would
have required the foresight of genius and the selflessness of
sainthood for the leaders of either country to have acted
substantially differently from the way they did in the midst of
one of the major upheavals of the twentieth century.

Once hostility, fear, and pride had crystallized Pakistan's
policies, it became doubly difficult to modify them, as the
leaders discovered in later years when they began to be
aware of the heavy costs of the course they had "chosen."
Moreover, several psychological factors entered into their
"decision" to pursue very ambitious goals. In bringing
Pakistan into being through sheer reliance on their will to
succeed, Pakistani leaders had in a decade done what most
observers had regarded as impossible. Having established a
nation, was it inconceivable they could surmount one more
obstacle and gain control of the additional territory that
would make their country complete? In the disorganized
conditions prevailing in the late 1940s, when boundaries
had not hardened, such goals may have not seemed unrealistic. Moreover, Pakistanis saw India's rejection of a
plebiscite in Kashmir as a rejection of the "Two Nation
Theory," and thus a threat to Pakistan's very existence.
Finally, in winning American support when U.S. superiority
in military and economic power was clear, in gaining Peking's
backing after Chinese armies had humiliated India in 1962,
and in securing Soviet neutrality for a time in the mid- and
late 1960s, Pakistani leaders had reason to think they had
found security—and perhaps leverage against India. But

they were wrong, and they, and their successors, paid dearly for their mistake.

Negotiating Successfully from Weakness

When Zulfikar Ali Bhutto became president of Pakistan on December 20, 1971, he inherited a country that was disoriented, demoralized, and diminished in status as well as in size. Its leadership had been both incompetent and brutal to a degree that had shamed most Pakistanis and shocked the country's friends — who had, in the end, stood by and permitted its dismemberment. Its traditional enemy was now ten times its size and had a leader — and, even more galling, a *woman* — who had demonstrated her mastery of international as well as domestic statecraft. The military establishment was discredited and sullen, and the economy required major reorientation. The treasury was empty and Pakistan's credit was shaky as a result of its suspension of debt repayments in 1971. The division of the country brought with it some potential benefits, such as better long-range economic prospects, and a less heterogenous population, but these seemed small consolation at the time.

Nor was President Bhutto without his personal liabilities. Although the Pakistan People's Party he had organized had won a majority in the December 1970 elections in West Pakistan, his role in the negotiations that led to the civil war left him saddled with some responsibility for the tragedy. If he had won popular support by his opposition to Ayub in the last years of his rule, he was known to be impetuous and was distrusted by many. Nonetheless, he was energetic, articulate, experienced, and skilled in domestic and foreign affairs, and possessed of great drive and self-confidence. Moreover, it was widely acknowledged that there was no alternative leader available — a recognition that was later to benefit him in his dealings with New Delhi.

Bhutto's initial foreign policy moves were designed to revive morale at home as well as to obtain external acceptance and support before beginning the inevitably difficult negotiations with India. On January 3, 1972, Bhutto announced the unconditional release of Sheikh Mujibur Rahman. In the next few months Bhutto visited more than twenty of the African and Asian countries that had supported Pakistan's effort to maintain its territorial integrity, thanking them for their understanding and seeking their continued support. Pakistan also severed diplomatic relations with a number of smaller countries for their recognition of Bangladesh—a measure it did not apply to the Soviet Union or the United Kingdom, although Pakistan had left the Commonwealth when Britain recognized Bangladesh. Bhutto visited first Peking and then Moscow in an attempt to retain Chinese support and mitigate Soviet hostility. He was, on the whole, successful in these missions, although Chinese support remained carefully limited, and he had no choice but to accept public chastisement by Soviet leaders over Pakistan's past policies when he visited Moscow in March 1972.

Bhutto moved quickly and dramatically on the domestic front as well—a strategy made easier by the fact that he was martial law administrator as well as president. He appointed his supporters as governors and martial law administrators of the four provinces, convened the National Assembly, and won approval of an interim constitution, and on two occasions he cracked down on the military establishment by removing its top leaders. He also cracked down on the "22 families" whose wealth and power were widely resented, nationalized various industries and business firms, and announced a land reform program. The people were shown that Pakistan, whatever its problems, was hardly moribund—a fact attested to by continued political turbulence, strikes, and protests.

By April Bhutto felt that he was in a strong enough position to respond affirmatively to Mrs. Gandhi's suggestion of summit talks to settle outstanding problems in the subcontinent. Moreover, he was under heavy pressures to secure the return of border territories held by Indian forces and the 93,000 Pakistani prisoners of war held in India—a group Mrs. Gandhi insisted would not be returned to augment Pakistani forces until India had reason to believe the two countries would live at peace.

It is worth appraising the relative strengths and weaknesses of the Indian and Pakistani positions as they approached the opening of the summit talks in Simla on June 28, 1972. India had decisively demonstrated its military superiority and held many strong cards, including Pakistani territory and prisoners. Mrs. Gandhi's sweeping political victory at the national level in 1971 had been repeated at the state level in March 1972. India's major supporter, the Soviet Union, had backed New Delhi strongly when the chips were down, while the United States and China had—for all their bluster—carefully stopped short of decisive support of Pakistan. The widespread support for Pakistan in the United Nations during the crisis was annoying and disappointing to Indians, but had no substantial effect on the outcome within the subcontinent.

If India was clearly in the stronger position, it is important to note that Pakistan was not so helpless as to have no choice but to accept any settlement proposed by New Delhi. Nor was India able to bring much additional pressure to bear on Pakistan, or to threaten it further. By 1972 India had done all it could to Pakistan without gravely damaging itself as well. Many Pakistanis believed that India had never accepted partition, and eventually planned to destroy and reabsorb Pakistan. The events of 1971 corroborated this suspicion, or conviction, in the minds of many.[7] Yet New Delhi was keenly

---

7. It seems more likely that most politically active Indians had ambivalent feelings about Pakistan's unity. Psychologically and emotionally they probably hoped for the country's demise, but they recognized that the ideal solution from India's standpoint was a united but democratic Pakistan in which the less hostile Bengali majority determined the country's foreign and defense policies.

aware of the difficulties the addition of tens of millions of additional Muslims into the Indian polity would involve. To be sure, the Bengalis in India and Bangladesh share a common language and elements of a common culture, and there is little logic in Bangladesh's insistence that the new nation is a secular state—but only for the Muslim-majority areas of Bengal. Yet the middle-class Muslims who control Bangladesh fear economic dominance by Hindu business and professional men in any united Bengal, while the Hindus in West Bengal fear that Muslim numerical superiority would be translated into political control—whether in an independent Bengal or one within India.[8] The attitude of most other Indians can be put succinctly: they want no more Muslims or Bengalis. If the Muslims of Bengal would create additional problems as Indians, the more militant Muslims of what was West Pakistan would be impossible to assimilate. Nor did New Delhi, which had already acquired a certain responsibility for Bangladesh, see how it would benefit from the instability or possible chaos that would follow if what was left of Pakistan descended into chaos or was divided into separate nations. Ironic as it was, India had acquired a stake in Bhutto's success.

Pakistan's position was also improving dramatically by mid-1972. One striking element of this is the way the government's export-promotion effort and its import curbs not only enabled a much smaller country to maintain (and later surpass) the export levels of the past but also to bring its trade into balance by 1973, before the great rise in oil prices. By mid-1972 Pakistan had secured extensive new aid from the International Monetary Fund, and the Aid-to-Pakistan Consortium had agreed to a short-term debt relief operation of $234 million and to provide $180 million in new aid dur-

8. For an appraisal of possible political arrangements involving the Bengalis, see Trevor Ling, "Creating a New State: The Bengalis of Bangladesh," *South Asian Review*, V. 5, No. 3 (April 1972), 221–29.

ing the year. Bhutto's blend of democratic politics and selective repression, while containing some ominous signs, was moving the country ahead politically.

The agreement reached at Simla and published on July 2, 1972, reflected the strength of the two countries' bargaining positions rather accurately. Pakistan, convinced that its position was improving, argued for a step-by-step approach to the many issues in dispute. India, which had favored the approach in the past but had been periodically rebuffed, now argued for a comprehensive agreement. When Pakistan made its refusal stick, India acquiesced in a partial agreement. It provided for a return to the status quo ante along the border, which meant India gave up the extensive Pakistani territories it held in return for the much smaller territories the Pakistani forces had captured. New Delhi was less flexible about the territory it had captured in Kashmir. India's major gain was Pakistan's acceptance of the line of control in Kashmir resulting from the cease-fire on December 17, 1971, although this was to be "without prejudice to the recognized position of either side." (New Delhi was soon to argue that this eliminated the role of the United Nations since the old cease-fire line no longer existed.) India also secured Pakistani acceptance—though less than clear-cut—that the two nations would henceforth settle their differences bilaterally. There were also general agreements to work for peace, trade, and cooperation—and to limit hostile propaganda—but decisions about the exchange of prisoners and civilian internees were left for future meetings.[9]

Although the agreements were quickly ratified by the national assemblies of the two countries, the provision that the withdrawals were to be carried out in thirty days proved naïvely optimistic. Ostensibly, the disagreements centered on the problems of determining the line of control (and India

9. The text of the Simla accord is in *Pakistan Horizon*, XXV, No. 3 (3rd quarter, 1972), 117–18.

made its withdrawal from areas along the international border conditional upon agreement on the Kashmir line), but other factors involving Bangladesh were affected. Pakistan pressed for the release of the 93,000 prisoners captured in East Pakistan (15,000 of whom were civilians). India, however, had to handle the prisoner issue in such a way as not to undermine its relations with Bangladesh and would not release them until Bangladesh agreed. Sheikh Mujibur Rahman not only insisted that the prisoners be held until Pakistan recognized Bangladesh's independence, but that it would try those guilty of war crimes — a number initially set at about 1,500. Bhutto was attempting to prepare his people for recognition by arguing that it was both necessary and inevitable, but he insisted that no war-crimes trials take place. If they were held, he hinted ominously that he could not guarantee the safety of the 400,000 Bengalis still held in Pakistan. (He also insisted — apparently for face-saving purposes — that he would not recognize Bangladesh until Mujib met with him personally.) Nor was Pakistan ready to accept the Biharis (non-Bengali Muslims who numbered somewhere between 600,000 and 1,000,000), who had generally believed in a united Pakistan and supported its soldiers and were in a precarious position in Bangladesh.

By late November events began to move again. India and Pakistan released the prisoners captured in the fighting on the western front. On December 7 agreement was reached on the line of control in Kashmir, and by December 20 — just over a year after the war ended — withdrawals were largely completed.

It was August 1973 before the next major step forward was taken. During the first half of that year two developments took place that weakened the bargaining power of India and further strengthened Pakistan's hand. The political and economic situation in India deteriorated. India's chronic factionalism returned as Mrs. Gandhi failed to use her dominant position to formulate and carry out effective measures to speed the pace of reform or economic development, a failure compounded by destructive monsoons and falling food production.[10] India's proud assertions of self-reliance soon gave way to the reality of its dependence on others. Second, the Pakistani prisoners of war were rapidly becoming a diminishing asset in India's hands. Not only were they costly to support, but Pakistani charges that India was acting contrary to the Geneva Convention attracted increasing support around the world — especially on those occasions when trouble broke out in the camps and prisoners were killed by Indian guards.

Finally, Pakistan had demonstrated that it could not only withhold a recognition of Bangladesh but could — through the assistance of China — keep the new nation out of the United Nations. Bangladesh's application for membership had been debated in the summer of 1972. Pakistan and China tried to have the question deferred, but failing that China on August 25 vetoed the application. (President Bhutto said on November 18, 1972, that while China had acted "on certain principles," he had also asked China to use the veto "if you are our friend.")[11] The debate in the General Assembly in December was also satisfactory to Pakistan, for that body passed two resolutions calling for the release of the Pakistani. prisoners and the admission of Bangladesh at an early date, and Pakistan could interpret the latter as being contingent upon implementation of the former.

India and Bangladesh were stalemated, and in an effort to break the deadlock they issued a joint declaration on April 17, 1973, that called for a compromise solution. They said they were ready to seek a solution through simultaneous repatriation of the Pakistani prisoners of war and civilian internees

10. Pakistan also experienced severe economic dislocations because of heavy floods but quickly secured extra outside assistance, and the economy soon recovered.

11. Zulfikar Ali Bhutto, President of Pakistan, *Speeches and Statements October 1, 1972–December 31, 1972* (Karachi: Department of Films and Publications, Government of Pakistan, 1973).

(except those Bangladesh insisted on holding for trial on criminal charges), and repatriation of the Bengalis in Pakistan and the Pakistanis in Bangladesh. The latter were defined as "all non-Bengalis who owe allegiance and have opted for repatriation to Pakistan." Bangladesh Foreign Minister Kamal Hossein announced publicly on the same day that 195 — not 1,500 — prisoners would be tried as war criminals.

Pakistan promptly expressed its continued opposition to *any* trials on both practical and legal grounds — that such trials would heighten tensions and make the position of Bengalis in Pakistan dangerous, and that whatever acts took place in 1971 took place in the territory of Pakistan, which gave it exclusive jurisdiction. Pakistan expressed its willingness to try any officials against whom evidence was available, and filed a petition in the International Court of Justice requesting the court to order India not to turn over any of the prisoners of Bangladesh. Nor was Pakistan ready to acknowledge an obligation to accept all the non-Bengalis who wanted to come to Pakistan.

Nonetheless, the stalemate was broken. In July and August new negotiations were undertaken, and on August 28 an agreement was signed between India and Pakistan. Bangladesh, which had been consulted by India, pronounced itself "fully satisfied with the agreement."[12] It provided for the repatriation of all the Pakistani prisoners save the 195 charged with war crimes, all the Bengalis in Pakistan, and a substantial (but unspecified) number of those non-Bengalis in Bangladesh who had indicated a desire to settle in Pakistan.[13]

Pakistan had made substantial progress in utilizing the negotiating process to achieve its goals. However, its continued refusal to recognize Bangladesh became a more difficult posture to sustain as time went on — just as India's

12. *The New York Times*, Aug. 29, 1973.
13. For a more detailed account of the negotiations during 1972–73, see S. M. Burke, "The Postwar Diplomacy of the Indo-Pakistani War of 1971," *Asian Survey*, XIII, No. 11 (Nov. 1973), 1036–49.

refusal to release the prisoners had gradually been transformed from an asset to a liability. On July 10, 1973, the Pakistan National Assembly had approved a resolution permitting the government to recognize Bangladesh when it decided "that such recognition is in the national interest." Yet when the time came to yield on the issue Bhutto did so under auspices that simultaneously protected his domestic flank while giving maximum discomfort to India. Bhutto had arranged for an Islamic Summit meeting to be held in Lahore on February 22–24, 1974, as part of his effort to demonstrate to his people (and to the world) that Pakistan had many friends, as well as to provide a symbol of Pakistan's place in the comity of nations. During the meeting several leaders from other Islamic countries made a strong (and prearranged?) plea for reconciliation between Pakistan and Bangladesh so that the latter could join its fellow Muslim nations at the conference. Yielding to such entreaties, Bhutto announced recognition of Bangladesh, and Sheikh Mujib promptly flew to Lahore. The recognition long sought by India had come about, but under auspices that New Delhi could hardly approve — especially in view of Bhutto's constant reference to Bangladesh as "Muslim Bengal." Nonetheless, sufficient momentum had been generated so that the foreign ministers of the three countries could meet, and on April 9, 1974 they agreed that Bangladesh would hold *no* war-crimes trials, and Pakistan demonstrated somewhat more flexibility about receiving non-Bengalis who wanted to live in Pakistan.[14] Important issues remained to be settled, but much had been accomplished in two years of diplomatic activity.

Domestic Pressures and Constraints

Scholars attempting to identify and analyze the determinants of different countries' foreign policies have adopted

14. The text of the tripartite agreement is in *The Overseas Hindustan Times*, April 18, 1974.

two approaches. Some have seen foreign policy as growing largely out of the values, aspirations, and fears of the people of each country, particularly its elites. Foreign policy is thus the projection of domestic politics onto the outer world.[15] This approach calls for appraisal of the culture, ideology, interest groups, and internal political dynamics of a society as an essential preliminary requirement to any understanding of the country's attitudes and policies toward its neighbors as well as the wider international community. The other approach places primary stress on foreign policy as the response of a country seeking to advance its national interests in the face of challenges and opportunities arising from the international environment, which is viewed as competitive if not always actively hostile.

Neither of these approaches is adequate by itself. No country is powerful enough to make the world conform to its values or preferences; all must, to a greater or lesser degree, operate in a system of independent nation-states whose values, interests, and styles differ from their own. On the other hand, the "national interest" is not a discernible objective reality readily apparent to all within a nation's borders. If it were, there would be few great debates on the subject—and far fewer opportunities for scholarly disputation. Arguments over the importance of "ideology" and "national interest" often overlook the fact that these concepts are not held in separate compartments of men's minds. Rather, men's concepts of the national interest are shaped to some degree by their ideology, values, and memories. Thus, the scholar who ignores domestic pressures and constraints operates as a one-dimensional man, with a corresponding distortion of reality.

Nonetheless, there are many difficulties one encounters in attempting to catalogue and evaluate the domestic influ-

15. One example of this is the bureaucratic politics approach set forth by Graham T. Allison in *Essence of Decision: Explaining the Cuban Missile Crisis* (Boston: Little Brown, 1971).

ences on Pakistan's foreign policy. Public opinion polling
was not—to put it mildly—looked upon with favor during the
years of authoritarian rule. The impact of public opinion was
important on only a few basic issues. Specific decisions were
made largely as a result of the views and interests of a few
key groups—senior military officers and civil servants, and
to a lesser extent powerful business and agricultural interests. Pakistani scholars, who were closest to the scene, gave
little attention to the subject of domestic influences on foreign policy except in the most general terms, and there has
been little time to analyze the new situation that has existed
since 1971. The press has been under governmental control
or influence for most of the last quarter-century. What criticisms there were of government policy were sometimes officially inspired demands that the government pursue a more
assertive and nationalistic policy, which the government
could cite in its dealings with other nations as proof of its
moderation in the face of a difficult climate of public opinion.
It is not clear that the situation in this regard has changed
since 1971.

Faced with such a paucity of data and lack of access to the
specific thinking of many key decision-makers, one can do
little more than list the basic domestic factors influencing
Pakistan's foreign policy, assess the strengths and weaknesses of certain key groups, appraise the manner in which
such factors and groups interact, and set forth some general
conclusions in the hope that they will encourage further research as well as shed some light on the probable direction of
Pakistan's foreign policy. There will be as many questions
as answers, and some of the latter will be based upon impressions and reflections, but they should help set the parameters
of the choices open to Pakistan's leaders. (Nor should we
overlook the impact of foreign policy successes or failures
on a government's domestic popularity. This is most obvious
when external support is acquired or wars are lost, but membership in international organizations and foreign visits by,

or to, leaders of powerful nations are only a few examples of activities that enable a political leader to claim he has won prestige and influence for his country.)

The existence of widespread Pakistani fear of and hostility toward India, and the fact that these emotions have a powerful impact on Pakistan's foreign policy, is obvious to any observer. But just how wide and deep is this fear and hostility among different groups within the country? If the fear could be lessened, would the hostility also diminish? (Most Indian commentators assert that the fear and hostility are largely generated and manipulated by elements within the Pakistani elite to enable them to maintain their dominant position, but these commentators underestimate the strength and depth of these emotions, just as the Congress party leaders underestimated the appeal of the Muslim League to the Muslim masses in the 1940s.) How has the situation changed as a result of the traumatic events of 1971? Did Indian actions serve to heighten already fierce animosities? For some Pakistanis they undoubtedly did, and they may be more determined than ever to avenge their humiliation if Indian weakness ever gives them the opportunity. But others apparently concluded that continued hostility (especially toward an India now ten times Pakistan's size) is futile if economic development is to proceed and the area is to become less vulnerable to manipulation by outside powers. (Ancient animosities do fade away in some cases, as witness Franco-German cooperation in recent decades – although neither country was ready for such change until it had suffered far greater destruction than recent wars have brought to India and Pakistan.) Few in the former group are clamoring for immediate military confrontation, just as few in the latter are willing to see Pakistan accept a position and policy of subservience vis-à-vis India. But differences exist, which provides some room for maneuver by skillful leadership.

One great unknown, of course, is the position and views of the Pakistani military – essentially the officer corps. The

military services were widely respected in West Pakistan as
the sword and shield of the country in the past, and military
officers received impressive emoluments and were accorded
high status. Respect — both public and self-respect — declined
in the years just after 1971, and the internal cohesion among
the officer corps is tempted to blame Ayub, Yahya, and their
immediate associates, the failure of governments dominated
by military men to forge an acceptable political system at
home or defend the country from its principal enemy has left
the military tarnished.[16] Nonetheless, along with the police
the officer corps retains a monopoly on coercive power and
thus is essential for ensuring domestic security as well as protecting the country from whatever designs India and Afghanistan are thought to have on it. The military leaders are probably quite wary of assuming direct political responsibility, a
caution that is likely to persist for some years. They are probably also less fearful of a democratic government than they
were when a majority of Pakistani citizens were Bengalis,
for the latter were less hostile toward India than were the
West Pakistanis and — even before Mujib's Six-Point Program
threatened the financial base of the military — less inclined
to give top priority to military spending.

How much influence over Pakistan's foreign policy does
the military have in this situation, and what policies does it
advocate within the government? While Bhutto has been
openly critical of the military at times, their voices — and
particularly when they voice their needs as to men and
equipment necessary to defend the country — must be accorded considerable weight. (Bhutto's exemption of military
officers' holdings from his land reform program is another
indication of his caution in threatening their interests.) Thus,
Bhutto "is attempting to confine the military to a role of participation rather than domination of politics. Further, he has

16. For an excellent appraisal of the role of the military in Pakistan, see Stephen
P. Cohen, *Arms and Politics in Bangladesh, India, and Pakistan* (Buffalo: State
University of New York, Nov. 1973, Special Study No. 49), esp. pp. 25–36.

tried to avoid threatening the honor and esprit of the military. To do so could invite another coup, but it also means that he must continue to make military and security matters one of the central concerns of the Pakistani government."[17] He hardly has to meet all of their requests—indeed, he cannot— to obtain their acquiescence in his rule, but he must make serious efforts to meet what they regard as their essential needs. Not parity with India, but a "credible deterrent" seems to be their goal. This demands a substantial budget allocation, and Pakistan has significantly increased the size of its armed forces and raised the level of its military budget in recent years.[18] On the international scene, the military requires a foreign policy that makes possible the acquisition of modern weapons. Given Pakistan's experience with the United States, it probably also means avoiding complete dependence upon any single source of arms.

If it is difficult to find hard evidence that the Pakistani military sees its own status and interests as served by continuing tension with India, it is equally difficult to imagine the military urging the government to be more accommodating toward New Delhi. Soldiers have rarely been the foremost advocates of beating swords into plowshares. Given the deeply ingrained Pakistani military bravado and Muslim contempt for Hindu soldiers, it is unlikely that even the 1971 defeat has brought about a fundamental change— in contrast to an increased wariness—in the attitude of the military. While the civil bureaucracy shares many of the views of the military officers because of somewhat overlapping backgrounds, positions in society, and basic outlooks, the bureaucracy's direct *interests* are not tied to high military budgets. Similarly, the Pakistani intelligence officials probably find it difficult to take a detached view of Indian intentions and tend to err on the side of expecting

17. *Ibid.*, p. 42.
18. See *The Military Balance 1975–76* (London: The International Institute for Strategic Studies, Sept. 1975).

the worst—much as Indian intelligence officials probably do with regard to China.

But the military no longer has the field of policy-making largely to itself. The victory of Bhutto and his Pakistan People's Party (PPP) in the elections of December 1970, and the position of Bhutto and the PPP today, project a group—or a coalition of groups—into the center of the struggle for power. The position and interests of the PPP are somewhat ambivalent. Bhutto not only made his early reputation as an antagonist of India, but the PPP made its most impressive electoral showing in 1970 in the districts along the Indian border where memories of the 1965 war were strongest. At the same time, the party owes part of its success to its appeal to the students, workers, and middle-class elements who resented their exclusion from political power and from the benefits of the country's economic growth under Ayub. Its moderate socialism, some of which has been put into practice, is designed to appeal to the "modernizing" elements in Pakistan. This has been discussed by Syed in chapter three.

However, Bhutto and his party face an important dilemma in reconciling domestic and foreign policy pressures. Continued confrontation with India probably would lead to such a central political role for the Pakistani military—and to such large budgetary allocations for it—as to reduce drastically if not doom the desires of Bhutto and the PPP for civilian government and more rapid economic development. Moreover, there are limits to the time, energy, and imagination of political leaders; if these are expended on a constant search for national security, domestic concerns often suffer. So far Bhutto has avoided a fundamental choice, but this may not be possible indefinitely.

Two further points need to be made about domestic influences on Pakistan's foreign policy. The first has to do with the urge for economic development. Put simply, there is general pressure on the government to pursue foreign economic policies that improve economic conditions by finding markets for Pakistan's exports, secure the needed imports, and obtain adequate levels of foreign assistance. Because of the small number of people knowledgeable about economics or personally involved in development or foreign trade, these pressures seldom take priority over perceived security needs. However, they cannot be ignored by political leaders, especially since aspirations are gradually increasing with the spread of education and urbanization.

The final point has to do with the role of Islam, which often creates perceptual problems for the non-Muslim observer. Islam has been an important but somewhat ambivalent element in the people's sense of national unity, and fierce conflicts periodically arise over questions involving Islam.[19] Pakistan has found it difficult to adopt and implement the principles of Islam in its domestic political life. The problem of constructing an "Islamic" foreign policy is even more complex and difficult, partly because the implications of such principles are hazy, but also because Pakistan has little control over its external environment. But frustrations over these difficulties only add to the importance of maintaining close relations with other Muslim states. The Westernized political leader who is attacked by the orthodox Muslim for failing to be true to the "teachings" of Islam often finds his best defense in regular visits from, and to, other Muslim leaders. Pakistan has devoted considerable effort to forging and maintaining such links, and if it has sometimes been rebuffed it sees little option but to continue along these paths.

These considerations suggest two conclusions. First, the possibility of Pakistan's seeking reconciliation with India is greater today than at any time — except perhaps in Ayub's

19. Such as the controversy and the ensuing riots in mid-1974 over the issue of whether or not members of the Ahmadi sect are true Muslims. Riots over this perennial dispute led to the death of an estimated two thousand people in 1953. *New York Times*, July 4, 1974.

first years in power. At a minimum, there are more people in West Pakistan today who see the disadvantages of continued conflict. In the first instance this involves an awareness of the dangers to a smaller Pakistan in any future war, especially after the Indian nuclear explosion.[20] But there probably is also a greater awareness of the difficulties of maintaining civilian government and fostering economic development without a normalization of relations with India. These conflicts within the society take many forms, such as the less enthusiastic attitude of Pakistanis in some provinces for a large army since a larger military benefits the already dominant Punjabis more than other groups. Second, the possibility of these pressures leading to a new relationship with India depends upon policy toward India becoming a legitimate subject of public debate, or if Bhutto (or some other leader) secures such a predominant position as to be able to *impose* a new policy upon the country. As long as the view persists that Pakistan is so beleaguered that anyone advocating a changed course is virtually a traitor, few will risk their reputations or positions in such a cause. Thus, the evolution of Pakistan's political system will influence its foreign policy—just as will the policies of the major powers and of India.

The Road Ahead

Pakistanis can take considerable satisfaction from their achievements since the dark days at the end of 1971. Despite their humiliation and defeat, they pulled themselves together and tackled the problems facing them with energy and imagination—just as they did a quarter-century earlier following the upheavals of partition. The adoption of a con-

20. Arguments that West Pakistan was the source of over 90 percent of the military manpower—and that East Pakistan required at least some protection—overlook not only the psychological dimensions of the events of 1971 but also the loss of budget revenue from the eastern wing. Pakistan's attractiveness to outside powers may also have declined.

stitution and the establishment of representative civilian government were major steps forward. The economy expanded by over 6 percent in 1973–74. Sharp price increases in oil and other goods put heavy strains on the balance of payments, and the economy experienced considerable difficulties in 1974–75 despite the fact that debt repayments of $650 million due to countries participating in the Aid-to-Pakistan consortium were rescheduled in mid-1974 — and in a period of rapid inflation a payment postponed is a payment reduced.[21] Pakistan has improved its ties with many of the oil-rich Middle Eastern nations and has received substantial help from some of them, and during 1975–76 the economy grew by about 5 percent. However, Pakistan's important ties with Iran, which provided a $580 million loan in 1974, were for a time strained by the Shah's irritation over Bhutto's cultivation of Libya's Qaddafi and Pakistan's concern over Iran's efforts to develop better relations with India.

But these achievements have a certain fragility about them. The political system is subject to many strains, and Pakistani culture and democracy have yet to adapt to each other. In the words of one observer, "One of the most disconcerting aspects of Bhutto's two years in office has been his continuance of the Pakistani habit of equating opposition with treason."[22] The task of building a strong and durable mass base is one that no previous political party has accomplished. The Pakistan People's Party still has shallow roots, and has increasingly become the personal instrument of Bhutto, and civil liberties are steadily being restricted.[23] Anwar Syed has commented that "During the first phase, the PPP became a movement to overthrow the existing political order on the basis of a winning ideological posture. Phase two has been a period of decay: the movement failed

---

21. *Pakistan Affairs*, July 16, 1974.
22. David Dunbar, "Bhutto — Two Years On," *The World Today* (Jan. 1974), p. 24.
23. Lewis Simons, "Bhutto Takes Gandhi's Path," *The Manchester Guardian Weekly*, Feb. 15, 1976.

Pakistan Foreign Trade: 1970; 1973–75 (Millions of U.S. dollars)

	1970		1973		1974		1975	
	Exports	Imports	Exports	Imports	Exports	Imports	Exports	Imports
Total World	724	1102	952	974	1116	1740	1051	2129
Developed Countries;	369	873	448	668	462	1158	405	1311
of which								
U.S.	85	313	40	250	52	402	46	269
U.K.	75	120	71	72	66	114	65	135
Developing Countries;	228	117	455	202	588	451	576	672
of which								
Asia*	93	50	285	96	268	179	232	257
Middle East	57	64	108	82	261	251	271	389
U.S.S.R.	31	29	17	12	34	16	30	50
China	39	28	13	48	11	54	13	54

*Not including China
Sources: International Monetary Fund, International Bank for Reconstruction and Development, *Direction of Trade, Annual 1968–1972*; IMF, IBRD, *Direction of Trade,* August 1976.

to convert itself into a party."[24] The final results are still not in, but the similarities with the record of the Muslim League are apparent and ominous, even though the PPP has a better elaborated domestic program. Finally, centrifugal pressures in Baluchistan and the Northwest Frontier Province raise questions about the country's ability to remain united and acquire greater cohesion. Bhutto's reliance on punitive military actions and playing off one tribal chief against another may keep thinly populated Baluchistan under control, but continued repression in the Northwest Frontier Province could lead to an explosive situation there. The Frontier problem was made more difficult by Daud's return to power in Afghanistan and his reactivation of the Pushtunistan issue, although during 1976 the two leaders met on two occasions and apparently made progress in working out a detente if not a complete rapprochement.[25]

Moreover, it is difficult to know how to appraise the trend in Indo-Pakistani relations. The accomplishments since 1971 could mean that a new era of reconciliation if not friendship has begun in South Asia.[26] But has Bhutto decided that accommodation rather than confrontation is essential even if distasteful, and if so can he carry his countrymen with him? (He has been careful to prepare "public opinion" for each of his accords with India lest he become vulnerable to the kind of attack *he* launched against Ayub for signing the Tashkent Agreement.) Or should one emphasize that until 1976 India and Pakistan still had not returned all the way to the status quo ante—although this represents faster progress than in the past, for by 1970 they had not returned to the status quo that obtained before the 1965 war?

Bhutto clearly is in a difficult position and faces many

24. See chap. 3 of this volume.
25. *Pakistan Affairs*, Sept. 1, 1976.
26. For such an interpretation, see K. P. Misra, "Trilateralism in South Asia," *Asian Survey*, XIV, No. 7 (July 1974), 627–36.

painful choices. Pakistan's ability to gain and hold extensive great power support has probably declined.[27] American support during 1971 was welcome but ineffectual, and President Nixon's comment during Bhutto's September 1973 visit to Washington that the "independence and integrity of Pakistan is a cornerstone of American foreign policy" was gratifying.[28] Nonetheless, Bhutto has cited such actions as recognition of the Sihanouk government, and of the North Vietnamese and the North Korean regimes, and Pakistan's withdrawal from SEATO to demonstrate that he was not subservient to the United States.[29] Little in the way of arms was provided by the Nixon administration, despite Bhutto's claims that the United States is obligated by its bilateral treaties to supply military equipment. Moreover, the United States is reducing its involvement in South Asia while making it known that it is disinclined to challenge India's position in the subcontinent. There is no reason to think that President Ford was more favorable to Pakistan than was Mr. Nixon. The lifting of the United States arms embargo on sales to South Asia in 1975 raised hopes in Pakistan and angered India, although through 1976 no significant sales of military equipment occurred. Moreover, United States opposition to Pakistan's purchase of a nuclear fuel reprocessing plant from France — essential to the development of an atomic bomb capability — was causing Washington to threaten to refuse to sell conventional arms, although both governments were anxious to avoid an impasse on this issue.[30]

27. India and Pakistan secured about $25 billion in external support during the past two decades, a level not likely to be maintained — at least in *real* terms — in the future. Nor was influence something that accrued only to the outside powers; their competition for the favor of the South Asian countries enabled the latter to maintain considerable freedom of maneuver as well as to exert some influence on the major powers.

28. *Department of State Bulletin*, Oct. 15, 1973, p. 482. Such statements have been repeated on numerous occasions by United States officials such as Secretary of State Kissinger in Lahore on August 8, 1976. *Department of State Bulletin*, Sept. 6, 1976, p. 318.

29. Karachi Domestic Service, Dec. 22, 1973; Foreign Broadcast Information Service, Middle East and Africa, Dec. 27, 1973.

30. *The New York Times*, Aug. 9, 10, and 26, 1976.

Nor can Pakistan expect much help from the U.S.S.R. Moscow has demonstrated that it wants to maintain a position in Pakistan, and in 1972 it renewed its agreement to provide aid for a steel mill in Karachi. But relations between the two countries are marked by suspicion and distrust as a result of Pakistan's cordial relations with Peking and Moscow's long record (interrupted only partially in the late 1960s) of supporting India when forced to choose in the subcontinent. Indeed, many Pakistanis fear that the Soviet Union, either directly or through Afghanistan, is stirring up trouble in Baluchistan and the Northwest Frontier Province in order to make Pakistan more amenable to Soviet desires or even to break up the country.[31] That Moscow wants to see Pakistan destroyed is unlikely, for when given the choice Soviet leaders appear to value stability over upheaval, especially in areas such as South Asia where they have a major stake.[32] But the Soviet leaders would like to receive Pakistani endorsement of Brezhnev's Asian collective security scheme, or Kosygin's proposed South Asian economic cooperation arrangements, or perhaps have Pakistan sign a bilateral friendship treaty with the U.S.S.R. Bhutto might be tempted to explore such possibilities at some point in an attempt to placate Moscow as well as limit its support for India. However, the mid-1974 postponement of his Moscow visit is only one indication that friction will continue to mark the relationship, and both Bhutto and the military leaders are likely to be extremely cautious about antagonizing China by moving markedly closer to the Soviet Union.

This reluctance to risk its ties with China does not stem from any Pakistani belief that Peking has fulfilled all of Pakistan's expectations or needs. (Enthusiasm for things Chinese declined sharply during the Cultural Revolution and has never fully revived.) China gave Pakistan strong

31. *The Economist* (London), Aug. 3, 1974.
32. For an appraisal of Soviet–South Asian relations, see William J. Barnds, "South Asia," in Kurt L. London, ed., *The Soviet Impact on World Politics* (New York: Hawthorne Books, 1974), pp. 156–81.

backing during the 1965 war, but its stand in 1971 was more cautious — partly because of its awareness that Pakistani leaders had made "serious mistakes" in handling the situation in East Pakistan, but more fundamentally because of the existence of nearly fifty Soviet divisions on China's northern frontier. Nor was Peking interested in Pakistan's suggestion of a defense pact in 1972. Chinese arms aid to Pakistan, while very important, has also been rather modest.[33] Pakistan is also aware that New Delhi would like to see a normalization of Sino-Indian relations. Peking, while still seeing India as acting under Soviet influence, finally responded to Indian overtures early in 1976 by agreeing to an exchange of ambassadors after a fifteen-year gap, but Pakistan's importance to Peking would decline if Peking ever decided to try to weaken Indo-Soviet links by substantially improving relations with New Delhi.

But if Pakistan has become aware of the limitations of Chinese support, it is fully aware that it has no alternative but to rely on China for whatever help it can extract.[34] Moreover, Sino-Pakistani relations were cordial if distant even before Sino-Indian relations deteriorated in the late 1950s.[35] Pakistani officials have consulted Chinese leaders regularly on the various Indo-Pakistani accords of the past few years, and have received official Chinese approval of their moves. The joint communiqué issued at the end of Prime Minister Bhutto's visit to Peking in May 1974 said:

33. Information is sparse on the amounts involved. The U.S. government has stated that such shipments amounted to $133,000,000 between 1965 and 1972. *U.S. Foreign Policy for the 1970s: The Emerging Structure of Peace—A Report to the Congress by Richard Nixon, President of the United States*, Feb. 7, 1972, p. 147.

34. In February 1972 China agreed to convert four of its past loans for economic assistance (amounting to $110,000,000) into grants and to defer the repayment period on the 1970 loan of $200,000,000 for twenty years. *Peking Review*, Feb. 4, 1972.

35. Sino-Pakistani relations are examined in William J. Barnds, "China's Relations with Pakistan: Durability Amidst Discontinuity," *The China Quarterly*, No. 63 (Sept. 1975), 463–89.

The two sides noted with pleasure that agreements had been reached among the countries concerned of the South Asian subcontinent, which had led to the implementation of the relevant resolutions of the United Nations General Assembly and Security Council and thus created favourable conditions for the normalization of relations among the countries of the subcontinent. The two sides hoped that the countries of the subcontinent would live in friendship in conformity with the principles of equality and mutual respect for sovereignty, and they expressed readiness to develop goodneighborly relations with the countries of the subcontinent on the basis of the Five Principles of Peaceful Coexistence.[36]

The expressed desire of both Pakistan and China to see the countries of the subcontinent live in harmony with each other and with outside powers was welcome to New Delhi. However, these bland assurances received less attention from Indians than did the reference to China's continued support of the right of the people of Kashmir to self-determination—a position that prompted a walkout by the Indian chargé d'affaires when expressed by Vice Premier Teng Hsiao-ping at a banquet for Mr. Bhutto. Bhutto quickly visited China after Peking and New Delhi agreed to exchange ambassadors in 1976, and won continued Chinese support on the important Kashmir issue.[37] The Indians were also suspicious about Chinese and Pakistani motivations in seeking more normal relations with Bangladesh. The Bangladesh government of Sheikh Mujib was officially very friendly to India, but New Delhi is aware that the fading dreams and the mounting frustrations of the Bengalis were leading to rising anti-Indian—and, more ominously, anti-Hindu—sentiments. Indians fear Pakistani manipulation of militant Islamic elements in Bangladesh as well as Chinese exploitation of radical forces—a dangerous combination from India's viewpoint. Prime Minister Bhutto failed to work out an agreed division of assets and liabilities of united

36. *Peking Review*, May 17, 1974.
37. *Peking Review*, June 4, 1976.

Pakistan or arrange for the establishment of diplomatic and trade relations during his June 1974 visit to Bangladesh, which was but one indication that major difficulties to any cooperation between the two states remained as long as Mujib was in power. However, the crowds that greeted him upon arrival indicate that a reservoir of pro-Pakistani sentiment still existed.[38] The overthrow of the Mujib government in mid-1975 caused apprehension in India and raised hopes in Pakistan. Since then relations between India and Bangladesh have deteriorated while Pakistani-Bangladesh relations have improved considerably.

Just as certain Pakistani moves have created apprehension in India, New Delhi has also taken actions that have intensified Pakistan's suspicions and fears. The Indian defense budget for 1974–75 increased by 20 percent, and the increases were in categories that suggest this was not simply an attempt to keep up with inflation.[39] India insists on being treated on the basis of equality by the major powers but criticizes the United States for "equating" India and Pakistan. Indian talk of the country's "special" or "dominant" position in the subcontinent—the Indian version of "manifest density"—New Delhi's insistence that Pakistan cease looking for support from outside the subcontinent, and India's double standard on arms imported by India and Pakistan, all increase the difficulties facing any Pakistani leader who attempts to work out a reconciliation. Pakistanis fear that what is "normalization" to India amounts to something close to "domination." Indians often appear not only

38. The International Bank for Reconstruction and Development has been attempting to determine how the $3.6 billion foreign debt liability should be divided. Bangladesh has accepted responsibility for only $500,000,000 so far, and argues that it should receive a share of the foreign exchange reserves and airlines and shipping assets. *The Economist* (London), April 27, 1974; *The Far Eastern Economic Review*, July 8, 1974.

39. Government of India, Explanatory Memorandum on the Budget of the Central Government for 1974–75. New Delhi, 1974. There was a further increase in the defense budget 1975–76. See *The Military Balance, 1975–76, op. cit.*

unable to deal with these concerns but unwilling to recognize them.[40]

The most disturbing Indian action was clearly its explosion of a nuclear device on May 18, 1974, an action that increased Pakistani fears and reduced its flexibility. New Delhi's claim that it was done because of the need for a peaceful explosions technology to speed up the country's economic development was widely discounted, even by those who saw the move as designed more to win international status and divert attention from domestic troubles than as the inevitable first step toward a weapons program.

India's nuclear explosion deepened but did not fundamentally alter Pakistan's dilemma; it made reconciliation with India more important but also more difficult. Bhutto at first stated that Pakistan "cannot afford" to develop a nuclear capability of its own, but that it would seek guarantees against "nuclear blackmail" from the major nuclear powers.[41] He also asserted that

we will never surrender our rights or claims because of India's nuclear status but . . . we will not be deflected from our policies by this fateful development.

In concrete terms, we will not compromise the rights of self-determination of the people of Jammu and Kashmir. Nor will we accept Indian hegemony or domination over the subcontinent. . . . What is needed is a joint undertaking in the nature of an obligation by all permanent members of the Security Council to act collectively or individually on behalf of a threatened state. In other words, a nuclear umbrella of all five great powers.[42]

But as India discovered in the mid-1960s, it is easier to seek a nuclear guarantee than to find a willing guarantor.

40. These matters are discussed in Anwar H. Syed, "Pakistan's Security Problem: A Bill of Constraints," *Orbis*, XVI, No. 4 (Winter 1973), 952–74; and in William J. Barnds, "Indian Conceptions of Asian Security," *Asian Forum* (Autumn 1976).

41. *Christian Science Monitor*, May 30, 1974.

42. *Far Eastern Economic Review*, June 3, 1974.

Neither the United States nor the Soviet Union is likely to come forth to provide any credible guarantee. Even the Chinese reacted very carefully to the Indian nuclear explosion and the Pakistani search for support. Peking simply repeated its standard statement supporting Pakistan's "national independence and state sovereignty."[43] While cautioning against expansionism and nuclear blackmail, China's years of complaints against great powers' effort to impose the nuclear hegemony on others probably limited their inclination to criticize the Indian action. Later moves by Bhutto indicate that Pakistan wanted to develop its nuclear capability to the extent that would enable it to produce nuclear weapons if it chose to do so.

Thus, in the final analysis Prime Minister Bhutto is faced with the same problem that has bedeviled every Pakistan government—the problem of living with India in the subcontinent, and, since mid-1975, of determining whether India's move away from democracy will affect its policies toward its neighbor in any significant manner. (The idea that Pakistan should become a Middle Eastern nation has much to commend it in terms of economics and psychology, but it overlooks the basic facts of geography. Moreover, the Middle Eastern states are largely unwilling as well as unable to provide the amount and kinds of support Pakistan would need to match Indian power.) Ultimately this comes back to the issue of Kashmir, which remains the focal point though hardly the totality of Indo-Pakistani hostility. On this issue India can show little flexibility, increasing the need for Indian sensitivity on other matters. India's 1974 efforts to work out a new arrangement for Kashmir acceptable to Sheikh Abdullah are an attempt to settle the issue without Pakistani involvement as well as an indication that New Delhi is still unsure of the loyalties and sympathies of the Kashmiris despite its claim that the issue is settled.

43. *Peking Review*, July 5, 1974.

Prime Minister Bhutto has occasionally sounded a note of flexibility on the Kashmir issue but has quickly reverted to Pakistan's traditional position. His ability to yield to India on this matter is untested but probably quite limited, at least in the near future. One major problem he faces is that many of the Pakistanis most committed to Kashmir are those with a national outlook, while those who are less concerned about Kashmir are basically oriented to their own region. Thus, any abandonment of the Kashmir issue would have complex implications for domestic politics and the development of a national outlook. Moreover, Bhutto must consider how a shift on Kashmir would affect those elements of his domestic constituency that are keen for economic reform but are also anti-Indian. Finally, the potential long-run benefits of any Indo-Pakistani reconciliation – greater trade, improved communications, and possibly lower military budgets – would be somewhat uncertain and thus hard to argue for within the Pakistani political context. On the other hand, the costs probably would be clear and immediate – if largely psychological. Nonetheless, while the pace of Indo-Pakistani normalization slowed, it did not stop between 1974 and 1976, for the two countries reached agreements concerning trade, postal arrangements, and travel. In April and May of 1976 each side made concessions that made possible a resumption of rail and civil air traffic, and also reestablished diplomatic relations. Mrs. Gandhi apparently wanted to offset India's deteriorating relations with Bangladesh by improved relations with Pakistan, which might limit the impact of a further Pakistani-Bangladesh rapprochement. Bhutto, despite continued Chinese support, probably feared that the trend of Sino-Indian relations was working against Pakistan and additional flexibility toward India was appropriate. Thus all of the active disputes between India and Pakistan have been settled – save Kashmir.

Looking at the subcontinent after the 1971 upheaval, Wayne Wilcox wrote:

While the prospects of Pakistan's foreign policy appear to be bleak, both because of domestic problems and insufficient resources, this prospect is not new. Since its creation, the state has operated under very great constraints and has been able to produce quite remarkable gains. Whether this will be possible in the future awaits tomorrow's opportunities. What is clear, however, is that Pakistan will continue to prove to be a dynamic state in world politics. Its setting, structure, domestic politics, and need for external resources are too great for it to become "isolationist." And the spilled blood of the communal riots, wars and clashes between India and West Pakistan do not appear to make a foreign policy of "subordinate reconciliation" possible. Neither peace nor war, but cold war will most probably continue to divide the two great countries of South Asia in the next decade.[44]

Despite the great progress made since early 1972, this unhappy prophecy remains to be disproved as long as the Kashmir dispute continues and the two countries are unable to devise a positive relationship acceptable to all.

44. Wilcox, *op. cit.*, p. 115.

14

Pakistan: The Long Search for Foreign Policy

Norman D. Palmer

Changes in a country's foreign policy are a consequence of changes in its internal situation and its international environment. This has been true of Pakistan during its relatively brief existence as an independent state. It is particularly true of the period since 1971, when a new and different Pakistan came into being. The Pakistan that existed from 1947 to 1971 is no more. It is smaller in size, in population, and in resources, but in spite of its persisting internal divisions, it is perhaps a more coherent entity.

The "new" Pakistan may prove better able than the old to solve the problems of national integrity and identity. But will it also be better able to evolve a consistent foreign policy, promote its national interests, and achieve greater influence abroad? Or must it reconcile itself to a lesser status in regional and world affairs, abandoning any hopes for "equality" or "parity" with an even stronger India? As a middle power, can it sustain mutually beneficial ties with the Muslim states of the Middle East and with the greater powers? Or will it no longer seek acceptance as a middle power, and become simply another small power, which has no real prospect of improving its position in the international hierarchy?

In exploring these fundamental questions, this chapter first considers a number of contrasting approaches to the understanding of Pakistan's foreign policy. It then analyzes numerous factors conditioning Pakistan's foreign policy over the years. The country's foreign policy objectives are then considered and certain recent events alluded to. The chapter concludes with a brief assessment of Pakistan's "long search" for a stable foreign policy.

Approaches to Pakistan's Foreign Policy

Continuities and Discontinuities

One could easily marshal evidence to support the thesis that Pakistan has generally sought to play, and has fancied that it has played, a much larger and more influential role in regional and world affairs than its circumstances and capabilities permitted or than in fact it has actually played. One could even argue further that Pakistan never really evolved a satisfactory foreign policy, i.e., one that managed a satisfactory relationship between capabilities and commitments. The "old" Pakistan seemed constantly to be aspiring to membership in exclusive clubs that were generally dominated by stronger players. Once it gained membership in these clubs, as in the case of the Commonwealth, SEATO, or the United Nations, it was not able to achieve the role and status that it felt it deserved, nor was it able to adapt the rules of the clubs to suit its national purposes. Moreover, until the "new" Pakistan becomes a stronger and more effective political system, it is likely to experience the same problems and frustrations as the "old" Pakistan.

It was difficult enough to discuss the constants and variables in the foreign policy of "old" Pakistan. The problem is now accentuated because we cannot ascertain whether and to what extent observations that may have been relevant in the past apply to Pakistan's foreign policy today. The future Pakistan is unique in the modern world; the successful secession of East Pakistan has no parallel among the developing nations. It is therefore necessary to ask: how sharp are the foreign policy discontinuities that flow from succession?[1]

Images and Reality

In considering the foreign policy of any country, it is difficult to distinguish accurately between images and reality, between professions and performance. The task is further complicated by problems of national sensitivity or of inadequate information.[2] These difficulties are compounded when considering Pakistan's foreign policy. In few cases has the gap between images and reality, between professions and performance, been more marked. In few cases have the intensity of sensitivity and the inadequacy of information outside inner government circles been as great.

With a few notable exceptions, most studies of foreign policy by Pakistani nationals have been little more than description-cum-justification of Pakistan's foreign policy, in all its stages and phases, often reflecting more accurately official declarations than a careful, objective analysis of interests, costs, and choices. More objective studies appear to have been ruled out under previous regimes by pressures on scholars to conform to the official line, by the paucity of source materials and the unwillingness of officials to encourage balanced analysis of alternative approaches to real and often anguishing foreign policy problems. Foreign scholars also had difficulty in applying the tools of systematic foreign policy analysis, whether because of their own biased national perceptions, their sometimes unconscious commitment to one side or another in the Indo-

1. See Oran R. Young, "Political Discontinuities in the International System," *World Politics*, XX (April 1968), 369–92.
2. See Kenneth E. Boulding, "National Images and International Systems," *The Journal of Conflict Resolution*, III (June 1959), 120–31; "The Learning and Reality-Testing Process in the International System," *The Journal of International Affairs*, XXI (1967), 1–15; and Robert Jervis, *The Logic of Images in International Relations* (Princeton: Princeton University Press, 1970).

Pakistan dispute, or because of their lack of basic knowledge of the nature and interactions of the social, economic, and political systems in an unfamiliar part of the world. Adequate and reliable data and other materials were scarce, and the kind of interview-access scholars sometimes have to foreign policy-makers in many parts of the world was simply not available in Pakistan. Presumably the situation is now changing; already some first-rate works on Pakistan's foreign policy have appeared or are in process. But the basic problems of access and lack of understanding remain.

Foreign Policy and Political Development

Pakistan provides an outstanding laboratory for analyzing the relationship between foreign policy and political development, an approach that has been sadly neglected in both political development and foreign policy studies. Much light could be shed on the course of Pakistan's external relations and behavior by investigating, with current methodological and conceptual tools, "such well-trodden and undoubtedly relevant subjects as the linkages between the internal and external environment, decision-making in foreign policy and the role of decision-making elites. . . , the processes of nation-building, and the concept of political development as a part of the total developmental process."[3] Of special value would be some analysis of these subjects, not as discrete topics but in terms of their interrelationships.

Obviously, the international environment impinges on a state in many ways. All states have the task of "coping with the international environment," to use Rajni Kothari's words, and all are affected, for better or for worse, by external conditions and events. Developing countries in particular are "penetrated systems" and may be seriously affected by

3. Norman D. Palmer, "Foreign Policy and Political Development: International and Comparative Dimensions," *The Indian Journal of Political Science,* XXXIII (July–Sept. 1972), 253–70, quoted on 253.

various external influences and, in some cases, outright intervention.[4] Even external assistance in the form of economic and military aid, may, under certain circumstances, have undesirable consequences. "Soft" states, in Gunnar Myrdal's terms, may be haunted by anxieties about overwhelming pressures from more powerful states, however distant they may be.

Developing countries are not well equipped to influence in their favor international events, and they are frequently at the mercy of events beyond their control. They often have to give more attention to foreign policy than they would like, or than they are capable of sustaining. On the other hand, several charismatic leaders of new states, in the early years of independence, gave excessive attention to foreign affairs and tried, with varying degrees of success, to use foreign policy for diversionary purposes, to gain prestige at home, to divert attention from internal problems and conflicts, or to promote national unity and integration.[5] Involvement in interstate conflict is a hazardous but not uncommon phenomenon for certain new states. At times this may have unifying effects internally, but this is not always the case. As Lloyd Jensen points out,

the utility of interstate conflict for diversionary purposes is dependent upon whether or not external threats can unify the population as a whole or whether it merely integrates the majority, while widening the breach with the minority. . . . The utilization of interstate conflict for diversionary purposes will also depend upon the level of economic progress whether or not an elite finds it necessary to take advantage of the short-term unifying capabilities of external conflict.

4. See Andrew W. Scott, *The Revolution in Statecraft: Informal Penetration* (New York: Random House, 1965). See also the chapter by Ralph Braibanti in this volume.

5. See W. Howard Wriggins, *The Ruler's Imperative: Strategies for Political Survival in Asia and Africa* (New York: Columbia University Press, 1969), esp. chap. 12.

The central question, as Jensen indicates, is that of "the exact relationship between internal political stability and interstate conflict."[6]

Students of international affairs are giving a great deal of attention to the question of the relationship between domestic and foreign conflict behavior.

Conventional wisdom seems to assume that there is a fairly direct and visible relationship between internal and external instability and conflict behavior. This relationship seems to be affected, in part, by the level of development of a political system, by the spill-over effects of internal disorders, by the extent to which national leaders try to divert attention from internal problems, by external adventurism, by the general nature of the external as well as internal environment, by types of conflict situations, and many other factors.[7]

Thus far, however, the findings are tentative, and frequently conflicting.[8]

The relationship between foreign policy and political development seems to be affected by the level of development of a state. This may be

a major factor in determining the type and style of that state's foreign policy, and indeed its overall external and internal behavior. . . . Two interesting questions to explore are: (1) Does the same state behave in different ways in the international system as its political and economic development evolves? (2) Do states at different levels of development behave in different ways in their international relations? Quite likely the answer to both questions is broadly in the affirmative.[9]

6. Lloyd Jensen, "Levels of Political Development and Interstate Conflict in South Asia," in Richard Butwell, ed., *Foreign Policy and the Developing Nation* (Lexington: University of Kentucky Press, 1969), pp. 205, 206.

7. Palmer, *op. cit.*, p. 266.

8. For a summary of some of these findings, especially those of Rudolph J. Rummel, Raymond Tanter, and Jonathan Wilkenfield, see *ibid.*, pp. 266–69; and Jonathan Wilkenfield, ed., *Conflict Behavior and Linkage Politics* (New York: David McKay, 1973).

9. Palmer, *op. cit.*, p. 265. See also Ivo K. and Rosalind L. Feierabend, "Levels of Development and International Behavior," in Butwell, ed., *op. cit.*, pp. 137, 143, 157, and 161.

"Foreign policy, therefore, is closely related to political development, and to the internal environment of a political system, as well as to the external behavior of a state."[10] But it is well to remember that foreign policy is a projection of the internal dynamics of a political system and has no independent existence or raison d'être. As Rudolph Rummel has noted, "participation in the international system is internally derived behavior. Participation is a resultant of the properties of a nation."[11]

These observations about the relationship of foreign policy and political development have a particular relevance to Pakistan.[12] Pakistan's foreign policy can usefully be analyzed from the point of view of this relationship and of such collateral approaches as the use of Indo-Pakistan conflicts for diversionary purposes, the effects of these conflicts on the internal scene, the impact of external pressures on internal politics and behavior, the relation of internal and external conflict behavior, and the spillover effects of civil war and internal violence, notably during the crisis of 1971, which began as an internal conflict, speedily expanded into a major crisis in Indo-Pakistan relations, and eventually took on larger international dimensions.

Ideological Confusion

Because the foreign policy of a nation-state and the nature of its participation in the international system are, in Rum-

---

10. Palmer, *op. cit.*, p. 270.

11. Rudolph J. Rummel, "Some Dimensions in the Foreign Policy of Nations," in James N. Rosenau, ed., *International Politics and Foreign Policy* (New York: The Free Press, rev. ed., 1969), pp. 611–12.

12. This point has been well brought out by Khalid B. Sayeed: "The foreign policy of a developing country has a decisive impact on political development. Pursuing an ambitious or independent foreign policy may help a country like Pakistan to promote national consensus or integration. . . . The government of Pakistan has also tried to rally support internally by pointing out that as a result of its independent foreign policy, Pakistan has become an influential country in international politics." *The Political System of Pakistan* (Boston: Houghton Mifflin, 1967), p. 289.

mel's words, "a resultant of the properties of a nation,"
the special "properties" and peculiar features of Pakistan
are highly relevant. From the beginning, as Ian Stephens
has pointed out, there was "confusion about the nature of the
Pakistani state, which has since perplexed not only foreigners, but many Pakistanis themselves."[13] This confusion
arising from the geographical and cultural division of pre-
1972 Pakistan has been largely resolved in the more compact
and integrated Pakistan that remains after the traumatic
events of 1971. But some forms of ideological confusion are
still apparent.

The ideological confusion was noticeable when the idea of
Pakistan was first publicized and in the years immediately
following the attainment of nationhood. Pakistan was conceived as an "Islamic state." But what was an "Islamic state"
in the twentieth-century world? To what extent would the
Pakistan nation be governed by the principles of Islam? Who
would determine whether Pakistan was following the true
Islamic path? There was even a Homeric battle, much of
which went on behind the scenes, that had broad societal as
well as religious and political implications and centered on
the desirability of creating a separate political unit at all.
Even Iqbal seemed to have reservations on this crucial issue.
As Sarwar Hasan pointed out, "Although Iqbal was the first
front-rank Muslim leader to put forward the idea of a separate
Muslim state. . . . [he] denounced the notion of territorial
nationalism as inconsistent with the Islamic conception of a
universal brotherhood."[14] Both concepts — nationalism and
Islamic unity — have been powerful factors in the evolving
world of modern Islam, and most Muslims apparently have
not found them irreconcilable on a pragmatic level. But to
many orthodox *ulema* the idea of cutting the seamless web of
Islam into distinct national fragments was close to anathema.

13. Ian Stephens, *Pakistan* (London: Ernest Benn, 3rd ed., 1967), p. 26.
14. K. Sarwar Hasan, *Pakistan and the United Nations* (New York: Manhattan
Publishing Co., 1960), pp. 29, 28.

This raises aspects of the Pakistani scene that foreign observers find hard to understand, and that seem to account in large part for the peculiar nature of the Pakistan state. Ian Stephens has called attention to the obvious gap between Western-educated Pakistanis and the more locally oriented Muslims of the countryside and how they pose dilemmas for the interested student of subcontinental affairs:

. . . the theologians, whom Westerners usually assume encouraged the concept [of Pakistan], actually opposed it almost to a man: not merely because those who advocated it were reformers, but on the broader ground of principle that it was nationalist, and nationalism, by implying fragmentation of the Muslim world into separate States, runs counter to Islamic theory. Indeed we may find in Pakistan, when experienced enough to know where to look for it, a strange, and for the connoisseur fascinating barrier between her professed theologians and her Westernized upper-middle classes, such as probably no other "under-developed" Afro-Asian country can offer. . . . This anomaly, a by-product of scholastic events in the later nineteenth century, explains much of the otherwise unpredictable quality of Pakistani national life, who [*sic*] so baffles many Western observers.[15]

To a student of international relations Pakistan offers a fascinating example of a political unit that has been both more and less than a nation-state. It has been more than a nation-state as a result of what might be called the extranational loyalties and identifications of many of its citizens and persisting uncertainties about its place in the larger world of Islam. As S. M. Burke has observed: "The unification of a part only of the Muslims of the world under the flag of Pakistan was thus not viewed by the founding fathers of Pakistan as the culmination of their efforts but merely as a necessary milestone on the journey towards the ultimate goal of universal Muslim solidarity."[16] Over the years the search for Pakistan's integrity, security, and identity became in-

15. Stephens, *op. cit.*, p. 26.
16. S. M. Burke, *Pakistan's Foreign Policy: An Historical Analysis* (London: Oxford University Press, 1973), p. 65.

creasingly emphasized, and the goal of Islamic unity, at least through political means, became increasingly remote. Moreover, most other Muslim states seemed to have less difficulty than Pakistan did, at least in the formative years, in reconciling their allegiance to the concept of Islamic unity with their functioning as nation-states. Gradually, most Pakistanis came to accept the prevailing pattern, whatever the reservations or qualms of many of its more religiously orthodox citizens, few of whom ever filled top positions in the Pakistan state. In the political arena the emphasis in the Muslim world seems to be less on the nebulous concept of Islamic unity in a non-national or supranational sense, and more on the promotion of "solidarity among Muslim Countries," to quote the language of the Lahore Declaration of February 24, 1974.

Pakistan has been less than a nation-state in the sense that it has never been able to resolve satisfactorily the basic problems of national integration and identity. It has had considerable success in state-building, but little success in nation-building, a defect that eventually led to the break-up of the Pakistan that came into existence in 1947. Its retarded development as a nation-state has affected the course and effectiveness of its foreign policy. It is difficult for a new nation to project a clear and strong image abroad when its image at home is still unclear, or to carry out an effective foreign policy when the nature of the political system is still so uncertain. Pakistan was never able to evolve a political system that seemed suited to its conditions and needs, although leaders like Jinnah and Ayub Khan appeared to have certain definite ideas about the kind of political system they thought the country should have. Its foreign policy, therefore, revolved around the related issues of national security and relations with India. It further distorted its quest by pursuing illusory goals, such as a larger role in the Islamic world than other Muslim states were willing to concede, or by playing a more influential position in regional and world affairs than its internal weaknesses and limited capabilities would seem to warrant.

Factors Conditioning Pakistan's Foreign Policy

Any analysis of the constants and variables in Pakistan's foreign policy must give some attention to the factors conditioning that policy. It is not necessary for present purposes to analyze at length the major conditioning factors. Three, however, stand out: namely, the historical, the geopolitical, and the ideological. The first two are basic factors conditioning the foreign policy of any state; the third is of considerable importance for most states, and of particular importance for some, including Pakistan.

Historical Background

Pakistani interpretations of the historical background of Pakistan are available in the four-volume *A History of the Freedom Movement* and in many other works.[17] These interpretations invariably stress the difficulties that the Muslims of the subcontinent experienced both with the majority Hindus and with the British. Some of the more balanced commentators would, however, agree with Khalid B. Sayeed that "the Muslim separatist movement that eventually culminated in the creation of Pakistan [was] not due just to Hindu short-sightedness and exclusiveness, or wrong tactical moves by the Congress Party in its dealings both with the British and the Muslim League," nor was it "a product entirely of British machinations."[18] The roots of Pakistan, it seems, are

17. I. H. Qureshi, *A History of the Freedom Movement* (Karachi: Pakistan Historical Society, 1970, 4 vols.).
18. Khalid B. Sayeed, *Pakistan: The Formative Phase* (London: Oxford University Press, 1968), p. vi.

to be sought mainly in fundamental Hindu-Muslim differences separating two ways of life and two civilizations.
These differences were accentuated and highlighted by the
varying experience of Muslims and Hindus during the period
from the "Mutiny" of 1857 to partition and independence in
1947. Among major events or aspects may be mentioned the
harsh treatment of the Muslims after the "Mutiny," the teachings and influence of Sir Sayyid Ahmad Khan, with his emphasis on Muslim separatism and dignity, the experience of
the two major organizations in the "freedom movement," the
Indian National Congress, which always included some
Muslims, and the Muslim League, which after a period of
initial if limited cooperation with the Congress was alienated
from the mainstream of the Indian independence struggle.
The partition of Bengal and its aftermath, the granting of
separate electorates, the Khilafat movement, and the role
of Mohammad Ali Jinnah, including his relations with the
Congress, with Gandhi, Nehru, and other Congress leaders,
were also important. More particularly, the provincial elections of 1936–37 and the subsequent refusal of the Congress
to allow members of the Muslim League to join any of its
ministries were watershed events. The latter decision, according to I. H. Qureshi, who reflects a widespread Muslim
view, "hastened the final rupture between the Congress and
the Muslim League and paved the way for Pakistan."[19]
The different attitudes and treatment of the Congress and the
League by the British during the Second World War also
played a part.

A very important aspect of the historical background is to
be found in the immediate circumstances leading to independence and partition, during the final stages of the transfer
of power, and the tragic aftermath of partition. All of these
aspects need further examination; they are obviously important pages in the Pakistan story. But sooner or later, one

19. Qureshi, *op. cit.*, "Introductory."

comes back to the basic factor of Hindu-Muslim differences, which were deep-seated and which proved to be irreconcilable, and whose roots, as Dr. Qureshi has written, "spread into the entire history and volume of the relations between the two peoples."[20] As the independence movements reached their climax, these basic differences led to a political parting of the ways. "In the main," concludes Khalid B. Sayeed, "Pakistan was the end product of Muslim anxiety at first to establish cultural and political autonomy within the framework of a federal India, and later of their bold assertion that Muslims, being a separate nation, must have sovereign status."[21] The famous "Two Nation Theory" was fundamental to the Muslim League's approach, but it was anathema to the leaders of the Indian National Congress. It has been a source of continued disagreement between India and Pakistan and has accounted in part for the insistence of Pakistan on equality of status and treatment with India in almost every respect. But the theory emerged as a guiding doctrine only in the later stages of the freedom movement. The fundamental reasons for Pakistan are to be sought in deeper causes, such as those that Sayeed has described. An even stronger statement of these fundamental reasons is presented by Qureshi:

. . . the phenomenal conception of Pakistan as an ideal . . . was the result of the instinctive attitudes of the Muslim community built up during the entire course of its history. What had been felt all the time in its subconscious, now came out into the open, removing all the cobwebs of confusion, making it as clear as daylight to the Muslims that their real destiny was neither a second class citizenship in a uninational Hindu state, nor even the doubtful partnership in a multinational India where the majority would consist of the Hindus whose most "nationalist" and liberal wing was represented by the Congress, but a separate nationhood with a separate homeland.[22]

20. *Ibid.*
21. Sayeed, *op. cit.*, p. 8.
22. Qureshi, *op. cit.*, p. 18.

Most standard Pakistani interpretations of the historical background and roots of Pakistan stress these points. It can only be conjectured to what extent this interpretation is based on myth, and to what extent it is based on reality. But whether myth or reality, it is the generally accepted Pakistani answer to the basic question, "Why Pakistan?"

Geopolitical Factors

Geopolitical factors have shaped the foreign as well as the internal policies of Pakistan. The importance of these factors is obvious to anyone familiar with the geography and history of South Asia. Pakistan's two wings were separated by a thousand miles of territory belonging to a larger, more powerful, and often hostile neighbor; its western wing was bounded by the historic invasion routes on the northwest and by India to the east. The western wing also lay in close proximity to the Soviet Union, China, and the Muslim states of the Middle East. By contrast, its eastern wing was almost completely surrounded by Indian territory and oriented toward Southeast Asia. The importance of its geopolitical position is suggested by the following factual observations of G. W. Choudhury:

> . . . Pakistan has inherited the traditional frontiers of this subcontinent. She is strategically located both in South and South East Asia as well as in [the] Middle East. Apart from the traditional frontiers of the subcontinent she is confronted with the task of safeguarding nearly three thousand miles of "inward frontier" with her bigger neighbor. It is this inward frontier which has caused real worries and anxieties to the foreign policy-makers in Pakistan.[23]

Ayub Khan, perhaps because of his military experience and interests, was particularly aware of the geopolitical factors conditioning Pakistan's foreign and defense policies. His two chapters on foreign policy in his autobiographical work,

23. G. W. Choudhury, "Pakistan Foreign Policy," unpublished paper, n.d., p. 4.

Friends Not Masters, are full of geopolitical reflections, as are many of his other writings and speeches. His geopolitical approach was broad, not confined simply to the frontiers of the subcontinent or to internal geopolitical considerations. For example, in an article in the American journal *Foreign Affairs* in 1960 he wrote: "As a student of war and strategy, I can see quite clearly the inexorable push of the north in the direction of the warm waters of the Indian Ocean."[24]

The present leader of Pakistan, Prime Minister Zulfikar Ali Bhutto, has also often called attention to geopolitical factors, which in his view support Pakistan's claims to being a nation worthy of special attention and support. In an interview with a correspondent of the French news weekly *L'Expresse* in early January 1974, he took a strongly geopolitical approach in asserting these claims. He argued that resumption of military aid to Pakistan was essential in view of Pakistan's geographical position and strategic importance, that Pakistan should be viewed "in the larger context of the interests of foreign powers, the vitality and importance of the Indian Ocean and its proximity to the Gulf and to the Middle East," and that "if it is viewed from a broader perspective, the importance and value of Pakistan would become much more apparent."[25] Ayub often stated that the geopolitical factors in Pakistan's foreign policy were not sufficiently appreciated, either within Pakistan or by other countries. Prime Minister Bhutto would probably agree with him, although he seems to be more inclined than Ayub was to emphasize other factors, including the ideological.

Ideological Factors

The ideological factors in Pakistan's foreign policy are the most difficult to understand and to evaluate, at least for non-Pakistanis. As G. W. Choudhury has observed, "Pakistan has

24. Mohammed Ayub Khan, "Pakistan Perspective," *Foreign Affairs,* XXXVIII (July 1960), 556.
25. Quoted in *Weekly Commentary and Pakistan News Digest,* Jan. 11, 1974, p. 5.

always stressed its ideological foundations."[26] In 1960 Ayub Khan, no great ideologue himself, wrote that "prior to 1947, our nationalism was based more on an idea than on any territorial definition."[27] The Objectives Resolution of March 12, 1949, contained the flat assertion that Pakistan was conceived as a state to enable Muslims to order their lives in accordance with the teachings of Islam, as set forth in the Holy Quran and the Sunnah. In 1953 Mahmud Husain declared in the Constituent Assembly: "Pakistan exists only on the basis— that Muslims were a separate nation—and on no other basis."[28] It can be concluded that ideology is fundamental to the Pakistan experience, to the raison d'être of its origin and to its continued existence.

The ideology on which Pakistan is said to have been founded is of course Islam, and the country is a leading example of an ideological state in the modern world. Nevertheless, there is no consensus within Pakistan regarding the nature of the "Islamic state," and there is no agreement regarding the nature of Islamic ideology. As an elusive concept, it is subject to interpretations and applications. Moreover, after the Pakistani state was launched its leaders played down ideological aspects and emphasized more pragmatic and practical considerations. As Keith Callard noted, "The struggle for Pakistan was led by men of politics rather than by men of religion,"[29] and the same observation could be made regarding Pakistan's leadership since independence. Nonetheless, even secular leaders, because of necessity or belief, have repeatedly referred to Pakistan's ideological foundations. And all of Pakistan's constitutions have in varying degrees enshrined Islamic ideology as the basis of the state. Even the Quaid-i-Azam Mohammad Ali Jinnah, who

---

26. Choudhury, *op. cit.*, p. 17.
27. Ayub Khan, *op. cit.*, p. 549.
28. Constituent Assembly of Pakistan, *Debates*, XV (Oct. 28, 1963), 540.
29. Keith Callard, *Pakistan: A Political Study* (London: George Allen & Unwin, 1957), p. 225.

was not a religiously orthodox Muslim, changed his position in an address before the inaugural session of the Constituent Assembly of Pakistan on August 11, 1947. He first expressed the hope that "in the course of time Hindus would cease to be Hindus and Muslims would cease to be Muslims, not in the religious sense, . . . but in the political sense as citizens of the State."[30] However, he soon began to emphasize Pakistan's dedication to the principles of Islam, in politics as in religion.

The break-up of united Pakistan in 1971 showed that a common ideology was not enough to transcend antagonism between the two wings of the country. All the same, Pakistan's new leadership sensed the necessity for reviving an Islamic ideology, and Bhutto has long recognized the ideological bases of the nation. In 1966 he declared: "Pakistan is an ideological state, and one of its main ideas is to strengthen Islamic unity."[31] Since assuming control of Pakistan in December 1971, Bhutto has used ideological appeals to rally support to his government and to provide a basis for national unity. Although such appeals can damage minority rights in Pakistan, they could also assist the country in coping with its problem of identity. Indeed, it might even help improve its relations with the Muslim nations of the Middle East and Southeast Asia.

Closed Circles and Limited Debate (1947–58)

Pakistan has labored under special handicaps in trying to evolve and support a satisfactory foreign policy. As S. M. Burke has noted in this volume, foreign policy has generally been conducted by a small group within the power elite, with little participation by members of elected legislative bodies and even less by the citizenry. The press has given a

30. *Quaid-e-Azam Speaks* (Karachi: Pak Publicity, n.d.), p. 11; quoted in Sangat Singh, *Pakistan's Foreign Policy: An Appraisal* (Bombay: Asia Publishing House, 1970), p. 10.
31. Quoted in *Dawn*, April 20, 1966.

great deal of attention to questions of foreign policy, but it has generally supported (by choice or because of subtle or less-than-subtle forms of pressure) the prevailing policies of the administration in power. With notable exceptions, few scholars have had any role or influence in official circles.

The founder of Pakistan, Mohammed Ali Jinnah, was markedly vague in his infrequent statements on foreign policy as his interests and preoccupations were elsewhere. In one of his longest foreign policy statements he said:

> Our foreign policy is one of friendliness and goodwill toward all the nations of the world. We do not cherish aggressive designs against any country or nation. We believe in the principles of honesty and fair play in national and international dealings and are prepared to make our utmost contribution to the promotion of peace and prosperity among the nations of the world. Pakistan will never be found lacking in extending material and moral support to the oppressed and suppressed peoples of the world and upholding the principles of the U.N. Charter.[32]

Prime Minister Liaquat Ali Khan gave more attention to foreign policy. During his visit to the United States in 1950, for example, he made a number of statements, most of which were quite general in nature. In a significant address in 1951 he stated flatly that Pakistan was "neither tied to the apron strings of the Anglo-American bloc nor was she a camp-follower of the Communist bloc,"[33] despite the fact that Pakistan's orientation at that time was clearly more toward the West than toward the Soviet Union.

There was no significant debate in the National Assembly until 1957, ten years after independence. On February 22, 1957, Prime Minister H. S. Suhrawardy made the longest and most significant statement on Pakistan's foreign policy that had ever been presented to the National Assembly. Speaking for two hours to a full chamber and crowded galleries, Suhrawardy reviewed the entire gamut of Pakistan's foreign

32. *Quaid-i-Azam Jinnah Speeches* (Karachi: Pakistan Publishers, n.d.), p. 65.
33. Quoted in *Dawn*, March 9, 1951.

policy and made a strong defense of the policy of alignment with the United States. "Isolation," he declared, "cannot be the policy of a country that is liable to be attacked. We have, therefore, to have allies." At the end of three days of debate he made still another speech. Although praising Pakistan's major ally, the United States, he also warned: "Those who have been responsible for the foreign policy of America must have blushed to some extent at the encomiums which have been showered on them. Let it be a lesson to them that we are wholeheartedly with them. But we expect them also to be wholeheartedly with us."[34] At the close of the debate the members of the Assembly approved the foreign policy of the government by a vote of forty to two (with sixteen abstentions).

Other Factors

Other factors conditioning Pakistan's foreign policy could be listed. Among these would be the nature, personality, images, and beliefs of the country's top leaders. They profoundly affect perceptions of external threat and opportunity and influence the way statesmen assess advantages and costs. The procedures and organization for the conduct of foreign policy are touched on in the chapter by S. M. Burke. Of no small importance would be a detailed study of the nature of Pakistan's leadership and how it dominates foreign as well as domestic policy.

Objectives of Foreign Policy

National Integrity and Security

Although there are many constants in Pakistan's foreign policy, priorities have been altered during different periods, and tactics to promote these objectives have also changed.

34. Quoted in *Dawn*, Feb. 23 and 26, 1957.

The primary objective has been to preserve the integrity and security of Pakistan. This is entirely understandable as the new state was in jeopardy from its inception as an independent entity. As Liaquat Ali Khan told the National Press Club in Washington during his official visit to the United States in May 1950: "Our strongest interests, therefore, are firstly the integrity of Pakistan."[35] "The inevitable first object of foreign policy," wrote Keith Callard, "had to be to show the world that Pakistan was a reality and was capable of maintaining its independence."[36] Pakistan had an acute problem of identity and urgently sought recognition and acceptance in the early years of its existence.

Today it is again faced with the same problems, even though its boundaries, political system, and leadership are different. Allied with the necessity of convincing the outside world that it exists as an integrated and functioning nation-state is the problem of national security. Pakistan has been obsessed with the threat from its more powerful and generally hostile larger neighbor. Relations with India have been very complicated. As C. A. Salahuddin has observed, they are "a complex of social, religious, historical, political and psychological forces all tending in a sinister combination to antagonise the two states."[37] This "fixation" on India has in fact largely shaped Pakistan's relations with and attitude toward other countries. In his book, *Friends Not Masters*, President Ayub wrote: "We have an enemy, an implacable enemy in India," and he referred to "India's ambition to absorb Pakistan and turn her into a satellite."[38] On March 16, 1966, at Rajshahi, he declared: "The crux of the problem between India and Pakistan was that leaders of India had not

35. Quoted in Liaquat Ali Khan, *Pakistan, the Heart of Asia* (Cambridge: Harvard University Press, 1950), p. 11.
36. Callard, *op. cit.*, p. 303.
37. C. A. Salahuddin, "Pakistan's Policy in the United Nations on the Political Settlement of the Italian Colonies" (M.A. thesis, Columbia University, 1954), p. 3.
38. Mohammad Ayub Khan, *Friends Not Masters* (London: Oxford University Press, 1967), pp. 52, 115.

yet reconciled themselves to the very existence of Pakistan."[39] The same idea has often been expressed by other leaders, including Z. A. Bhutto, who in the past has voiced his fears of India. On March 19, 1966, he asserted that "India cannot tolerate the existence of Pakistan" and that "In the destruction of Pakistan lay India's most sublime and finest dreams."[40]

In Pakistan's quest for security against India—a constant factor in its foreign policy—may be found the keys to the broad changes in Pakistan's foreign policy orientations since independence. This point has been illustrated by G. W. Choudhury:

> The quest for security had been the dominating factor in her foreign policy objectives. In search for security against a potential Indian threat, Pakistan turned to the Commonwealth and to the Muslim countries in the early years of her independence (1947–53); then she turned to the USA by entering into a number of bilateral and multilateral defensive pacts. Then in the 1960's Pakistan found that her Western allies had upset the balance of power in the subcontinent by arming India against China, arms which Pakistanis felt could well be used against them; the Russians also joined in helping the Indians in their huge military build-up after the Sino-Indian border conflicts of 1962. Pakistan, therefore, turned to new friends, if not allies, in her same search for security.[41]

Islamic Unity and Close Relations with Muslim Countries

The quest for national integrity and security, particularly vis-à-vis India, has been the primary and most constant theme in Pakistan's foreign policy. An important secondary objective has been the cultivation of close relations with other Muslim countries, especially with the Muslim states of Southwest Asia. This effort has led to equal frustrations

39. As reported in *Morning News* (Dacca), March 17, 1966.
40. National Assembly of Pakistan, *Debates*, March 15, 1966, p. 496.
41. G. W. Choudhury, "The Major Powers and the Indian Subcontinent," unpublished manuscript, n.d., chap. 9, pp. 3–4.

and even greater variations of policy and approach. As Keith Callard noted many years ago:

... The principal secondary theme in foreign policy has been support for other Muslim countries, especially for Muslim colonial peoples seeking independence and for Arab countries against Israel. This policy, stressing the special bonds that unite Muslims, is a logical extension of the fundamental assertion of Muslim nationhood in India. . . . The belief in the essential unity of purpose and outlook in the Muslim world has been an illusion that has been much cherished in Pakistan.[42]

This objective was clearly related to "the fundamental assertion of Muslim nationhood in India," to repeat Callard's words, and to the ideological underpinnings of the Pakistan state. In 1951

Prime Minister Liaquat Ali Khan eloquently expressed the true aspirations of all Pakistanis when he stated that Pakistan came into being as a result of the urge of the Muslims of the subcontinent to secure a territory where Islamic ideology could be practiced and demonstrated to the world, and since a cardinal feature of this ideology [was] to make Muslim brotherhood a reality, it was a part of her mission to do everything in her power to promote fellowship and cooperation between Muslim countries.[43]

From the very beginning, and more particularly since 1949, Pakistan made efforts to come closer to the Muslim countries of West Asia and to bring Muslim governments closer together. An unofficial Muslim World Conference was organised in Karachi which was attended in February 1949 by delegates from 19 Muslim countries. Prime Minister Liaquat Ali Khan emphasised in London in May 1949 that Muslim nations between Cairo and Karachi could play an important role between the two power blocs. . . . The same year, the President of the Muslim League . . . visited West Asian countries to promote the idea of an Islamic bloc. In November 1949 the first International Islamic Economic Conference was held in Karachi, and was presented with a major presidential address by Ghulam Mohammad, the Finance Minister of Pakistan. . . . At the second Muslim World Conference held in

42. Callard, *op. cit.*, pp. 18, 314.
43. Burke, *op. cit.*, p. 65.

Karachi in February 1951, Prime Minister Liaquat Ali Khan talked of Pakistan's "mission . . . to do everything in its power to promote closer fellowship and cooperation between Muslim countries." In early 1952 Pakistan's Muslim Peoples' Organisation held a conference attended by delegates from several Muslim countries. In 1949 and 1952 abortive attempts were also made by Pakistan to arrange official or inter-governmental Islamic conferences. In 1953 an attempt was similarly made to set up a permanent consultative organization of Muslim states. Contacts with heads of State and Prime Ministers of Muslim countries were maintained through frequent visits. Pakistan similarly championed the Arab cause against Israel and otherwise tried to support every Muslim cause in the United Nations.[44]

Most of these efforts proved to be abortive, however, and produced disillusionment and frustration in Pakistan. "The belief in the essential unity of purpose and outlook in the Muslim world," to use Callard's words, did indeed prove to be "an illusion."[45] Other Muslim states did not take the same view of the relation between religion and nationalism, and the concepts of Islamic unity and brotherhood were less decisive on the political level than national interests and priorities. While "Pakistan sought to build an Islamic bloc and to obtain friendship and support of Muslim countries which could be mobilized against its principal enemy, India,"[46] the leaders of most Muslim states wanted to avoid involvement in Indo-Pakistan disputes. Indeed, Gamal Abdel Nasser seemed more sympathetic with and closer to India than to Pakistan.

Relations have been cool with the neighboring Muslim state of Afghanistan. Tensions have often erupted in border skirmishes, and occasionally have caused the severance of diplomatic relations. The Pakhtunistan issue that Afghanistan has intermittently pressed, allegedly with the encourage-

44. D. C. Jha, "Pakistan's Foreign Policy: An Analytical Study," *The Indian Journal of Political Science*, XXXI (April–June 1970), 123.

45. Callard, *op. cit.*, p. 314.

46. Jha, *op. cit.*, p. 123.

ment of the Soviet Union, has seriously complicated Pakistan-Afghanistan relations. Pakistan has enjoyed better relations with the non-Arab Muslim states of West Asia, i.e., Turkey and Iran. The three countries have been associated with CENTO since 1955 and the Regional Cooperation for Development (RCD) since 1964. Turkey, however, is distant in more than a geographic sense, while the Shah of Iran provides tangible and intangible support to Pakistan but also shows interest in India. Moreover, the Shah's actions around the Persian Gulf make the Pakistanis uneasy. A special relationship seemed to be developing with Indonesia during the Sukarno era; and references were sometimes made to a "Peking-Djakarta-Pindi axis." But Sukarno's fall neutralized this effort. Nevertheless, these two largest Muslim countries are friendly toward one another.

Pakistan has been disappointed with its program of Islamic unity, more so because it did not receive significant support in its conflict with India. Disillusionment with the Muslim states forced Pakistan in 1953–55 to turn to the West for support. This turn caused the country to enter into mutual security agreements with and to accept military aid from the United States. It also led Pakistan to join the Baghdad Pact (CENTO) and later SEATO, even though these actions alienated Pakistan from the Arab countries and dimmed any hope for close Muslim cooperation.

When Pakistan became disillusioned with its Western allies in the early 1960s, it turned to a policy of "bilateralism" and began to cultivate the People's Republic of China and the Soviet Union without severing its ties with the United States. It also renewed efforts at developing satisfactory relations with the Arab states. Pakistan was disappointed with the lack of Western support during the Indo-Pakistan war of 1965. However, it did receive sympathy and military assistance from some Arab countries as well as from its RCD partners, Turkey and Iran, during the crisis of 1971.

Since Bhutto assumed control of Pakistan in December

1971, the Southwest Asian orientation of his foreign policy has been particularly marked. "President Bhutto's first visit abroad after the war was paid to Afghanistan and the next to the Middle East and North Africa, and he called these travels 'a journey among brothers.'"[47] Deprived of its eastern wing and more than half of its population, and facing an even stronger India, Pakistan needs good relations with both the United States and the Soviet Union. But only China appears to be a steadfast supporter. Therefore, Pakistan is bound to look more and more to Southwest Asia and the world of Islam. Some Pakistani spokesmen go so far as to assert that Pakistan should consider itself a Southwest Asian as much as a South Asian state. This approach may provide balm for hurt pride, but it remains to be seen whether it can provide Pakistan with real security.

The Islamic Summit Conference, held with great pomp and publicity in Lahore on February 22–24, 1974, gave Pakistan an occasion for reaffirmation of Islamic unity and solidarity as well as an opportunity to cement its ties with other Muslim countries. Pakistan also reaffirmed its support of the Arab cause in the Middle East. In addition, the conference became the vehicle for the recognition of Bangladesh by Pakistan. In his address opening the historic conference, Prime Minister Bhutto said that the Muslim countries were now able to play "a most constructive role" in promoting cooperation among themselves and with the other Third World countries, and that the time for translating the concept of Islamic unity into concrete programs had arrived. "Let not posterity say," he urged, "we were presented with an historic, possibly unrepeatable, opportunity to release ourselves from the injustices inflicted on us for many centuries and we proved ourselves unequal to it."[48] In the Lahore Declaration, issued at the conclusion of the conference, "the

47. Burke, *op. cit.*, p. 407.
48. Quoted in *Weekly Commentary and Pakistan News Digest*, March 8, 1974, p. 6.

Kings, Heads of State and Government and the Representatives of the Islamic countries and Organisations" proclaimed "their determination to preserve and promote solidarity among Muslim countries, to respect each other's independence and territorial integrity, to refrain from interference in each other's internal affairs, to resolve their differences through peaceful means in a fraternal spirit and, whenever possible to utilize the mediatory influence or good offices of a fraternal Muslim State or States for such resolution."[49] Thus, the Declaration subscribed both to the goals of Islamic solidarity and to that of national independence.

The Long Search: An Evaluation

In 1962 Pakistan began turning away from its alliances and close relations with the United States. It was moving toward a policy that was later characterized as "bilateralism" but was really a mixture of disillusionment with past policies and "friends" and also a realistic reappraisal of changing circumstances. At that time, Mahmud Husain concluded his remarks at a symposium on foreign policy by saying: "I have a feeling that Pakistan is still in search of a foreign policy which should help us in safeguarding our national interests. Unfortunately, so far we have not had a settled foreign policy. This is a precarious situation."[50] And the search for a viable foreign policy continued without attaining the "settled foreign policy" that Mahmud Husain had hoped for; now under Prime Minister Bhutto this search continues. Wayne

49. The text of the Lahore Declaration of February 24, 1974, is given in *ibid.*, pp. 15–19.
50. Mahmud Husain, "Concluding Remarks," in L. A. Sherwani et al., *Foreign Policy of Pakistan* (Karachi: The Allies Book Corporation, 1964), pp. 97, 98. Professor Husain made this comment at the conclusion of a symposium on Pakistan's foreign policy, conducted by the Department of International Relations, University of Karachi, in March 1962.

Wilcox, to whose memory this volume is fittingly dedicated, noted:

> Judged against any reasonable criteria, Pakistan's foreign policy for the first twenty five years of its independence has been creative and successful . . . it brought more economic and military support than Pakistan's resources, power and importance would appear to justify, and it did so while allowing the consistent pursuit of Pakistan's interests *vis-a-vis* India.[51]

Much depends, no doubt, on the resolution of the question of what are "reasonable criteria" for judging the foreign policy of Pakistan. Under the circumstances of internal weaknesses and divisions, changing political structures and leadership, and external pressures and dangers, Pakistan's record in foreign policy could be described as a truly remarkable one. It might be argued that at least during the heyday of its alignment, and perhaps at the present time, the country, in its different forms, has been able to evolve "settled" foreign policies that are well suited to promote basic national objectives. But the story of Pakistan is, in general, a sad, and even tragic one, whatever its successes at various times. And since its foreign policies were mainly projections of domestic policies and of political experiments which eventually, whatever their temporary successes, did not work, it is hard now to give very high marks to many major aspects of its national achievements. After all, even Pakistan's "economic miracle" did not last long. In the area of politics and foreign policy "miracles" were even fewer and generally proved to be mirages. Hence it may be wiser to continue to suspend judgment on the success or failure of Pakistan's foreign policy to date, and to take the more detached view that for Pakistan the search for a viable foreign policy, as indeed for a viable basis of national organization and existence, goes on, with the outcome still very much in doubt.

51. Wayne A. Wilcox, "Pakistan," in Wayne A. Wilcox, Leo E. Rose, and Gavin Boyd, eds., *Asia and the International System* (Cambridge, Mass.: Winthrop, 1972), pp. 113, 114.

15

The Research Potential of Pakistan's Development

Ralph Braibanti

I

Concepts of political development emerged significantly in American thought from 1960 to 1974 and, measured by published analysis, reached a peak from 1966 to 1972. This period coincided with depressed official American interest in Pakistan, and an unsympathetic Pakistani attitude toward American research in that country. The end of the peak period and after (1970–74) was marked by an emotionally charged preoccupation of relevant American scholarship with the trauma surrounding the secession of East Pakistan. This unfortunate conjunction of the near maturation of an important idiom in American intellectual history, i.e., development theory, with a sequence of attitudinal changes and events in the world of realpolitik results in a condition almost entirely excluding Pakistan from consideration as a major political system in the main corpus of political development analytics. Thus, development theory is deprived of Pakistan's explanatory potential for influencing, corroborating, or disproving generalizations which, in characteristic fits of intellectual hubris, are often accorded canonical status.

The discontinuity between experience in political development and rumination about the development process is an obvious and oft-reported deficiency. In the perennial reconstruction of intellectual perspectives this dialectic appears inevitable, for congruence between reality and its abstraction for analysis is uncommonly achieved. Nor is it necessarily aided by cybernetic technology, for the spiraling universe of referrents oscillating between psychic, physiological, and sociological determinants and spatially from tribal to global arenas outpaces cybernetic capacity to order, retrieve, and interpret perennially changing perspectives.

It is useless to dwell on the reasons for disarticulation of experience and concept-building or on the failure to relate the experience of Pakistan not only to concept-building but even to textbook or casebook exegesis. Rather, Section III of this chapter deals with positive measures for the correction of this condition.

In academic comparative studies we face a remarkable opportunity for transfer of insights and experience from one culture area to another. The gradual abandonment of structures of knowledge based on an area approach is, in many ways, a distinct advantage to the scholar. The universe of comparable phenomena thus easily crosses cultural lines that we find to be far more permeable than we imagined and, indeed, far more artificial than real.

II

There are several indicators of this sterile condition of scholarship on Pakistan. (1) The total number of major works relating to political development published in the United States and England approximates 120, about a third of which are collections of articles earlier published in journals. This total includes the work of such sociologists as Eisenstadt, Myrdal, and Nettl, and economists such as Millikan and Rostow who crossed the threshold to political analysis. It also includes the seven-volume series of the Committee on Comparative Politics of the Social Science Research Council and the ten-volume series on development administration of the Comparative Administration

Group of the American Society for Public Administration. Further, it includes ten SAGE Professional Papers in the SAGE Comparative Politics Series, which began publication in 1970 and now totals sixty volumes. Here the selection of the ten SAGE volumes is somewhat arbitrary since most of the sixty volumes are peripherally related to development problems. The ten selected (listed in note 15 in this chapter) deal explicitly and exclusively with political development.

Not included among these 120 volumes are substantial works exclusively on Pakistan. Of these there are many — some of a high order of analysis — published in the United States, England, Pakistan, and India. Their exclusion arises from a generic difference, i.e., they are discrete country analyses with no analytical synaptic bond with the main corpus of development theory. Of these 120 volumes there are approximately thirteen specifically using case materials that might easily and advantageously have included Pakistan as a referrent. Some of these thirteen use cases merely as examples, often in appendices, loosely connected or even unconnected with analysis in the text. A few articulate with varying degrees of rigor the case experience to a paradigm explicated in the text. Only three of these works make use of Pakistan's twenty-nine year experience in any systematic or significant way.[1] These three do not include books of readings in which Pakistan is treated marginally, e.g., Fickett's reader in which only six pages are devoted to Pakistan.[2]

This pervasive omission of a political system that for nearly

1. These are Gabriel A. Almond and James S. Coleman, eds., *The Politics of the Developing Areas* (Princeton: Princeton University Press, 1960); Douglas E. Ashford, *National Development and Local Government Reform: Political Participation in Morocco, Tunisia and Pakistan* (Princeton: Princeton University Press, 1967); Gunnar Myrdal, *Asian Drama: An Inquiry into the Poverty of Nations* (New York: Pantheon, 1968), Vol. I.

2. Lewis P. Fickett, Jr., ed., *Problems of the Developing Nations* (New York: Thomas Y. Crowell, 1966).

a quarter century was the world's largest Muslim nation was certainly not due to its unimportance or to its analytical sterility. Indeed, the countries included as cases in the remaining ten volumes reveal no greater analytical potential than Pakistan. The following survey of use of these cases, arranged chronologically, suggests the absence of any superiority of potential. Silvert uses reports of the American Universities Field Staff from Afghanistan, Argentina, Bolivia, Brazil, Indonesia, Israel, India, Japan, the Philippines, Saudi Arabia, and South Africa.[3] Fickett includes cases from Algeria, Tunisia, India, Indonesia, and Thailand, and six pages on Pakistan. In the Finkle and Gable collection of readings, Ethiopia, Tunisia, Morocco, Sri Lanka, Turkey, and Japan are included.[4] In the reader edited by Welch, Iraq, Ghana, Uganda, Japan, Turkey, Iran, Sri Lanka, the Soviet Union, and the People's Republic of China are used as cases.[5] Shaffer and Prybyla draw on the experience of five countries: Japan, India, Israel, Egypt, and Yugoslavia.[6] Kebschull draws on materials from Africa and Latin America and abstracts the article by Marguerite J. Fisher, "New Concepts of Democracy in Southern Asia," in such a manner to include only India and (in unjustifiable expansion of the area—"Southern Asia") the Philippines.[7] Albinski draws on China, Japan, Indonesia, and India for cases.[8] Rostow, purporting to construct development theory based on global experience, scarcely mentions Pakistan, and his forty-six tables and charts

3. K. H. Silvert, ed., *Expectant Peoples: Nationalism and Development* (New York: Random House, 1963).

4. Jason L. Finkle and Richard W. Gable, eds., *Political Development and Social Change* (New York: John Wiley & Sons, 1966).

5. Claude E. Welch, Jr., ed., *Political Modernization: A Reader in Comparative Political Change* (Belmont, Calif.: Wadsworth, 1967).

6. Harry G. Shaffer and Jan S. Prybyla, eds., *From Underdevelopment to Affluence: Western, Soviet and Chinese Views* (New York: Appleton-Century-Crofts, 1968).

7. Harvey Kebschull, ed., *Politics in Transitional Societies* (New York: Appleton-Century-Crofts, 1968). See esp. pp. 141–48.

8. Henry S. Albinski, *Asian Political Processes: Essays and Readings* (Boston: Allyn and Bacon, 1971).

include none on Pakistani data.[9] This omission is made despite the Ford Foundation's quite reasonable judgment that as of 1965 "the documentary basis of Pakistan's development plans [was] considerably above that of most emerging countries."[10] Eisenstadt analyzes Burma, Sri Lanka, Thailand, India, Turkey, and the Maghrib.[11] Almond and his colleagues, "taking the historical cure," look to the history only of Britain, France, Germany, Mexico, Japan, and India.[12]

(2) A second indicator is the seven-volume series "Studies in Political Development" mentioned earlier. This series of approximately three thousand pages apportioned into some eighty chapters by a similar number of contributors has only one chapter of eighty-one pages on Pakistan.[13]

(3) The ten-volume series of the Comparative Administration Group suggests the same proportionate omission of Pakistan. This series consists of nearly 4,800 pages divided into some 124 chapters by a similar number of contributors.

9. W. W. Rostow, *Politics and the Stages of Growth* (Cambridge: Cambridge University Press, 1971).

10. Ford Foundation, *Design for Pakistan: A Report on Assistance to the Pakistan Planning Commission by the Ford Foundation and Harvard University* (New York: Ford Foundation, February 1965), p. 21.

11. S. N. Eisenstadt, ed., *Post-Traditional Societies* (New York: W. W. Norton, 1972). The omission of Pakistan is not due to classificatory delimitation since, according to the preface by Stephen R. Graubard, Pakistan is one of fifteen "principal" post-traditional societies (p. x). The book's dust cover claims that Pakistan is "treated" as a post-traditional society. Both statements are deceptive, however, for only peripheral attention is given to Pakistan on pages 147–149 and then only as an instance of efforts to "modernize" Islam.

12. Gabriel Almond, Scott Flanagan, Robert Mundt, eds., *Crisis, Choice and Change: Historical Studies in Political Development* (Boston: Little, Brown, 1973).

13. This series, published by Princeton University Press, includes Lucian W. Pye, ed., *Communications and Political Development* (1963); Joseph La Palombara, ed., *Bureaucracy and Political Development* (1963); Robert E. Ward and Dankwart A. Rustow, eds., *Political Modernization in Japan and Turkey* (1964); James S. Coleman, ed., *Education and Political Development* (1965); Lucian W. Pye and Sidney Verba, eds., *Political Culture and Political Development* (1965); Joseph La Palombara and Myron Weiner, eds., *Political Parties and Political Development* (1969); Leonard Binder et al., *Crises and Sequences in Political Development* (1971). The single chapter on Pakistan is Ralph Braibanti, "Public Bureaucracy and Judiciary in Pakistan," in La Palombara, ed., *Bureaucracy and Political Development*, pp. 360–441.

Only two chapters totaling fifty-eight pages make explicit use of Pakistan as a case reference.[14]

(4) The fourth indicator of this condition of Pakistan's use in comparative development analysis is the SAGE Comparative Politics Series, edited by Harry Eckstein, Ted Robert Gurr, and, since 1973, Aristide Zolberg. This series, with a heavy methodological orientation, is likely to be as influential as the SSRC and CAG series were in a broader configurative approach. Of the ten papers[15] dealing explicitly with political development methodology and in which it might

14. The first two volumes of this series were published by McGraw-Hill (New York City) and were part of the McGraw-Hill Series in International Development, which otherwise has a predominantly economic orientation: John D. Montgomery and William J. Siffin, eds., *Approaches to Development: Politics, Administration and Change* (1966); Bertram M. Gross, ed., *Action Under Planning* (1966). The third volume was published by SAGE Publications (Beverly Hills, California): Robert T. Daland, ed., *Comparative Urban Research* (1969). The remaining seven volumes, under the general editorship of Ralph Braibanti, were published by Duke University Press (Durham, North Carolina): Ralph Braibanti and Associates, *Political and Administrative Development* (1969); Dwight Waldo, ed., *Temporal Dimensions of Development Administration* (1970); Edward W. Weidner, *Development Administration in Asia* (1970); Allan Kornberg and Lloyd P. Musolf, eds., *Legislatures in Developmental Perspective* (1970); Fred W. Riggs, ed., *Frontiers of Development Administration* (1971); James Heaphey, ed., *Spatial Dimensions of Administrative Development* (1971); Clarence E. Thurber and Lawrence S. Graham, eds., *Development Administration in Latin America* (1973). The two chapters on Pakistan are Harry J. Friedman, "Administrative Roles in Local Governments," and Inayatullah, "Local Administration in a Developing Country: The Pakistan Case," both in Weidner, ed., *Development Administration in Asia*, pp. 251–300.

15. The ten papers surveyed here, all published by SAGE Publications, Beverly Hills, California, are M. C. Hudson, *Conditions of Political Violence and Instability* (1970); Sidney Verba, Norman H. Nie, and Jae-on Kim, *The Modes of Democratic Participation: A Cross-National Comparison* (1971); Lee Sigelman, *Modernization and the Political System: A Critique and Preliminary Empirical Analysis* (1971); Harry Eckstein, *The Evaluation of Political Performance: Problems and Dimensions* (1971); Ted Robert Gurr and Muriel McClelland, *Political Performance: A Twelve-Nation Study* (1971); Roland F. Moy, *A Computer Simulation of Democratic Political Development: Tests of the Lipset and Moore Models* (1971); Ronald Rogowski and Lois Wasserspring, *Does Political Development Exist? Corporatism in Old and New Societies* (1971); James R. Scarritt, *Political Development and Culture Change Theory: A Propositional Synthesis with Application to Africa* (1972); Andrew J. Sofrank and Robert C. Bealer, *Unbalanced Modernization and Domestic Instability: A Comparative Analysis* (1972); Robert B. Stauffer, *Nation-Building in a Global Economy: The Role of the Multinational Corporation* (1973).

have been feasible and rewarding to incorporate Pakistan as a case, that country is not used either substantially or marginally. One of the ten papers is an important study of twelve nations in which an effort is made to evaluate political performance. Pakistan is not one of the twelve, although Colombia, Tunisia, the Philippines, and Mexico are.[16] In another study Pakistan is listed among the 115 nations used in the Banks and Textor survey—a list commonly used in research of this type.[17] But this inclusion is routine; neither Pakistan nor any other country is singled out for special analysis. Hence, this listing does not in the least invalidate the argument presented here.

(5) It is revealing also to ascertain the extent to which Pakistan's experience has been fed back into United States foreign assistance operations. An assessment of this influence is more difficult to make. The principal entity for bridging academic work on development and government foreign assistance programs is the Southeast Asia Development Advisory Group (SEADAG), administered by the Asia Society under contract with the United States Agency for International Development[18] (USAID).

Because assistance to Vietnam was a major activity of USAID for many years, the budgetary policy funding SEADAG made it applicable only to the geographical area that embraced Vietnam, i.e., Southeast Asia. By definition, Pakistan was not included. For this reason, no research or even extended reference to Pakistan is found in the 114 mimeographed *SEADAG Papers* that appeared from 1965 through September 1974. *SEADAG Papers*, presented at international seminars and subsequently revised in the light

16. Gurr and McClelland cited in n. 15 above.
17. Sigelman cited in n. 15 above.
18. A more detailed analysis of SEADAG can be found in Ralph Braibanti, "External Inducement of Political-Administrative Development—An Institutional Strategy," in Braibanti, ed., *Political and Administrative Development*, cited in n. 14 above, pp. 26–30.

of seminar discussion, are a significant indicator of development thought in the SEADAG operation. The exclusion of Pakistan as well as East and South Asian countries because of budgetary-definitional limitations has been unrealistic and unfortunate. The Asia Society had proposed to USAID a revised contract for its operation beginning in 1975 that would have converted SEADAG into an Asian Development Advisory Program (ADAP). ADAP was to have included South and East Asia as well as the South Pacific. This proposal was not approved; hence, research structure with potential for relating Pakistan's development to United States foreign aid activity will continue not to exist. The implication should not be drawn that this proposal would have made Pakistan's experience meaningful or influential, but only that a base would have been built. It should be noted that, quite apart from SEADAG, other means, largely unstructured, exist within USAID for relating Pakistan's experience to that agency's development policy. Since the AID program in Pakistan has been (with Vietnam, Taiwan, and South Korea) one of the largest and oldest of the AID programs, Pakistan's experience has had informal influence through transfer of personnel who worked in Pakistan and by means of policy-formulation structures generally. That influence, however, is dependent upon the internal efficacy of policy formation processes of USAID.

(6) A similar state of affairs is found in British scholarship. The Institute for Development Studies, created in 1966 at the University of Sussex primarily by the Ministry of Overseas Development, has given little attention to Pakistan in its 120 papers issued as *IDS Communications Series*.[19] Its most ambitious undertaking relevant to this analysis was Shaffer's comparative evaluation of administrative training in four countries, one of which was Pakistan.[20] The Development

19. See reference in n. 18 above, pp. 30–32.
20. Bernard Shaffer, *Administrative Training and Development: A Comparative Study of East Africa, Zambia, Pakistan and India* (New York: Praeger, 1974).

Administration Group, which is part of the Department of Local Government and Administration at the University of Birmingham, has manifested equally little interest in Pakistan, if we use doctoral dissertations as an indicator. Of the twenty-four doctoral dissertations completed there from 1965 to 1973, only one was on Pakistan.[21] This condition of British scholarship persisted for a quarter-century despite Pakistan's membership in the Commonwealth. A mitigating circumstance was that interest in development as a process developed much later in Britain than in the United States. Indeed, only now in the 1970s do we find the ferment there that was characteristic of American scholarship in the 1960s. The earlier period in Britain was dominated by issues of post-colonialism, transfer of power, and historical memoirs of colonial officers. Some excellent studies moving toward conceptualization have appeared, among them *India and Ceylon: Unity and Diversity*,[22] edited by Philip Mason. Yet this volume itself epitomizes the condition here described. It was in Pakistan that the first successful secession occurred in the post-independence period—a case of diversity converting unity to disunity. Yet this otherwise excellent study is silent on modern Pakistan.

The six indices analyzed above suggest that this condition is worse than Pakistan specialists had imagined. This experiential discontinuity is a special loss to academic development thought since no other new nation which gained independence after 1947 has experienced the variety or the intensity of traumas that Pakistan has suffered. It is appropriate to survey these traumas briefly. (1) Pakistan is unique in having had four constitutions in a quarter of a century. These were the Indian Independence Act of 1947 (derivative juridically from the Government of India Act of 1935) and the con-

21. University of Birmingham, *Development Administration Group* (Birmingham, Feb. 1974), No. S.46305, pp. 10–11.
22. Philip Mason, ed., *India and Ceylon: Unity and Diversity* (London: Oxford University Press, 1967).

stitutions of 1956, 1962, and 1973. (2) No other new state has rearranged the crucial relationship of space, power, and culture four times — from five provinces to two (under the Establishment of West Pakistan Act, 1955) — then again to five provinces and, with the secession of East Pakistan, to four provinces. (3) No other state outside the communist system has tried to depart from the colonial heritage of local government and the global ideological suasion of community development theory by devising a structure — Basic Democracies — that, while not totally original, was an ingenious adaptation to cultural context. This emerged at a time when adaptation in the direction of indigenization was considered unmodish, even backward. Yet comparable efforts in other nations in the mid-1970s are applauded as "appropriate technology." (4) Pakistan was also the major exemplar of an effort to sedate the participation explosion while building institutional capability. This effort to control the timing of the sequence of phases of development, while doomed to failure, was nevertheless an experiment that might have tested a major hypothesis of development theorists, i.e., sequential rates of development in various sectors or phases. (5) Nor has any other new state changed its basic structure of government from a parliamentary to a presidential system, then returned to a parliamentary form and simultaneously adjusted from a unicameral to a bicameral legislative system. (6) As though these major changes in polity and power were not enough, there was also a long period in which both the legislative and political party processes were suspended. (7) These changes occurred within the context of two periods of martial law, three wars with India, including the only successful war of secession among new states in the post-independence period. (8) Further, few new nations (with the possible exceptions of South Korea, Taiwan, and South Vietnam) have had such a massive infusion of technological and economic aid from the United States or allied themselves in foreign policy so closely with that country. Nor have many

new nations so shrewdly and intelligently adjusted their foreign policy to a highly multilateral set of relations coupled
with a renaissance of Islamic connections, once the futility
of exclusivity with the United States was realized.

III

The condition described above for the past need not characterize the relationship between Pakistan and development
scholarship in the future. Indeed, this is a revolutionary moment in this nexus—a moment in which scholarly developments of the last quarter-century on this front can be dramatically reversed. The possibility of this reversal is affected by
several new attitudes and events. Foremost is the current
posture of the Government of Pakistan—more facilitative
of American research in Pakistan than at any other time in
twenty-nine years. Thus, in 1974 and 1975 all twenty-five
fellowships of the American Institute for Pakistan Studies,
created in 1973, submitted to the government were confirmed with no difficulty and visas were issued promptly at
the direction of the Prime Minister. During the summer of
1974, approximately ninety college and secondary school
teachers were on eight-week study tours in Pakistan. These,
combined with miscellaneous research awards, total somewhat more than one hundred American researchers in Pakistan almost at the same time in the summer of 1974. Even
during the regular academic year 1974–75, there were some
thirty predoctoral and senior researchers at work in Pakistan. When these figures are compared with those of a decade
ago when fewer than five researchers were there, the change
is obvious and requires no elaboration.

A second factor is the contraction and consolidation of the
cultural heartland of Pakistan resulting from the establishment of Bangladesh. This greatly simplifies research and
lessens the distortion and imprecision consequent to the

formulation of generalizations of proximate nationwide validity. No longer do we have to qualify our observations by limiting them to half the country. Nor do we have to immerse ourselves in two cultures and life-styles to understand one nation. The regionalization that exists can be exaggerated in the interest of national disunity and can be underestimated by euphoric nationalism. But on balance it is no more than that of Belgium, Lebanon, the United Kingdom, and certainly less than that of India. From the perspective of scholarly research, consolidation of a heartland with reinforced psychic and political bonds with the Middle East is a distinct advantage.

Third, both academic and operational perspectives of political development are changing. There is a movement away from the hubris of unilinear political growth ethnocentrically premised on Western models. Concurrently, in academic development studies especially, we perceive a gradual retreat from an ahistorical position as a search is made for the relevance of early development experiences of older nations. A teleological dimension is also in evidence, not exclusively generated by ecclesiastical sources such as Paul VI's *Populorum Progressio* of 1967 but arising also from segments of the radical youth movement of the 1960s with its emphasis on quality of life. This teleological dimension[23] – the disposition to ask "development for what?" – is analogous to the emergence of growth limitation notions in development economics and to anti-development thought generated by an awareness of the finitude of global resources.[24]

23. It is not inferred here that this teleological dimension is yet regnant in development literature. On the contrary, only four of the thirty formulations in the synoptic chart on pp. 455–62 can be said to be explicitly concerned with this dimension. They are Pennock, *Populorum Progressio*, Braibanti, and Goulet (items 16, 19, 22, 29). Nevertheless it is bound to be a major idiom in the course of the next decade in part for reasons analyzed in this chapter, pp. 440–54.

24. Salient differences between growth economics and political development as subdisciplines are analyzed in further detail in Ralph Braibanti, "The Relevance of Political Science to the Study of Underdeveloped Areas," in Ralph Braibanti and

Further, a national, if not global, mood of introspection and self-analysis conduces to a greater appreciation of man's psychic needs, the role of religion and tradition in nurturing such needs, and to the regenerative, even innovative, role of tradition. Intellectual accommodations among religions once antagonistic to each other are significantly emerging. A new perception of non-Christian religions by Christians is evident in both Roman Catholicism and in some Protestant denominations. This is strikingly evident in the proceedings of the Fourth Synod of (Roman Catholic) Bishops meeting in the Vatican in September 1974, which urged greater emphasis on local traditions, culture, and social structure and more study of Buddhism, Hinduism, and Islam.[25] This is in marked contrast to earlier attitudes of rigidity and hubris that greeted the efforts of Jesuits in India in 1623 and in China in 1742.[26]

Joseph J. Spengler, eds., *Tradition, Values, and Socio-Economic Development* (Durham, N.C.: Duke University Press, 1961). The movement toward anti-development theory is illustrated by Donella H. Meadows et al., *Limits to Growth* (New York: Universe Books, 1972); Jay W. Forrester, *World Dynamics* (New York: Wright-Allen Press, 1971); Walter A. Weiskopf, *Alienation and Economics* (New York: E. P. Dutton, 1971); Edward J. Mishan, *Technology and Growth: The Price We Pay* (New York: Praeger, 1970); Denis Goulet, *The Cruel Choice: A New Concept in Political Development* (New York: Atheneum, 1973); John H. Hallowell, ed., *Development for What?* (Durham, N.C.: Duke University Press, 1964); Robert A. Nisbet, *Social Change and History: Aspects of the Western Theory of Development* (New York: Oxford University Press, 1969). For a critique of the view reflected in these, see the *Wall Street Journal*, Sept. 28, 1971, Dec. 29, 1971, and March 17, 1972. cf. Peter Passell and Leonard Ross, *The Retreat from Riches* (New York: Viking Press, 1973). See also P. T. Bauer, *Dissent on Development* (Cambridge: Harvard University Press, 1973) and his *Economic Analysis and Policy in Underdeveloped Countries* (Durham, N.C.: Duke University Press, 1951); and Peter T. Bauer, "The Case Against Foreign Aid," *Wall Street Journal*, Oct. 3, 1972, p. 22, and the accompanying editorial. See also a special issue of *Daedalus* entitled *The No-Growth Society*, No. 102 (Fall 1973).

25. As reported in *New York Times*, Sept. 29, 1974, p. 12; *Raleigh News and Observer*, Sept. 29, 1974, p. 1; *Durham Morning Herald*, Sept. 29, 1974, p. 1.

26. In the former case, the papal constitution of Gregory XV, *Romanae sedis antistes* of January 31, 1623, resolved issues of adaptation to Brahminism in favor of Roberto di Nobili. This toleration faded with di Nobili's death and passed with deportation of the Jesuits from India in 1759. See Vincent Cronin, *A Pearl to India: The Life of Roberto di Nobili* (New York: E. P. Dutton, 1959) and P. Thomas, *Christians and Christianity in India and Pakistan* (London: George Allen and Unwin, 1954), pp. 63-76. As to the latter, the papal bull of Benedict XIV, *Ex quo singulari*

Earlier notions of Christian superiority are less obviously expressed and have even been abandoned. While references to heathenism may remain in hymnology and other residuary sources, such words as "heathen," "pagan," "unbeliever," and "infidel" have silently vanished from common usage in much theological and even popular exposition.

Efforts to synthesize Christian and Asian non-Christian beliefs are equally noteworthy. Thus, Thomas Merton,[27] the converted Roman Catholic Trappist monk, and the Roman Catholic William Johnston[28] write with uncommon spiritual insight and understanding of Buddhism. The Anglican Benedictine, Dom Aelred, shows similar mastery of Buddhism.[29] Alan Watts, an Anglican priest who became a strong advocate of Zen Buddhism, developed the same theme in a less theologically rigorous but insightful journalistic style in many volumes that attracted widespread attention.[30] Similar though fewer efforts have marked an assessment of Hinduism. Erik Erikson's comparison of the Hindu stages of life (āśrama-dharma) with his own eight periods in the life cycle is perhaps the most important of such recent efforts.[31] It is noteworthy that Erikson's first encounter with India was his

---

of 1742 resolved the Rites Controversy by ruling against Matteo Ricci and other Jesuits who sought to equate the concept of *T'ien* with God and to allow ancestor "worship" by Christian converts. See *Catholic Encyclopedia* (London, 1908), III, 671–72.

27. Thomas Merton, *Zen and the Birds of Appetite* (New York: New Directions, 1968); and Naomi B. Stone et al., eds., *The Asian Journal of Thomas Merton* (New York: New Directions, 1973).

28. William Johnston, *Christian Zen* (New York: Harper & Row, 1971); and his *Still Point: Reflections on Zen and Christian Mysticism* (New York: Fordham University Press, 1970).

29. Aelred Graham, *Zen Catholicism: A Suggestion* (New York: Harcourt, Brace, and Jovanovich, 1963).

30. See, *inter alia*, Alan Watts, *In My Own Way: An Autobiography 1915–1945* (New York: Pantheon, 1972).

31. See Erik Erikson's *Gandhi's Truth* (New York: W. W. Norton, 1969), esp. pp. 33–52; also his *Childhood and Society* (New York: W. W. Norton, 2nd enlarged ed., 1950), pp. 219–35; and his *Identity and the Life Cycle: Selected Papers by Erik H. Erikson* (New York: International Universities Press, 1959), *passim*, esp. p. 120, revised in *Identity, Youth and Crisis* (New York: W. W. Norton, 1968).

leadership of a seminar in Ahmedabad in 1962 on human life cycles. Beatrice Bruteau, one of the founders of the Teilhard Research Institute of Fordham University, has attempted to reconcile Hindu traditions with the Catholic theology of Teilhard de Chardin.[32] These more recent interpretations of Buddhism and Hinduism have earlier equivalents in Islam. Unlike Buddhism and Hinduism, Islam postdates Christianity. It canonically embraces part of its scriptures, part of its prophethood, and some of its theology. It appears to have an intrinsic reconciliation that partially fills the need for a contemporary theological search for equivalence. The work of Cragg, Smith, and Hodgson must be mentioned as teleological reconciliations comparable to those mentioned above for Buddhism and Hinduism.[33] Nor can we neglect Sir Thomas Arnold's earlier *The Preaching of Islam,*[34] or Sir Mohammad Iqbal whose thought was influenced by Arnold, his teacher. The relationship between Iqbal's thought and phenomenology and between Sufism and Christian mysticism make further overtures to intercreedal equivalence.[35] The mystical component of Islam has fascinated Henry Corbin, well known in France, whose major work, *En Islam Iranien,* is now being translated at McGill University. Corbin is convinced that mysticism is the most profound element in all religious thought and that it is the basis for sharing and un-

32. Beatrice Bruteau, *Evolution Toward Divinity* (Wheaton, Ill.: Theosophical Publishing House, 1974).

33. See, *inter alia,* Kenneth Cragg, "Each Other's Face," *The Muslim World,* XLV (1955), 172–82, his *Call of the Minaret* (Oxford: Oxford University Press, 1956), and *Sandals at the Mosque: Christian Presence Amid Islam* (Oxford: Oxford University Press, 1959); Wilfred Cantwell Smith, *Islam in Modern History* (Princeton: Princeton University Press, 1957); Marshall G. S. Hodgson, "A Comparison of Islam and Christianity as Framework for Religious Life," *Diogenes,* XXXII (1960), 49–74.

34. *The Preaching of Islam* was first published in England in 1896. The fourth edition, published by Sultan Ahmad at the Printing Palace in Lahore, n.d. (ca. 1933), is used here.

35. *The Reconstruction of Religious Thought in Islam* (Lahore: Sheikh Muhammad Ashraf, 1930). Accounts of Iqbal's intellectual development can be found in chapters under various authorship in Hafeez Malik, ed., *Iqbal: Poet Philosopher of Pakistan* (New York: Columbia University Press, 1971).

derstanding among religions. He has analyzed especially the mysticism of the Ishraqi school of the Iranian Shias. Of special interest is the work of French-speaking Roman Catholics such as Louis Massignon, who emphasizes Abraham and the Virgin Mary as crucial points of contact between Islamic and Judaeo-Christian traditions.[36]

Further, there is a new appreciation of indigenous modes of behavior and attitudes implicit in such new terms in development as "appropriate technology" and moves toward a labor-intensive rather than a capital-intensive development strategy. Economists assume they have discovered a new concept, although the term "appropriate technology" means nothing more than the use of human and other resources at hand and of techniques compatible with the culture and economy. The contribution of contemporary development economics to this analysis lies in the empirical validation of assumptions that labor-intensive methods and indigenous techniques can in some cases be cheaper and more productive than capital-intensive programs using exogenous techniques.[37] The potential of labor-intensive methods may be far greater than is commonly realized. Edgar Owens asserts that labor-intensity applied to agriculture would increase crop yields sufficiently to eliminate the global food shortage.

36. I am indebted to Professor Charles J. Adams, director of the Institute of Islamic Studies of McGill University, for a critical reading of these comments on Islam and for his calling my attention to the work of Corbin and Massignon.

37. The SEADAG development administration panel held a seminar in Singapore in July 1973 on the topic "Administrative Requirements for Labor-Intensive Development." See also William A. McCleary, "Foreign Aid and the Choice of Technique in Road Construction in Thailand," *SEADAG Papers* (No. 74–8) mimeographed (New York: The Asia Society, SEADAG, 1974); Larry E. Westphal, "Research on Appropriate Technology," in Lawrence J. White, ed., *Technology, Employment and Development* (Manila: University of the Philippines, 1975); Lawrence J. White, "Appropriate Technology and A Competitive Environment: Some Evidence from Pakistan," Discussion paper No. 46, Research Program in Economic Development, Woodrow Wilson School, Princeton University (May 1974), mimeographed. Also Samuel A. Morley and Gordon W. Smith, "Managerial Discretion and the Choice of Technology by Multinational Firms in Brazil," Paper No. 56, Rice University Program of Development Studies, Houston, (Fall 1974), mimeographed.

In the past the effectiveness of such labor intensity in agriculture was associated with total societal revolution as in the People's Republic of China. Owens rightly reminds us that spectacular success in crop yields has also marked agricultural reform on Taiwan.[38] The origins of systematic attention to adapting technique to context (a simpler way of describing "appropriate technology") can be traced at least as far back as Gandhi in 1946 and to E. F. Schumacher, whose ideas led to official use of the term at the first conference held in Hyderabad in 1964 at the Small Industry Extension Training Institute. Earlier there was resistance to notions of a "second-hand" or "indigenous technology," and the new term seemed not so pejorative. Now the Government of India has established an Appropriate Technology Cell in the Ministry of Industrial Development and contemplates establishing a National Center for the Promotion of Appropriate Technology.[39] The widespread rejection of Gandhi's economic views by the Indian intelligentsia in the 1960s has given way to a new appreciation of his emphasis on indigenization of techniques of development.[40] The rise of a neo-Gandhian movement in India coincides with a globally dispersed emphasis on "appropriate technology."

Even family planning technicians, long the most brazen of social engineers in their exclusive reliance on technology detached from cultural realities, now confront their problem with a new humility and awareness that cultural change must precede demographic reform. Thus, the Erlichs urge control of outside agencies, especially multinational corporations, and the pursuit of measures appropriate to each country (as

38. Edgar Owens, "World's Lilliputs Hold the Answer to Famine Threat," *Washington Post,* Oct. 13, 1974, p. C2. An elaboration of Owens' perspective can be found in Edgar Owens and Robert Shaw, *Development Reconsidered: Bridging the Gap between Government and People* (Lexington, Mass.: Lexington Books, 1972).

39. *News-INDIA* (New Delhi), I (May 1974), 5.

40. *Ibid.,* I (Oct. 1974), 1.

in China) as prerequisites to successful control of population growth.[41]

The United States Congress appears to have abandoned the ethnocentrism implicit in Title IX of the Foreign Assistance Act of 1967 in its successor Act of 1973.[42] The new version aims foreign aid directly at "improving the lives of the poorest of [the] people." This aid, if implemented, will go directly to small, poor farmers who are the majority. Disillusionment with the "green revolution" and with agricultural technology incompatible with realities of small scale, in conjunction with this new congressional idiom of aid, will create a context highly favorable to the use of technologies appropriate to context.

This new appreciation of the distinctiveness and power of cultural forms is undergirded by an implicit belief in the relativity of cultural values and form as well as by the demand of communal, ethnic, or pluralistic groups for parity of esteem and respect. The inevitable concomitant result of these forces is new respect for existing attitudes and belief systems and the replacing of cultural absolutism with cultural relativism.[43]

This emerging emotional and intellectual idiom that favors esteem for distinctive national and subnational cultural modes is reinforced by the international political context.

41. Paul R. Ehrlich and Anne H. Ehrlich, "Misconceptions," *New York Times Magazine*, June 16, 1974, pp. 9, 30, 31, 34.

42. For discussion of Title IX of the Foreign Assistance Act of 1967 (Public Law 89–583; 80 Stat. 795), see Ralph Braibanti, "External Inducement of Political-Administrative Development: An Institutional Strategy," in Braibanti and Associates, *Political and Administrative Development*, pp. 11–21. The new legislation referred to in the text is par. 5, Section 2, Public Law 93–189 (81 Stat. 445), December 1973, amendment to the Foreign Assistance Act of 1967.

43. This trend carries with it profound risks for mankind, among them the loss of standards and values, hence the loss of a moral basis for civilization. On this point, see Brand Blanshard, "Morality and Politics," in Richard T. De George, ed., *Ethics and Society* (Garden City, N.Y.: Anchor Books, 1966), pp. 1–25, esp. pp. 4–7.

Even economists, long resistant to non-economic factors, have adopted a new humility.[44] Thus, Madden predicts a new universe of relevance for economists, reflecting a world view marked by "holism, naturalism, immanentism, configuration of processes . . . ," and he concludes that these ideas "redefine capitalism, environmental balance and the quality of life."[45] The dynamic of ethnocentric interventionism, which once characterized American foreign assistance manifesting itself as cultural and ideological imperialism, is fading. Signaled by the Nixon Doctrine[46] and a preoccupation with domestic problems, this retreat from an imperial posture is well known.[47]

But other forces in Pakistan and Asia have been at work. Foremost among these has been a dramatic change from uncritical acquiescence in American advice to a more realistic assessment of American capability and intentions. Multilateralization of international relations is the hallmark of this new idiom in Pakistan. Beginning with friendship with China, this new policy matured with withdrawal from SEATO, strengthening the Regional Cooperation for Development (RCD) regional structure, and reinforcing the Arab connection. This new idiom is of significance. The emergence of multilateral and regional sources of advice, assistance, and inspiration will require reconstructed modes for regulating, controlling, and correlating these sources with indigenous values in Pakistan. Formerly, the principal source of new ideas was a single radiating system—the United States. This was especially true in those activities in which the United States exerted almost exclusive influence.

44. *The Wall Street Journal*, Sept. 6, 1974, p. 1.
45. Carl H. Madden, "The Greening of Economics," *Virginia Quarterly Review*, L (1974), 169.
46. *United States Foreign Policy for the 1970's: Building for Peace—A Report to The Congress by Richard Nixon, President of The United States*, February 25, 1971; *Department of State Bulletin*, March 22, 1971, LXIV (No. 1656), 341–432.
47. See Henry Brandon, *The Retreat of American Power* (New York: Doubleday, 1973); Raymond Aron, *The Imperial Republic* (Cambridge, Mass.: Winthrop, 1974).

These were military technology (through Military Assistance Advisory Groups [MAAG]), community development (Michigan State University and the Ford Foundation), administrative reform (University of Southern California, AID, and Ford Foundation), population planning (AID and Ford Foundation), scientific agriculture (AID and Washington State University), foreign affairs (training of foreign service officers at the Fletcher School of Law and Diplomacy), economic planning (Ford Foundation and Harvard Advisory Services), and technical training (Texas Agricultural and Mechanical College and AID). Thus, the idiosyncracies of that system were mastered in a decade or so by officials trained in the United States. But intellectual mastery did not result in Pakistan's capacity to control such induced change. This was because the change was generated in the context of American foreign policy and derived its momentum from the dynamics of the radiating technology of the United States disarticulated from the realities of the recipient context. The precarious and neo-colonial nature of this relationship was manifest in the title of President Ayub's book, *Friends Not Masters.*[48] With multilateralization Pakistan has developed a new capacity to deal with ideas from a variety of systems—to seek equivalences from such variety. The capacity to comprehend, integrate, and control these diffused forces calls for attitudes and skills attuned to several cultural systems rather than to one or two. This process of cultural translation, or equivalency identification, will inevitably stimulate reexamination of Pakistan's own system and techniques.

It may be that the intuitive grasp of this multilateral condition, rather than mere showmanship, prompts Prime Minister Bhutto to adopt such diverse sartorial transformations as Maoist peaked cap and tunic, *chola* and *pugri*, goldbraid-adorned uniform faintly reminiscent of Persian

48. (Karachi, 1967).

imperial splendor, and Western suits resembling the tailoring of Savile Row.

Mention must be made of the deliberations of developing nations at the Sixth Special Session of the United Nations General Assembly in April 1974.[49] These deliberations mark a turning point in history—a moment in which a common assumption of the relations of nations is being overturned. Again we find the beginnings of congruence between global thought of nation-states and academic thought. This arises in the work of Goulet, whose criteria for development reflect these assumptions of access to natural resources and to manufacturing and distributive technology on an "equitable," "non-colonial" basis.[50] Just as it was once assumed that colonialism was a natural state of affairs, so in a post-colonial period it was assumed that a dependent economic relationship of 80 percent of the globe's population and a concomitant dependent relationship of resources to manufacture and distribution was a normal state of affairs. This theme is reiterated with singular force and cogency in United Nations–sponsored conferences on population and on food. The Bucharest conference in the summer of 1974 emphasized that population control was not necessarily desirable, rather redistribution of resources could sustain existing and even

49. See text of speech of Dr. Mubashir Hasan, Pakistan's minister for finance, planning and development, at the Sixth Special Session of the United Nations General Assembly, April 22, 1974. See also James Reston's comment on the immense significance of this statement and the revolutionary concept implicit in it (*New York Times*, April 24, 1974). This position had for some time been espoused by the United Nations Conference on Trade and Development (UNCTAD) and is the official and unofficial view of most governments and analysts in developing systems. See a similar Indian position in *News-INDIA* (New Delhi), I (May 1974), 4, and the cogent comments of one of Indonesia's keenest analysts, Mochtar Lubis, editor and publisher of *Indonesia Raja*, writing in *Newsweek*, March 11, 1974, p. 11. See also *World Bank Annual Report 1974* (Washington, D.C., 1974) and mimeographed statements of various governors of the International Bank for Reconstruction and Development (World Bank) at the 1974 annual meeting of the Board of Governors, variously dated September and October 1974, Washington, D.C. See also Robert S. McNamara, *Address to the Board of Governors [of the International Bank for Reconstruction and Development]* (Washington, D.C., Sept. 30, 1974).

50. See Goulet's criteria in my Synoptic Chart, pp. 461–62, item 29, with relevant citation.

increased levels of population density. The symposium in Cocoyoc, Mexico, sponsored by the United Nations Conference on Trade and Development (UNCTAD) and the United Nations Environment Program, asserted that only massive redistribution of economic wealth and resources can save a large part of the world from starvation. The World Food Conference sponsored by the United Nations in Rome in November 1974 emphasized the same idiom. Developing nations are consistent in their belief that their hunger and poverty are the responsibility of developed nations. Jagivan Ram, India's minister of agriculture and irrigation, addressing the World Food Conference on November 6, 1974, put it bluntly: "It is obvious that developed nations can be held responsible for their [underdeveloped nations'] plight. . . . Whatever help is rendered to them now should not be regarded as charity but as a deferred compensation for what has been done to them in the past by the developed countries."[51] This view of a globally diffused, retrospectively applied responsibility runs counter to notions of individual responsibility that are commonly applied to nations.[52] Now the use of oil as an economic weapon and the growing institutional unity of Muslim nations has given meaningful force to the use of natural resources to compel a global restructuring of economic relations and resource allocation. The political use of economic cartelization is by no means new, but its invocation by less developed nations mobilized advantageously within the global arena is strikingly novel.[53] The beginnings of new patterns of redistribution are in evi-

51. *News-INDIA* (New Delhi), XIII (Nov. 22, 1974), 2.
52. For further analysis of the notion of globally diffused responsibility, see Charles W. Maynes, Jr., "The Hungry New World and the American Ethic," *Washington Post-Outlook*, Dec. 1, 1974, p. B1.
53. The feasibility of such political cartelization should not be lightly dismissed. Analyzing the obstacles to such action, two World Bank economists conclude that "in a basic situation where developing countries urgently need resources for development, the chances of their resorting to such drastic measures could depend, in the last analysis, on the overall state of relations between rich and poor countries." Bension Varon and Kenji Takeuchi, "Developing Countries and Non-Fuel Minerals," *Foreign Affairs*, LII (April 1974), 497–510.

dence, and this new idiom of our time will be sustained both by regionalism and by the vestigial remnants of a tri-polarized world in which China, the Soviet Union, and the United States can be used shrewdly to the advantage of developing nations.

Finally, it is of significance that Pakistan now rediscovers a position of some importance in a Muslim world growing in self-esteem, unity, and power. This is in consequence of newly acquired oil wealth, new Muslim leadership (Faisal and Khalid), the political use of economic cartelization start-ing with oil, and a new global context of decolonized freedom that permits the prideful assertion of an Islamic identity. The League of Arab States has expanded to include certain non-Arab states (notably Pakistan) as associate members. An Islamic Development Bank, established in Jeddah, may ultimately be as significant as the Asian Development Bank. The Arab Investment Company, a joint stock company capitalized at $463 million, based in Riyadh, includes Saudi Arabia and other Gulf nations among its seven Arab member states. The establishment of the Islamic Secretariat with the distinguished Malaysian statesman, Tunku Abdul Rahman, as its first secretary-general has already achieved importance. It was the Secretariat that sponsored an historic event in the Muslim world—a summit conference of Muslim states, held for the first time in a non-Arab state, in Lahore, Pakistan, in February 1974. This was followed by a technical conference in Kuala Lumpur in March 1974 to plan for distribution of supplies of oil to Muslim nations. The summit conference was hailed with uncommon enthusiasm in all Muslim nations.[54] Pakistan's proposal for creation of an Islamic Scientific Foundation, financed by 1 percent of the export income of Muslim nations for four years, will establish

54. See, e.g., comments in *The Sunday Times—Malaysia*, March 3, 1974, p. 1; *The Straits Times*, Feb. 26, 1974, p. 8; *ibid.*, March 4, 1974, p. 8; *Pakistan Times*, Feb. 26, 1974, p. 4; *ibid.*, March 5, 1974, p. 3.

scientific institutes and train scientists in Muslim countries. These structural developments are made more meaningful by the obvious rise in prestige of the Arab states as the developed world woos Arab dispensers of oil and the wealth derived from it. Both the World Bank and the Asian Development Bank seek to sell bonds to Arab states as a means of recycling Arab oil money.[55] Whether this effort will be vitiated by ties to the Islamic Development Bank remains to be seen. But the growing power of Arab wealth is regarded with concern by the non-Muslim world.

A typically social science appraisal of these moves within the Muslim world focuses on the weakness of structures and the divisive forces within the Islamic sphere. But of greater importance is the tacit dimension, the psychic, indwelling[56] nature of Islam which, interacting with the new forces described earlier, might well signal a renaissance of Islamic political power. Pakistan moves increasingly into the sphere of Middle Eastern concerns which is its authentic cultural heritage and will be its meaningful economic and strategic arena as well. It is not accidental that in organizing committees or "constituencies" for the Committee on Reform of the International Monetary System and Related Issues (Committee of Twenty) the International Monetary Fund grouped Pakistan not with India, Sri Lanka, Bangladesh, but with the Middle East and Gulf states.[57] This propulsion to the fountainhead of its heritage strengthens Pakistan's Islamic bonds with the Middle East, thus increasing pride in Islam and enhancing resilience against Western intervention and social engineering that in an earlier era would have been accepted as a panacea for all social ills.

55. *South China Morning Post*, Business News supplement, Feb. 25, 1974, p. 1.
56. Here I have used the terms and followed the analysis of Michael Polanyi. See his *The Tacit Dimension* (New York: Doubleday, 1966).
57. For a list of these constituencies and their composition, see International Monetary Fund, *International Monetary Reform: Documents of The Committee of Twenty* (Washington, D.C.: International Monetary Fund, 1974), p. 252.

IV

Academic perceptions of the attributes of political development vary greatly. No neat formulation after the manner of
growth economics has been possible, simply because the
issues in political development deal with the total cultural
configuration rather than merely with gross national product,
per capita income, and the accumulation and distribution of
capital resources. The synoptic chart on the following pages
chronologically arranges abstracts of formulations of thirty
from a universe of approximately forty development specialists. The thirty selected have attracted some attention in
academic literature. Some of these formulations are syntheses
of other writers' work; others are group efforts; a few are
efforts of economists and sociologists (Lerner, Millikan,
Eisenstadt, Black, Myrdal, Rostow) whose influence has
seeped into political development literature. These thirty
formulations are not at the same level of sophistication.
Some were loosely designed as suggestive characteristics;
others are more rigorously worked out as potential research
designs. There is, notwithstanding, surprising conceptual
equivalence among the thirty formulations, partly hidden
though it is by terminological variety. But there are also
fundamental differences in value premises implicit in these
formulations. These appear especially in the degree of ethnocentrism, in respect for individuation of political modes,
and in concern for psychic aspects of man's well-being within
the context of his own culture. Hence, the selection of a
formulation within which Pakistan can be analyzed is a
serious step with important methodological and intellectual
consequences. This is not the place to debate the comparative merits, especially the analytical utility, of any single set
of characteristics. My proposal at this point is that specialists
on Pakistan use any set of characteristics, or mixture of sets,
or indeed formulate sets of their own, into which Pakistan's

Synoptic Chart Showing Selected Perceptions of Concepts of Political Development (R. Braibanti, 1974)

1. Lerner 1958	Sequence of phases reciprocally related: 1. Urbanization: urban matrix develops modernizing skills and resources, especially literacy and communications. 2. Political participation: voter turnout. 3. Popular responsiveness to felt needs of population.

Source: Daniel Lerner, *The Passing of Traditional Society Modernizing the Middle East* (Glencoe, Ill.: The Free Press, 1958).

2. Millikan and Blackmer 1960	1. Interest groups. 2. Popular participation. 3. Governmental structures and administrative organization. 4. Sensitive political mechanisms for relating demands to public power. 5. National unity and political consensus. 6. Peaceful transfer of power. 7. Political competitiveness.

Source: Extrapolated from Max F. Millikan and Donald L. M. Blackmer, eds., *The Emerging Nations* (Boston: Little, Brown, 1961), pp. 68–90. This was a report for the Senate Committee on Foreign Relations.

3. Almond
1960
	Seven functional categories of all political systems:
	A. Input
	  1. Political socialization and recruitment.
	  2. Interest articulation.
	  3. Interest aggregation.
	  4. Political communication.
	B. Output
	  5. Rule-making.
	  6. Rule application.
	  7. Rule adjudication.

Source: Gabriel A. Almond, "Introduction: A Functional Approach to Comparative Politics," in Almond and James S. Coleman, eds., *The Politics of Developing Areas* (Princeton: Princeton University Press, 1960), p. 17.

4. Wriggins 1962	1. Minimum public order. 2. Essential services. 3. Common defense and foreign policy. 4. Resolution of conflicts.

4. Wriggins
1962 *(cont.)*

5. Orderly expression of public demands and discontent.
6. Orderly transfer of legitimacy of power.
7. National unity melding diversities.
8. Recognition for elites and prospective elites.
9. Increased distribution of worldly goods.

Source: Abbreviated from Howard Wriggins, "Foreign Assistance and Political Development," in Robert Asher et al., *Development of the Emerging Countries: An Agenda for Research* (Washington, D.C.: The Brookings Institution, 1962), pp. 181–214.

---

5. Almond
1963

1. Integrative capability.
2. International accommodative capability.
3. Participation.
4. Welfare or distribution.

Source: Gabriel A. Almond, "Political Systems and Political Change," *The American Behavioral Scientist,* VI (1963), 3–10. This perspective was subsequently expanded in other works by Almond.

---

6. Eisenstadt
1963

1. Differentiation, unification, and centralization of political system.
2. Continuous development of high level of "free-floating" resources and political power.
3. Continuous spread of political power to all groups and individuals.
4. Weakening of traditional elites and legitimations and their replacement by modernizing elites and legitimations.

Source: S. N. Eisenstadt, "Bureaucracy and Political Development," in Joseph La Palombara, ed., *Bureaucracy and Political Development* (Princeton: Princeton University Press, 1963), pp. 96–119.

---

7. von der Mehden
1964

1. Goal consensus.
2. Communications between leaders and masses.
3. National integration of minority groups.
4. Secularization of politics.
5. High literacy rates.
6. Large well-educated elite.
7. Trained civil service.
8. Political competitiveness.
9. Institutions with specific and differentiated functions.
10. Widespread political activity.
11. Infusion of Western values.

| 7. von der Mehden 1964 *(cont.)* | 12. Associational interest groups. 13. Political mobility. 14. Constitutional government; no anomic disturbances. 15. Civilian control of military. |

Source: Fred von der Mehden, *Politics of the Developing Nations* (Englewood Cliffs, N.J.: Prentice-Hall, 1964), p. 6.

| 8. Packenham 1965 | Surveying earlier writers such as W. Wilson, J. W. Burgess, and Max Weber, as well as AID documents, reduces their emphasis to: 1. Constitution. 2. Economic base. 3. Administrative capacity. 4. Social system. 5. Political culture. |

Source: Robert A. Packenham, "Approaches to the Study of Political Development," *World Politics,* XVII (1965), 108–21.

| 9. Lasswell 1965 | 1. Self-sustaining power accumulation. 2. Power-sharing. 3. National independence. 4. Responsible role in world politics. 5. Internal decision-making process conducing to wider participation in all values. 6. Timing of elements in sequence of development. |

Source: Harold D. Lasswell, "The Policy Sciences of Development," *World Politics,* XVII (1965), 286–310.

| 10. Apter 1965 | Main guides to modernization that can be compared most easily: 1. Roles and growth indexes. 2. Careers and entrepreneurship roles. 3. Technology. 4. Per capita income. |

Source: David E. Apter, *The Politics of Modernization* (Chicago: University of Chicago Press, 1965), p. 70.

| 11. Huntington 1965 | Surveying other writers such as Ward and Rustow, Emerson, Pye, and Eisenstadt, reduces their emphasis to: 1. Rationalization. 2. National integration. |

11. Huntington　　3. Democratization.
　　1965 (*cont.*)　　4. Participation.
　　　　　　　　Deploring inattention to institutionalization, he advances that as a prime requisite of political development.

Source: Samuel P. Huntington, "Political Development and Political Decay," *World Politics,* XVII (1965), 386–430; and his *Political Order in Changing Societies* (New Haven: Yale University Press, 1968), pp. 12–24.

---

12. Pye　　　Three points of view: equality, capacity, differen-
　　1966　　tiation.
　　　　　Forecasting SSRC formulation:
　　　　　1. Identity.
　　　　　2. Legitimacy.
　　　　　3. Penetration.
　　　　　4. Participation.
　　　　　5. Integration.
　　　　　6. Distribution.
　　　　　These crises occur in relation to a sequence.

Source: Lucian Pye, *Aspects of Political Development* (Boston: Little, Brown, 1966), pp. 45–58.

---

13. Black　　1. Increased centralization.
　　1966　　2. Bureaucracy.
　　　　　3. Rapport between state and every member in society.
　　　　　4. Participation.

Source: Cyril E. Black, *Dynamics of Modernization* (New York, 1966), p. 14.

---

14. Diamant　　1. Ability to sustain new social goals and create
　　1966　　　new social organizations.
　　　　　2. Differentiated polity.
　　　　　3. Centralized polity.
　　　　　4. Increasing power of more spheres of society.
　　　　　5. Increased participation in political power.

Source: Alfred Diamant, "Political Development: Approaches to Theory and Strategy," in John D. Montgomery and William Siffin, eds., *Approaches to Development, Politics, Administration and Change* (New York: McGraw-Hill, 1966), pp. 25–26.

---

15. Almond　　Five capabilities:
　　and　　　1. Regulative.
　　Powell　　2. Extractive.
　　1966　　　3. Distributive.
　　　　　4. Symbolic.
　　　　　5. Responsive.

Source: Gabriel A. Almond and G. B. Powell, *Comparative Politics — A Developmental Approach* (Boston: Little, Brown, 1966).

16. Pennock   1. Security
     1966   2. Liberty
                     3. Welfare
                     4. Justice

Source: J. Roland Pennock, "Political Development, Political Systems and Political Goods," *World Politics,* XVIII (1966), 418.

17. Rustow   1. Growth of authority.
     1967   2. Formation of national identity.
                     3. Quest for political equality and participation.
                     4. Political leadership.

Source: Dankwart A. Rustow, *A World of Nations* (Washington, D.C., 1967), and "Modernization and Comparative Politics," *Comparative Politics,* I (1968), 37–51.

18. Welch   1. Centralization of power.
     1967   2. Weakening of traditional sources of authority.
                     3. Differentiation and specialization of institutions.
                     4. Increased popular participation in politics.
                     5. Greater identification of individuals with the whole system.

Source: Claude E. Welsh, Jr., ed., *Political Modernization* (Belmont, Calif.: Wadsworth, 1967), p. 7.

19. Populorum   1. To do more.
     Progressio   2. To know more.
     1967   3. To have more in order.
                     4. To be more (ut ideo pluris valeant).

Source: Encyclical Letter of His Holiness, Paul VI, Pope. *On the Development of Peoples (Populorum Progressio),* March 29, 1967.

20. Myrdal   Value Premises:
     1967   Modernization Ideals:
                     1. Rationality.
                     2. Planning.
                     3. Rise in productivity.
                     4. Rise in levels of living.
                     5. Social and economic equalization.
                     6. Improved institutions and attitudes.
                     7. National consolidation.
                     8. National independence.
                     9. Political democracy.
                     10. Democracy at grass roots.
                     11. Social discipline.

Source: Gunnar Myrdal, *Asian Drama* (New York: Pantheon, 1967), I, 55–69.

21. Friedrich 1969	1. Cope with technical problems of survival.
	2. Enforcible restraints on government.
	3. Operative popular participation in rule-making.
	4. General rules reflecting shared beliefs.
	5. Judicial interpretation of rules.
	6. Voluntary associations.

Above six elements based on need for security, external peace, prosperity, internal peace, and sub-objectives of justice, freedom, and equality.

Source: Carl J. Friedrich, "Political Development and the Objectives of Modern Government," in Ralph Braibanti, ed., *Political and Administrative Development* (Durham, N.C.: Duke University Press, 1969), pp. 107–36.

22. Braibanti 1969	1. Architectonics.
	2. Institutionality.
	3. Participation.
	4. Innovation.

Source: Ralph Braibanti, "External Inducement of Political Administrative Development: An Institutional Strategy," in Braibanti, ed., *Political and Administrative Development* (Durham, N.C.: Duke University Press, 1969), pp. 3–107.

23. Albinski 1971	1. Socialization.
	2. Interest articulation.
	3. Public participation.
	4. Political leadership.
	5. Political development of public policy.

Source: Henry S. Albinski, *Asian Political Processes: Essays and Readings* (Boston: Allyn and Bacon, 1971), pp. v, vi.

24. Rostow 1971	1. Concentrate on modernization of society rather than on external adventure.
	2. Modernize in loyalty to the society's culture.
	3. Steady growth in the economy and resources available for public purposes.
	4. National political party, or coalition of parties, containing legitimate representatives of the key groups within the society, among which compromise agreements must be reached before an effective national policy can be pursued by the government.
	5. Participation.
	6. Cooperative regionalism in foreign affairs.

Source: W. W. Rostow, *Politics and the Stages of Growth* (Cambridge: Cambridge University Press, 1971), pp. 300–1.

25. SSRC   Syndrome Components:
    1971   Equality.
                  Capacity.
                  Differentiation.
                  Five Crises:
                  1. Identity.
                  2. Legitimacy.
                  3. Participation.
                  4. Distribution.
                  5. Penetration.

Source: Leonard Binder, "The Crises of Political Development," in Binder et al., *Crises and Sequences in Political Development* (Princeton: Princeton University Press, 1971), p. 65.

26. Eckstein   1. Durability.
    1971   2. Civil Order.
                  3. Legitimacy.
                  4. Decisional Efficacy.

Source: Harry Eckstein, *The Evaluation of Political Performance: Problems and Dimensions* (Beverly Hills, Calif.: SAGE Publications, 1971). Eckstein's characteristics are tested in Ted Robert Gurr and Muriel McClelland, *Political Performance: A Twelve-Nation Study* (Beverly Hills, Calif: SAGE Publications, 1971).

27. Huntington   1. Culture.
    1971   2. Structure.
                  3. Groups.
                  4. Leadership.
                  5. Policies.

Source: Samuel P. Huntington, "The Change to Change: Modernization, Development and Politics," *Comparative Politics,* III (1971), 283–323.

28. Brunner and   Model of complex change: 22 variables, 20 pa-
    Brewer   rameters. Relations between variables and
    1971   parameters expressed in 12 equations con-
                  structed from other theories and analysis of
                  development in Turkey and the Philippines.

Source: Ronald D. Brunner and Garry D. Brewer, *Organized Complexity: Empirical Theories of Political Development* (New York: The Free Press, 1971).

29. Goulet   1. National access to resources to provide
    1973   minimum life-sustaining goods to all nation's
                  members.
                  2. Poor nations have prior claim to resources
                  within their boundaries independently of
                  sufficiency of capital for exploitation.

29. Goulet
1973 (*cont.*)

3. Nations with abundant resources are obligated to grant needier nations access to part of their resources.
4. Precise form of such access (item 3) to be determined by practical needs.
5. Rights of access to resources also apply to groups and individuals within nation.
6. Recognition or esteem must be accorded poor nations and esteem of its citizens must not be based on wealth or functional excellence.

"Structures" of poor nations must be replaced by:
   a. Reciprocal obligations between wealthy and poor.
   b. Decision-making at all levels minimizing paternalism.
   c. Ability of each man and group to resist manipulation by others.
   d. Interpersonal and intersocietal solidarities promoting both self-interest and communality.
   e. Sharing in collective knowledge of human race.

Source: Denis Goulet, *The Cruel Choice: A New Concept in the Theory of Development* (New York: Atheneum, 1973), pp. 119–20.

---

30. Almond
1973

"Taking the historical cure." Analysis of cases in historical perspective using five time periods:
1. Preexistent system.
2. Environmental changes.
3. "Within system" changes.
4. Linked changes.
5. Resultant system.

Source: Gabriel A. Almond, "Approaches to Developmental Causation," in Almond, Scott C. Flanagan, Robert J. Mundt, eds., *Crisis, Choice and Change: Historical Studies of Political Development* (Boston: Little, Brown, 1973), pp. 24–25.

---

experience can be fitted.[58] If this were done, the impact of that experience on revised formulations leading ultimately to a theory of political development would be profound.

58. The first such effort to come to my attention is an unpublished paper, "Political Development Theory and Its Application in Pakistan," by Jeffrey A. James, presented at a seminar on Modernization at the Administrative Staff College in

By way of provocative suggestion, and not because of any qualitative judgment, I have set forth below my own set of four characteristics into which are blended (or subsumed) certain elements given particular emphasis by Lasswell. After analyzing the conceptual issues raised under each characteristic, I have then outlined some possible issues that Pakistan's experience would illuminate. These issues are by no means exhaustive; rather they are a tentative beginning suggestive of research directions.

1. *Characteristic I — Architectonics and the Correlative Problem of Polycommunality*

By architectonics we refer to common agreement on a fundamental polity of the state — an overarching purpose that gives form, cohesion, and direction to all public action within a sensed community. "Constitutionalism" is not an adequate term because it merely is a first step in molding a political order. "National integration" connotes submersion, deflection, conversion, or elimination of differential ethnicities or subnational cultures, and this is precisely what is not occurring. "Community" or communalism suggests too much sharing of values and is too closely related to utopian, monastic experiences or to the peculiar phenomenon in India.

Architectonics is the "consensus of sentiment" as defined by Cicero. It is concord, as Ortega defines it, on "the dogmas about life and the universe, moral norms, legal principles, rules regulating the very form of the struggle." Architectonics must be analyzed in the context of a major revolution of our time, i.e., the demand of national and subnational cultural entities for parity of esteem and respect, and the concomitant assumption by the state of a responsibility actively to nurture rather than dilute such differences. Hence, there is simul-

---

Lahore, July–August 1974. Using the Almond and Powell five-capability formulation (item 15 in my Synoptic Chart), James fits in a portion of Pakistan's experience. Economists have done much more such research of this kind, of which the paper by Lawrence J. White, cited above in n. 37, is an example.

taneous fragmentation and consolidation within the nation-
state. Indeed, the conditions, real and alleged, leading to
fragmentation seem to increase. A recently identified determinant of cleavage is that in Andhra Pradesh, India, where
even in the context of common language, nearly common
religion, and common ethnicity, the single factor of economic
disparity threatened the cohesion of the state. It is likely that
demands for equitable distribution of political and economic
goods will focus attention increasingly on this determinant.

More recently in Pakistan, the Rabwah incident over the
status of the Ahmediyas, declared by the National Assembly
to be a non-Muslim minority, raises a clearly sectarian cleavage within a common ethnic-linguistic-religious group.
Here the cleavage arises from the narrowest of causes. Ahmediyas are Punjabis, hence there is no ethnic or cultural
differential. According to their own views, they are Muslims.
Their interpretation of the Quranic suras relating to a prophet
following Mohammed differs from that of other Muslims.
Moreover, there is ambiguity in their alleged claims of the
"prophethood" of their founder, Mirza Ghulam Ahmed. On
the basis of these claims, the constitution of Pakistan was
amended in 1974 to declare them a non-Muslim minority.
The oath of office for the president and prime minister prescribed by the constitution includes an affirmation that the
swearer is a Muslim and that he believes that Mohammad
was the final prophet of Allah. This oath combined with the
new amendment effectively bars Ahmediyas from holding
offices of president and prime minister. This resolution of the
Ahmediya issue, festering at least since the Punjab disturbances of 1953, can be a dangerous precedent. Judgments
based on textual exegesis can easily be extended in application. It is conceivable, for example, that Ismaili Muslims
(followers of Prince Karim, the Agha Khan) can be declared
non-Muslims or that the Shia community can be so defined.
Such interpretations of membership exclusivity in the body
of Islam can strengthen other tendencies toward fragmentation of Pakistan. Since such fragmentation, manifest pre-

dominantly among Pathans and Baluch, presents a serious threat to Pakistan's national integrity, an astute government should judge explosive religious divisions in the larger context of preserving the nation and the Islamic unity that is one of its greatest strengths.

In some countries (e.g., Pakistan, India, Uganda, Libya, and in the case of Palestinian refugees) refugees or immigrants (*muhajirs*) constitute significant subnational groups, even though often their inadequate organization may reduce their political influence. Transnational manipulation of latent subnational forces must also be noted. Obvious examples are: interest of Libya and other Muslim states in the Filipino Muslims of Mindanao; Iraq's concern for Baluchistan and Afghanistan's interest in the Northwest Frontier Province; India's interest in Bengal, which assisted in creating Bangladesh; Israeli interest in Soviet Jewry; Irish-American interest in Northern Ireland. Some of the Asian states are faced not only with diverse groups but also with insurrectionist or secessionist movements aided by outside powers. In southern Thailand and in northwest Malaysia are Muslims whose secessionist proclivities are encouraged by local Maoist Chinese guerrillas along the Thai-Malaysian border. In India, Naga tribes were helped by outside sources. The Kurds of Iraq were openly supported by Iran until March 1975 when Iran achieved detente with Iraq and agreed to cease all support of Iraqi Kurds. These potential secessionist movements necessarily make for military frontier administration that cannot easily be reconstructed along civil developmental lines.

The term "ethnicity"[59] is convenient in referring to forms

59. For general analysis, see Wendell Bell and Walter E. Freeman, eds., *Ethnicity and Nation-Building* (Beverly Hills, Calif.: SAGE Publications, 1972); Cynthia H. Enloe, *Ethnic Conflict and Political Development* (Boston: Little, Brown, 1973); and Abdul A. Said, *Protagonists of Change: Subcultures in Development and Revolution* (Englewood Cliffs, N.J.: Prentice-Hall, 1971); Alvin Rabushka and Kenneth A. Shepsle, *Politics in Plural Societies: A Theory of Democratic Instability* (Columbus, Ohio: Charles E. Merrill, 1972), esp. pp. 10–22. See also the important effort to categorize variations of this phenomenon in Donald L. Horowitz, "Three Dimensions of Ethnic Politics," *World Politics*, XXIII (1971), 232–44.

of this event in the United States, but is inadequate in referring to more complex manifestations in India, Pakistan, and elsewhere in which linguistic, ethnic, religious, and cultural factors are mixed and overlaid in almost kaleidoscopic design. The confusion in terms, reflecting inadequate understanding of the phenomenon abroad, and facile, though ignorant, transfer of the paradigm from American to foreign experience is neatly illustrated by the new journal *Ethnicity*, first published in 1974, described as "an interdisciplinary journal of the study of ethnic relations," edited at the Center for the Study of American Pluralism of the University of Chicago. It deals with "ethnic relations throughout the world." Note the curious use of the term of lesser generality, "ethnic," to refer to the phenomenon (polycommunality) embracing far more than ethnicity, and the more embracing term "pluralism" to describe the more restrictive, essentially ethnic American phenomenon. The term "confessionalism" used in Lebanon is as restrictive as the term "ethnicity," for each of them refers only to one factor in the complicated mix of differentials. The term "corporatism" recently revived from the Fascist context of prewar Italy is equally unsatisfactory because of its reference to economic and occupational grouping. This phenomenon is also referred to in the context of Europe as "consociational democracy,"[60] an adequate term but connoting excessive emphasis on political-structural elements and insufficient emphasis on communal-tribal aspects somewhat more dominant in systems such as Pakistan.

An historical study of this phenomenon in Austria, Belgium, Luxembourg, Netherlands, and Switzerland uses the term "segmented pluralism" in distinction from the plural society of Furnivall.[61] This study traces the Dutch concept of *verzuiling*, a neologism derived from the Dutch word *zuil*

60. Arend Lijphart, "Consociational Democracy," *World Politics*, XXI (1969), 207–25.
61. Val R. Lorwin, "Segmented Pluralism: Ideological Cleavage and Political Cohesion in the Smaller European Democracies," *Comparative Politics*, III (1971), 141–77.

(pillar). The Dutch thought of ideological groups as pillars — each vertical and separate, but supporting an overarching unity. This is a valuable and clarifying construct, although it is not as useful for Pakistan (except for the Ahmediya) as it might be for India or Malaysia. Another mode of analysis is "bimodalism," used especially in Malaysia to describe a basic cleavage between indigenes (Malays) and nonindigenes. The latter can then further be divided by their ethnic-religious-cultural, i.e., polycommunal characteristics.[62]

A more useful term "plural societies" (sometimes interchanged with pluralism) was first used by J. S. Furnivall, a distinguished British officer of the colonial service who was also an accomplished scholar in political economy. Furnivall first used the term to describe the phenomenon in 1939 in the Netherlands East Indies (now Indonesia), and nearly a decade later he extended his analysis comparatively to include Burma.[63] Furnivall's term has been discovered by Europeanists via Dutch scholars, conditioned by their colonial contacts with the then Netherlands East Indies, and has been introduced into analysis of this ancient phenomenon in European states.[64] An important journal published at The Hague since 1969 is called *Plural Societies.* The terminology and concept have been transferred to other disciplines and other areas, especially the Caribbean,[65] and their applicability seriously debated.[66]

62. Stephen Chee, "Rural Development and Development Administration in Malaysia," *SEADAG Papers* (No. 74–5) mimeographed (New York: The Asia Society, SEADAG, 1974).

63. John S. Furnivall, *Netherlands India: A Study of Plural Economy* (Cambridge: The University Press, 1938). The comparative extension to Burma appeared in his *Colonial Policy and Practice* (London: Cambridge University Press, 1948).

64. Furnivall's term was used by Rabushka and Shepsle, cited above in n. 59, and by R. Rogowski and L. Wasserspring, *Does Political Development Exist? Corporatism in Old and New Societies* (Beverly Hills, Calif.: SAGE Professional Paper No. 01–024, 1971).

65. See, e.g., M. G. Smith, *The Plural Society in the British West Indies* (Berkeley and Los Angeles: University of California Press, 1965).

66. An account of this debate can be found in A. W. Singham, *The Hero and the Crowd in a Colonial Polity* (New Haven: Yale University Press, 1968), pp. 1–30, and in Rabushka and Shepsle, cited in n. 59 above.

Unfortunately, the term "pluralism" has been used in American studies to refer both to participation at different levels of government (especially local) and to the existence of competing interest groups in American society. Indeed, if that term had not come more recently to be associated with the United States and with these other phenomena, it would be entirely satisfactory. A term more global in application, though less felicitous in style, is "polycommunality." Few are the nations (perhaps only Japan and South Korea) that are not confronted with this paradox of fragmentation and integration. Only time will resolve the terminological inconsistency.

In the meantime, the phenomenon continues to emerge as a major revolution of our time. In the United States, Congress passed Title IX, Ethnic Heritage Studies, as part of the Education Amendments of 1972,[67] appropriating $10 million for its implementation for fiscal year 1972 and double that amount for fiscal year 1973. A $170 million a year program supporting bilingual education in public schools was included in the 1974 Education Act.[68] This gives further support to the nurture of esteem and respect for ethnic differences and hastens the demise of a "melting pot" theory that once characterized an "Americanization" process. There has been what has been called an "upthrust of ethnicity,"[69] or what Novak calls the "unmeltable ethnics."[70] In the United States, television series starring such "ethnic" personalities as Kojak, Colombo, Banacek, Petrocelli, Chico, Rhoda, Sanford, and many others, each proclaiming his ethnic origin at least once on each program, increase. This is reflected further

67. Title IX, Public Law 92–318 (86 Stat. 235), June 23, 1972. See also Easy Klein, "The New Ethnic Studies," *Change* (Summer 1974), pp. 13–16.
68. Public Law 93–380, Aug. 21, 1974. See also Nathan Glazer, "Ethnicity and the Schools," *Commentary* (1974), pp. 58–59.
69. Robert Nisbet, "The Decline of Academic Nationalism," *Change* (Summer 1974), p. 28.
70. Michael Novak, *The Rise of the Unmeltable Ethnics: The New Political Force of the Seventies* (New York: Macmillan, 1972).

in candidacy for political office, rise of small ethnic religious groups, cultural associations, and restaurants, as well as a spurt of literature.[71]

The problem of polycommunality can be expressed in terms of an equation, the parts of which are space (territoriality), political power, economic viability, and culture. It is typical for nations to develop only the economic and political portions of this equation. Culture, the tacit or unseen dimension, like the submerged portion of an iceberg, may be more significant and fraught with greater potential for the dissolution of the nation. It is likely that Pakistan did not pay sufficient attention to public manifestations of esteem for Bengali culture. Elsewhere I have described this failure in some detail.[72] Reluctance to deal positively with the language question, to recognize Tagore in a manner similar to the recognition given Iqbal, failure to give equal treatment to newspapers published in both East and West Pakistan are but a few of many examples. It is not sufficient that the central government acted to establish equity after crises of cultural inequity were articulated by political agitation. Such sensitivity should have been manifested in a predictive and therapeutic manner. Under this rubric it would be fruitful to study the relative influence of government actions dealing with this problem through politics and administration. Since we have the experience of the first successful secession in the postwar period, it would be even more fruitful to analyze what Pakistan has learned from this experience as it seeks to maintain its national integrity with the four major cultural groups within its boundaries. It is evident that religion alone and alleged

71. See an account of bilingual instruction in the United States, *Wall Street Journal*, Dec. 15, 1972, p. 1. See also *ibid.*, July 11, 1973, p. 1; *ibid.*, Sept. 7, 1973, p. 1. Among the books are Andrew M. Greeley, *Why Can't They Be Like Us?* (New York: American Jewish Committee, 1971); Mark R. Levy and Michael S. Kramer, *The Ethnic Factor: How America's Minorities Decide Elections* (New York: Simon & Schuster 1972), and those cited above in notes 67 through 70.

72. Ralph Braibanti, "Pakistan's Experience in Political Development," *ASIA*, *Supplement No. 1* (Fall 1974), pp. 25–43, esp. pp. 29–33.

economic parity would not appear sufficient to hold the nation together. The subtle behaviors of cultural sensitivity were almost totally absent until the last five years of a united Pakistan. The legendary cultural arrogance of the Punjab was in many ways a reality. Innumerable small episodes of insensitivity that, added together, constituted a tissue of cultural arrogance contributed to the secession. Structures must be established that, through economics, politics, and administration, hold the state together while maximizing cultural individuality. It is likely that representativeness must characterize more than merely the legislative structures—the classic locus for that quality. It is also likely that the older ideal of a bureaucracy recruited exclusively on merit and "neutral" in its administration of policy will have to give way to a bureaucracy deliberately and scrupulously articulated to communal representativeness. Under such conditions, bureaucracy must probably become representative of the composition of the larger society. Where there is disparity in experience, education, or civic morality among constituent groups there is likely to be impairment of bureaucratic efficiency and productivity. Another consequence is likely to be increased politicization of administration. Where recruitment is on a communal representative basis, segmented communal, hence political considerations, become important factors in administrative decision-making.

The foregoing issues may be encapsulated in the following way. To what extent has the total governmental apparatus of Pakistan been infused with the awareness that all parts of the equation mentioned above are important? To what extent is this awareness reflected in the organization of government, in the policies pursued, and in statements made by government officials? To answer these questions, the poly-communality of Pakistan would first have to be fitted into the general schema described earlier in this section. Resulting insights can then be translated into the main body of development thought with minimum friction.

2. Characteristic II — Institutionality

The second characteristic of political development — institutionality — received very little attention until about a decade ago.[73] Three systems for analyzing institutionality have thus far appeared in political science. The first and earliest analytical formulation was that of Huntington, published in 1965.[74] His criteria for measuring institutionalization were four: adaptability, complexity, autonomy, and coherence. The most ambitious undertaking was that of a consortium financed by the Agency for International Development.[75] The consortium set forth two categories of variables: (1) "institution variables," which are leadership, doctrine, program, resources, internal structure; and (2) "linkages," described as enabling, functional, normative, and diffused. The third is my own formulation identified by the acronymn RABCIRR by which I seek to appraise characteristics of institutions identified as Receptivity, Autonomy, Balance, Congruence, Internality, Reformulation, and Roles. This analysis was first presented at a conference at the Villa Serbelloni in 1967 and published two years later.[76] Subsequently, this formulation was refined and linked to the problem of value diffusion in the administrative process of

73. For a review of the evolution of this concept, see Ralph Braibanti, "Introduction: The Concept of Institutionality," in Robert S. Robins, *Political Institutionalization and the Integration of Elites* (Beverly Hills, Calif.: SAGE Publications, 1976), pp. 1–10.

74. Samuel P. Huntington, "Political Development and Political Decay," *World Politics*, XVII (1965), 386–430.

75. A substantial inter-university research effort was headed by Milton Esman at the University of Pittsburgh on "institution-building." For a review of this effort, see Ralph Braibanti, "External Inducement of Political-Administrative Development: An Institutional Strategy," in Braibanti and Associates, *Political and Administrative Development*, pp. 52–53, esp. n. 128. See also Joseph W. Eaton, ed., *Institution Building and Development: From Concepts to Application* (Beverly Hills, Calif.: SAGE Publications, 1972). Cf. Martin Landau, "Linkage, Coding, and Intermediacy: A Strategy for Institution-Building," *Journal of Comparative Administration*, II (1971), 401–29.

76. Ralph Braibanti, "External Inducement of Political-Administrative Development: An Institutional Strategy," in Braibanti and Associates, *Political and Administrative Development*, pp. 3–107, esp. pp. 52–56.

developing systems.[77] The definition of institution used as a basis for this analysis is the following. *Institutions are patterns of recurring acts structured in a manner conditioning the behavior of members within the institution, shaping a particular value or set of values, and projecting values in the social system in terms of attitudes or acts.* This definition reflects an earlier definition of Talcott Parsons and makes more explicit the psychoanalytic insights of personality formation implicit in Lasswell and Kaplan's concept of value distribution.

Classic institutions that may be selected for analysis include civil bureaucracy, military bureaucracy, judiciary, legislature, ecclesiastical entities, voluntary associations, education, communications, private commerce. Any of the three measurement formularies (Huntington, Pittsburgh consortium, or Braibanti) may be used to appraise the level of institutionality in Pakistan. Differences in levels may suggest a condition of unbalanced or asymmetrical institutional development. The measurement of institutional effectiveness will enable us to determine what institutions require strengthening, hence can assist in a strategy for development.

In the case of Pakistan it would be uncommonly rewarding to apply Lasswell's principle of a self-sustaining level of power accumulation to the appraisal of institutions.[78] In a viable political system there should be a relative degree of stability and certainty as to the locus and quantum of power exercised in the total system. The traumas of Pakistan, listed at the end of Section II of this chapter, theoretically drastically relocated and redistributed power at least every two years for a quarter of a century. How did this system

77. Ralph Braibanti, "Values in Institutional Processes," in Harold D. Lasswell, Daniel Lerner, and John D. Montgomery, eds., *Values and Development: The Asian Experience* (Cambridge, Mass.: M.I.T. Press, 1976), pp. 133–52.

78. Harold D. Lasswell, "The Policy Sciences of Development," *World Politics,* XVII (1965), 286–310. See also item 9 in my Synoptic Chart in this chapter.

survive such major dislocations of power? Were the dislocations real or merely theoretical? Despite such dislocations, it is likely that institutionalization in Pakistan may be judged of a high order.

3. *Characteristic III — Power Diffusion*

Analysis of a third characteristic of development, diffusion of power (participation) must be considered with institutionality. Power diffusion is the involvement of the entire population in political life. Ideologically, this characteristic derives from concern for enhancement of human dignity, reflected juridically in the concept of popular sovereignty and implemented institutionally in universal franchise, political parties, and participative entities such as community development. This attribute has been variously alluded to as participant society,[79] social and political mobilization,[80] power-sharing,[81] participation explosion,[82] and channelment of mass society.[83] Rapid diffusion of power to the periphery of the social order changes the nature and quantum of political demands, thus increasing the strain on the capability of institutions to convert such demands into effective governmental action. This condition has been discussed in terms of "load," the handling of crises, and the demand-conversion crisis. The sequence or timing of institution-building and acceleration of power diffusion is crucial. Ideally, rapid and effective institutionalization should precede mass suffrage and the formation of political

79. Daniel Lerner, *The Passing of Traditional Society* (Glencoe, Ill.: The Free Press, 1958), pp. 48–50.

80. Karl W. Deutsch, "Social Mobilization and Political Development," *The American Political Science Review*, LV (1961), 493–514.

81. Lasswell, "The Policy Sciences of Development," p. 290, cited in n. 78 above.

82. Gabriel A. Almond and Sidney Verba, *The Civic Culture* (Princeton: Princeton University Press, 1963), pp. 2–3.

83. Giovanni Sartori, "Political Development and Political Engineering," in John D. Montgomery and Albert O. Hirschman, eds., *Public Policy*, XVII (1968), 273.

parties. Yet this sequence has rarely been put into practice. Among noncommunist developing systems of 1974, probably only Iran, South Africa, and Pakistan can be said to have engineered such a sequence. The experience of Pakistan is unique in this respect. During the Ayub regime, institutions were greatly strengthened. Simultaneously, participation was deflected and sedated. Political parties and the legislative process were suspended. Through the Elective Bodies (Disqualification) Order, 1959 (EBDO), a generation of politicians, judged guilty of misconduct after August 14, 1947, was debarred from politics until December 31, 1966.[84] Thus, it was thought that a twenty-year encrustation of human corruption would be replaced by a new innocence emerging untainted by previous evils of politics. Simultaneously, a new system of indirect elections utilizing a community development structure—renamed Basic Democracies—would provide a fresh apparatus for the gradual channeling of slow participation by the new innocents. The fall of the Ayub regime doomed the experiment to failure. Careful research might reveal the causes and shed light on the syndrome of sequential phases. I venture some speculations to suggest the importance of the theme. It is doubtful if participation can be effectively curtailed among a people who have experienced broad participation. Without a compelling ideology sustained by an authoritarian regime (e.g., communist systems), quasi-authoritarianism (such as Ayub's martial law) could not suppress what had once been effervescent. It was particularly difficult to sedate participation when India, whose historical experience prior to 1941 was shared by Pakistan, had five general direct elections. Probably it is naïve to assume that new power will long remain any more innocent than old power. The theory of EBDO was hence in defiance of the older and more realistic Actonian

84. President's Order No. 13 of 1959. Elective Bodies (Disqualification) Order, 1959. *Gazette of Pakistan, Extraordinary,* Aug. 7, 1959.

dictum. The Pakistan experience may well show us that the political process must somehow be accommodated concurrently with strengthening of institutions, perhaps even at the risk of institutional strength. This would go far toward resolving the arguments between "balanced growth" and "unbalanced growth" proponents.[85]

4. Characteristic IV — Innovation

Obviously every political system deals with the problem of change. Endemic or regular change occurs constantly, often imperceptibly. This involves rapidly changing incidence of demands, the substantive content of demands, and the oscillating roles played by institutions in attempting to fulfill these demands. Here the concept of spiraling contextuality is important.[86] The adjective "spiraling" is used deliberately to convey a significant perception. By contextuality we mean a changing universe of referrents that are perceived as having an associational, perhaps even a causal, relationship with an event or segment of knowledge. This context can expand or contract and it can move in either of two directions; hence, the metaphor of the spiral, which also has these qualities, seems to be of some explicative utility.

The context within which relationships are analyzed can change in at least three ways. The first can be called *episodic;* that is, a major discovery of new knowledge that substantially, dramatically, and often immediately modifies a paradigm and hence the context. Such discoveries as Harvey's

---

85. An analysis of these arguments can be found in Ralph Braibanti, "Administrative Reform in the Context of Political Growth," in Fred W. Riggs, ed., *Frontiers of Development Administration* (Durham, N.C.: Duke University Press, 1971), pp. 227–46.

86. For a fuller treatment of this concept, see Ralph Braibanti, "Conceptual Prerequisites for the Evolution of Asian Bureaucratic Systems," in Inayatullah, ed., *Administrative Change in Asia* (Kuala Lumpur: United Nations, Economic and Social Commission for Asia and the Pacific, Asian Centre for Development Administration, 1975), pp. 185–231. See also Ralph Braibanti, "Political Development: A Contextual Nonlinear Perspective," *Politikon* 3 (Oct. 1976), 1–25.

circulatory system of the living body, Pasteur's germ theory of disease, Watson's definition of the DNA molecule, Darwin's theory of evolution, Freud's exploration of the layers of the mind, Einstein's theory of relativity—to name but a few—are obvious examples by which contextuality was dramatically modified.

A second determinant of change can be the result of *technological invention.* Such devices as the microscope and its electronic successors, X-ray, the computer, the space satellite, are obvious examples that often create new knowledge and almost always enable new arrangements of knowledge, hence new perceptions. Space exploration, for example, not only revealed new knowledge but dramatically called our attention to the finite nature of the planet on which we live and the necessity for the recycling of resources on that planet.

A third determinant of change may be characterized as being *reformulative.* In this category, we do not necessarily find dramatic new discoveries in knowledge. Rather an event or an episode either reformulates existing knowledge or directs attention to a different perception of relationships of existing knowledge. Such reformulation may set in motion a substantial change in contextuality. Illustrative of the latter would be Rachael Carson's *Silent Spring,* which directed attention to ecological concerns. Other examples are Norbert Wiener's formulation of cybernetics and Lasswell and Lerner's formulation of policy science. Included in this third category are archeological discoveries that compel reformulations of existing knowledge, recast historical periodization, revise hypotheses of derivation and diffusion of cultural forms and of reciprocity in the relationship of civilizations, and expand the temporal and spatial dimensions of insights into man's behavior. Examples of this are the Egyptian excavations that made possible a scientific archeological system, discovery of the Rosetta Stone (1799) that made Egyptian hieroglyphics decipherable, Leakey's discovery of Rama (Kenya) pithecus (1968), the Mohen-jodaro excavations of the Indus Valley civilization (1950), and the Xabis discoveries in Iran (1973) that may prove that true writing originated in Iran and moved westward into Mesopotamia instead of vice versa.

It cannot be said that any one of these determinants — episodic, technological invention, reformulative — acts in isolation of the others or that any one is more influential than the others in changing the contours of contextuality. Each class of determinant shades into the next class and each has effect on the others.

Change in contextuality produced by these three determinants occurs at two levels: in the perceptions of men and in the actions of institutions in consequence of changed perceptions. There is a reciprocal relationship between these two levels. Spiraling contextuality manifests itself spatially as when knowledge or technique from two distant points on the earth are associated together. Hence, the importance of global satellite communications as now being developed in India. There is also a temporal manifestation as when a body of knowledge reaches into the past and invests a doctrine once discarded (e.g., acupuncture, tribal medicine, midwifery) with a legitimation based on new perceptions.

This changing context complicates the diffusion of new knowledge and its application among nations in disparate stages of development. The ideas emanating from a post-technetronic system and propelled with all the force of the distributive technology of that system into a developing system can do much damage.

A developing nation can best deal with this threat by maintaining pride in its own culture (the instrumental behavior is the use of appropriate technology), by being wary of all external technological intervention, and by establishing a structure (reduction-gears) for mediating between the high technology and the low technology of the recipient system.

Pakistan's experience can be neatly fitted into this paradigm. There is enormous pride in the indigenous, sustained principally by the distinctiveness of Islam and the militant posture it has assumed in the Hindu cultural context. There has also been significant experimentation with indigenous forms, particularly in local government. While there has been acceptance of massive technical assistance, mostly from the United States, there has been significant disenchantment with that assistance, especially since 1971 when East Pakistan seceded.

V

The systematic application of Pakistan's experience to the construction of a theory of political development is a challenge of uncommon dimensions. This chapter has demonstrated the virtually total omission of Pakistan from such an endeavor. The time to pursue such studies, both by individuals and groups, has probably never been more propitious. At least thirty paradigms of development of varying degrees of sophistication and of differing methodological modalities exist. These will satisfy most students or will provoke original and perhaps more useful formulations.

We find a fortuitous congruence of two sets of factors. (1) Changes occurring in the intellectual stance of academic development studies are conducive to a more appreciative understanding of the total configuration of Pakistan's culture and of the impact of that configuration on the evolution of distinctive development modes not necessarily in imitation of specified Western models. As this new appreciation perceptibly erodes attitudes of hubris and cultural imperialism, there is likely to be expanded receptivity of research and scholarship. A reciprocal consequence may well be an even more accelerated understanding of configurative forces. (2) Concurrently, the global configuration of political power diversifies Pakistan's interests and allegiances into a healthier structure.

This is the potential of a new intellectual context for research in Pakistan. If such research is pursued responsibly, maturely, with humility, with empathy for national sensitivities, devoid of frenetic emotional attachments to ideologies or regimes of the moment, there will be reason to expect useful insights into Pakistan's experience.

Index

DATE DUE

11. 24 '83	
6. 06. '85	
1 29. '86	
6 17 '87	
MAR 15 '89	
NOV 2 2 89	
MAY 0 9 '90	
OCT 31 '90	
NOV 14 '90	
Ref 12/4	
JUN 12 31	
JAN 0 2 2001	
JAN 0 2 2001	

BRODART, INC.

Cat. No. 23-221